Mencken's America

H. L. Mencken

Mencken's

AMERICA

EDITED BY
S. T. JOSHI

Ohio University Press   •   Athens

Ohio University Press, Athens, Ohio 45701
© 2004 by S. T. Joshi
Printed in the United States of America
All rights reserved

Ohio University Press books are printed on acid-free paper ⊗ ™

12 11 10 09 08 07 06 05 04   5 4 3 2 1

Permission to publish H. L. Mencken's articles is granted
by the Enoch Pratt Free Library of Baltimore, in accordance
with the terms of the will of H. L. Mencken.

Cover, title page, and chapter opening art courtesy of Tom Chalkley.

Library of Congress Cataloging-in-Publication Data

Mencken, H. L. (Henry Louis)
    Mencken's America / edited by S. T. Joshi.
        p. cm. 302/ 4984 3/04
    Includes bibliographical references and index.
    ISBN 0-8214-1531-X (cloth : alk. paper) — ISBN 0-8214-1532-8 (paper : alk.
paper)
        1. United States—Civilization—1865–1918. 2. United States—Civilization—
1918–1945. 3. National characteristics, American. 4. United States—Politics and
government—1901–1953. I. Joshi, S. T., 1958– II. Title.

E169.M5195 2004
973.8—dc22

2003056755

Contents

Introduction

Americans have developed an enviable skill at remaining impervious to criticism. Perhaps it is merely the defense mechanism of a relatively new people facing the intimidating cultural antiquity of Europe and Asia; perhaps America's remarkably sudden rise to political and economic supremacy has engendered an arrogance that leads its citizens to vaunt size, speed, power, and money as intrinsic goods; perhaps, conversely, the nation's founding by religious dissenters has produced a holier-than-thou attitude that blandly overlooks instances of American hypocrisy, duplicity, and cultural inadequacy as insignificant counterweights to American morality and piety. Educated Americans can hardly be unaware that, from the earliest days of the republic, a nearly uninterrupted succession of overseas visitors has seized upon American political, social, and cultural deficiencies and held them up scornfully to the light of day; but it has become routine to pass these off as the maunderings of ignorant foreigners.

H. L. Mencken, although the son of immigrants, can be considered neither foreign nor ignorant. Why, then, did he take so dim a view of his fellow citizens? Why did he regard the U.S. government as "corrupt, ignorant, incompetent and disgusting" and its people as "the most timorous, sniveling, poltroonish, ignominious mob of serfs and goose-steppers ever gathered under one flag in Christendom since the fall of the Eastern Empire"? Mencken uttered this towering condemnation at about the midpoint in his long career as a journalist and cultural commentator, a career that began just prior to the turn of the twentieth century and continued until a stroke in 1949 suddenly stilled his pen; and in that fifty-year span, his opinion of Americans does not seem to have altered to any significant degree, either for the better or for the worse. Mencken claimed that rancor or indignation were foreign to his temperament, and that in spite of his dim view of his countrymen he was "curiously happy." Where, after all, could one find such a good show as that provided by an unending succession of American buffooneries?

As a journalist—first for the *Baltimore Herald* and then, beginning in 1906 and continuing almost without a hiatus until 1948, for the *Baltimore Sun* and *Evening Sun*—Mencken was in a good position to view these buffooneries at first hand. He attended nearly every Republican and Democratic national convention from 1904 to 1948, and his pungent reporting of the political shenanigans that regularly turned them into grotesque farces is well known.[1] In his "Free Lance" column in the *Evening Sun*—a column he wrote six days a week for four and a half years, from 1911 to 1915—he found an inexhaustible fund of absurdity in his native city of Baltimore, although he gradually broadened his scope to cover the entire nation and the world as it lurched into war. From 1914 to 1923 he added the responsibilities of coediting, with George Jean Nathan, the *Smart Set*, turning it into a leading American cultural organ and gaining celebrity for himself by his tart and uncompromising monthly review column. In these reviews, as in his later review columns for the *American Mercury* (1924–33), he rarely restricted himself to works of pure literature; instead, he extended his intellectual range to cover such things as the political tracts of Walter Lippmann, a new translation of the Bible, a brace of works on Freudian psychology, and any other book that caught his fancy. His final review, in the *American Mercury* for December 1933, was an examination of Hitler's *Mein Kampf* and other works of "Hitlerismus." Few reviewers have demonstrated such intellectual range; it was no surprise that these reviews, many of them the equivalent of substantial essays, served as the basis for the early volumes of Mencken's landmark six-volume series of *Prejudices* (1919–27), which cemented his reputation as the leading American cultural critic of the 1920s.

Mencken's productivity was such that he himself could scarcely trouble to assemble all his disparate writings into books, so that the task must be fulfilled by others. In particular, six papers he wrote for the *Smart Set* in 1913–14, about a year before he assumed the editorship of the magazine, are among his most scintillating screeds on American life; I have gathered them here under the rubric "The American: A Treatise." He incorporated one of these papers, with revisions, in the long essay "Puritanism as a Literary Force" (a chapter in *A Book of Prefaces*, 1917), but the rest remained unreprinted, although they manifestly served as a continual reservoir of ideas that Mencken drew upon for much of his later writing on the subject. A succession of other essays—accounts of travels throughout the country, meditations on American political and religious life, thoughts on the American literary tradition, even his views of the nascent film industry—fills out this volume, and presents a comprehensive account of American culture as Mencken saw it, rivaling and complementing such well-known essays in *Prejudices* as "The National Letters," "The Sahara of the Bozart," and "On Being an American."

What, then, did Mencken find so offensive about Americans? The matter can be summed up in one word: Puritanism. It is of no consequence that Mencken's use of this term may have been historically inaccurate—that the Puritans of the seventeenth century may not have had the exact attributes that he had in mind under the rubric of Puritanism; for Mencken, the issue was more one of psychology than of history. While it is true that he dates the emergence of the "new Puritanism" to the generation after the Civil War, he was aware that its fundamental premises had colored American politics, society, and morals from the beginning; and while dogmatic religion may have been at its base, its ramifications went well beyond theology and entered into nearly every facet of American life.

Puritanism, in Mencken's memorable phrase, "assum[es] that every human act must be either right or wrong, and that ninety-nine percent of them are wrong." It was, in his view, Americans' inveterate habit to judge all thoughts and actions from an ethical perspective, and to disapprove of the great majority of them as subversive of "good morals." It was this that engendered Americans' suspicion of the fine arts as somehow morally dangerous. It was not simply that Americans were *indifferent* to art; they were actively *hostile* to it as a potentially corrupting influence. The notion that art could civilize, could soothe the asperities of daily life, or could merely supply some harmless amusement, was absent from their consciousness. Art, in any case, was the province of the few, and Americans did not look with favor upon any aspect of life that could not be readily appreciated by all. The principle of equality was illegitimately extended from the political and legal realms into the realms of intellect and culture: if a book or a painting or a piece of music could not be understood and enjoyed by everyone, then it should not be enjoyed by anyone.

It was Puritanism, too, that assumed the moral "wrongness" of many thoughts and actions that the rest of the world deemed harmless and pleasurable, and, further, that demanded the suppression of these thoughts and actions by "the secular arm." Mencken may have been in error in deeming the seventeenth-century Puritan society of New England a "theocracy," but he was quick to detect the ever-increasing encroachments upon freedom by crusaders whose quest for moral purity impelled them closer and closer to tyranny and fascism. The censorship campaigns of Anthony Comstock and his Society for the Suppression of Vice; the long, tortured, agonizing lurch toward the Eighteenth Amendment, fueled by the hardball political tactics of the Anti-Saloon League; the chasing of Reds and other undesirables in the post–World War I period—all these things were witnessed at first hand by Mencken and elicited his relentless and towering condemnation. Mencken frankly referred to himself as a libertarian; but unlike many present libertarians, who envision only the freedom of business to engage in economic manipulation without irritating government interference, Mencken knew that the cornerstone of liberty was freedom of thought: "As for me, my literary theory, like my politics, is based chiefly upon one main idea, to wit, the idea of freedom. I am, in brief, a libertarian of the most extreme variety, and know of no human right that is one-tenth as valuable as the simple right to utter what seems (at the moment) to be the truth. Take away this right, and none other is worth a hoot; nor, indeed, can any other long exist."[2]

Mencken himself exercised that "simple right" on every possible occasion, and never more vigorously and iconoclastically than in the realm of politics. It was not merely that he tirelessly exposed the blatant and undisguised hypocrisy and duplicity of self-serving politicians, whom he considered merely jobholders intent on keeping their positions from one election to the next with the least amount of effort; it was that he boldly challenged the most cherished shibboleths of American political thought. Specifically, he presented—briefly in some of the essays in this book and more exhaustively in the treatise *Notes on Democracy* (1926)—a systematic critique of the very principle of American democracy. Democracy, in his judgment, was flawed in its very conception; as he wrote in "What Ails the Republic" (1922), it "always resolves itself, in the end, into a scheme for enabling weak and inferior men to force their notions and desires, by mass action, upon strong and superior men. Its essence is this substitution of mere numbers for every other sort of superiority—this fundamental assumption that a group of idiots, if only its numbers be large enough, is wiser and more virtuous than any conceivable individual who is not an idiot." Mencken would have agreed emphatically with his erstwhile correspondent Ambrose Bierce, who only a few years earlier had written a "future history" in which the downfall of the American republic was memorably etched: "An inherent weakness in republican government was that it assumed the honesty and intelligence of the majority, 'the masses,' who were neither honest nor intelligent."[3] And Mencken would have agreed with both facets of Bierce's condemnation: the American people were not merely uneducated (and therefore unable to grasp the complexity of the political, economic, and social issues that they were called upon to adjudicate), they were also fundamentally dishonest. The "liberty" they touted was in reality liberty for themselves and restraint for everyone else; the moral "evils" they condemned were those they had neither the desire nor the capacity to commit themselves, or those they knew they could commit without detection.

The whole issue of the viability of democracy as a political principle is well beyond the scope of this introduction, but some further thoughts on Mencken's attitudes may be in order. The basis of his critique of democracy was the very low opinion he held of both the abstract intelligence and the educability of the "plain people":

> I doubt that the art of thinking can be taught at all—at any rate, by school-teachers. It is not acquired, but congenital. Some persons are born with it. Their ideas flow in straight channels; they are capable of lucid reasoning; when they say anything it is instantly understandable, when they write anything it is clear and persuasive. They constitute, I should say, about one-eighth of one per cent. of the human race. The rest of God's children are just as incapable of logical thought as they are incapable of jumping over the moon. Trying to teach them to think is as vain an enterprise as trying to teach a streptococcus the principles of Americanism.[4]

In the absence of an educated electorate, it would then appear that every politician is obliged, in order to be elected at all, to become a demagogue; and the end result (as he states in his contribution to Harold Stearns's *Civilization in the United States*, included here under the title "The American Politician") is that "It is almost impossible to imagine a man of genuine self-respect and dignity offering himself as a candidate" for political office. Mencken was not naive enough to imagine that pure intelligence was sufficient to transform a person into a sensible voter; rather, he was looking for what might might be termed political savvy—an ability to sniff out the insincerities, hypocrisies, and rhetorical smokescreens that so many politicians use to bamboozle the electorate and to win favor for policies that they secretly support for quite other (and usually self-serving or doctrinaire) reasons.

This brings up the vexed issue of what the *purpose* of democracy actually is. Is the principle of "majority rules" valid in itself, and in every circumstance? Should a majority of people not be allowed to determine what policies its government is to follow? It is here, as Mencken saw, that both intelligence and morality (what he habitually termed "common decency") come into play. What if, for example, a majority of the American people decided to imprison, exile, or even execute all African Americans, or homosexuals, or atheists? For large periods of American history such policies would probably have been supported by substantial majorities. It is no argument that the Constitution—specifically the Bill of Rights—prevents such decrees from taking effect; Mencken was well aware that the Constitution could be changed with suitable doses of demagoguery from politicians or pressure groups, as happened with Prohibition. It would then seem that, in the absence of an intelligent and morally sound electorate, democracy cannot function even in principle.

Mencken, of course, was hardly inclined to offer any solutions to this dilemma or the others that he faced when contemplating American society and culture; probably he felt that that there were no viable solutions to be had. Remember that Mencken believed the American people were not merely *uneducated*, but *ineducable*: no amount of education, and no amount of reform of educational practice, could ever allow more than a tiny fraction of the American (or human) populace to attain a sufficient modicum of intelligence to make politically astute decisions. And that ineducability, Mencken well knew, played itself out in many other aspects of social and cultural life.

One of those other aspects was religion. Mencken does not discuss the exact place of religion in American life and morals explicitly or concentratedly in his 1913–14 papers on "The American" nor in *Treatise on the Gods* (1930), an unwontedly sober study that is chiefly concerned with the anthropology of religion.[5] In "The American: His New Puritanism" he does discuss the religious origins of the new Puritanism, but one must turn to other, later writings—specifically his editorials in the *American Mercury*—for his views of the state of American religion in the 1920s. It is not surprising that, in an editorial published in the November 1925 issue, Mencken—still relishing the firestorm of controversy he had provoked by his pungently satirical reporting of the Scopes trial that summer, which concluded with several kicks in the stomach to the late lamented William Jennings Bryan—would address himself to the "divine ignoramuses" of the Fundamentalist sects, a group that Mencken presciently saw as a growing threat to American freedoms. Nor is it surprising that in another editorial, written just prior to the presidential election of 1928, he should actually welcome the widespread anti-Catholic prejudice that emerged, notably from the Ku Klux Klan, with the nomination of Alfred E. Smith as the Democratic candidate. Advocate of free speech that he was, Mencken was not inclined to propose the restriction of even the ugliest kinds of religious or racial bigotry, so long as it was limited to speech—and so long as others, like himself, were equally free to have their own say in turn.

In an editorial of 1931 Mencken identifies a tendency that would come to dominate American religious thought and practice for the rest of the century: a kind of homogenization of religion into a bland and doctrine-free Christianity, offensive to no one and capable of incorporating the views of nearly all religious groups, with only atheists and agnostics left beyond the pale. Mencken himself was far from being an atheist, but his skeptical credentials were well established far in advance of the Scopes trial; and one cannot help feeling that he looked with something like wistful regret at the decline of religious infighting, especially since this suggested as a corollary that criticism of anyone's religion had suddenly fallen beyond the bounds of good taste. Mencken knew that the numerous follies embedded in the doctrines of every religion could be exposed only by freewheeling debate, even if that debate occasionally verged on abuse and billingsgate; and he was opposed to the granting of some unspecified "respect" for a person's religious views merely on the ground that he or she held them. Nothing is to be gained by sealing off religion, or any other facet of life, from critical scrutiny, even in the interests of social harmony.

Mencken devoted the great proportion of his career in pointing to the deficiencies of the American character; but in so doing he was necessarily relying, albeit at times implicitly, upon a conception of proper social, political, and moral behavior as he saw it. What, then, was Mencken's ideal? What was his antidote to the pathological Puritanism of American life? He summed it up in a single word: civilization. Behind this word lurked a complex network of conceptions that is difficult to elucidate. It was not merely that civilized persons are capable of appreciating the great literature, art, and thought that represent the highest pinnacles of human endeavor; it was that such persons have the self-restraint to keep their moral fervor in check, to resist bringing in the secular arm in regard to thoughts or actions that do not encroach upon anyone else's freedoms. Moreover, civilized persons can take their pleasures sanely and level-headedly; they can enjoy liquor, dancing, and even sex without running amok; they were unthreatened by difference—difference in opinion, in behavior, in philosophical or political orientation. Civilized persons are even willing to allow Puritans "the private practice of their rococo asceticism on their remote farms or in the galvanized-iron tabernacles that they erect on suburban dumps," so long as those Puritans do not make any efforts to railroad them into those tabernacles without their consent. That this kind of restraint comes only after centuries of civilized life, such as we find in the mellow societies of Europe and Asia, Mencken assumed as a foregone conclusion, hence his lack of enthusiasm for waging a campaign for civilizing the raw American. The effort, he knew, would be doomed from the start.

It was, indeed, as a function of his spanning the globe—from the Caribbean so early as 1900 to Germany in 1917 and the Middle East in the 1930s—that Mencken arrived at many of his views on the American character. Nor did he refrain from canvassing the American continent as time and circumstances permitted. His reporting of the quadrennial political conventions caused him to crisscross the country several times over; other journeys were taken for less strenuous purposes, although he rarely allowed himself to kick up his heels in some vacation spot without writing at least one or two accounts of it.

And yet, Baltimore remained close to his heart, as the early essay "Good Old Baltimore" (1913) attests. Let it pass that a large part of this essay is devoted to Maryland cuisine, with the suggestion that the finest days of its culinary preeminence are in fact over. The real issue is whether we are meant to see any contradiction between the unfeignedly positive portrayal of his native city ("A quaint town! A singular people! And yet the charm is there!") embodied in this essay and the rather glum portrayal we find only nine years later in "Maryland: Apex of Normalcy" (1922). Perhaps the contradiction is only on the surface. It is not sufficient to say that the later essay was written as Prohibition had gained its stranglehold upon the American populace and upon American civil liberties; what is more pertinent is that the lugubrious assessment we find there—life "is dull . . . it is depressing . . . it steadily grows worse"—is really implicit in the earlier piece as well, which could be read as a nostalgic elegy for a Baltimore that, even in 1913, had already seen its apogee as a haven for the civilized.

Mencken was, accordingly, forced to seek that haven elsewhere, even if temporarily. He would never abandon Baltimore, but he could at least sample what the rest of the country had to offer. How about nearby Philadelphia? Not likely: this "city of seven Sundays"—a reference not to the Philadelphians' excess of piety but to their moral and aesthetic timidity—did not offer the mellow civilization Mencken sought, and the worst thing he can find to say of it is that "Philadelphia is the least un-American city in the nation." Washington, D.C., is even closer to Baltimore, but it too is found wanting: its architecture is a chaotic congeries of classic grandeur and appalling lack of taste, and its citizens (particularly the politicians) are barefaced hypocrites in the wake of Prohibition. New York? No doubt Mencken enjoyed his frequent visits to New York as editor of the *Smart Set*; but it is telling that he agreed to take on the editorship only if he could edit the magazine at long distance, making trips to the editorial offices only "every third or fourth week."[6] One gains the impression, surveying his many discussions of New York over the course of his career, that Mencken felt an unacknowledged envy at the megalopolis that so overshadowed his native city in its size, its wealth, and its role as a magnet for artists and writers hoping to cash in on their proximity to the nation's major publishers. In the later essay, "Metropolis" (originally an editorial in the *American Mercury*, October 1926, and reprinted in *Prejudices: Sixth Series*, 1927), he repeats the contention made in the essay "New York" (1923) that the city has not figured prominently in much of the major American literature of the recent past; he singles out Chicago as the source of much of the inspiration of such writers as Frank Norris and Theodore Dreiser. In light of recent events, it is of course chilling to read of Mencken's bland prediction of the ease with which a foreign attack could be undertaken on that exposed and underdefended city.

It is no surprise that Mencken found his civilized paradise in San Francisco, a city he visited only twice, once in 1920 for the Democratic National Convention, and again in 1926, in the course of a lengthy stay in both southern and central California. What else did San Francisco represent to him but a "subtle but unmistakable sense of escape from the United States"? Of all the cities in the United States, it perhaps came the closest to replicating the civilized mellowness of the great cities of Europe, although Mencken was aware that its orientation was eastward, to Asia. But consider the specific points on which Mencken bases his praise of the city by the bay: "here, at last, was an American city that somehow managed to hold itself above pollution by the national philistinism and craze for standardization, the appalling progress of 100% Americanism, the sordid and pathetic dreams of unimaginative, timorous and inferior men." It defied the American hostility to art; it rejected that absence of independent thought that caused so many Americans to be joiners of safe groups of like-minded individuals; it had eyes for values other than the acquisition of wealth and power. It was, in a word, un-American.

It is interesting to note that the one aspect of American civilization that gained Mencken's approval was what he termed the "American language." And yet, it becomes evident that no small element of prejudice entered into his approbation — specifically, prejudice against the cultural hegemony of the British (hateful to a German American who excoriated his adopted country for siding with the Allies during World War I) and his unrelenting scorn for the "schoolmarm" and other pedagogues, whose pedantry and inflexibility he never tired of skewering. A careful reading of the essay "The American: His Language" (1913)—which could serve as a radical condensation of what became *The American Language* (1919)—reveals its share of fallacies and contradictions. Firstly, the championing of ungrammatical lower-class speech comes oddly from one who otherwise spared no occasion to lampoon the intellectual failings of that class. Secondly, Mencken far exaggerates the degree to which even this class actually uses the ungrammatical and slang-ridden formulations he attributes to them. Indeed, in an awkward moment in his last revision of *The American Language,* he was forced to admit, after an analysis of statistics he himself endorsed, that "the schoolmarm's efforts to inculcate 'good grammar' have some effect."[7] Mencken himself never utilized these formulations in his own writing except for parodic purposes. Nevertheless, he was unquestionably right in asserting that the impetus for change in the English language now came largely from Americans—not only by virtue of their sheer numbers, but because they did indeed seem to have a gift for piquant and novel utterance, perhaps because their fluid and dynamic society created a greater degree of social and technological change than the stratified British society of the period.

But when it came to studying American literature, Mencken saw himself as judge, jury, and executioner. He was relentless in condemning the timid, hackneyed, and simply mediocre writing that bulked so large in the history of American literature—and was more relentless still in crucifying the timid, hackneyed, and mediocre critics who vaunted this literature over the bold and dynamic work that crept in, almost by accident, along the edges of the prevailing desert of conformity. On the one side were Irving, Longfellow, Lowell, and Whittier; on the other side, Poe, Twain, Whitman, and Dreiser. Dreiser in particular was the watershed, heralding the advent of such other writers of social realism as David Graham Phillips, Sinclair Lewis, and Willa Cather. What Mencken sought was originality, iconoclasm, a freedom from moral convention—and it could be embodied as well in the gritty work of a Dreiser as in the languid and satirical fantasy of a James Branch Cabell.[8]

But Mencken knew that the kind of writing he sought faced numerous obstacles, and the greatest of them was that American hostility to art that went to the extreme of censorship of purportedly objectionable material. In "Puritanism as a Literary Force," one of his most impressive works of scholarly exposition, Mencken assembles a prodigious array of evidence from court cases of the late nineteenth and early twentieth centuries demonstrating the degree to which the campaigns by the "Comstocks" (the Society for the Suppression of Vice and its analogues) inhibited the free expression of literary work by threats of censorship, heavy fines, and even prison. It made no difference that many of these campaigns failed; the threat still hung over authors—and, more particularly, publishers, who stood to suffer heavy financial loss even in the case of ultimate victory in court—and also over the editors of magazines. Mencken was perennially looking over his shoulder in preparing issues of the *Smart Set,* which under his tenure had gained the reputation of a ribald and even, on occasion, a somewhat risqué magazine; and his battle with the Watch and Ward Society of Boston over a story he published in 1926 in the *American Mercury* is well known.[9]

Mencken also identified another, very different kind of obstacle to the production of a sound American literature: the lure of big money presented to authors by middlebrow magazines like the *Saturday Evening Post,* by publishers looking for best-sellers to tickle an aesthetically crude reading public, and by film magnates looking for pablum for the yokels who flock to the movies. Now-forgotten hacks like Robert W. Chambers, Ethel M. Dell, and Elinor Glyn far outsold the Dreisers and the Cathers, just as the Stephen Kings and John Grishams of today cast the Toni Morrisons and Gore Vidals in the shade, at least as regards the size of their bank balances. The problem was inveterate and incurable, for again no amount of education would ever raise a statistically significant number of readers to the level where they could appreciate the Dreisers and scorn the Chamberses; one could only rely on the integrity of those few authors who held out for aesthetic sincerity and passed up the chance for financial comfort. In the film industry, which Mencken witnessed at first hand in Hollywood in late 1926, the situation was the same: in "The Low-Down on Hollywood" (an interview of Mencken by James R. Quirk, published in *Photoplay* for April 1927), he stated without equivocation that "the present movie folk . . . think too much about money." But of course they had no choice: they "are on the hooks of a sad dilemma. In order to meet the immense cost of making a gaudy modern film they have to make it appeal to a gigantic audience. And in order to make it appeal to a gigantic audience they have to keep it within a narrow range of ideas and emotions, fatal to genuine ingenuity." What will be the upshot? In one of his most insightful comments, Mencken came to this conclusion: "Soon or late the movies will have to split into two halves. There will be movies for the mob, and there will be movies for the relatively civilized minority."

H. L. Mencken would be the last to consider himself a prophet or prognosticator, but it may be worth devoting a few final words as to the continuing relevance of his judgments on American life and thought. More specifically, what would Mencken make of the political, social, and cultural tendencies of the present age, and to what degree have his own writings played a role in bringing those tendencies about?

One would have to admit that his verdict on our time would be a mixed one. To be sure, intellectual freedom could be said to have made substantial advances since the 1920s: we no longer live in an age of oppressive, religiously inspired blue laws, under which it is a criminal act for an orchestra to play Beethoven's Fifth Symphony on a Sunday; and the very notion of censoring or even boycotting a book or play or film because of some perceived moral or religious offense is sufficient to engender either mirth or an augmented interest in the work in question. And there seems no doubt that Mencken's own tireless championing of free speech—in spite of his suspicion of the general effectiveness of the ACLU and other groups that he regarded as part of the moral crusading he despised—has played its role in the liberalization of American thought and behavior on this point. But we should be wary of declaring the battle won. Recent events suggest that the protection of civil liberties is an ongoing and perennially difficult task, especially when the government perceives that its own concerns outweigh the freedoms granted by the Constitution; Mencken was correct in believing that the people at large are far more concerned about their comfort than their freedom, so they are not likely to be of much help even in blatant instances of the restriction of liberty. And if freedom of expression has perhaps been enlarged since Mencken's time, there remain subjects or points of view that are for all practical purposes *verboten*. Mencken himself identified one of them: "Dispute about democracy's failures all you please, but don't argue that democracy itself is a failure!" The notion that democracy (with universal suffrage) is and must be the only viable and morally sound political system is so entrenched, not only among the general public but even among political philosophers, that one despairs of ever conducting an honest debate on the issue. One could add that the frank espousal of atheism, socialism, and other heresies is virtually a guarantee of intellectual marginalization, as no major newspaper, magazine, publishing house, or television or radio station is likely to risk offending large segments of its audience with the expression of such views, given the inevitable economic consequences. It is then that we long for a Mencken who not only spoke his mind fearlessly on these and other issues but who realized that there is a higher value to be sought in intellectual debate than inoffensiveness.

As we have seen, Mencken in a sense predicted the rise of religious fundamentalism under the influence of charismatic ministers, although the humiliation they suffered as a result of the Scopes trial delayed their emergence for half a century. On a related subject, Mencken was sadly in error when, in the late paper "The Burden of Credulity" (1931), he recommended that African Americans give up the "barnyard theology" preached to them by their own fundamentalist pastors; African Americans remain among the most consistently religious segments of the American populace, and one can scarcely resist the conclusion that their piety is at least in part a defense mechanism against the continuing prejudice to which they find themselves subject. On the other hand, Mencken's adjuration to African Americans, in "Notes on Negro Strategy" (1934), to fight for the liberties that white society denies them appear to have been taken to heart, albeit a generation or two later.

It is in the realm of contemporary politics that Mencken would probably find the chiefest cause for cynical merriment. The monumental scorn he heaped upon the local and national politicians of his day ("What they know of sound literature is what one may get out of McGuffey's Fifth Reader. What they know of political science is the nonsense preached in the chautauquas and on the stump. What they know of history is the childish stuff taught in grammar-schools. What they know of the arts and sciences—of all the great body of knowledge that is the chief intellectual baggage of modern man—is absolutely nothing") would seem scarcely less relevant to the trimmers and hacks who occupy the halls of legislation today. Mencken could not have foreseen the corrosive effect of big money in the corruption of political leaders; but his words on the insidious power of lobbyists in affecting legislation are strikingly prescient; or perhaps they only appear so because we forget how pervasive that power has always been in American politics. Given the single-minded quest of the great majority of politicians to secure reelection at all costs, it is no surprise that they are readily subject to outside influences; all that has changed in the present age is that politicians have less of a need to kowtow to the pressure of the mob (although there is certainly plenty of that) and more of a need to lick the boots of their wealthy campaign contributors. Elizabeth Drew, among others, has lamented the decline in the level of intellectual debate in Congress;[10] but it is a fair question whether current debates over gun control or abortion or terrorism are any less foolish, self-serving, or hypocritical than the debates over the prohibition amendment in the late 1910s.

Were Mencken alive today, he would probably say that America has changed for the better, changed for the worse, or stayed pretty much the same, depending on what facet of politics, society, or culture was under discussion. Americans, by and large, still seem hostile to artistic expression, still translate every political or social cause into a moral crusade, still prefer the acquisition of property to the acquisition of culture, still endure restrictions to their liberty with insouciance so long as their material comforts are not jeopardized, and still make religion, politics, and art into commodities to be hawked like soap or patent medicines. But, as Mencken was the first to admit, no one can deny that it is all a good show to anyone capable of viewing the spectacle from a safe and unassailable pinnacle of sardonic indifference.

S. T. JOSHI

A Note on This Edition

This book contains a wide sampling of H. L. Mencken's writings—most of them uncollected—on American culture. A few items have appeared in Mencken's books in different form: "On Living in the United States" was incorporated into the essay "On Being an American" (*Prejudices: Third Series*, 1922); "New York" was reprinted in part as "Totentanz" (*Prejudices: Fourth Series*, 1924); the editorial I have titled "Evangelical Pastors" was included in the essay "Protestantism in the Republic" (*Prejudices: Fifth Series*, 1926); "The American Tradition" was incorporated into the essay of that title (*Prejudices: Fourth Series*). In these cases, I have gone back to the original appearances in magazines or newspapers because of their historical interest and because these versions are more capable of standing independently than their later revisions.

I have reprinted the essays without alteration aside from minor emendations in spelling and punctuation so that they are stylistically consistent with Mencken's habitual usages. (For example, Mencken did not use the serial comma, but several of the magazines in which he published added the serial comma as part of their house style; the serial comma has therefore been omitted in those essays in which it was found.) I have also systematized Mencken's use of titles, printing titles of novels and other book-length works in italics and titles of short stories, articles, and other such works in quotation marks. Many other idiosyncratic usages by Mencken have been preserved. I have supplied titles for some editorials in the *American Mercury* and a few other works; in the list of sources in the rear of the volume, I print my titles in brackets.

Mencken was very fond of name dropping, and many of the names he cites are now little known. To minimize the number of explanatory notes, I have chosen to prepare a glossary of names in which relevant information on these individuals is supplied. Names the reader can be expected to know are omitted; a few such names of well-known people are included only to point to Mencken's writings about them or to supply information on specific works cited in the essays. In some cases I have found it more convenient to elucidate the names in the notes rather than in the glossary. The essay "Puritanism as a Literary Force" included a number of footnotes by Mencken; these have been placed among my own notes, appended with the abbreviation [HLM].

Abbreviations used in the notes, glossary, and list of sources are as follows:

AM = *American Mercury*
BES = *Baltimore Evening Sun*
CST = *Chicago Sunday Tribune*
P1–6 = *Prejudices: First–Sixth Series* (1919–27)
SS = *Smart Set*

Works by Mencken mentioned in the glossary (chiefly his book reviews in the *Smart Set* and *American Mercury*) are often cited in abbreviated form; full bibliographical information on them can be found in Betty Adler's *H.L.M.: The Mencken Bibliography* (Baltimore: Enoch Pratt Free Library/Johns Hopkins University Press, 1961).

I am grateful to Douglas A. Anderson, Paul Boytinck, Scott Briggs, and Scott Connors for assistance in securing the texts of some of the articles included in the book. I have learned much about Mencken from such colleagues as Ray Stevens, Richard J. Schrader, and other members of the Mencken Society.

Prologue: On Living in the United States

It is one of my firmest and most sacred beliefs, reached after due prayer, that the Government of the United States, in both its legislative and its executive arms, is corrupt, ignorant, incompetent and disgusting—and from this judgment I except no more than twenty lawmakers and no more than twenty executioners of their laws. It is a belief no less piously cherished that the administration of justice in the Republic is stupid, dishonest and against all reason and equity—and from this judgment I except no more than twenty judges. It is another that the foreign policy of the United States—its habitual manner of dealing with other nations, whether friends or foes—is hypocritical, disingenuous, knavish and dishonorable—and from this judgment I consent to no exceptions whatsoever. And it is yet another that the American people, taking them by and large, are the most timorous, sniveling, poltroonish, ignominious mob of serfs and goose-steppers ever gathered under one flag in Christendom since the fall of the Eastern Empire.

Such is my unbreakable faith, held passionately since my nonage and now growing stronger and stronger as I gradually disintegrate into my component carbon, oxygen, hydrogen, phosphorus, calcium, sodium, nitrogen and iron. Yet here I am, a loyal American, even a chauvinist—paying taxes without complaint, obeying all laws that are physiologically obeyable, accepting all the duties and responsibilities of citizenship unprotestingly, investing the usufructs of my toil in the obligations of the government, contributing my mite toward the glory of the national arts and sciences, spurning all lures (and even all invitations) to get out and stay out—here am I, a bachelor of forty-one, able to go wherever I please and to stay as long as I please, remaining contentedly and even smugly beneath the folds of the Stars and Stripes—a better citizen, I daresay, and certainly a less mercurial and exigent one, than thousands who hold the Hon. Warren Gamaliel Harding in superstitious devotion, and regard the Supreme Court of the United States as directly inspired by the Holy Spirit, and belong ardently to every Rotary Club, Ku Klux Klan and Anti-Saloon League,[1] and believe with the faith of little children that any one of Our Boys taken at random could dispose in a fair fight of ten Englishmen, twenty Germans, thirty Frenchmen, or fifty Japanese.

Well, why am I still here? In particular, why am I so complacent (perhaps even to the point of offensiveness), so free from indignation, so curiously happy? Why

1

did I answer only with a few academic and polite *Hochs* when Henry James, Ezra Pound, and Harold Stearns issued their successive calls to the native intelligentsia to flee the shambles, escape to fairer lands, throw off the curse forever? The answer is to be sought in the nature of happiness. To me (and I can only follow my own nose) it presents itself in an aspect that is tripartite. To be happy one must be (*a*) well fed, unhounded by sordid cares, at ease in Zion, (*b*) full of a comfortable feeling of superiority to the masses of one's fellow men, and (*c*) delicately and unceasingly amused according to one's taste. It is my contention that, if this definition be accepted, there is no country in the world wherein a man constituted as I am—a man of my peculiar weakness, vanities, appetites and aversions—can be so happy as he can be in the United States. Going further, I lay down the doctrine that it is a sheer physical impossibility for such a man to live in the United States and *not* be happy. If he says he isn't, then he either lies or is insane. Here the business of getting a living is enormously easier than it is anywhere else in Christendom—so easy, in fact, that an educated and unsqueamish man who fails at it must actually make deliberate efforts to that end. Here the general average of intelligence, of knowledge, of competence, of self-respect, of honor is so low that any man who knows his trade, does not fear ghosts, believes in nothing that is palpably idiotic and practises the common decencies stands out as brilliantly as a wart on a bald head, and is thrown willy-nilly into a meager and exclusive aristocracy. And here, more than anywhere else in the world, the daily panorama of human existence—the unending procession of governmental extortions and chicaneries, of commercial brigandages and throat-slittings, of theological buffooneries, of aesthetic ribaldries, of legal swindles and harlotries—is so inordinately extravagant, so perfectly brought up to the highest conceivable amperage, that only the man who was born with a petrified diaphragm can fail to go to bed every night grinning from ear to ear, and awake every morning with the eager, unflagging expectations of a Sunday-school superintendent touring the Paris peep-shows.

A certain sough of rhetoric is here. I yield to words as an evangelist yields to them, depicting the almost intolerable bliss of the New Jerusalem. But fundamentally I am quite as sincere as he is. For example, in the matter of attaining to ease in Zion, of getting a fair share of the national swag. It seems to me that the only man who fails to do this in the United States is the man who is somehow stupid—perhaps not superficially, but certainly deep down. Either he is one who cripples himself imprudently, say by setting up a family before he can care for it, or by trusting too naïvely to the skill and decency of an employer, or by submitting his fortunes to the gross frauds and imbecilities of labor leaders; or he is one who endeavors fatuously to sell something that no normal American wants. When I hear a professor of philosophy complain that his wife has eloped with a moving-picture actor who can properly feed her, my natural sympathy for the man is greatly corrupted by contempt for his lack of sense. Would it be regarded as sane and laudable for a man to travel the Sudan trying to sell fountain-pens, or Greenland offering to teach double-entry bookkeeping? Coming closer, would the judicious pity or laugh at a man who opened a shop for the sale of incunabula in Little Rock, Ark., or who demanded a living in McKeesport, Pa., on the ground that he was a first-rate conductor of grand opera? In precisely the same way it seems to me to be nonsensical for a man to offer generally some commodity that only a few rare and dubious Americans want, and then weep because he is not patronized. One seeking to make a living in a country must pay due regard to the needs and tastes of that country. Here in the United States we have no jobs for grand dukes, and none for *Wirklicke Geheimräte*,[2] and none for palace eunuchs, and none for masters of the buckhounds—and very few for contrapuntists, metaphysicians, astro-physicists, assyriologists, grammarians, watercolorists and epic poets. Well, then, why practise such trades—that is, as trades? The man of independent means may venture into them prudently; it may even be argued that he performs a public service by adopting them. But the man who has a living to make is simply silly if he goes into them. Let him abandon the vain enterprise, and go into the chautauquas or the uplift instead, as, indeed, thousands of Ph.D.'s have already done. Let him bear in mind the fact that, whatever its neglect of the humanities and their monks, the Republic has never got half enough bond salesmen, quack doctors, ward politicians, phrenologists, evangelists, circus clowns, magicians, soldiers, farmers, popular song-writers, chautauqua orators, bootleggers, policemen, detectives, spies, snoopers and *agents provocateurs*. The rules are set; the discreet man observes them. Observing them, he is safe, in fair weather or foul. The boob is a bird that knows no closed season—and if he won't come down to Texas oil-stock or a one-night cure for diabetes, he will always come down to Inspiration and Optimism, whether political, theological, pedagogical, literary or economic.

If it is thus easy to get money in the United States, given ordinary prudence and resourcefulness, it is equally easy to get balm for the ego, given ordinary dignity and decency. Simply to exist, indeed, on the plane of a civilized man is to attain to a distinction that should be enough for most of us; it is even likely to be too much, as the frequent challenges of the Klu Klux Klan, the American Legion and other such patriotic societies testify. Here is a country in which all political thought and activity is concentrated upon the scramble for jobs. Go into politics, then, without seeking or wanting a job, and at once you are as conspicuous, almost, as the Cid was in Spain. Here is a country in which it is an axiom that a business man shall be a member of the Rotary Club, an admirer of Charles M. Schwab, a reader of the *Saturday Evening Post*, and a golfer—in brief, a vegetable. Spend your hours of escape from *Geschäft* reading Rémy de Gourmont and practising the violoncello, and the local Sunday newspaper will infallibly find you out and hymn the marvel.

Here is a land in which women rule and men are slaves. Train your women to get your slippers for you, and your ill fame will match Galileo's or Darwin's. Here is the Paradise of democrats, of back-slappers. Maintain ordinary reserve, and you will arrest instant attention—and have your hand kissed by multitudes who, despite democracy, have all the inferior man's unquenchable thirst to worship superiors. Nowhere else on earth is superiority more facilely attained or more eagerly admitted. The most conspicuous and respected American in nearly every field of endeavor, saving only the purely commercial (I even exclude the financial and the manufacturing) is a man who would attract absolutely no attention in any other country. The leading American critic of literature, after twenty years of incessant exposition, has yet to make it clear what he is in favor of.[3] The leading American musical director, if he went to Leipzig, would be put to polishing trombones. The chief living American military genius belongs to the Elks.[4] The leading American philosopher (now dead, with no successor) spent a lifetime erecting an epistemological defense for the national maxim "I don't know nothing about——, but I know what I like."[5] The greatest statesman the United States has produced since Lincoln was fooled by Arthur James Balfour, and miscalculated his public support by more than 5,000,000 votes.[6]

I refrain from marshaling evidence that life in the United States offers the greatest show in the world; the proofs are too numerous and too insistent. We have clowns in constant practise among us who are as far above the clowns of any other great state as a Jack Dempsey is above a Y.M.C.A. secretary—and not one, but whole herds of them. Human enterprises that, in all other countries, are resigned despairingly to an incurable dullness—things that seem devoid of exhilarating amusement by their very nature—are here lifted to such inordinate buffoonery that contemplating them tears the very midriff from its moorings. I cite one example, and pass on: the worship of God. Everywhere else on earth it is carried on in a solemn and dispiriting manner; in England, of course, the bishops are obscene, but the average man seldom gets a chance to see them. Now come home. Here we not only have bishops who are vastly more obscene than even the most gifted of the English bishops; we have also a great force of superlative specialists in ecclesiastical mountebankery—the Rev. Dr. Billy Sunday and his host of disciples. Every American town has one of its own: a holy clerk with such superb talent for introducing the arts of jazz into the salvation of the damned that his performance takes on all the gaudiness of a four-ring circus, and the bald announcement that he will raid Hell on such and such a night is enough to empty all the town blind-pigs and bordellos and pack his sanctuary to the doors. Personally, I have been overfed with such ribaldries, and prefer politics, patriotism and the Ziegfeld Follies. But within the limits of my prejudices I have quite as much fun as you do, and a great deal more than any imaginable European. Lately, within the space of two weeks, I was torn with such mirth that I actually came down with a severe tetany. First, I read the returns of the New York municipal election.[7] Then I made a tour of the New York cafés and observed the results of Prohibition. Then I went to Washington and viewed the triumphal arch erected in honor of the delegates to the Disarmament Conference:[8] an exact replica of the façade of Mrs. Jack Johnson at the last inaugural ball. Then I passed the guards and heard Dr. Harding's opening address to the Conference. And then—

But to think of the appointment of young Teddy Roosevelt, Jr., as American naval expert brings me, even now, to such hysterical snickers, such orgiastic and unhygienic cackles, that I put away the memory on the advice of my medical adviser. This episode, in fact, assaults me from two sides. Not only is it intrinsically almost beyond the grasp of the most cynical imagination—a feat of imbecility that lifts itself to truly epic heights—a masterpiece comparable to the Fifth Symphony, the Sistine frescoes, or the human eye. In addition it is something more. It is a subtle and devastating *attentat* upon democracy, a proof that there is nothing, after all, in that superstition. We subscribe to the doctrine of human equality—and the Rooseveltii reduce it to absurdity as brilliantly as the sons of Veit Bach. Where is your equal opportunity now? Here in this Eden of clowns, with the high rewards and usufructs of clowning theoretically open to every poor boy—here in the very citadel of freedom we found and cherish a clown *dynasty*!

one

The American: A Treatise

The American

Does he exist? Is there actually such a fowl as the *Homo Americanus?* Has he yet emerged from his welter of parent races, his wallow of mongrelism, different, divergent, distinct? Does the thought of him bring up a picture of a definite human type, set off sharply from all other types? Is he recognizable physically; does he think and feel in his own peculiar way? Finally, does he show any signs of what the biologists call fixity of species: is he handing on to his children a something that is ponderable and characteristic, a something apart from and rarer than their common human heritage of hands and eyes, kidneys and warts, lusts and rascalities, *malaises* and *pediculidæ?*

There was a time, of course, when the answer to every one of these questions would have been a ready and perhaps accurate negative. That was during the Colonial era, and down to the War of 1812. The American who then flourished and begot his kind was merely an Englishman living in America, or, more rarely, a German or Dutchman or Irishman or Scotchman. If he showed any separate character it was only in small and unimportant ways. Physically and mentally he was practically identical with his brothers in blood across the sea. Even his revolt against English misrule was a revolt essentially English in principle and method; even his Puritanism was an imported madness. But once the young republic stood firmly on its own four legs, the American began to develop into a creature that had never been on land or sea. Physically and by habit he took on a certain gawkiness and *gaucherie:* he ceased to be a gentleman, or even the larva of a gentleman, by any European standard. And psychically he proceeded to processes of mind and a theory of life

7

which departed more and more from the characteristics and ideas of his grand-fathers. Finally he stood forth boldly: distinct, unprecedented, incomparable, a new man under the sun. And when strangers came from overseas to sell out and share his land he forthwith swallowed them up, so that the children they presently spawned were more *his* children than their own, and their grandchildren were his entirely.

Today, I take it, there is no longer any serious doubt of his differentiation. Ethnologists may argue learnedly that he does not and cannot exist, but the world in general recognizes him at sight. In all his grosser characters he is marked off plainly from the races that have contributed corpuscles to his blood. Every schoolboy knows that he is taller than the Italian, and lighter than the Spaniard, and darker than the Scandinavian, and leaner than the South German, and less moon-faced than the Slav. Again, on the psychic side, it is patent that he is less imaginative than the Frenchman, and more mercurial than the Englishman, and more optimistic than the Russian, and less stolid than the Scotchman, and more practical than the Irishman. So much indeed is visible to the naked eye: no proof is needed of what everyone admits. But if, in an effort to make the obvious doubly plain, such proof is actually sought out, with tape line, callipers and scale, it will be found beyond peradventure that the American differs, in some way or other, from every other type of white man, sometimes only in small details, but often very widely and strikingly.

Consider one element: his height. Measurements made of hundreds of thousands of native-born Americans, of all lines of ancestry, show that the average lies somewhere between five feet seven and one-half inches and five feet seven and two-thirds. That is the mean height of the normal adult American male, and it is substantially the same East, West, North and South. Now, how does this American compare to the men of other races? Is he larger or smaller? A study of the figure shows that only the Scotchman overtops him. The Swede, a tall, well made man, is nearly half an inch shorter. So is the North German. So is the Sikh, the tallest of all Orientals. The Welshman is a full inch shorter. The Greek, the Turk, the Italian, the Russian and the Swiss are two inches shorter. The Pole is three inches shorter, the Russian Jew is four. The Spaniard and the Hun, full five inches shorter, scarcely come up to the American's nose: he can look over them and into the eyes of the Norwegian, the Irishman and the Englishman, who are exactly his own height. But does this last prove merely that he is still an Englishman himself, perhaps with a dash of the Scotchman to draw him up and a dash of the German to draw him down, and dashes of the Irishman and Norwegian to keep him steady? Not at all. If you will examine the measurements lately made by Dr. Franz Boas, a very able and careful man, you will find that the American tends to be five feet seven and a half inches in height *even when he hasn't a drop of English blood in his body*. When immigrants come here who are shorter—and all of them now are—their children promptly shoot up toward the average. Thus the invading Bohemian, who is but five feet six inches in height, produces children who grow to five feet seven and a half. And thus the Pole, the Slovak, the Hungarian and the Russian Jew, who are from three to five inches shorter than the American, gain between an inch and two inches in the first American born generation, and will probably reach the American average in the second.

This same curious movement toward a racial mean is visible in all other measurements. For example, in weight. It used to be thought that lean immigrants fattened in this country simply because they got more and better food, but now it appears that the process is far more subtle, for children born abroad, even when brought here while still very young, do not develop into as heavy men and women as those born on this side of the water. Perhaps the better feeding of the mothers explains it. But how explain the fact that, while the height and weight increase, the shape of the skull also changes? How is it, for example, that a Russian Jew born in this country has a rounder head than his brother born in Kief? And how is it that a South Italian has a longer head? Here we come upon movements toward the American mean from both directions. The American, as the anthropologists have it, is sub-brachycephalic. That is to say, his head is about four-fifths as wide as it is long: his cephalic index oscillates between 80 and 82. The Jew, on the other hand, is more brachycephalic: his index runs beyond 83. And the Italian tends to be dolichocephalic, or long-headed: his index is below 78. But the children of Jews, born in America, show an average index of 81.4, and the children of Italians show an index of 81.5. In brief, both lose their original characters and take on American characters. Both, in the very first generation, sprout essentially American skulls.

But all this by the way. The present bright day is not one for exploring too intimately the persons of immigrants, an enterprise trying to the patience and the nose. Nor is it worth the trouble it takes. We all know very well how perfectly the diverse stocks of past generations have been absorbed and amalgamated, and we see the same process going on around us today. With bell and book and by procedures less pious the strangers that come pouring into our ports are intermating and interbreeding with the native stock and with each other. Young Jewish bucks marry Irish girls, and Lithuanians take fair Bohemians to wife. Their children will marry the children of Italians and Greeks, Huns and Slovaks, Swedes and Danes. And into the cauldron, from time to time, there will shoot streams of English blood— English blood, that is, tinctured with German blood, Scotch blood and Spanish blood. I myself bear a German name, but one-fourth of me is a fantastic of English and Irish, and the only girl I am sorry I didn't marry was half German, a quarter Irish and a quarter French. The fellow who carried her off was a Scotchman with vague New England quarterings. Their children will be as thoroughly American as Theodore Roosevelt. Their grandchildren will be more American than Abraham Lincoln, or Thomas Jefferson, or Andrew Jackson, or George Washington.

No, the immigrant does not last. A few whirls in the machine and he emerges wrapped in the Star-Spangled Banner, with American slang in his mouth, American sentimentality in his heart, and an American indictment hanging over him. He may hold to his national customs for a generation, but no longer. Ridicule makes him ashamed of them; ambition makes him abandon them. His highest aim is to speak American without an accent, to belong to an American lodge, to *be* an American. Nature helps him by lengthening his legs, by squeezing in his high cheekbones, by blocking his head to the national model. Nature helps still further by the process known as alternating heredity, whereby so-called dominant or strong characters crowd out recessive or weak ones, not by compromise and coalescence but by actual obliteration. The characters of the native type are dominant; they fit the American's environment. Thus they fasten themselves upon the stranger, helping out his sub-brachycephalic noddle, his elongating shank. And before this physical transformation has gone halfway, the psychical metamorphosis is in full force and effect. The German-American's view of things, even of things German, gradually becomes an American view. The Irish-American, for all his ferocious loyalty to Ireland, ends by seeing her remotely, darkly, almost as he sees Armenia. And the gorged Italian-American, going back to his sunny vineland to drowse away his days, is urged into politics by some force beyond him, and plays the game American style, his hands outstretched, his eyes alert for spoil.

But back to the American, the native and indubitable American, two long generations removed from the swarming immigrant ships! Back to that sub-brachycephalous and sentimental fellow, with his sudden sobs and rages, his brummagem Puritanism, his childish braggadocio, his chronic waste of motion, his elemental humor, his great dislike of arts and artists, his fondness for the grotesque and melodramatic, his pious faith in quacks and panaceas, his curious ignorance of foreigners, his bad sportsmanship, his primitive feeding, his eternal self-medication, his weakness for tin pot display and strutting, his jealous distrust of all genuine distinction, his abounding optimism, his agile pursuit of the dollar. Of all these habits and qualities, which is the dominant one? Which lies over and vitalizes all the others, as the grail motive vitalizes *Lohengrin?* Which may be said to give the American his peculiar cut and color, setting him off, not only in his actions but also in his way of thinking, his theory of life, his attitude toward the great problems of life and living, from all other civilized white men?

The average intelligent foreigner, I dare say, will offer a ready and easy answer to all these questions. He will tell you at once that the outstanding mark of the American is his money madness, and assume it thereafter as a primary and immutable premise. He will point, in support of it, to the huge fortunes of American millionaires, swollen beyond all estimate and dreaming; to the graft which penetrates to every nook and cranny of the public service, national, state and municipal;

to the vast structure of privilege that has been built up by the mere power of money, so that the worst of all aristocracies is nurtured at the breast of the greatest of all democracies. And behind him, in this estimate, will be the practically unanimous public opinion of the world. It is rare, indeed, for America to be mentioned by a European without some reference, direct or indirect, to the American pursuit of the dollar. It is rarer still for an immigrant to come to these shores without the fixed intent to join in the chase. It is unheard of for a visitor to go home without carrying marvelous tales of American riches, American cupidity and American prodigality. In all European languages, and in most of those more remote, the United States is frankly spelled "United $tate$."

For all this weight and circumstance of evidence, this universal concord of opinion, I doubt that the indictment of dollar worship is one that may be fairly brought against the American people. In that idolatry, indeed, there are devotees overseas who make the pale ardor of the Yankee seem almost atheistic. For example, the French. For example, the Scotch. For example, the Germans. What a Frenchman regards as no more than prudence and thrift, the average American would regard as avarice; what a Scotchman or German looks upon as decent economy, the American would reject as hoggishness. The American, true enough, receives more for his labor than these other fellows, not only actually but even perhaps relatively. He demands far more pay for his short day than they are able to get for their long one. But the money he thus acquires with ease he at once spends with prodigality. No other man of the same degree of civilization saves a smaller proportion of his net income in hard cash, or puts less of it into permanent property. No man is more swindled by useless middlemen and criers of gewgaws. He is poorer in all those goods which represent shrewd bargaining and self-denial than either the German or the Scandinavian: it is only the enormous natural wealth of his country, so vast as to be almost waste-proof, that makes him seem richer. And even counting in this natural wealth, he is poorer than the Britisher and the Frenchman. He has less money in the bank, he is less a lender, his annual excess of income over outgo is relatively smaller. In brief, his alleged worship of the dollar is a great deal more an appearance than a reality. His mania for getting it is outmatched and overshadowed by his mania for getting rid of it. If he must be given a financial label, then let it be that of spendthrift, and not that of money grubber. No man in Christendom is less a hoarder-up of riches. No man has less genuine reverence for money.

This is shown plainly by the American attitude toward men of great wealth. Are they heaped with admiration and adulation? Are they revered as superior beings? Are they held up as models for the youth of the country? Are they showered with honors by the nation? Of course they are not. As Maurice Low has sagaciously pointed out, the United States is perhaps the only country in the world in which money, in itself, carries no public honor with it, and in which even the most lavish heaving of coins to the rabble goes unrewarded. An English Carnegie would have had a seat in the House of Lords twenty years ago; a French Rockefeller would have sported the grand cordon of the Legion of Honor before ever he sported a toupee; a German Morgan could never have escaped the Red Eagle and Privy Council. But in the United States a great fortune is the most effective of all bars to public dignity and preferment, and even to private respect. Our Ryans and Harrimans are not idols but targets: the one sure way to make a stir in politics is to attack them successfully, or, failing that, merely savagely. And our spectacular philanthropists, our Rockefellers, Carnegies and Sages, get only mocking for their philanthropy. They are public butts, fair game for every wayside clown and spellbinder. Imagine the roar that would go up if it were proposed to erect a monument to one of them, or to send him to Congress or to make him President! Now and then, true enough, a millionaire buys his way into the Senate, but it is seldom that he lasts long or gains any appreciable influence there: he has scarcely taken his seat before a hue and cry is raised against him. The immorality of wealth, in truth, has been one of the fundamental doctrines of the American people since they first developed a settled public opinion. The whole history of our politics, from the day of Jackson's historic rousing of the chandala,[1] has been a history of incessant warfare upon opulence. Every first-rate leader that the country has produced, from Jefferson to Bryan, has pictured wealth as something loathsome in itself and its possessors as familiars of the devil, and no open preacher of the contrary principle has ever won to an elective office of national importance.

But if all this is true, if the foreigner is wrong in his view, if the American is not the dollaromaniac that he is usually thought to be—even by himself, if the elegies of his moralists truly represent him—then what *is* he? What salient lust or weakness is his hallmark, as unruliness is the hallmark of the Latin-American, and melancholy of the Russian, and molelike patience of the German? What habit of thinking gives color to all his ideas, and direction to his aspirations, and form and substance to his character? Let me answer with a habit that is not really a habit of thinking at all, but rather a habit of feeling. A habit of dramatizing, of romanticising, of sentimentalizing. A habit of reasoning almost wholly by emotion, abruptly, irrationally, extravagantly, even when the problem to be solved is as intrinsically devoid of emotional content as a theorem in geometry. In brief, the American thinks with his nerve ends, his liver and his lachrymal ducts, and only revises and regrets with his cerebellum. A member of the most numerous democracy ever seen upon earth, he pushes the tricks and weaknesses of democracies to lengths never matched in history. A unit in the largest crowd ever brought into reciprocal understanding and accord, his psychology is frankly the egregious, preposterous psychology of the mob. The men of other nations, true enough, also have their national saturnalia, their occasional debauches of enthusiasm and rage, their orgies of hero worship and their butcheries of heroes following after, but it is only in the United States that the body politic is chronically in this state of tumescence, it is only here that a pathological state is almost the normal state. Say that the American is the master money grubber of the world and you do him wrong, for there are fellows overseas who grub for money harder; but say that he is the master sentimentalist, and you come close to giving him his authentic label, for there is no man in Christendom who puts pretty poetry higher above sober prose, or who views cold logic with a more bilious suspicion, or who is misled more easily or more systematically by undisguised appeals to his prejudices, his superstitions and his infantile vanities.

Perhaps we may find the first cause of all this in his fantastic mixture of blood, with its warring and irreconcilable feeding streams. No doubt it takes years for such a compound to settle. Much the same excess of emotion is visible in other mongrel races, for example, the Iberian, the Southern Italian and the Latin-American. A restless bubbling goes on until one element conquers all the others, or until some new and stable combination is precipitated. In the veins of the American, of course, this process is constantly interrupted by the entrance of new elements. Before the original mixture of English, Scotch and Dutch plasmas could arrive at equilibrium, there came an acid dash of Irish, and then a heavy stream of German, and now, in our own time, there are toxic, epileptogenic additions of Slavic and Scandinavian, Latin and Semitic. Add to this incessant stirring up within the individual or small group the ease with which ideas and emotions are communicated from one group to another, and you may come to some understanding, perhaps, of the peculiar excitability of the American people. No high wall, physical or psychical, separates one part of the country from the other parts. There is unanimity of language, of ideals, of present interests, of fundamental assumptions. The same theory of virtue runs from Maine to Texas, and the same theory of truth, and the same theory of heroism. It is impossible for the Pacific Slope to be profoundly moved without awakening some echo of its feeling in New England and the South. With a thousand foci of possible inoculation, there is almost perfect machinery for spreading the infection. Let a new divine healer arise in some Arkansas hill town, or a new trust buster come forward with his panacea in Oregon, or a new kidnapping flabbergast the gendarmes in New York, or a new muckraker toss up a city dungpile in Ohio, or a new divorce inflame the pulpit thumpers in Boston—and in five days the whole country will rock with the news, and Americans three thousand miles away will miss meals to gabble over it, and make enemies in maintaining their views of it.

A cause contributing to this circular hysteria, this incurable eagerness to be startled and astounded, this childish interest in the trivial, this firm faith in the preposterous, is to be found in the large leisure of the American people. In their own view, of course, they have no leisure at all: they like to think of themselves as the prime hustlers of the world, the race *prestissimo*, the champion burners of the candle. But, as a matter of fact, they work less and play more than any other civilized nation. Their hours of labor are the shortest in the world; they increase their holidays yearly; they show none of that meticulous and insatiable diligence which characterizes, for example, the Germans and French. The result, on the one hand, is a general frowziness: a spick and span community is rare in the United States, and so is a spick and span home. And, on the other hand, the effect is to put a premium upon a host of devices, all more or less banal, for occupying the lengthening hours of ease. Nowhere in Europe will you find a people who devote as much time to any communal recreation, not even excepting religious rowdyism, as the American people devote to baseball. Nowhere will you find a people with so much time for the fripperies and futilities of fraternal orders, Christian Endeavor Societies,[2] "pleasure" clubs, idle visiting, interminable card playing, precinct politics and other such time-wasters. And nowhere, finally, will you find a people with less disposition to consider the sober things of life with that care and patience which they demand. The typical American is all for the short cut, the dramatization of a situation, the quick, spectacular solution. As Dr. Münsterburg puts it, he suffers from a congenital "inability to suppress and inhibit." He is perpetually drunk upon his own chromatic and effervescent blood.

Naturally enough, this attitude toward life in general leads to a wholesale corruption of those institutions which depend for their dignity and value upon their philosophical remoteness, their superiority to transient passions. For example, the judicial system. A court of law, in the United States, is not a thing above and apart from the stream of everyday life, but a bobbing craft upon that stream, subject to infinite suctions and hazards. The least citizen is competent to criticise the highest judge, and he exercises that divine right whenever he is sufficiently attracted by the judge's doings. Nine times out of ten, of course, he is not attracted by them, and could not understand them if he were, but the tenth time he lifts his voice in hideous objurgation, and brave indeed is the rare Taney who disregards him. The result is that a case of any public interest whatever commonly resolves itself into a mixture of circus and camp meeting, with the newspapers in the dual role of clown and exhorter. Whether the defendant be a corporation accused of making money or an individual accused of murder, the actual weighing of the evidence is conducted outside the courtroom, and the verdict reached within is merely a weak echo and ratification of the circumambient *vox populi*. In the case of the corporation, of course, that verdict is always one of guilt, whatever be the merits of the defense. So thoroughly is this true, indeed, that no sane corporation lawyer ever goes into court with any notion of trying such a case upon its merits alone. His one effort is to keep its merits out of it, to combat public prejudice and passion with professional ingenuity, to convert the issue from one of fact into one of mere procedure and etiquette, and so to achieve the salvation of his client by his superior knowledge of those recondite sciences. Technicalities have saved many an American criminal from his just dues, but for every criminal so favored, they have probably saved ten innocent men from legal lynching. Even so, the prisons of the United States are full of scapegoats—the helpless victims of popular prejudice, superstition and rage.

No sense of abstract justice seems to reside in the soul of the American. A mob man in his ways of thinking, he shows all of the mob's sentimentality, suggestibility, credulity, irascibility, bad sportsmanship and lust for cruelty. On the one hand, the United States is probably the only country in Christendom in which Christ might reappear and preach to the people without danger from the police; and on the other hand, it is the only country, save perhaps England, in which utter social and political extinction is the portion of the man who departs in the slightest from the current fashions in morals, theology, political theory or dress. It is but a few years since it was almost certain ruin for an American politician, save in a few large cities, to wear dress clothes; it is still ruin for him to wear court costume at a foreign court, or to defend its wearing by others. To prove that a man is an agnostic—*i.e.*, that his private attitude toward religion is that of such giants as Huxley and Spencer, Haeckel and Ibsen—is to debar him automatically from all public office save the most degraded. To convict him of adultery is even worse, despite the fact that fully sixty per cent. of all American men are unchaste, and the further fact that most of the rest would be likewise if they had the courage. It is a definite crime in the United States for a man to argue publicly against many of the doctrines set forth in the Declaration of Independence: he may actually get into jail for it. Republican France has her royalists and all the kingdoms of Europe have their republicans, but it would be almost suicide for an American to propose the overthrow of the republic and the election of a king.[3]

Much of this sharp rage against heretics, of course, is mere thirst for butchery. The fact that someone has committed a crime is of far less interest to the American than the fact that someone is being punished for a crime. This is shown by his readiness to pursue and brickbat his heroes of yesterday, for crimes purely theoretical or for no crime at all. The dramatic downfall and savage excoriation of Chauncey M. Depew, a favorite of the mob for years, afford a case in point. Chauncey was not taken in unsuspected deviltry: he merely admitted freely, being asked, what everyone already knew about him. But the demand of the moment was for a shining mark, and so the jester found himself suddenly chased by bloodhounds. The same appetite for torture explains the easy success of most so-called "good government" campaigns in American cities, and their quick collapse after succeeding. Let a newspaper but announce the discovery that some notorious political rogue is stealing, and at once the whole community takes to his trail. He is commonly very game, or at least very well intrenched; and so the pursuit of him is good sport. First, there is the fun of shaking him loose from his grafts, and secondly, there is the greater fun of forcing him into prison. But the moment he is behind the bars all interest in the business evaporates. The chances are two to one that the reformer who has followed him in power will be grafting himself within two years, and if, by any excess of virtue, he refrains, then he is sure to be succeeded by a professional grafter at the end of his service. It is rare, indeed, for an American reform movement to last longer than the term of the incendiary reformer. The public resents the tedium of decency. Its thirst for a good show is vastly more powerful than its thirst for an honest man.

But here I invade the domain of American morals, the which will engage us at length in a future essay. What I really want to do, in the short space remaining, is to call attention (*a*) to the American's lack of individual enterprise, and (*b*) to his lack of communal enterprise. The first of these accusations, of course, he will sharply resent, as a statement of a palpable and libelous absurdity. His chief boast, indeed, is that the civilization he adorns puts a high premium upon enterprise and originality, that his country is preëminently the land of opportunity. But opportunity to do what? To make money, yes. To launch new religions, to market new patent medicines, to combine the two in new and bizarre ways—yes again. To change the old platitudes into new platitudes, the superstitions of yesterday into the superstitions of today—yes a third time. But certainly not opportunity to tackle head on and with a surgeon's courage the greater and graver problems of being and becoming, to draw a sword upon the timeworn and doddering delusions of the race, to clear away the corruptions that make government a game for thieves and morals a petty vice for old maids and patriotism the last refuge of scoundrels—to think, in brief, as men think whose thinking is worth while, cleanly, innocently, ruthlessly! Alas, no. The American is not hospitable to such toying with his *principia*. Tell him that Mrs. Eddy was divine and he will be all ears, but tell him that his other dead gods were *not* divine and he will be for burning you. Dispute about democracy's failures all you please, but don't argue that democracy itself is a failure! Attack his party program until you are tired, but don't attack his party! If you start out from one of his fallacies he will hear you, but if you start out *against* his fallacies he will damn you—and it will make but slight difference whether the concrete thing you are advocating be aristocracy or cannibalism, the disfranchisement of job holders or polygamy, the foolishness of preachers or the assassination of Presidents.

And as he thus represses, with all the force of a national taboo, the free cavorting of individualists, he clings with sentimental hunkerousness to the ideas and customs that would perish by their freedom. The United States is the largest democracy ever seen on earth, but it has never been a leader of other democracies, it has never made pioneer experiments with new democratic inventions. After nearly a century and a half of starting forward and going back, it is still far from universal manhood suffrage—a commonplace in all other republics, and a probability of tomorrow in most monarchies. It has hesitated over giving the vote to women for forty years, and is still afraid to make the trial. It waited for Australia to devise a fair and secret ballot. It debates today, as perilous novelties, democratic contrivances that have already grown hoary elsewhere—the direct primary, the initiative and referendum, minimum wage laws, compulsory arbitration in labor disputes, the recall of erring office holders, the commission form of city government, old age pensions, workingmen's accident insurance, the public ownership of public utilities, the federal control of corporations. It was the last civilized country to adopt the merit system in public office—*i.e.*, the thoroughly democratic rule of putting a man's intrinsic value above the influence of his friends and family. It was the last civilized country to abolish slavery.

Thus the American, viewed in his outlines, and not too closely. In the main he clings close to his archetype, the mob man. He shows the same disordered emotionalism, the same incapacity for sober self-analysis, the same distrust of distinction, the same great fondness for ready and sophistical formulæ. But in detail he departs widely from this mean. In detail he has lusts and weaknesses, habits and axioms that are all his own. Of these anon.

The American: His Morals

"More than any other people," said Wendell Phillips, in one of his penetrating flashes, "we Americans are afraid of one another." He might have added, as an obvious corollary, "and merciless to one another." The national fear of giving offense, in truth, has the soundest of prudence in it: it is fed constantly by new evidence of what happens to the man who treads upon the communal corns. A scream of rage—and he is flat upon his spine. And swiftly upon the heels of that condign felling, before ever he can lift his voice in his defense, or even in apology and appeal for grace, the process continues as follows:

1. The removal of his liver and lights.
2. The deposit of a cake of ice in the cavity.
3. The burial of the corpse.

A natural consequence, perhaps, of democracy. An inevitable symptom of that emotional mob-thinking which distrusts all genuine distinction on the one hand, and is eternally eager for an *auto-da-fé* on the other. Wherever and whenever the mob has ruled, it has leaned to like proceedings. You remember, of course, the program of Wat Tyler and his honest hinds—how they stopped each stranger they met on the road to London and demanded to know if he could read and write; and how, if he said yes, they bawled, "He confesses!" and forthwith hanged him to the nearest oak. So, again, in the French Revolution: if there was one thing more astounding than the mob's fickleness, it was the mob's senseless savagery. It killed men for crimes that were improbable and even incredible, and its favorite for killing was always some amateur messiah whose hand it had licked the day before.

So, too, in the Rome of the First Triumvirate and in the English Commonwealth: democracy is the same forever. It makes for an irrational, explosive, get-a-rope way of doing things. It puts the wayward passion and biliousness of the hour above all settled conviction and policy. Menaced everlastingly by the chance that the minority of today may become the majority of tomorrow, that black may turn suddenly white, that the wholly virtuous may become the wholly vile, it falls into the habit of striking from the shoulder while a nose is actually within reach. In other words, the majority heaps penalties upon the minority in the hope of crippling it beyond recovery, or, failing that, of drawing out its recovery as long as possible. And the method thus pursued in the field of purely political combat is used again in the field of morals. Immorality, in the abstract, is not frowned upon by democracy. On the contrary, democracy is itself immoral, and its highest rewards go to successful acts of immorality. Its central doctrine, indeed, is that all human valuations are subject to change overnight, and it holds that there is a positive merit in thus overturning them. But the man who makes the attempt *and fails* must pay a swift and staggering penalty for his failure. His sin is not against any ideal of abstract and immutable virtue, not against any *jure divino* or *jus naturæ*,[4] but against the security and *amour-propre* of the majority. And the punishment for that sin does not flow from any remote and icy fountain of justice, but from the blind rage of a mob.

Thus we find in the very constitution of the American commonwealth a reason for the strange timorousness which marks the American—a timorousness noted by Harriet Martineau, De Tocqueville, Follen, Emerson and Channing before ever Phillips pointed it out and moralized upon it, and by Maurice Low, Nicholas Murray Butler, Hugo Münsterberg and many another anatomist of the national character after him. But this reason is not the whole reason. It accounts for the fear of the individual, but it does not account for the moral obsession of the mass. It explains why the punishment of the erring is so devastating, but it does not explain why the community should be so eager to smell the erring out.

That further explanation is to be found, I believe, in the continued survival of a dominating taint of Puritanism in the American character—a survival no less real and corrupting because many of its outward evidences have been concealed by time. Since the very dawn of his separate history, the American has been ruled by what may be called a moral conception of life. He has thought of all things as either right or wrong, and of the greater number of them, perhaps, as wrong. He has ever tended, apparently irresistibly, to reduce all questions of politics, of industrial

THE AMERICAN: A TREATISE

organization, of art, of education, and even of fashion and social etiquette, to questions of ethics. Every one of his great political movements has been a moral movement; in almost every line of his literature there is what Nietzsche used to call moralic acid; he never thinks of great men and common men, of valuable men and useless men, but only of good men and bad men. And to this moral way of thinking he adds a moral way of acting. That is to say, he feels that he is bound to make an active war upon whatever is bad, that his silence is equivalent to his consent, that he will be held personally responsible, by a sharp-eyed, long-nosed God, for all the deviltry that goes on around him. The result, on the one hand, is a ceaseless buzzing and slobbering over moral issues, many of them wholly artificial and ridiculous, and on the other hand, an incessant snouting into private conduct, in the hope of bringing new issues to light. In brief, the result is Puritanism.

This national Puritanism, of course, has been considerably modified, in materials if not in method, by the passage of the years, and is still in process of laborious evolution. At the start, as everyone knows, it was inextricably mingled with purely theological ideas. In all of the early colonies, at least in the North, it was a great deal more dangerous for a man to go astray in exegesis than to go astray in conduct. Under the Massachusetts theocracy, for example, the punishment for heresy was far heavier than the punishment for adultery, or even than the punishment for ordinary murder. But by the time the constitution of the new republic came to be framed, this old snorting over the affairs of heaven had been eased, in a measure, by the pressing importance of the affairs of this earth, and so the hostile factions were ready to accept the compromise proposed by Thomas Jefferson and other such neutrals, declaring a permanent truce of God in religion. As Maurice Low points out, it was the bitter need of the hour and not any genuine toleration that lay at the bottom of this truce. The breach between Quaker and Catholic, churchman and dissenter, was still unspanable, but they chose to forget it in the face of common perils and a common hatred. Each faction held hunkerously to its own creed, but it was ready to abandon its right to damn and penalize the creeds of the others.

But this very sacrifice in the department of theology made for an increase of activity in the department of morality. The scope of puritanical endeavor was suddenly narrowed, but the puritanical spirit remained. If it was now impossible to throw a fellow man to the wolves for confusing the Hebrew vowel points, it was still possible to throw him to the wolves for mistaking some other fellow's wife for his own, and to this and like ferocities the Americans addressed themselves with holy fire. The country became, in brief, a bull ring of malignant moralists, each bent upon forcing the whole population to greater and greater feats of personal asepsis, and all bawling like the devil. Religion, ceasing to be a conflict of principles—intelligible at least, however absurd—became a mere debauch of unordered and gaudy emotions, an orgy of enthusiasms, a frenzy almost pathological and wholly obscene. This was the period of great revivals, of entire counties converted to holiness *en masse* and brought bellowing to the mourners' bench. Thus and then was prohibition born, and the jehad against tobacco with it, and the campaign against swearing, and the vice crusade, and a dozen such donkeyish ecstasies and outrageous invasions of private morals. The camp meeting, invented by negroes but once removed from cannibalism, was adopted by the whole population—and survives today as the chautauqua. Morality raged like a pestilence. No human act, however natural and innocent, escaped a destructive moral analysis. Even the language, as Bartlett tells us in his *Dictionary of Americanisms*, was spayed and fitted with skirts. Such words as "bull" and "mare," in the forties and fifties, became "male cow" and "female horse." "Stomach" (held virtuous for some reason unknown) was stretched to include the whole region from the nipples to the pelvic arch. The forthright nouns and adjectives of a franker if no less moral day were covered with such gossamers as "the social evil," "a statutory offense," "a house of ill fame" and "an interesting condition."

In politics appeared the same exaltation of moral issues and moral reasoning. There has been no great political movement in the United States since Jefferson's day without some purely moral balderdash at its center. The long battle against slavery, for example, was led from first to last by men obsessed by the wickedness of the slaveowners, and eager to put it down at any cost in blood and sweat. The historians, true enough, show us that slavery was economically unsound, and that irresistible natural laws worked toward its destruction, but no one thought of its economical unsoundness during the two decades before the Civil War. It was the *moral* unsoundness of the thing that inflamed the North and sent John Brown across the Potomac and provoked four years of unparalleled wrath and butchery. The Abolitionists were not moved by any fear that the South was going bankrupt, nor even by any tangible feeling that the North was suffering unfair competition, but simply and solely by an uncontrollable craving, entirely puritanical in character, to make the Southerners change their brand of virtue. It was their unalterable conviction that they themselves were wholly good and that the Southerners were wholly bad, and they thought it was their supreme duty, as custodians of the divine grace, to purge and punish the erring. In brief, they were Puritans of the purest ray. They were willing to sacrifice everything, including even the State itself, to force their private morals upon unwilling sinners.

The same mania, always taking extremely hysterical forms, is evident in all our other political experiments and revolutions. A new political idea, however persuasively it may be set forth, never takes hold upon the American imagination until it is put into terms of a sonorous morality. I need not point out how our political mountebanks have always given poignancy to their issues by the simple process of finding (or inventing) villains to denounce. The great heroes of the common people have seldom brought anything actually new to the problems they have presumed to solve. Jackson was not the author of the so-called Jacksonian scheme of mob rule, and Bryan was not the discoverer of the free silver panacea, and Roosevelt was not the father of any of his vast and irreconcilable brood of remedies. But Jackson *did* convince the chandala that their betters were robbing them, and Bryan *did* convince them that the trusts were crucifying them, and Roosevelt *did* convince them there were vast, horrible and unintelligible conspiracies against them, and so these rabble-rousers got their ears and inflamed them to multitudinous follies. The touchstone, in every case, was their moral hyperesthesia, their weakness for reducing all ideas to terms of right and wrong, their eternal eagerness to burn a concrete and screaming sinner.

But how does it happen that this Puritan point of view has survived the swift and radical changes of a century? How, for one thing, has it survived the opposition of the 30,000,000 immigrants who have poured into the country since 1830—many of them from lands untouched by Puritanism, some of them from environments bitterly hostile to it? And how, for another thing, has it survived the changing conditions of life at home—from the spaciousness and leisure of the country to the crowded competition of the towns, from pastoral simplicity of interests to commercial and industrial complexity? The first of these two questions answers itself if you reflect upon the newly-arrived immigrant's dominating desire to lose his differentiation as soon as possible. That differentiation is a heavy burden to him. It costs him a lot every day, not only in actual wages but also in social opportunity and public respect, to be a Mick, a Dutchman, a Bohick, a squarehead, a dago or a guiney. He is impatient to be accepted as an American, and if, by any ossification of habits, he is personally deprived of that boon, he makes sure that his children enjoy it. And public opinion supports him in his effort. All the little tricks of manner that he brought with him are laughed at, and so are his inherited ways of thinking. So long as he remains a palpable foreigner, he is a common butt, and on no higher level than the native blackamoor. No wonder he tries his best to lose his stigmata! No wonder his one hope is to speak American as the Americans speak it, to look and eat and see and smell like an American, to outfit his mind with a full stock of American ideas! And no wonder he is especially hospitable, whatever his initial repugnance, to those ideas which Americans seem to set most value upon—in other words, to the great root ideas of their national Puritanism.

This absorption of the foreigner, of course, is not wholly without its compensatory coloring of the absorbing mass. The German has ceased to be a German in the United States, and the Russian Jew is ceasing to be either Russian or a Jew, but the American, by the same token, has become a bit of a German, and a bit of a Jew. Where large numbers of an invading race have settled together, they have broken down the native morality by their sheer weight, and substituted a sort of compromise between it and their own morality. Thus the Irish introduced their peculiar weakness for political chicanery into most of the large cities of the East—often finding a fertile soil for it, one may observe, in a native weakness almost as marked. And thus the Germans and Scandinavians in such cities as Cincinnati, St. Louis, Milwaukee and Chicago have made Puritanism draw in more than one of its horns. But in general the immigrant has done nine-tenths of the yielding. I was somewhat startled lately, for example, to hear that a number of German- American pastors had joined the Lord's Day Alliance,[5] one of the most violent and vicious of all our native camorras of puritanical snouters. And everyone must have noticed how the Roman Catholic Church in the United States has taken on something of the national austerity and distrust of joy. On its own soil the church is far from puritanical. Its bishops in Austria, Bavaria, Spain and Italy would never think of prohibiting innocent sports on Sunday afternoons, or of arguing that a man who buys a lottery ticket will go to hell; but their brethren in this country, while perhaps not actually preaching such doctrines, have at least remained silent while other shepherds have preached them, and while complaisant legislators have sought to reinforce them with pharisaical and unenforceable laws.

As for the second question—how Puritanism has survived the changing conditions of life at home—its answer is that Puritanism has changed with them. In principle, perhaps, that yielding has been very slight. The American's point of view is still essentially puritanical. He still sees the devil's snares on all sides of him; he is still enormously interested in the private morals of his fellow men; he is still eager to display his abhorrence of sin by cleaving off the hide of a sinner. But his repertoire of sins has been overhauled more than once: he has taken out old ones and put in new ones. In the main, it will be noted, on examination, that those he has taken out are sins that he has found it expedient or convenient to commit himself with increasing frequency and lack of concealment. And those that he has put in are sins for which he has lost all use or taste, or which he has learned to commit without having to admit it. The primitive Puritan, as we have seen, was more interested in theology than in anything else under the sun, and so he placed the discussion of it above all other enterprises, and was ever ready to hang or burn the man whose view of it offended him. But the American of today, having lost his notion of the supreme importance of theology, is impatient of the turmoil which its discussion entails, and so he has actually erected that discussion, once the first of pious duties, into a sin. Thus he has turned a complete somersault in morals and robbed Puritanism of its original aim and excuse. Religious freedom, in the few American colonies which offered it, meant the right of every man to state his belief boldly and without risk of being disemboweled. But in the republic of today it has come to mean the duty of every man to approve the belief of the other fellow, if not on the ground that he holds it himself, then at least on the ground that it is made reasonable by the other fellow's assent, and is, in any case, not worth rowing about. Once the sin lay in questioning that which happened to be orthodox; now the sin lies in the simple fact of questioning. The American still thinks that it is virtuous to crack the skull of a sinner who professes no faith at all, but he has learned to keep his hands off the sinner who merely professes the wrong one.

To be a sin, under a moral democracy, an act must meet one of two conditions: either it must be something which the majority of persons have no taste or capacity for committing, or it must be something which the average man can commit without serious risk of being found out. To the first class, in the United States, belongs the new sin we have just been discussing. The American of today has no taste for serious religious controversy—he believes, in his normal moods, that one route to heaven is about as good as another and that all sinners will go to the same hell—and so he holds that such controversy is evil. Into the same class he puts acts that are beyond his imagination and talents—for example, seduction, piracy upon the high seas, polygamy, homicide in all the forms that require courage, usury, duelling, bull fighting, acts in restraint of free competition (*i.e.*, against the artificial security of the weak and incompetent), gambling upon any but the pettiest scale, rebellions against the marriage laws, originality in dress, efforts to overthrow the Constitution and set up a better one, and armed resistance to the tyrannies of the police and to statutes passed by corrupt and imbecile legislatures. Such acts, the delight of many undoubtedly first-rate men in all ages, are viewed with horror by the American. He groups a great many of them under the generic name of "anarchy"—and then flees from the name as from a plague. He would regard it as an act of "anarchy" to propose that the President of the United States be shipped to the Philippines and a king put in his place. And by the same token, he would regard it as "anarchy" to go about with naked legs, or to live in amity with two or three wives, or to substitute the cleanly killing of slum babies for their slow starvation, or to teach the poor how to limit their offspring, or to halt the evil-doing of a camorra of political thieves with machine guns, or to extend the masculine standard of morals to women. His chief complaint against the trusts is that they are "anarchistic." By this he means that they accomplish successfully, by straightforward and intelligent means, the things that the average man is unable to accomplish by his clumsy and stupid means.

To the same class belong many offenses which carry us somewhat deeper into the congenital Puritanism of the American. Call them acts of joy and you have described them pretty accurately. The American views joy with unscotchable suspicion, whatever its visible form: his attitude toward it, in general, is exactly opposite to that of the Periclean Greek. Some of its agents, true enough, have wormed themselves, after a fashion, into his reluctant affections—the theater and the dance may serve as examples—but he is still full of a vague feeling that the devil sent them, he is still disposed to apologize for them. When he flings his legs in air, it is by no means in innocence, but with a full sense that the act is subtly lascivious; that it will lay him up no stores in heaven. In principle, indeed, he is wholly against dancing, as he is against card playing and wine-bibbing, and the largest of his native religious sects specifically prohibits all three.[6] Unable, by a defect of the imagination, to penetrate to their spiritual uses or to apprehend the joy they symbolize as a thing in itself, he sees only their element of carnality, and so he feels uncomfortably mocked every time he yields. In the theater his conscience is always with him, sitting sepulchrally at his side and favoring him with a clammy smack ever and anon. The result is a constant effort to stave it off, to placate it, to compromise with it. That is to say, his choice is ever for plays that tickle it at least as much as they outrage it—plays that end safely upon some sonorous and preposterous platitude—plays teaching the general doctrine that virtue is not only possible in this life, but even profitable and agreeable. If the American shows a willingness, now and then, to venture a rod or two into the moral Bad Lands, it is only because of the excuse it gives him for an affecting rush back. He will stand for a play in which John Doe casts a libidinous eye upon Mrs. Richard Roe, but not for a play in which John gets away with it. No, there must be a sad finish for John, and a reconciliation between Mrs. Roe and Richard. And, as a rule, the American feels that even this small toleration of immorality is rather too much. He greatly prefers, indeed, a play in which John picks a virgin for his dalliance, and in which the virgin remains in that blessed state until after the final curtain. In brief, he insists upon what he calls a happy ending.

All sports except baseball are held to be immoral by the American. He may go to see a horse race or a boxing match once in a while, just as he may play poker or view a hoochee-coochee dance or get drunk, but always there will be protests from his conscience. Such diversions, and fox hunting and joy riding with them, are on his roster of iniquities, and he would not dare to yield to any of them if he thought he were going to die next week. The persons who patronize them habitually constitute a recognized and abhorrent caste of sinners: the follower of horses or of royal flushes is just as sure to go to hell as the follower of skirts. Baseball escapes from this general ban for two reasons: the first is that its essential immorality, as an expression of joy, is covered up by its stimulation of a childish and orgiastic local pride, a typically American weakness, and the second of which, flowing from the first, is that it offers an admirable escape for that bad sportsmanship and savage bloodlust which appear in all the rest of the American's diversions. An American crowd does not go to a baseball game to see a fair and honest contest, but to see the visiting club walloped and humiliated. If the home club can't achieve the walloping unaided, the crowd helps—usually by means no worse than mocking and reviling, but sometimes with fists and beer bottles. And if, even then, the home club is drubbed, it becomes the butt itself, and is lambasted even more brutally than the visitors. The thirst of the crowd is for victims, and if it can't get them in one way it will get them in another.

This hot yearning to rowel and punish someone—preferably a sinner, but failing that, anyone handy—is one of the distinguishing marks of the American. The energies which the Germans put into bacchanalian and military enterprise, and the English into idle sport and vapid charity, are chiefly devoted, in this fair land, to moral endeavor, and particularly to punitive moral endeavor. The nation is forever in the throes of loud, barbaric campaigns against this sin or that. It is difficult to think of a human act that has not been denounced and combated at some time or other. Thousands of self-consecrated archangels go roaring from one end of the country to the other, raising the *posse comitatus* against the Rum Demon, or cocaine, or the hobble skirt, or Mormonism, or the cigarette, or horse racing, or bucket shops, or vivisection, or divorce, or the army canteen, or profanity, or race suicide, or moving picture shows, or graft, or the negro, or the trusts, or Sunday recreations, or dance halls, or child labor. The management of such crusades is a well organized and highly remunerative business: it enlists a great multitude of snide preachers and unsuccessful lawyers, and converts them into public characters of the first eminence. Candidates for public office are forced to join in the bellowing; objectors are crushed with accusations of personal guilt; inquisitorial and unconstitutional laws are put upon the statute books; the courts, always so flabby under a democracy, are bullied into complaisance. In the large cities, of course, there is considerable opposition to these puritanical frenzies, if only on the ground that they hurt trade, but the laws of most American cities, it must be remembered, are not made by their citizens but by peasant legislators from the country districts, and no protest can ever prevail against the rural madness for chemical purity.

Such donkeyish enactments, of course, do not actually put down the sins they are aimed at. Their one certain effect, indeed, is quite the contrary: they reinforce mere immorality with positive crime. Thus, in New York City, the effect of prohibiting prostitution, a wholly ineradicable evil, has been to convert it into a mammoth and predatory business, with thousands of petty politicians fattening upon it; and the effect of the unenforceable laws against gambling has been to turn the police into blackmailers. But this inevitable failure doesn't daunt the moral American. The way he gets his fun is not by stamping out sin, but by giving chase to sinners. He likes to catch a few of them now and then and put them to the torture—but it would give him bitter disappointment if they all came in and surrendered. Prohibition, a typically American imbecility, is kept alive by the very fact that it won't work. Its appeal lies almost wholly in the endless sport it affords. First there is the fun of prohibiting the chief solace and recreation of a horde of protesting sinners, and then there is the fun of hunting down all those who refuse to come over to well water—*i e.*, about 99.99 per cent. There is just as much drunkenness in a dry town as in a wet town, and sometimes even more—but there is also more moral excitement. The constant raids and denunciations thrill the pure heart. There is infinite opportunity for exhilarating, spying, threatening, roweling, punishing. The liquor seller who was a licensed merchant yesterday "and felony for to shoot," is now an outlaw, a fugitive from justice, *feræ naturæ*.[7] The breeding and pursuit of such game is the national sport of the American.

The same ferocious impulse is at the bottom of most of the "anti-ring" and "reform" movements which periodically rack American cities. For grafting, in itself, the American has only a theoretical horror, just as he has only a theoretical horror of drunkenness. Whether in public office or in private office, he is commonly a grafter himself, at least in a modest way, and what is more, the fact is universally recognized and taken into account. The cash register is omnipresent in the United States—and for a reason. In no other land in Christendom is the bonding business one-fifth as prosperous. Nowhere else are the public service corporations—such as street car and gas companies, for example—put to greater ingenuity to protect themselves from their customers. But this petty dishonesty—the natural fruit, perhaps, of the hypocrisies engendered by the national Puritanism—does not interfere with the rapturous chase of grafters of more heroic cut. Let but a newspaper announce solemnly that a given public official is taking bribes—a fact already known, or at least strongly suspected, by every reasonable man in the community—and at once the mob is up in arms, and a rousing hunt has begun. Loud demands are made that the trial of the accused be rushed, that he be jailed as quickly as possible, that he be given the maximum sentence under the law. All persons who appear in his behalf, if only to plead for his plain rights, are denounced as accomplices and scoundrels. The whole population yells for his gore; the racial bloodlust demands an immediate victim. But once he is safely behind the bars, once the chase is over, all interest in it dries up. A year or so later the felon is turned out. Sentimentality now rescues him, as savagery once condemned him.

Here we come at last (and it is high time, for these papers must be short) upon the second of the two classes of sins mentioned two or three pages back—that is to say, the sins which the man of average talents can commit without serious risk of being found out. This sin of grafting is a shining example: it is almost always possible, as the vernacular has it, to get away with the goods. Probably the majority of all American public officials, federal, state or municipal, may be "reached" with more or less ease, but not one in a thousand is ever caught and punished. And in private life the ratio of the guilty to the convicted is certainly no larger. (How many men are ever jailed for beating the street cars? Or for using lead nickels in slot machines?) So it is perfectly safe for the American to arraign graft fiercely when a peculiarly inept practitioner is taken in the act: the more he bellows, indeed, the more he diverts suspicion from himself. And not only is it safe and profitable, but in addition, it is urged by a sort of subconscious psychological necessity, for, as Dr. Freud tells us, it is always our own salient weakness that we combat most violently.

The wildest foes of the Rum Demons are drunkards under their skins; the Sunday school superintendent is a bad man to trust with orphans' money; the most rigidly perfect table manners are found in persons whose childhood meals were eaten in the kitchen and to the raucous music of father's gurgitation. And the loudest excoriators of graft, perhaps, are those who know its snares too well.

But an even better example of the sin subterranean is adultery, an act punished in the United States by penalties unmatched in any other civilized land. All our moralists, however far they roam, come back to it soon or late. The wars upon cigarettes, bridge whist and peekaboo waists are passing madnesses; the war for the Seventh Commandment is with us always. It is the inspiration and foundation of innumerable laws, uncompromising, preposterous, unenforceable. It is the theme perpetual of all pious dervishes and rabble-rousers, tear-squeezers and mad mullahs. To be taken in adultery, dramatically, publicly, is to forfeit all qualification to public office under the republic. The simple accusation of a weeping woman, even of a weeping charwoman, might have ruined a Lincoln or a Grant. It *did* ruin — but I name no names! In nearly half the territorial area of the United States a man accused of one form of adultery becomes an outlaw *ipso facto*; he may be shot down without trial, and public opinion will applaud his slayer. And from end to end of the country, the woman who makes an open departure from the cold, straight path is practically expelled from the human race. There is no room is our national life for a George Sand, nor even for a George Eliot. Gorky the patriot and Gorky the artist were swallowed up instanter by Gorky the adulterer. Of the two chief questions that every immigrant must answer before he may enter the gates of the nation, one gives him plain notice that he must not shoot the President and the other gives him plain notice that he must not deny monogamy. Only once in our history has a whole State faced the penalty of disenfranchisement for crime, and then it was for allowing polygamists to admit it.[8]

But does all this show an unexampled purity of national character, a unique frenzy for virtue, a unanimous worship of virginity? Is the American, then, the most chaste of living creatures? Is he a frigid, ascetic archangel, remote from all the low passions and appetites of the brute? Alas, I fear I cannot tell you that he is! I wish I could, but I can't—and he isn't. On the contrary, he is one of the lustiest rogues in all Christendom, a fellow grievously over-sexed, the constant victim of his own fevers, a natural adventurer in amour. All his so-called chivalry, indeed, is no more than evidence of one of his projecting defects: his inability, to wit, to think of women save as servitors to his uses. It is costing him great effort to acquire a more complex view of them; he is still somewhat scandalized whenever they show intelligence and individuality. He would much prefer them to remain his simple property—his cherished, coddled, well defended property, perhaps, but still unmistakably his property. The things he asks of them in return for that jealous cherishing are services almost purely sexual: he wants them to be assiduous wives and willing mothers: it displeases him to picture them in any other role. This view, of course, reacts viciously upon the women themselves. There is no land in which the holding out of the sexual lure is less covered up by artificialities and disguises. The American girl is turned loose upon the reluctant male at seventeen, and she practises her frank magic until she is long past forty. Scarcely a single restraint is upon her; no crippling conventions hamper her display of goods; she is free to snare a man however she may.

And in a score of less open and innocent ways the crude sexuality of the American makes itself evident. His cities reek with prostitution; his newspapers devote enormous space to matters of amour; his one permanent intellectual exercise is the exchange of obscene and witless anecdotes. Recognizing this weakness himself, he makes elaborate efforts to armor himself against it. No other civilized white man is so full of hypocritical pruderies. He is afraid of all "suggestion," as he calls it, in books, pictures and plays. He cannot look at a nude statue innocently; he cannot even imagine a nude woman innocently. Words and images that have no more effect upon a German or a Frenchman than the multiplication table are subtly salacious to the American, and lead him into evil. He is forbidden to kiss his girl in the public parks because he cannot be trusted to stop at kissing. His laws solemnly proscribe, as incitements to debauchery, the very weapons that professional moralists aim at—for example, the report of the Chicago Vice Commission.[9] The ordinances of all his large cities embody a specific denial that he has kidneys; he is afraid to face squarely the commonplaces of physiology. A man eternally tortured by the animal within him, a man forever yielding to brute passion and instinct, his one abiding fear is that he may be mistaken for a mammal.

The American: His Language

If it were not for the fact that school teachers, as a class, are the most hunkerous and unobservant folk in all the world, the teaching of orthodox English in the public schools of America would have been abandoned long ago. Thomas Jefferson, that sure-sighted fellow, saw clearly that the language could not serve permanently the complex and expanding needs of the American people. "The new circumstances under which we are placed," he wrote to John Waldo on August 16, 1813, "call for new words, new phrases, and for the transfer of old words to new objects. An American dialect will therefore be formed."[10]

This prediction, as every attentive man must know, has been amply fulfilled. American is now so rich in new words, new phrases and old words transferred to new objects that it is utterly unintelligible to an educated Englishman, and, as I shall presently show, its grammar and pronunciation have undergone great changes as its vocabulary has developed. But the poor little martyrs in the schools are still taught English instead of American—and not the fluent, racy, loose-jointed Eng-

THE AMERICAN: A TREATISE

lish of living and breathing Englishmen, but the heavy, precise, classical, esoteric English of Macaulay, Addison, Herbert Spencer and Matthew Arnold. Even an Englishman, native to the soil and bred in English schools, does not find this grammar book language ready to his tongue. When he sits down to write a book, a speech or a letter to *The Times*, he has to think the thing out in one language—the spoken English of his particular class and year—and then translate it laboriously into another language—the petrified, bloodless, clumsy English of the pundits.

Some Englishmen, true enough, know this artificial language well enough to write it almost spontaneously, just as many medieval scholars knew Latin, and as a few stray Jews, even today, know the pure Hebrew of the days before the Babylonian captivity. But the great majority of Englishmen know it only imperfectly. Some can read it without being able to write it; some can read it and understand, say, seventy-five per cent. of it; others can understand only fifty per cent., or twenty-five per cent.

Finally, there are the millions who can understand only those elements of it which it has in common with the English of the people—a few of its root words and most of its connectives. When such Englishmen read a leader in *The Times* (which they seldom do more than once in a lifetime) they do not get the exact sense of it, nor even half the sense of it, but only the general drift of it, just as the average Jew gets only the general drift of the Talmud, and the average Italian and Russian get only the general drift of the Latin and Old Slavonic masses.

But, as I have said, the American schoolboy is forced to master the complex and senseless grammar of this foreign and mummified tongue, and even to listen to lectures upon its orthodox pronunciation. It is the master bugbear of his first six years of schooling, and it usually so disgusts him with learning that he never opens a textbook of any sort after he has once left school. And what he is thus forced to learn, unwillingly and against the sharp common sense of childhood, is not only useless to him, but even a bit dangerous. That is to say, he would bring down social odium upon himself, and often actual punishment, if he essayed to speak such a strutting, artificial language outside the schoolroom. His companions, on the one hand, would laugh at him as a prig, and his parents, on the other hand, would probably cane him as an impertinent critic of their own speech. Once he has made his farewell to the schoolmarm, all her effort upon him goes to waste, and all his own effort with it. The boys with whom he plays baseball speak American, and not English, and so do the youths with whom he will begin learning a trade tomorrow, and the girl he will marry later on, and the saloonkeepers, vaudeville comedians, shyster lawyers, business sharpers, and political mountebanks he will look up to and try to imitate all the rest of his life.

It is a bitter waste of time to teach this boy the difference, in transcendental English, between *will* and *shall*, *should* and *would*, *who* and *whom*, for in the American language no such distinctions exist. It is perfectly proper, in American, to say, "I *will* be forty years old tomorrow," or "The girl *who* you introduced me to." Again, it is useless to teach him that the double negative is a contradiction in terms, for he knows very well that "I don't want no more" has a precise and intelligible meaning, and so do his sisters and his cousins and his aunts. Yet again, it is ridiculous to warn him against such forms as "I have gotten," "Him and her were married," "He loaned me a dollar," "I blowed in the money," "The bee stang him," "The man was found $2," "His wife give him hell," "The baby et the soap," "Give everybody whatever is theirn," "It's me," "We taken a trip to Atlantic City," and "Us boys killed a cat." These transformations of the verb and the pronoun, whatever their immorality in English, are perfectly allowable in American. Some of them, such as *gotten* for *got*, are merely archaic English forms, surviving in America long after their disappearance in England, just as many other archaic English forms have survived in Ireland. But others, such as the use of the objective pronoun in the nominative case, have reached so elaborate and separate a development in the United States that their affinity with English dialectic mutations has grown almost imperceptible. And there are corresponding peculiarities in the adjective, in the verb and even in some of the prepositions. Not one of the parts of speech, indeed, has failed to yield something of its English rigidity of tense and case to the special demands of the American people.

But let us begin with the simple personal pronouns. Here is an attempt at their declension in American:

FIRST PERSON

	Singular	*Plural*
Nom.	I	We
Poss.	My	Our (ourn)
Obj.	Me	Us

SECOND PERSON

Nom.	You	Yous
Poss.	Your (yourn)	Your (yourn)
Obj.	You	Yous

THIRD PERSON

Nom.	He, she, it	They
Poss.	His, her, hisn, hern, its	Their (theirn)
Obj.	Him, her, it	Them

So far, so good. This declension accounts for many familiar Americanisms. For example, "Give everybody whatever is theirn." For example, "Yous usen't to use it." For example, "Don't mix up ourn and yourn." And many others of a familiar sound. But a brief inspection is sufficient to show that it does *not* account for a form equally familiar—to wit, the form revealed in "Us fellows have often went broke." Here, it must be plain, we have a transfer of *us*, in the first person plural, from the objective case to the nominative. And much the same phenomenon is seen in "Them men are Swedes," and in "Him and her are brothers and sisters," and in "Us and them are neighbors." An American does not say "*we* and *they*"; he says "*us* and *them*." He does not say "*those* men"; he says "*them* men." He does not use "*he* and *she*" as a subject; he uses "*him* and *her*."

Well, what does all this indicate? It indicates, in the first place, that the plural pronoun in American, whenever it is hitched to its corresponding noun so as to form the subject of a sentence, takes the inflectional form of the objective case. It indicates, in the second place, that two or more singular pronouns, whenever they are joined together by prepositions for the same purpose, undergo the same change. The which may be reduced, for convenience, to a single rule—the first scientific contribution, so far as I know, to the grammar of the American language—to wit:

Whenever an American pronoun used as the subject of a sentence is joined to its corresponding noun or to another pronoun, it takes the form of the objective case.

But is this the whole story? Isn't it a fact that certain plural pronouns undergo the same change, even when standing alone? For example, what of "*Them* are the kind I like"? What of "*Them* were the men I seen"? Here we have plain inflections to the objective form, and yet the pronouns stand alone and are not connected with their corresponding nouns. An apparent extension of our pioneer rule, but, after all, it is only apparent. The truth is that in both of these examples, and in all other such examples, the corresponding noun is either concealed by ellipses, or standing a step or two away. "*Them* are the kind I like" is merely a shorter form of "*Them* kind are the *kind* I like," and three times out of five the American actually inserts the missing noun. And even when he doesn't, he commonly makes up for it with interest by inserting a more specific noun, as in "Them *men* (or *oysters*, or *poker hands*, or *false teeth*, or *clergymen*) are the kind I like." In brief, this change of the plural pronoun to the objective case is fully covered by our rule, and so no extension is needed to account for it. When the plural pronoun stands indubitably alone—*i.e.*, when its corresponding noun would be obviously redundant, or must be imagined as part of a preceding and wholly separate sentence—then it retains the nominative form. The American does not say "*Them* went home"; he says, "*They* went home." And in the same way he does not say, "*Us* are soused"; he says, "*We* are soused."

If we now turn to the verbs, we shall find a similar disharmony between English and American, though here the American forms are often matched by identical forms in archaic or dialectic English. The American perfect participle of *get*, for example, was in good usage in England in Dryden's day and is still encountered in a number of county dialects. But not many educated Englishmen of today use *gotten*: they prefer the more euphonious if less regular *got*. In the same way they prefer the irregular *struck* to the regular *stricken* as the perfect participle of *to strike* in the passive voice. An English lawyer moves in court that certain testimony be struck out; his predecessor in Coke's day moved that it be stricken out; his American colleague of today clings to the older form. Thus with other American conjugations. The tendency to make irregular verbs regular, as revealed in such forms of the past tense as *throwed, knowed, blowed, drawed* and *heared,* is one which spoken American shows in common with most of the other colloquial forms of English. And so is the tendency to bring the irregular conjugation of verbs of similar sound into harmony, as, for instance, in the use of *skun* for *skinned,* obviously a false analogy from *spin* and *spun, win* and *won.*

But beside these widespread aberrations, met with in Irish-English, Scotch, Cockney and other English dialects as well as in American, there are a number of American forms, in use from end to end of the United States, which are native to the soil. For example, the use of *left* as the past tense form of *to let* and the similar transformation of *to fine* into *found.* It is true enough that an American newspaper reporter, deliberately trying to write book English, will say that a magistrate *let* one prisoner off with a warning and *fined* another a dollar, but it is equally true that every policeman in the courtroom will say that the first prisoner was *left* off and that the other was *found.* But perhaps I had better present a few typical American conjugations, illustrative of this and other points:

PRESENT	PAST	PERFECT PARTICIPLE
Arrive	Arrove	Arriven
Be	Bean	Ben
Begin	Begun	Began
Bring	Brung	Brang
Bust	Busted	Bust
Climb	Clumb	Clumb
Cling	Clang	Clung
Creep	Crep	Crep
Come	Come	Came
Crow	Crowed	Crew
Deal	Dole	Dole
Dive	Dove (*pro.* doave)	Dove
Do	Done	Did

Drag	Drug	Drug
Draw	Drawed	Drew
Drink	Drunk	Drank
Drown	Drownded	Drownded
Eat	Et	Ate
Fight	Fought	Fitten
Fine	Found	Found
Fling	Flang	Flung
Flow	Flew	Flown
Fly	Flew	Flew
Freeze	Froze	Friz
Get	Got	Gotten
Give	Give	Gave
Go	Went	Went
Hear	Heerd	Heerd
Heat	Het	Het
Hide	Hidden	Hid
Keep	Kep	Kep
Know	Knowed	Knew
Lend	Loaned	Lent
Lie	Laid	Laid
Ring	Rung	Rang
Run	Run	Ran
Say	Sez	Said
Sing	Sung	Sang
Sit	Set	Set
Skin	Skun	Skun
Slide	Slid	Slidden
Sling	Slang	Slung
Sneak	Snuk	Snuk
Spin	Span	Spun
String	Strang	Strang
Sting	Stang	Stung
Swim	Swum	Swam
Swing	Swang	Swung
Throw	Throwed	Threwn
Wring	Wrang	Wrung

Here we have examples of a number of characteristically American peculiarities of conjugation. For example, there is the confusion of words apparently identical, such as *fine* and *find*, leading to the use of *found* for *fined*. Again, there is the drawing of false analogies between words which rhyme but are otherwise unrelated, such as *deal* and *steal*, leading to *dole* instead of *dealt*, and *dive* and *drive*, leading to *dove* instead of *dived*. Yet again, there is the persistence of an original vowel sound through one or both inflections, as in *give* and *hear*. Yet again, there is the smoothing down and easing of speech by apocope, as in the use of *kep* for *kept*, *crep* for *crept* and *het* for *heated*. Yet again, there is the transfer of an error in the conjugation of one word to the conjugation of other words of similar sound, as in the case of *brung* and *rung* as past tense forms of *bring* and *ring*: a borrowing from the American inflection of *sing*, which is *sung* and not *sang* in the past tense. Yet again, there is the obvious tendency to heighten the effectiveness of speech by substituting harsh, brassy vowels for soft ones, as in the use of *stang*, *swang*, *slang* and *flang*. Finally, there is the persistent transfer of the English perfect participle into the simple past tense, and *vice versa*, as in the use of *throwed* for *threw* and *drawed* for *drew*, and in the confusion of *did* and *done*, *saw* and *seen*, *run* and *ran*, *drank* and *drunk*.

This last tendency is visible in Irish-English and Cockney as well as in American, but in no other dialect is the change carried to such lengths. There is gradually growing up in American, indeed, a habit of introducing it into the conjugation of *all* irregular verbs, regardless of whether their inflections are otherwise orthodox or not. Thus, an American is now very apt to say "I *taken* a trip," and "I *written* a letter," just as glibly as he says "I *seen*" or "I *done*," and in the opposite direction he is almost as full of "I would have *wrote*" and "I oughtn't to have *took*," as he is of "I have *began*" and "The milkman has *came*." The causes of this muddling of tenses I do not profess to know: all I want to point out is its effect of simplifying grammar. When the past form of *to write* is changed from *wrote* to *writ* or *written*, the verb becomes measurably more regular, following the example of *to bite*, and so its use becomes measurably easier. I am well aware that there is a corresponding lessening of regularity in the past perfect, but that lessening is far from compensatory, for the American keeps out of the past perfect tense as much as possible, just as he keeps out of the present perfect and the future perfect. These complex tenses are opposed to the genius of his language, which has ease of use as its first principle, and no doubt he will get rid of them entirely by and by. Already, indeed, he has well-nigh abandoned the present perfect tense: he never says "I have dined," but always "I am through." And the future perfect exists in American only as a fossil. Even the American newspapers, which still profess to cling to English grammar, though they make frank use of the American vocabulary, are now almost free of "will haves." I have been unable to find a single specimen in two issues of the New York *Sun*. The simple future tense serves all purposes nearly as well, and in spoken American it is used exclusively.

Now add to this movement toward simplicity a strong habit of strengthening the original forms of verbs by elisions, reinforcements and other changes, as in *bust, un-*

loosen, ketch, et, sez, rile and *rench* (for *rinse*); and an equally strong habit of manu-facturing entirely new ones out of nouns, adjectives or the empty air—for example, *bulldoze, lynch, slump, lexow, electrocute, muss, swat, filibuster, gerrymander, dicker, boost, belly-ache, boodle* and *bluff*—and you come to an understanding, not only of the growing philological autonomy of the spoken American of the common people, but also of its peculiar vigor. It is, indeed, an extraordinarily succinct, nervous and clangorous speech. None other of modern times is better adapted to the terse and dramatic conveyance of ideas. It would be impossible, in orthodox English, or in French or German or Italian, to get so much of assurance and command and fi-nality into three words as the American gets into "Swat the fly!" The Englishman says "I shall"; the American says "I will"—and ten times the resolution and cer-tainty of the English form is in the American. "I went broke" is better than "I was broken"; "het up" is vivider than "heated up"; even Professor Lounsbury admits the vast superiority of "It's me" to "It is I." Finally, compare "He saw his duty and he did it" and "He seen his duty and he done it": the one is a mere statement of fact, the other is a statement plus an enthusiastic ratification and defiance.

That American is much richer than English, even than the loosest spoken Eng-lish, in concise and picturesque words, precipitating ideas of considerable com-plexity into one or two *sforzando* syllables, must be evident to anyone who studies the vocabularies of the two languages. The former is full of comparatively new words—nouns, verbs and adjectives—which serve a very real need of expression, but are yet looked at askance by the English, as outlaws of speech. Of such sort are the nouns *crank, boss, bluff, boodle, graft, dicker, hobo, lasso* and *stampede* and their derivative verbs and adjectives. All of these are in universal use in America, but the English still regard them as slang. A few such American words—for example, *cau-cus, hoodlum, lynch, maverick* and *canoe*—have gone over into English, but a hun-dred times as many remain purely American. An Englishman, unless he has been in the United States, does not know the meaning of *sucker, wire-puller, crackerjack, wildcat, shanty, picayune, mugwump, bonehead, powwow, windup, deadhead, cut-off, highbinder, holdup, grubstake, lockout, gerrymander, filibuster, logroller, ham-mock* and *ranch.* The ideas conveyed by such words, vividly and economically, he can convey only by long and flaccid circumlocutions. The language he speaks is hunkerously inhospitable, in these later years, to reinforcement from without. Time was when every British adventurer brought home new words, but that time is past. When the Boer War gave the language *mafeking,* the word was immediately attacked, and today it survives only as a vulgarism. But American is constantly ab-sorbing the foreign words brought in by immigrants, just as the American people are constantly absorbing the superstitions, prejudices and *pediculidæ* of those im-migrants. Such needed words as *rathskeller, bock-beer, pumpernickel, sauer-kraut, frankfurter* and *wienerwurst* came into it from the German, and such words as *café* (pronounced *kaif*) and *fête* (pronounced *feet*) from the French, and in the same way many Yiddish words, such as *kosher* and *gonov*, for example, are fast forcing themselves into general usage.

What is more important, American is being enriched constantly by new words of native origin, and particularly by new words formed by compounding. The facility with which these agglutinates are manufactured does not result in clumsiness, as in German, but in an increasing clarity and ease of utterance. Such compounds as *cut-off, lock-out, ice-cream, log-roller, hold-up, horse-sense, ward-heeler, hog-wash, grab-bag, desk-room, dead-head, skin-game, wind-up, spell-binder, wild-cat, stamping-ground, wire-puller, monkey-shine, office-seeker, job-holder, kill-joy, crazy-quilt, dyed-in-the-wool* and *rabble-rouser* have not only a plentiful picturesqueness, but also a genuine value. The language is the richer and the more fluent for their invention: it grows in economy as it grows in vocabulary. And that same striving for vividness and forcefulness, when applied to the sentence instead of to the single word, produces the extraordinarily lush and vigorous thing called American slang. Not even French can show a slang with more in it of novelty, daring and penetrating impudence. Such phrases as *like greased lightning, like a snowball in hell, a land office business, by the skin of his teeth, beaten to a frazzle, like a dirty deuce, he handed me a lemon, from hell to breakfast, Pike's Peak or bust,* and *till the cows come home,* are apt, lucid and racy of the soil. And so are all the minor coins of American phrase — *to make good, to go back on, to face the music, to peter out, to fill the bill, to bury the hatchet, to chew the rag, to hit the booze, to kick the bucket, to scratch the ticket, to stump the state, to acknowledge the corn, to nurse a grouch, small potatoes, marble heart, glad rags, on the fence, on the hog, down and out, under the weather, in the neck, cold snap, up in the air, glad eye, second time on earth.* What language has ever produced a more incisive and detaining phrase than *yellow journal*? Or better humorous words than *skedaddle, sockdolager, guyascutis, scalawag* and *rambunctious*? Or more useful abbreviations than *O. K., N. G.* and *P. D. Q.*?

Naturally enough, a tongue so remarkably hospitable to reinforcements, however humble in origin, is noticeably rich in similes. There is scarcely a noun or adjective in common use, indeed, that hasn't at least two exact synonyms, instantly understood by ninety per cent. of all Americans. And about such universal words as *dead, married, food, whiskers, clergyman, drink, drunk* and *girl* there cluster picturesque equivalents in almost countless swarms. I take, for example, the word *whiskers*. In Farmer and Henley's *Dictionary of Slang and Colloquial English*[11] I can find but a dozen or so synonyms for it, and most of these are really special words used to describe facial flora of peculiar design, such as *mutton chops, imperial* and *goatee*. But here are no less than fifty American synonyms for *whiskers* in the general sense, and every one of them, I venture to say, would be immediately intelligible to eight Americans out of ten:[12]

Alfalfa	Ivy
Arbutus	Jimpsons
Asparagus	Jungle
Bib	Kraut
Brush	Lilacs
Bunch	Mattress
Bush	Moss
Buzzers	Muff
Chest protector	Muffler
Chinlash	Oleanders
Crape	Plush
Cyprus	Seaweed
Dogwood	Shrubbery
Duster	Slaw
Excelsior	Soup trap
Ferns	Spaghetti
Fine-cut	Spinach
Flax	Sprouts
Foliage	Sweet Williams
Furs	Tanglefoot
Fuzz	Tolstois
Grandpas	Vines
Grass	Weeping willows
Greens	Wild oats
Hedge	Windshield

Slang? To be sure. But a language such as American, the common tongue of a curious and talkative people, is necessarily composed largely, if not chiefly, of what the intransigeant school teacher would call slang. Slang in itself, it must be obvious, does not differ essentially from any other material of speech. All that may be validly said against it is that it is new, that it has not yet won the support of the conventional. No other objection uncovers a character that you will not find in equal flower in wholly orthodox metaphor. Say that it is extravagant and far-fetched and you also attack some of our noblest similes and hyperboles. Say that it is vulgar and you also attack Shakespeare's "There's the rub,"[13] a figure grounded upon the fact that a tight shoe is uncomfortable and causes corns. No man can write English without using the slang of yesteryear; no man can speak English without using more or less of the slang of today. The distinguished trait of the American is simply his tendency to use slang without any false sense of impropriety, his eager hospitality to its most audacious novelties, his ingenuous yearning to augment the conciseness, the sprightliness, and, in particular, what may be called the dramatic punch of his language. It is ever his effort to translate ideas into terms of overt acts, to give the intellectual a visual and striking quality. The idea of defeat, of bafflement, of ludicrous defrauding, he puts into the saying that he has been handed a lemon. The idea that whiskers are, in some subtle sense, ridiculous—that the man who devotes care to their nurture indulges a foolish weakness—this he makes vivid by a host of synonyms giving concrete and visual embodiment to the concept of comedy. And so he deals, too, with other complex and difficult concepts—for example, that of sexual charm. The English poet, feeling the inadequacy of mere description, goes to timid metaphor and calls his best girl a lily or a rose; the everyday American, moved by the same impulse and less shackled by fastidious restraints, calls her a peach, a daisy, a pansy, a pippin, or a bird.

Always his one desire is to make speech lucid, lively, dramatic, staccato, arresting, clear—and to that end he is willing to sacrifice every purely æsthetic consideration. He judges language as he judges poetry, not at all by its grace of form but wholly by its clarity and poignancy of content. He has no true sense of the sough and sweetness of words: all he can understand is their crash and brilliance. He is like—or, more accurately, he is himself—a musician with an abnormal development of feeling for rhythm and resonance, and no feeling whatever for phrasing and tone-color. Thus he is ever willing, on the one hand, to adopt words and expressions that are harsh and barbarous in themselves, such as *sour-belly, hog-wash, shin-dig, frazzle, scalawag* and *bulldoze,* and on the other hand he is constantly boiling down and making more pungent the words that belong to orthodox English. To an Englishman there is a sharp distinction between *don't* and *doesn't*; to an American *don't* seems just as proper in the singular as in the plural. In the same way, he always uses *won't* for the more difficult *sha'n't,* and always substitutes *ain't,* a monosyllable, for *aren't,* a dissyllable. Years ago he turned *burst* into *bust, copper* into *cop,* and *confidence* into *con*; of late he has continued the process by turning *bunco,* a simplified derivative of *buncombe,* into the still simpler *bunk.* The more subdued forms of the vowels he rejects in favor of sterner, more discordant forms Thus the short *e* is yanked out of *deaf, chest* and *kettle,* and the words become *deef, chist* and *kittle.* Thus the English *a* in *sauce* gives way to a more American *a* and the word becomes *sass.* Thus the diphthong in *roil, choice* and *hoist* is reduced to a simple vowel, and we have *rile, chice* and *hist.* This last tendency was early noted by visiting Englishmen. It is probable, indeed, that it was more powerful two generations ago than it is today—as witness *j'int, sile, p'int, jine, bile, ile* and *rej'ice,* now seldom heard—but it is still far from decadent. To the American a *quoit* is yet a *quait,* and *Hofbräu,* it is probable, will always remain *Huffbrow.*

Such is American, a language preeminent among the tongues of the earth for its eager hospitality to new words, and no less for its compactness, its naked directness, and its disdain of all academic obfuscations and restraints. The English from which it sprung was already a language of notably simple grammar—a language that had been gradually shedding its inflections for five hundred years. But American has progressed much faster than English. As we have seen, it has already reduced its tenses from six to three, and broken down the old barriers between the nominative case and the objective, and brought about an occasional marriage between singular and plural, and declared war upon the superfluous consonant and the disguised vowel. How far it will go in each of these several directions, and in new directions perhaps yet to be indicated, is beyond all prophecy. On the one hand, its tendency to reduce grammar to mere common sense is obviously very powerful, but on the other hand, its natural evolution is constantly combated by the conservatism of school teachers, who cling fanatically to book English and devote their best energies to rehabilitating it. To what issue that war will come remains to be seen. On the one hand the spread of schools may bring the teachers a substantial victory, and American may recoalesce with English, in grammar if not in vocabulary. But on the other hand, the teachers may have to make a frank compromise, as the newspapers have already begun to make it, and as a few daring scholars—for example, the late Prof. William James, of Harvard—have showed signs of making it. If such a compromise is ever reached, the result, in short order, will be an entirely new language, as distinct from orthodox English as the *langue d'oil* was from the *langue d'oc*, or as Russian is from that compound of Slavic, Arabic and Greek elements which goes by the name of modern Bulgarian.

The American: His Ideas of Beauty

Of all the *beaux arts*, whether graphic, symbolic or tonal, the American has his doubts and suspicions, holding them to be enervating and effeminate, and their practitioners no better than they should be.

For example, the notion that a grown man, sound in wind and with hair on his chest, should make a living playing the piano is to him a horror and an abomination. Such tricks are for milksops and scoundrels. Even that fellow who dallies with the keys for the mere fun of it, and without open claim to applause and reward, is one who pursues perilously a corrupting vice. Not, of course, that this amateur is without his saving justifications, his occasional uses. There are moments, God wot, when even the malest male is moved to sing, when "Old Uncle Ned" springs irresistibly from the sternest larynx, when music is not only lawful but almost laudable, and at such moments it is convenient to have an accompanist at hand, a performer tried and true, one familiar with the traditional airs and not apt to pass the hat. But the American, let it be remembered, ventures into brothels only on rare and careless nights, and so his need for such an accompanist is but slight, and his attendant toleration but transient. Taking one day with another, he clings faithfully to his theory that piano playing is a saccharine and unmanly pastime, fit only for women and machines, and to be abandoned even by a woman, if she would be thought wholly decent, after her first child.

For fiddlers, strangely enough, he has rather more respect, but only in proportion as they are genuine fiddlers and not violinists. That is to say, he esteems the fellow who can perform bouncingly a jig or reel, but views biliously the fellow who runs to sonatas and concertos. This bile is in part made up of a dislike of sonatas and concertos as such, on the ground that they are cacophonous and incomprehensible, and in part of a deep-seated distrust of all professional artists. The American, in brief, agrees thoroughly with George Bernard Shaw in the doctrine that artists and vagabonds are of the selfsame stock. The essential thing about both, as he sees them, is that they are unwilling to earn a living in a respectable and useful way. The hobo on the blind baggage is simply a farm hand who is too lazy to go on milking cows, or a city apprentice who has succumbed to dime novels and cigarettes; and the professional musician, by the same token, is simply a loafer who has grafted upon his reluctant father during an over-prolonged youth, and now maintains himself in idleness by inflaming the concupiscence of women who ought to be better occupied at home, darning socks and beating their children.

It is always easy to convince the American that any given artist is a debauchee and a rogue. He believes faithfully, for example, that all painters live in adultery with their models, that the great majority of poets are drunkards, that all dramatists of any pretensions are pornographers, that opera singers, male and female, are almost unanimously immoral, that all actors are polygamists, and that practically every actress, high or low, has her price. In many parts of the United States, indeed, the word "actress" is a common synonym for "prostitute," as the phrase "chorus girl" is in all parts. And when, a few years ago, one of the leading woman's magazines made the discovery that certain fair members of the Metropolitan Opera Company were honest wives and mothers, the mere statement of the fact, repeated in various accents of astonishment, was sufficient material for half a dozen articles.

No artist, purely as such, has ever evoked any manifestation of general respect in the United States. True enough, there have been temporary rages for such persons as Paderewski, Sarah Bernhardt and Jenny Lind, but in every such case it has been skillful press-agenting, appealing frankly to a childish weakness for the marvelous, that has primarily inflamed the vulgar. Paderewski won by his hair, his high pay and his general aspect of romance, and not at all by his indubitable skill at a difficult craft. Sarah Bernhardt conquered by elevating the art of acting to the level of bear-baiting, not only by her fantastic methods of advertising, but more especially by her choice of sensational plays. And as for Jenny Lind, she was exploited by P. T. Barnum in exactly the same deliberate, unconscionable way that he exploited Jumbo and Tom Thumb, and her own share in her success lay as much in her ostentatious alms-giving and her lack of artistic conscience as in her genuine magic of voice. Better artists, in all that separates the artist from the mere artisan, have come to the United States and failed, at least in the popular sense. I need only refer, among piano players, to Von Bülow, Rosenthal and Busoni; and, among actresses, to Duse and Agnes Sorma; and among singers, to Sembrich. Every one of these, of course, aroused a certain enthusiasm among the discriminating few, and now and then a faint echo of it got into the newspapers, but they never attained to the public celebrity of Paderewski, Bernhardt and Lind, nor to anything remotely approaching it. The one apparent exception to the rule is Enrico Caruso, but even in his case it is his ability to bellow a staggering high C that makes him famous, and not his more worthy (and far more difficult) feats of *bel canto*. In brief, he is venerated as a freak before he is appreciated as an artist, and no doubt a good part of his renown is due to his exploits and misadventures outside the opera house.

On turning from purely interpretive art to creative art, one finds a still lower development of intelligent appreciation. The United States, despite a poll parrot opinion to the contrary, has produced more than one great artist and many lesser ones of respectable capacity, and some of the latter have been intensely national in feeling, but there is no record of any spontaneous recognition of such a lord of dreams. That electric mixture of pride, patriotism and intelligent admiration which brought Norway to the feet of Ibsen and Björnson, and turned the fiftieth birthday of Joseph Victor von Scheffel into a German national holiday, and made all Poland mourn the too-early death of Stanislaw Wyspianski, and forced a glorious forgiveness from the Swedes for August Strindberg, and gave Tennyson an English barony, and raised Frédéric Mistral in Southern France to the place that Pushkin had in Russia and Burns in Scotland—such a universal acclaim of an imaginative artist is unheard of in this republic, and well-nigh unimaginable. While Poe lived, not one American in fifty was aware of his existence, and since his death it is chiefly in foreign lands that his fame has grown. The Americans of today buy his books from the book agents and even read them and enjoy them, but there is certainly not apparent any pressing sense of his greatness, any widespread pride in his daring and his achievement. In the city of Baltimore, where he won his first recognition, did his best work, came to his melodramatic death and now lies buried, it has been found impossible, after forty years of effort, to raise the ten thousand dollars needed to give him a decent monument.[14] Baltimore, during that time, has opened thirty new parks and two hundred new streets, but not one of them bears the poet's name. During the same time the city has spent more than three hundred thousand dollars upon monuments and memorials to fourth-rate soldiers and petty politicians, but until recently the very grave of Poe was hidden behind the dirty wall of a frowzy churchyard, and a private enthusiast had to furnish the few dollars necessary to cut a gate in that wall.

So with all the rest of our great makers and dreamers. If, now and then, one of them has attained to something approaching popular celebrity, it has always been in some capacity sharply differentiated from the purely artistic. Emerson, I dare say, was the most famous of the New England brahmans—he came closest, that is, to a truly national renown—but Emerson, it must be plain, was always far more the soothsayer than the artist, and it was precisely his banal soothsaying, and not his mild art, that made him a hero. In brief, he was the father of the New Thought of today, that typically American balderdash. Mrs. Stowe, in the same way, was a rabble-rouser and not an artist: there is little more esthetic merit in *Uncle Tom's Cabin* than in the average college yell. The *prima donna* preachers, lyceum stars and other such rhetoricians of the ante-bellum period go the same route: if there was any artistic merit in their whoopings, it was no more than the smoke accompanying the more important discharge of shells, and their glory did not grow out of it. When we come to a genuine artist, Walt Whitman, to wit, we come to a man who made no more impression upon his countrymen, taken in the mass, than a third-rate pugilist. If they thought of him at all, during his seventy-three years of life among them, it was chiefly, if not wholly, as a wholesaler of the obscene. He never appealed to them as a great poet, as an eloquent and impassioned prophet of their democracy, but merely as a man who took long chances with the postal laws. When, in reward for *Leaves of Grass*, he was deprived of his modest place in the Interior Department and denounced donkeyishly by some forgotten Tartuffe, public sentiment approved both the dismissal and the denunciation. Even today, by one of fate's little ironies, all appreciation of Whitman is confined to a narrow circle of admirers, most of whom are professed immoralists. That average American in whom he believed so resolutely, and whose thirsts and struggles he celebrated so feelingly, is no more moved by him than by Johann Sebastian Bach.

Comes now an exception—Mark Twain. But *is* he really an exception? I doubt it. It is a fact, I grant you freely, that he tasted the sweets of popular adulation in his later years, that he died a famous and honored man, that his celebrity was not only intense in degree but also widespread in extent—but was it, at bottom, the celebrity of a literary artist? Was it comparable, in other words, to the celebrity of Ibsen, or to that of Swinburne, or yet to that of Tolstoi? I am convinced that it was not. Mark Twain's countrymen, even today, have no true comprehension of his rank and dignity as an artist. They think of him, when they think of him at all, as a sort of super-clever clown, as the blood brother of Artemus Ward, Bill Nye and Chauncey M. Depew. They connect him, not with such magnificent pieces of imaginative work as *A Connecticut Yankee* and *Joan of Arc*, nor even with the penetrating, highly sophisticated humor of *Captain Stormfield* and *Huckleberry Finn*, but with the artificial hoaxes and buffooneries of his days and nights of idleness. It is the after-dinner jester, the extravagant lecturer, the wearer of white clothes that lingers in their memory, and not the incomparable literary artist. Of all the things he wrote, the one that made the greatest initial success and is oftenest referred to by his country-men today is "The Jumping Frog," a mere anecdote, borrowed in its substance and but little dignified in the telling. Whatever appreciation of Mark the artist is now visible in the United States is an appreciation confined to a remarkably small num-ber of persons. In Europe, and especially in England and Germany, he was earlier recognized and better understood: in his own country even professional critics got no genuine sense of his towering stature, of his kinship with Cervantes, Swift and Molière, until he was safely in his grave. The obituaries were the first accounts of him that did the half of justice to him, and here, no doubt, it was American senti-mentality, a great deal more than intelligent understanding, that set the tune.

So the list might be prolonged, but we must pass on from artists to art itself. On the way, it is sufficient to call attention to the long neglect of American singers, to the enforced exile of American painters, and to the public indifference to such na-tional bards as Key and Randall. America has been producing first-rate operatic singers, particularly sopranos and basses, for a generation, and since the early nineties they have swarmed in the opera houses of Europe, but it is still well-nigh impossi-ble for one of them to succeed at home without first gaining approval abroad. A few striking exceptions merely prove the rule. No spontaneous appreciation of merit ex-ists among us; the thing the American understands and applauds is not really singing at all, but notoriety. When it comes to painting not even notoriety attracts him. The two most famous English speaking painters of our time have been Whistler and Sargent, both of them Americans, and yet there is not the slightest sign of national pride in their achievements, and to the majority of Americans their very names are unknown. So are the names of Childe Hassam, John W. Alexander, Winslow Homer and Gutzon Borglum.

In the case of the patriotic poets, the authors of our national anthems, there has been rather more appreciation, but little more reward. Every schoolboy knows that Key wrote "The Star-Spangled Banner," but it was not until nearly a century after its composition that anyone thought to raise a monument to him, and even then the business had to be proposed and carried through by his descendants: our cities are full of memorials to undistinguished soldiers and forgotten politicians, but the one man who imbedded the high resolves and great daring of the War of 1812 in sonorous and electric stanzas has been neglected alike by government and by people. As for Randall, I remember well the pathos of his last days. The South, while still bawling his clarion call to arms, had forgotten its author, and so he came to Maryland in search of stronger memories. He was an old man and poor, and he frankly desired a pat on the back, a round of applause. But Maryland, My Maryland was too busy to heed him. A few woman's clubs offered him tea, as they might have offered it to a passing French lecturer or matinee idol; a survivor or two of the old regime invited him to dinner; the newspapers mentioned him a bit tolerantly, apologizing for the fervor of his youth. He died, in the end, almost unnoticed. Maryland was engrossed by peanut politics; the South was trying to forget the War.

But all of this, of course, may be dismissed as no proof of the American's indifference to artistic expression; he may disdain the artist, and yet hold the art itself in high respect. Æsop's fables delighted the Greeks, but Æsop himself, if we hear aright, remained a slave to the end of his days. *Hamlet* has been a first favorite among English tragedies since the afternoon of its first performance, but it took the English people so long to pay honors to the author that they found him, when the time came at last, already half a myth. I doubt, however, that any such common weakness of humanity may be pleaded in confession and avoidance of the American's apathy to artists. The truth is that his apathy to art is no less intense and unshakable. It is apparently impossible for him to think of beauty as a thing in itself. Even when he appears to be moved by a purely esthetic impulse, it is nearly always easy to show some other and less civilized impulse lurking in the background.

For example, his interest in the marvelously varied and beautiful scenery of his country is almost entirely a childish delight in mere bigness and singularity. He is impressed by Niagara chiefly because no other country in Christendom has so large a waterfall. He glories in Yellowstone Park because it is a sort of natural circus, an incredible geological debauch. He goes to the Grand Cañon of the Colorado and to Pike's Peak and to the redwood groves of California because these things are unparalleled and astounding, and not at all because they are beautiful. The one river that appeals to his imagination is the Mississippi, which is as deficient in attractive scenery as the average sewage disposal plant, but enchants his imagination by its mere hugeness. For Nature in her gentler, more normal, less prodigal moods he seems to have no feeling whatever. He is no wanderer in the woods, as the German is: he prefers a city park, with its paved ways and hideous flower beds, to the open country, and the intolerable garishness of a so-called summer park to either. The wide spaces of his Western prairies have never awakened the poetry in him, as the *steppe* has awakened the poetry of the Russian, and the *pussta* that of the Bohemian. Among all the lowly songs that make up his folk music, there is no single song of spring, nor one that celebrates the singing of birds, nor one that hymns the mountains, nor one that brings back to him the balsam and silence of the woods. His sentimentality often takes melodious form: he has many songs of home, of mother, of young love. But he has no "Goldene Abend Sonne" and no "Im Wald und auf der Heide" and no "Winter, Adieu!"

And if he is thus almost anesthetic to the beauties of nature, he is even less responsive to those beauties which spring from the hand of man. So long as art stands bravely on its own legs, disdaining the support of mere lavishness and bombast on the one hand and of morality and sentimentality on the other hand, he will have none of it. Thus he shows little interest in music until it becomes noisy and spectacular. The Germans, the Welsh and the Bohemians brought choral singing with them when they immigrated, and wherever they have settled they have founded large and excellent male and mixed choruses and give frequent concerts on a large scale, but the native American has remained entirely uninfluenced by this example. It is seldom, indeed, that his ear is acute enough for him to sing in tune, and almost unheard of for him to read music. Like the savage, however, he has a sharp sense of rhythm—so sharp, indeed, that he gets delight out of rhythmic eccentricities which affect the more cultivated hearer disagreeably. Hence his liking for the elaborate measures of ragtime and his equal liking for the thunderous step of band music. There is scarcely a county town in the United States that lacks its "silver cornet band," and not a large city that does not offer a ceaseless bray of brass in summer; but in the entire country there is not a single first-rate orchestra supported wholly by the public. Good orchestras exist, true enough—perhaps a dozen of them in all, or one to each 7,500,000 of population—but they are maintained by a very small class of rich amateurs, and their members are practically all foreigners. To so-called "light" music—i.e., to jingles combined with dancing and clowning— the American is very hospitable, but that is chiefly for the sake of the auxiliary attractions. It was a dance that made him rave over *The Merry Widow* and a dance that charmed him in *Florodora*. But for serious opera he has only scorn, and his view of so elemental a music drama as *Lohengrin* remains that of the Weimar audience which yawned over it in 1850.[15]

Here in music, of course, it must be noted and allowed in fairness that public taste, whatever its present crudity, is still measurably less crude than it used to be. The influence of the big orchestras and opera companies, true enough, is not felt directly by the common people. Such organizations are maintained by a very small number of rich men, and the persons who patronize them belong chiefly to that pushing, half-educated class which supports drama leagues, goes into raptures over each new fashionable philosopher and is hotly eager for every other such means to intellectual distinction. Add the social climbers pure and simple, hospitable to caterwauling because it is heard in dress clothes, and the small class of professional musicians and intelligent amateurs, and you have the typical American opera audience. The common people are not in it: its gallery, in so far as it has one, is made up almost entirely of foreigners. But if there is thus no direct inoculation of the American democrat and freeman with the hideous *cocci* of counterpoint and recitative, he is at least hospitable to an occasional small dose at second hand. That is to say, his appetite for marvels is aroused by newspaper tales of opera house prodigies, deficits and amorous intrigues, and so he is led to make a compromise with his prejudices. He still holds to his doctrine that grand opera is all bosh, and he is still reluctant to sit through it, even when the price is reduced; but he is curious to hear

Caruso earn a thousand dollars at one miraculous laryngeal blast, and so his phono-graph records begin to be sprinkled with high C's and he scrapes a far-away, unin-telligent acquaintance with "Celeste Aïda," the *Pagliacci* prologue and the quartette in *Rigoletto*.[16]

The Italian bands have helped in this modest progress, perhaps even more than the phonograph. When they first appeared in the summer parks, at the dawn of the new century, the union men of the native bands were immersed in the Rosey and Sousa marches, and it was only on national holidays that they ever tackled things so "hard" as the Pilgrims' Chorus from *Tannhäuser*, and the "Light Cavalry" over-ture.[17] The Italians, more brave and fluent, introduced the *Il Trovatore* tower duet for cornet and trombone, and the *Rigoletto* quartette for four loud trumpets, and the *Lucia* sextette for the whole brass choir,[18] and so the American began to acquire a tolerance for such mildly "classical" stuff, and even to demand it. But he has not gone into it very deeply. A band with sound wind could play his whole repertoire in an hour, and he would probably be begging for "My Old Kentucky Home" at the three-quarters.

Meanwhile, an indubitably American school of music has sprung up, as dis-tinctive in its markings as the Spanish school, or the Magyar or the Irish. There are pundits who deny this with great fuming and sophistry, just as there are pundits who deny that the jubilee songs were genuinely niggerish, but the fact remains that specimens of this American music are instantly recognized abroad, and that no other country produces it in any quantity. Its dominant characteristic I have already mentioned: it exalts mere rhythm to an importance elsewhere unattained in civi-lized music. No melodic invention is necessary to write this primitive stuff. So small are its demands in that direction, indeed, that its most eminent professors borrow shamelessly, from Methodist hymns[19] and comic opera tunes on the one hand and from such things as Mendelssohn's "Spring Song"[20] and the *Pagliacci* prologue on the other. Nor does it admit any emotional content: it cannot be made to express love or courage or hope or even simple reverie. Its one function is to set the knees and ankles to jerking. It is music bound by the closest of ties to the tom-tom rata-plan of the savage. It belongs in the sub-cellar of the tonal art, along with the end-less chants of the Bedouins, the inept and ludicrous dance music of the Chinese and the monotonic tunes made by children with their rattles. Compare it to the average Hungarian *czardas* or German *volkslied* or Polish *mazurka*, or even to the average Scotch pipe air or darkey "spiritual," and you will at once perceive its hol-lowness and nakedness.

In all the other arts that he presumes to dally with the American shows a like preference for elementals. His first demand of all of them is that they shall make no demands themselves, that they shall not burden him with any sense of their sig-nificance and value. And his second and last demand, whenever he goes beyond the first, is that they shall subordinate themselves, even in their lightest moods, to utility. The fruit of this attitude is visible in the household utensils and ornaments of the typical American home. They are not only unspeakably hideous, but also meaningless. You will not find in them any of that subtle symbolism which gives dignity to the peasant art of most other countries, and to the still lowlier art of savages. A Navajo blanket *means* something: it not only keeps out the cold, but also stands for a tradition of the past and an interpretation of the present. And so with the wood carvings of the Swiss mountaineers, the jewelry of the Tyrol *bauern*, the gaudy *ikons* of the Russian *muzhiks*, the peasant laces of Ireland, the pottery of a hundred races and tribes. These things not only meet the daily needs of the folk who make and use them, but they also, in a very real sense, voice the aspiration of those folk. A vision is in them. It may be a very humble one, but still it is a vision. In the stage properties of the American's life drama, however, there is no such esoteric element. He is surrounded by things made in factories, sordidly, without inspiration and at wholesale. In the design of his furniture the main object of the craftsman is to get as many chair legs as possible out of a hundred feet of wood. His carpets and wallpapers are deliriums of ugliness, with no meaning or intent save that of overwhelming the dazzled eye. His common ornaments are mere brummagem, dishonest imitations of antagonistic and puerile models—"bronzes" made of plaster, ormolus stamped by steam, "cut" glass full of mold marks. His beautiful native woods, by the time they reach his home, have been ridiculously disguised as mahogany or Flemish oak. The pictures on his walls, when they are not grisly caricatures of his dead relatives, are sentimental abominations of the "Playing Grandpa" school or shoddy reproductions of idiotic water colors.

No, I am not forgetting the arts and crafts movement, nor the appearance of Rookwood pottery, nor the invention of so-called mission furniture, that one purely American contribution to domestic art. But it must be obvious that these outreachings toward a greater decency in environment have usually ended in extravagance and absurdity, and that when they have escaped that peril they have made but little impression upon the American people. Not one American in a thousand has ever heard of Rookwood pottery, and not one in five thousand is taken with chills in the presence of a Brussels carpet. And not one in ten thousand, I dare say, could be made to see any offense against the eye and the midriff in putting mission furniture into a ten by twelve room. The home of the average American, as homes go in this inhospitable world, is richly furnished. That is to say, its contents represent a considerable expenditure—perhaps the equivalent, taking one with another, of a full year's income. But the effect of all this somewhat lavish outlay is never one of unity, of fitness, of character. That simple dignity which you will find in a German peasant house, and in an English cottage, and even in a remote Swiss châlet is wholly missing. Wall swears at floor, floor swears at furniture, and all three swear at the house itself. There is no feeling for beauty of arrangement, no effort at self-expression, no striving to make decoration a factor in the art of life. We have, in brief, no peasant art, no people's art, spontaneous, native and racy of the soil, as every other race in Christendom has, and nine-tenths of those in the heathendoms without.

But it is in architecture, perhaps, more than in any lesser art, that this national lack makes itself most manifest. Twice we have made wholesale architectural thefts from other people—and quickly reduced the loot to hideousness. The first time was during the early years of the young republic—the so-called "Colonial period"—when we borrowed various beautiful Georgian details from the English and essayed to combine them with details borrowed from the Greeks upon our soap box houses. The second time was just after the Civil War, when we got the mansard roof from France, added towers and jigsaw scrollwork, and achieved the most appalling architectural monstrosities in history. Each time the piracy failed to leave any impress of permanent value—and the same failure has pursued the more ambitious and delirious piracies of later years. There is scarcely an American city of one hundred thousand inhabitants that cannot show examples of every architectural style known to the handbooks, and yet no distinctively American style has arisen, and the average American home—the true test of national architecture—remains as ugly and as undistinguished as a Zulu kraal. In its essence, it is simply a square box. And from that archetype it proceeds upward, not through degrees of beauty, but through degrees of hideousness. The more it is plastered with ornament, the more vulgar and forbidding it becomes. The more it is adorned with color, the more that color becomes a madness, a debauch, a public indecency. Take a train ride through any American State and you will be sickened by the chaotic ugliness of the flitting villages—houses sprawling and shapeless, green shutters upon lemon yellow churches, a huge advertising sign upon every flat wall, an intolerable effect of carelessness, ignorance, squalor, bad taste and downright viciousness.[21] But make the same sort of journey through France or Germany—say from Bremen to Munich or from Paris to Lyons—or through Austria or Italy or Switzerland, and you will be charmed by the beautiful harmony visible on all sides, the subordination of details to general effects, the instinctive feeling for color, the sound grouping, the constant presence of a tradition and a style. The design of the peasant houses changes twenty times between the Westphalian plain and the foothills of the Alps, but in every change there is a subtle reflection of the physical environment, and an unmistakable expression of human aspiration, worldly estate and character. I don't know any ugly village between Bremen and Munich, nor even a village without its distinction, its special beauty, its individual charm. But I don't know of a village between Washington and Chicago that is not frankly appalling.

So goes space, and the profound business of accounting for all this remains untackled and undone. I have argued with great fuming and fury that the American is a foe to the beautiful, but I have not proceeded to the wherefore and the why. Well, let the grim labors and laparotomies of the inquiry go over to some other day. All I desire to do here is to throw out a suggestion, to wit, that the blame rests upon that lingering Puritanism of which I discoursed in July—a Puritanism which still poisons and characterizes the American, for all his latter-day dallying with the fleshpots. How strongly this Puritan tide yet runs in his veins you will begin to understand when you have read Mr. Maurice Low's *The American People*, a painstaking and searching book, too little studied in this fair land. The one thing to recall now is the undying opposition between the Puritan view of life and what may be called, in deference to current critical slang, the pagan view of life. The moving impulse of the Puritan is always moral: he cannot imagine anything that is neither right nor wrong. And naturally enough, his repertoire of things that are wrong tends to maintain a marked fatness, and to suck into it most things that are fleshly. And so regarding the world, suspiciously, sourly, biliously, he has no liking for life's eases and usufructs. The thing that is not indubitably moral must be necessarily *im*moral. There is no halfway house. There can be no honorable compromise between ethics and esthetics. The true and the beautiful are unthinkable save as symptoms and complications of the good.

Such is the Puritan. Such, I believe, is the American. He steers clear of beauty because he is afraid of beauty, because it is the author of all his own flings and backslidings. Music is the devil's whisper. The Medicean Venus has bare legs, and is hence no company for a family man. The books that so-called critics recommend are apt to deal with adultery. Paris, the home of art, is also the home of unspeakable levities. Pantheons go with *hetairæ*: cathedrals of Cologne with Rhine wine; colosseums with carnality. Poets drink; painters forget No. 7; composers swap wives; actors are polygamists. The American sniffs and pricks up his ears. Art is long—and licentious.

The American: His Freedom

It is one of the fixed faiths of the American that he is a sturdy and unfettered individualist, and that no sort of barrier, whether within or without, hinders the free play of his ego. He holds it as a truth almost self-evident that he has the maximum of political liberty attainable under civilization, and he commonly adds that he has the maximum of personal liberty, too. One of his favorite exercises in patriotism consists in comparing his lordly lot to that of the poor Englishman, borne down by armaments and rowelled by a haughty aristocracy; or to that of the poor German, burdened by taxes and barons no less, and by drill sergeants and the *polizei* to boot; or to that of the poor Russian, oppressed eternally by inexorable and incomprehensible tyrants; or to that of the Pole, Finn and Irishman, slaves in the lands of their fathers.

He is sincerely sorry for these unfortunate fellows, but a touch of contempt conditions his sympathy, for in the back of his mind there is always the feeling that their wrongs are due, at least in part, to their own supineness and lack of enterprise. He blames the Germans, for example, for their alleged sufferings at the hands of the police—sufferings which seem to him to be wholly incompatible with civilized freedom and national self-respect. The German he really esteems is that one who has cast off the hideous yoke—*i.e.*, that one who has sought escape from official despotism by coming to America. He regards the German who remains and bears it as a man of a distinctly inferior species, just as he regards the colonial loyalist as a man of an inferior species. He has no doubt whatever that this German is forced into the army unwillingly and ordered about by the police in violation of his inalienable rights, and that his submission is proof of a congenital weakness of character; and he often puts this theory into the doctrine that the German army is made up of stupid and sullen automata, and that a few dozen regiments of American freemen could easily dispose of it.

This conceit of the American in his own unparalleled liberty goes back to the period of exuberance following the War of the Revolution, and has been the dominant note in all his political literature ever since. The European, when he lifts his voice in patriotic song, commonly testifies to his holy passion by promising some definite service, either to his country or to his king. He will guard the Rhine, he will die for the tricolor, he will pray to God for King George. His hymn doesn't boast an achievement; it voices an ideal and an aspiration. But the American, when he sings of his country, quickly drops into frank praise of himself. He doesn't say that he longs for freedom, that he approves of freedom, that he would die for freedom: he says that he *has* freedom, that he has wrested it bravely from fate, that he defies fate to take it away from him. His country, as he sees it, is not *a* land of the free, but *the* land of the free. And not only the land of the free, but the home of the brave, for most of his pride in his freedom is pride in his valor. He looks down upon all folk who bend the knee, whether to kings, nobles, bishops, drill sergeants or police, and he looks down upon them most of all when they seek to justify the bending intellectually. To him there is never any virtue in such subservience, however lofty its ostensible aims. The philosophy he subscribes to is that of the successful and unrestricted act. He cannot give his approval to a philosophy which runs to restraints and inhibitions.

And yet, for all that glorious celebration of his unfettered state, and all that pitying disdain of those who do not share it, there is probably no civilized man who knows less of genuine liberty, either personal or political, than the American. He is the constant prey, not of one tyranny, but of an endless succession of tyrannies, some of them forced on him by the universal laws that govern human society, but more of them springing out of his own peculiar weaknesses, stupidities and traditional habits of mind. Morally, as we saw in July, he is hedged about by a vast and complex fabric of taboos, the visible symbol of his incurable puritanism: not only is he forbidden to do a host of things that are wholly innocuous in themselves, but he is even forbidden to object to the prohibitions. What is more, the number of such prohibitions is eternally increasing, so that it has become almost impossible for a citizen of the republic to get through a day without violating at least one of them. And this despotism in major morals is matched by a parallel and even worse despotism in minor morals. In every relation of life the private conduct of the American is minutely regulated. He is forbidden to dispose of his property as he pleases; he is forbidden to amuse himself as he pleases on his holidays; he is forbidden to read what books he pleases and to look at what pictures he pleases; he is even forbidden to dress, think, drink and die as he pleases.

Many of these restrictions, true enough, are founded upon a muddled conception of the public good: their aim would seem to be to protect the innocent bystander. But how does the bystander profit when the free citizen is forbidden to go fishing on Sunday, or to cut off his wife as Shakespeare cut off Ann Hathaway, or to get the reports of the Chicago and Philadelphia Vice Commissions through the mails, or to play poker in his own club, or to keep fighting cocks, or to see the play of *The Easiest Way*,[22] or to kiss his girl in the parks, or (being female) to smoke in public, or to commit suicide? And yet all of these things, and a thousand other such acts with them, are forbidden in many American States, and some of them in all States, severally or by federal statute.

If all this piling up of laws made for the security and peace of the citizen—if it protected him more than it harassed him—there might be some excuse for it, as there is for the omnipresent *Verboten* sign in Germany. The German's freedom is invaded by that sign, but at the same time his rights are safeguarded. The same police who forbid him to do this or that also forbid anyone else to bother him. He must cease his harmonic caterwauling at 11 P. M.—but so must his neighbor in the flat above. He must not discharge his kitchen wench without just cause—but neither may she depart without just cause. He must obey all police regulations—but those regulations may not be changed without due and public notice, and the privilege of breaking them is not for sale. In brief, the German gets a valuable consideration for his surrender of small liberties: putting one thing with another, he makes a distinct gain by his bargain. But the American gets little if any profit, either in security of life and property or in mere freedom from annoyance, out of his inquisitorial and meticulous laws. What does it benefit him that his neighbor is forbidden to hear opera on Sunday afternoons, or to spread the secrets of race suicide, or to send a flask of whisky by parcels post, or to preach atheism from a soap box? These prohibitions, it must be obvious, burden the individual without conferring any appreciable advantage upon the mass, or even upon other individuals. They are merely evidences of a peculiarly American weakness, the wanton exercise of the po-lice power for its own sake—and behind them lies another peculiarly American weakness, the failure of the police power when and where it is actually needed.

I will not bore you with a recital of the grosser proofs. You know as well as I do that the homicide rate in the United States is vastly greater than that of any other civilized country, and that the accident rate on all public carriers is many times as great, and that the fire risk, in any average American city, is five times as high as in the average German, English or French city. If liberty means, first of all, the rea-sonable security of life and property, the right to go unmolested, the protection of equitable and efficient laws—if such is its primary meaning, then the American has little more of it than the Finn, the Spaniard and the Turk.

And not only in these large ways, but also in a multitude of small ways, his enor-mous body of laws fails to serve him. Why do such private organizations as the Con-sumers' League, the S. P. C. A., the Society Against Unnecessary Noises, the Society for the Suppression of Vice, the Travelers' Aid Society, the Legal Aid Soci-ety, and the various City Clubs and Good Government Leagues—why do such organizations flourish so amazingly in the United States? Simply because the American, if he would enjoy his common rights, must fight for them extra-legally. Simply because his government does not protect him. It is wholly unnecessary in Germany for housewives to meet in council and issue diplomas to honest grocers: the government sees to it that *all* grocers are honest, that a pound is a full pound of sixteen ounces, that fresh food is actually fresh. No specific complaint is neces-sary. The private citizen doesn't have to play the detective. All such things are watched and regulated as a matter of course: the regulation of them is regarded as a prime duty of government. And so, though perhaps less thoroughly, in England. Imagine a fleet of Thames tugboats keeping all Lambeth and Pimlico awake at night—not of necessity, but out of sheer deviltry! The Thames Authority would stop it at once. And yet the only way to stop the din in the Hudson was for private citi-zens to band themselves together, and besiege the newspapers with lamentations, and go for relief at last to the courts of equity. The statute law was inadequate to protect them in their common right to sleep at night, and its officers made no move to help them.

Into most such crusades in the United States, of course, there enters a good deal of the Puritan spirit—that is to say, the pious yearning to put sinners to the torture. The S. P. C. A., for example, commonly estimates its success, not by the number of horses it has saved, but by the number of drivers it has jailed. And the various breeds of vice crusaders, whether their specific target be drunkenness, gambling or prostitution, are obviously moved by what may be called a glorified sporting in-stinct. They are hunters before they are reformers, and differ from ordinary hunters only in the fact that they hunt men and women instead of lions and rabbits. But for

THE AMERICAN: A TREATISE

all this, there is always an intelligible excuse at the bottom of their fine frenzy, and that is the excuse that the things they oppose are actually nuisances, and that the existence of such nuisances invades the rights of peaceful citizens. No sane householder, I take it, is pleased by the news that a brothel has been opened in the house next door or a faro game in the house opposite. However little these enterprises may outrage his pruderies, he is at least keenly conscious that they damage his property, and so he is against them. Here the law should aid him—and here the law almost invariably fails him. At best he must gather evidence at his own cost and risk, and with it break down the chronic indifference and incapacity of the police. At worst he must do battle with the police frankly against him—perhaps as the actual partners of the lawbreakers he is trying to dispose of. In brief, there is no automatic machinery for his relief and protection, no redress of his wrongs as a matter of course. What machinery there is must be started by his own effort, and too often the operation of it is beyond his strength. In all the countries of Europe, including even moral England, the business of prostitution, to take one example, is strictly regulated by the police. They determine the conditions under which prostitutes may practise the ancient art, and they take care that those conditions are not violated, to the loss and annoyance of the people in general. It is only in the United States that prostitutes are *feræ naturæ*, and free to go wherever the neighbors are not powerful enough to exclude them. It is only in the United States that their proper regulation—one of the most difficult problems of city life—is left, in the main, to private enterprise.

Thus, on inspection, the advertised liberties of the American begin to shrink a bit. If liberty means, on its negative side, a freedom from vexatious molestation, it must be plain that he has a good deal less of it than he might have—and perhaps a good deal less than many Europeans. On the one hand, he is constantly molested in his private actions by petty and tyrannical laws, and on the other hand, he gets but feeble protection against the slings and arrows of unsocial neighbors and professional lawbreakers. Imagine the state of a man who is forbidden to go to hear an orchestral concert on Sunday afternoon, and forced to listen to the ragtime issuing from the automatic piano next door! Imagine this, and you have a pretty accurate image of the normal state of the American. I am speaking here, of course, of the average American, of the American in the average American town. In some of the large cities, as everyone knows, the picture must be changed a bit to be accurate. In these cities, for example—or, at all events, in a few of them—the Sunday laws are relatively liberal, and almost all amusements that are lawful on six days of the week are also lawful on the seventh. But this liberality in one direction is always counterbalanced by increased oppression in some other direction. The New Yorker may do many things on Sunday that are unlawful in Roanoke, Va., or even in Boston, Philadelphia and Baltimore, but he has lost his constitutional right to bear arms, and his right of free speech is amazingly circumscribed by the police. So with the Chicagoan: he is under no obligation whatever to obey two-thirds of the moral statutes of his lawmakers, but if he were to go into one of the parks and argue that anarchy is reasonable or that abortion should be permitted by law, or if he should put either argument into a pamphlet and circulate it on the streets, the police would quickly clap him into jail. Yet the Englishman has the one right and the German has the other, and both are exercised as a matter of course.

And this change of restrictions is accompanied, as one mounts the scale of American communities, by a slackening of protections. The only American towns that may be said to be well policed are those so small that they have no police. So long as the exercise of the police power is a private duty, charged upon the neighbors, it is accomplished with reasonable zeal, but the moment it is laid upon professionals, it becomes nobody's business and is neglected accordingly. Government by neighbors, of course, has many disadvantages: it makes for innumerable petty invasions of personal property. But it lacks the two great drawbacks of all the more complex forms of government in America: it is not inefficient and it is not corrupt. The small-town American, whatever his surrender of civilized rights, is at least protected in the enjoyment of those that he retains. He is not forced, for example, to live in direct contact with prostitution. He is not bludgeoned by one set of officials, and compelled to submit to outrage by the criminal partners of another set of officials. He is not habitually robbed under the forms of law, and knocked about, and turned loose among rogues. But that is the lot of the American living in an incorporated town, and year by year the American living in an incorporated town is coming to represent, more and more closely, the American average, the true *Homo Americanus*. His grandfather was a pioneer, whether of the prairies or of the immigrant ships, and his father was a farmer, but he himself is used to paved streets, and his son will die a cockney.

But what of this American's liberties on the positive side? What of his independence of thought, his passion for individualism? Does it really exist, or is it merely an illusion? Two-thirds of it, I am convinced, has no more reality than his thrift, and scarcely more than his virtue. As a matter of fact, he is so little the soul-free individualist that it is almost impossible for him to imagine himself save as a member of a crowd. All of his thinking is done, and most of his acts are done, not as a free individual but as one of a muddled mass of individuals. When the impulse to function seizes him, he does not function and have done, but looks about him for others who yearn to function in the same way. In two words, he is a chronic joiner. He does not stand for something; he belongs to something. And whether that something be a political party, a trades union, a fraternal order or a church, it quickly reduces him to the condition of an automaton, so that in a short while his opinions and acts become nothing more than weak reflections of *its* opinions and acts. The result is visible in one of the most curious characteristics of the American: his extraordinary fealty to party. This fealty vastly transcends all intelligible theory and purpose. In the South, for example, a Democrat is a Democrat, not primarily because he approves the principles of the Democratic party, but simply because he is a Democrat. He puts the organization far above its aim; the name is more to him than the thing itself. He was a Democrat in 1892, when to be a Democrat meant to be in favor of the gold standard; he was a Democrat in 1896 and 1900, when it meant to be in favor of bimetallism; and he was still a Democrat in 1904, when it meant approval of the gold standard once more. And to match him there is the hide-bound Northern Republican, faithful to his party through a dozen changes of policy, and following leaders as unlike as ever were Gladstone and Disraeli.

This loyalty to party, and the relative permanence of party which goes with it, have been explained more than once on the ground that the two great political divisions in the United States represent the two great divisions of human thought. The Republican party, it is argued, is simply the Conservative party, the party jealous of settled ways, while the Democratic party is that of experiment and innovation. It is in some such way, roughly speaking, that all men are divided, not only in America, but everywhere else. Every civilized nation has its Liberals and Tories, its advocates of change and its foes of change. But this theory quickly goes to pieces when it is applied to the facts of American political history. The most radical political innovation ever proposed in the United States, at least since Jackson's day, was put forward and carried through by the Republican party. This was the abandonment of the republic's traditional insularity and the acquirement of colonies overseas, held by the sword.[23] And the most hunkerous clinging to old idols ever seen in our politics must go to the credit of the Democratic party—the party of experiment and progress. I allude, of course, to its extraordiriary fidelity to the doctrines of State's rights—a doctrine under heavy fire from the very beginnings of the republic, and long since exploded by the necessities of national development.[24] The whole history of the United States, indeed, is a history of successful attacks upon this doctrine. And yet the alleged party of progress solemnly reaffirms it every four years, and creates for it the mythical sanctity of a pious dogma, and seeks to make it appear as the supreme achievement of the fathers.

No; it is impossible to explain the American's devotion to party as a devotion to ideas. Now and then, when an extraordinary event (such as the revolt of Col. Roosevelt, for example)[25] introduces faction into a party, it is suddenly revealed that radical differences have existed for years. And at other times, as in 1908, two great parties come so close together that it is well-nigh impossible to distinguish them. The difference between the means of the two parties in the year mentioned, as shown by the national platforms, was obviously less than the difference between the two main wings of the Republican party, as shown by the dramatic quarrel of 1912, and yet both wings remained faithful and voted as a unit, and the election was carried by a strict party vote. A split came, it is true, four years after, but to ascribe it to an antagonism of ideas is to be rather too facile in explanations, for in the first place that antagonism had existed for a long period without causing a rupture, nor even any considerable desertion of forces, and in the second place the actual clash, when it came at last, revolved around personalities rather than around principles. Or, to be more accurate, it revolved around emotions rather than around ideas. On the one hand was loyalty to the party and on the other hand was enthusiasm for an heroic chieftain. These diverse emotions split the Republican party. They are the emotions which lie at the bottom of party organization and party fidelity in the United States. The American does not put ideas above party; he puts party above ideas. And after party he puts personalities; he is an incurable hero worshiper, an easy victim of gifted rabble rousers. If he has room for ideas at all, they go in third and last place. He sticks to his party long after it has repudiated all of his convictions. Witness the Democrats of the Southern sugar country, bawling for Cleveland and praying for protection. Witness, again, the failure of the Gold Democrat movement and the heavy vote for Bryan in 1896, despite the opposition to bimetallism among Eastern Democrats. Witness, yet again, the easy *volte-face* of the Democratic party in 1904.

But here I get into the troubled field of the party history, with its dubious records and conflicting testimonies, and had better turn back at once. The one point I want to make is that the boasted independence of the American vanishes into thin air at the very place where it would be most valuable if it really existed—to wit, at the polls. A democracy made up of assertive individualists, each reacting upon all the others, would be a democracy extremely jealous of human rights and extremely sensitive to new ideas. But the democracy actually flourishing in the United States is made up of two disorderly mobs, each wholly careless of the rights of the other, and of the rights, no less, of the individuals within its own ranks, and both highly resistant to purely intellectual suggestion. The chief mark of each is its extraordinary development of the herding instinct, its childish subservience to professional mob masters, its ruthless crushing out of originality. There is no room in American politics for the man of acute and inventive mind: this and not the prevalence of corruption explains the political timidity of the vast majority of educated and intelligent Americans. The very fact that a man proposes something new or says something new is sufficient evidence against him: he is dismissed at once as a heretic, a mugwump, a traitor to all decent thinking. In the long run, of course, he may see his ideas adopted by the people, but only after they have been translated into terms of conventional sentimentality, either by his own voluntary stooping to the mob's level, or by the aid (usually unwelcome) of some expert appropriator and popularizer. I once heard William J. Bryan confess that his own *armamentarium* of ideas was made up entirely of borrowings. It is doubtful that a single one of the actual authors of these ideas ever attained to enough prominence to make him remembered, even by Mr. Bryan, or that any one of them would have recognized his contribution after Mr. Bryan had salted and sauced it to the public taste. They were mugwumps, one and all, and they paid the inevitable penalty of their mugwumpery.

But as I have said, this distrust of new ideas in politics is by no means a loyalty to old ideas, at least in any intellectual sense. Nor is it, generally speaking, a loyalty to tradition, for only in the South is there an active tradition in politics, and even there it is dying. Nor is it, save in a small minority of cases, a selfish interest in a going concern, for not one American in a hundred makes any personal profit out of politics. What the American is actually loyal to is the mere party abstraction, the bald notion of order and discipline, the conception of undeviating, unintelligent direction — and after that, to great bravos, mighty chiefs, heaven-kissing heroes. In a word, his political thinking is not marked by independence, but by the very reverse: its essential quality is its doglike subservience. On the one hand he avoids innovation as something accursed, and on the other hand he bends a limber knee to bosses of his own creation. His dominant passion is not for self-expression, but for self-effacement. He performs the functions of a citizen, not as a free ego, but as a mere cipher, a nameless soldier in a large army. The one sure way to shake his party loyalty is to convince him that his party candidates are doomed, that the other side will have a walkover. In such an event, it is not unusual for him to vote for the opposing candidates, on the ground that he doesn't want to "lose his vote." The thing he most esteems in his party is success. It pleases him to think that he is part of a powerful organization, and that he is led by the powerful chiefs of that organization.

Reformers commonly make the mistake of denouncing party rings as things apart from and antagonistic to party. That is to say, they picture the bosses as rogues who have imposed themselves, by dark and devious arts, upon the innocent rank and file, and their whole propaganda is an effort to awaken the rank and file to the deception. No wonder they always fail! The alleged deception, of course, is no deception at all. The bosses obtain and hold their power by the free consent of the rank and file, and that consent springs out of the American's ineradicable distrust of himself, his ready servility to loud and forthright men, his irresistible tendency to join a crowd. There is probably not a single sane voter in the United States who is under any illusion whatever as to the aims and methods of his party bosses: that they pursue politics as a trade, and for their personal advantage only, is universally known. And yet there is not a single community in the United States which lacks a boss chosen by the free suffrages of the party members, most of whom are honest men, as honesty goes, and get no recompense, direct or indirect, from the boss. No recompense, that is, save the satisfaction of their inherent impulse to serve, their chronic repugnance to independent action. These men, if they so desired, could overthrow the boss with ease. When their lust for cruelty is properly inflamed and played upon by rhetoricians more skillful than the boss himself, they sometimes actually do it. But soon or late they always return to their vassalage. Soon or late they always return to the boss. And if not to the boss dethroned, then to some other boss. The whole Progressive movement in the United States is no more than wholesale change of bosses. The people are just as slavish to the new bosses as ever they were to the old bosses. In more than one State, indeed, the new bosses are merely the old bosses in new falsefaces.

This thirst of the American to be ruled, this ready acquiescence in the setting up of authority over him, is visible in nine-tenths of his daily acts, and casts a curious light upon his theoretical abhorrence of aristocracies. The fact is, of course, that human society would be impossible without aristocracies, and the American can no more emancipate himself from that organic necessity than the Russian, the Chinaman or the Englishman. Next to the craving for distinction, the most powerful psychic appetite in man is the impulse to admit and honor distinction. Within the ranks of a genuine aristocracy—i.e., among the intelligent minority of any people— the distinction that is honored is commonly real enough. That is to say, it is based upon some valuable achievement, or upon the possession of some tangible dignity. But in a democracy the tendency is always to pay homage to the spurious and meretricious; and nowhere is this tendency more marked than in the United States. Men are estimated by the American according to a scale that is almost inverse to the scale of their intrinsic worth. If such a man as Tschaikowsky or Darwin or Von Behring were to go to live in the average American community, he would be outranked in public eminence by the local political boss, by all the noisier preachers, by the principal fraternal order magnates, and by a great host of even lowlier mountebanks. His fame would be less, and his influence upon the communal life and thought would be less.

I once had an object lesson in an American city of considerable size, the seat of a great university. One day, walking down the main street, I overtook the president of this university, a man of distinguished scientific attainment and international renown. As I dropped into step behind him, I noticed that the political boss of the city, an extremely gross and ignorant man, was ten paces ahead of him. Thus I followed the pair for three or four blocks. The boss got bows and cringing smiles from two score citizens, including a leading banker, a high public official and a clergyman within the shadow of a bishopric, and many others craned their necks to stare at him. But not a soul showed any sign of respect for the great scientist, and I doubt that half a dozen passers-by even recognized him.[26]

The scientist was a man whose distinction resided in his personal merit, while the boss was a man whose distinction had no higher source than the doggish servility of the people. All through the United States the landscape is thick with such brummagem notables, and the people revere and follow them. A dozen tin-roofers meet in the back room of a saloon, organize a lodge and elect one of their number "grand worthy potentate." A year later they are "honored" by his presence at their meetings; in ten years he may be so eminent a magnate that they will travel miles for the privilege of shaking hands with him. All our bogus titles—"honorable," "colonel," "professor" and so on—are far more than empty names. They are the symbols, nine times out of ten, of a very real public position, though often that public position has no better basis than their gratuitous assumption. The American feels himself subtly honored by the acquaintance and notice of such magnificoes; he bows to them as willingly and as proudly as an Englishman bows to a baronet. Our whole repertoire of bogus titles, in truth, is proof that the average American, like every other commonplace man, is born with an ineradicable propensity to submit himself to his betters. The men who put the prohibition of "titles and orders of nobility" into the Constitution were not genuine commoners, but aristocrats subtly jealous of one another, and perhaps eager to prove their intrinsic distinction by theatrically resigning all external distinction. The thing was not without precedents: certain Frenchmen had but lately shown the way, and the history of England was strewn with examples. But the common people of the United States did not acquiesce in that arrangement very long. There was never, indeed, any "Citizen" Washington, he was "General" from the start, and in the First Congress it was formally proposed that he be made "His Excellency" or "His Highness." The motion failed, but its underlying doctrine remained.

Today we have our enormous hierarchy of "excellencies" and "honorables," "generals" and "colonels," "judges" and "doctors." We have generals of the army, generals by brevet, generals of the militia, generals of the governors' staffs, generals of the Boys' Brigade, generals of the Knights Templar, the Hibernian Rifles, the Patriarchs Militant, the G. A. R., the Spanish War Veterans. A man who has once been attorney-general of his State remains a general to the end of his days. And all the lesser titles cling as stickily—"major," "captain," "professor," "marshal," "sheriff," "squire." This is not private vanity: it is public opinion. The American's one true exercise of the infinite freedom he boasts of is revealed in his creation of innumerable and complex aristocracies. He must have lords to look up to; he must have bosses to lead him; he must have heroes to admire. The one guide he distrusts eternally is his own unfettered spirit.

The American: His New Puritanism

Not, of course, that the Puritan spirit of 1620 has ever gone into actual eclipse in These States, or suffered more than a temporary damping. Far from it, indeed!

Make the most cursory review of American history that you will, and you must surely be impressed by the persistence of the Puritan outlook upon the world, the Puritan conviction of the pervasiveness of sin, the Puritan lust to make a sinner sweat and yell. If there is one mental vice, indeed, which sets off the American people from all other folks who walk the earth, not excepting the devil-fearing Scotch, it is that of assuming that every human act must be either right or wrong, and that ninety-nine percent of them are wrong. This is the one great American contribution to the science of ethics, and the cornerstone of the American philosophy.

There has never been a large political or social question before the American people which did not quickly resolve itself into a moral question. Even so dull a row as that over the currency produced its vast crop of saints and succubi, of Iokanaans and Pontius Pilates, of crimes, heathenries and crowns of thorns. Nor has there ever been any letting up of that spiritual eagerness which lay at the bottom of the original Puritan's moral obsession: the American has remained, from the very beginning, a man genuinely interested in the eternal riddles. The frank theocracy of the New England beach had scarcely succumbed to the libertarianism of a licentious Crown before there came the Great Awakening of 1734, with its orgies of homiletics and its chase of sinners. The Revolution, of course, brought another setback. But the moment the young Republic got out of the nursery and could protect itself from foes abroad, its citizens resumed the glad business of dragging one another up to grace, and the Asbury revival made that of Whitefield, Wesley and Jonathan Edwards seem a mild and puerile thing.

Thereafter, down to the outbreak of the Civil War, the whole populace joined in pulling the devil's tail. On the one hand, this great campaign took a purely theological form, with a hundred new and outlandish cults as its fruits; on the other hand, it crystallized into the hysterical temperance movement of the thirties and forties, with its Good Templars on horseback and its drunkards in cages; and on the third hand, as it were, it established a prudery in thought and speech from which we are still but half-delivered. Such ancient and innocent words as "wench" and "bastard" disappeared from the American language; we are told by Bartlett, indeed, that even "bull" was softened to "male cow." The word "woman" became a term of opprobrium, verging close upon downright libel; legs became the inimitable "limbs"; the "stomach" began to run from the "bosom" to the pelvic arch; pantaloons faded into "unmentionables"; the newspapers spun their parts of speech into such gossamer webs as "a statutory offense," "an interesting condition" and "a house of questionable repute." And meanwhile evangelists of all sorts swarmed in the land like a plague of locusts, and the lyceum and the camp meeting, father and mother to the chautauqua of a later day, were born. State after State went "dry"; legislature after legislature stepped up to sign the pledge. Even the national House of Representatives was penetrated by this primeval uplift, and on more than one occasion it offered its rostrum to some eminent flayer of the Rum Demon, and spread his excoriations upon its minutes.

Beneath all this gay bubbling on the surface, of course, ran the deep and swift current of anti-slavery feeling—a tide of passion which historians now attempt to account for on economic grounds, but which showed no trace of economic origin while it lasted. Its true quality was moral, devout, ecstatic; it culminated, to change the figure, in a supreme discharge of moral electricity, almost fatal to the nation. The crack of that great spark emptied the jar: the American people forgot all their pledges and their pruderies during the four years of the Civil War. The Good Templars, indeed, were seldom heard of again, and with them into memory went many other singular virtuosi of virtue—for example, the Millerites.[27] But this truce with the devil was for the moment only: it was no more than the adjournment of the patent medicine show while the circus parade went by. The instant the smoke of the battlefields cleared away, the Puritans returned to their old sport of shaking up the erring, and by the middle of the seventies they were at it in full fuming and fury. The high points of that holy war halt the backward-looking eye: the Moody and Sankey uproar;[28] the recrudescence of the temperance agitation and its culmination in prohibition; the rise of the Young Men's Christian Association,[29] the Sunday school and the Christian Endeavor movement; the triumphal entry of the Salvation Army, regardless of all the warnings of Thomas Henry Huxley;[30] the dim beginnings of the vice crusade; the injection of moral concepts and rages into party politics (the "crime" of 1873!);[31] the loud preaching of baroque Utopias (Populism, Bellamyism, "If Christ Came to Chicago," Bryanism); the invention of muckraking and trust busting; the mad, glad war of extermination upon the Mormons, the anarchists, the Spaniards; the hysteria over the Breckinridge-Pollard case;[32] the enormous multiplication of moral and religious associations, each with its sure cure for all the sorrows of the world; the spread of zoöphilia, the dawn of the uplift, and last but far from least, Comstockery.

In Comstockery, if I do not err, the new Puritanism took its formal departure from the old, and moral endeavor suffered a general overhauling and tightening of screws. The difference between the two forms is very well represented by the difference between the program of the half-forgotten Good Templars and the program set forth in the Webb Law of 1913,[33] or by that between the somewhat diffident prudery of the forties and the astoundingly ferocious and uncompromising crusading of today. In brief, a difference between *renunciation* and *denunciation*, asceticisin and Mohammedanism, the hair shirt and the flaming sword. The distinguishing mark of the elder Puritanism, at least after it had attained to the stature of a national philosophy, was its appeal to the individual conscience, its exclusive concern with the demon within, its strong flavor of self-accusing. Even the rage against slavery was, in large measure, an emotion of the mourner's bench. The thing that worried the more ecstatic Abolitionists was their sneaking sense of responsibility, the fear that they themselves were flouting the fire by letting slavery go on. The thirst to punish the concrete slaveowner, as an end in itself, did not appear until opposition had added exasperation to fervor. In most of the earlier harangues against the sinful Southern planter, indeed, you will find a perfect willingness to grant his good faith, and even to compensate him for his property.

But the new Puritanism—or, perhaps more accurately, considering the shades of prefixes, the neo-Puritanism—is a frank harking back to the primitive spirit. The *stammvater* Puritan of the bleak New England coast was not content to flay his own wayward carcass: full satisfaction did not sit upon him until he had also butchered a Quaker. That is to say, the sinner who excited his highest zeal and passion was not so much himself as the other fellow; to borrow a term from psychopathology, he was less the masochist than the sadist. And it is that very peculiarity which sets off his descendant of today from the milder Puritan of the period between the Revolution and the Civil War. The new Puritanism is not ascetic but militant. Its aim is not to lift up the saint but to knock down the sinner. Its supreme manifestation is the vice crusade, an armed pursuit of helpless outcasts by the whole military and naval forces of the Republic, a wild scramble into Heaven on the backs of harlots. Its supreme hero is Comstock Himself, with his pious glory in the fact that the sinners he has jailed, if gathered into one penitential party, would fill a train of sixty-one railroad coaches, allowing sixty to the coach.

But how are we to account for this turning inside out? How did the Puritan come to transfer his holy ire from the Old Adam within him to the happy rascal across the street? In what direction are we to look for the springs and causes of that revolutionary change? In the direction, I venture to opine, of the Golden Calf. In the direction of the fat fields of our midlands, the full nets of our lakes and coasts, the belching factory smoke of our cities—even in the direction of Wall Street, that devil's chasm. In brief, Puritanism has become militant by becoming rich. Moral endeavor has become a huge and well organized business, heavily capitalized, superbly officered, perfectly armed. Wealth, coming to the aid of piety, has reached out its long arms to grab the distant and innumerable evildoer, the far-flung rebel, the happy runaway; it has gone down into its deep pockets to pay for his capture, his extradition, his flaying; it has created the Puritan *de luxe*, the daring organizer of Puritanism, the moral Lorenzo the Magnificent, the czar and pope of snoutery, the busybody of the fourth dimension. And by the same token, it has created a new science and art of sinner hunting, and issued its letters of marque to the Puritan mercenary, the professional hound of Heaven, the specialist in crusading, the moral "expert."

The Puritans of the elder generation, with few exceptions, were poor. All Americans, down to the Civil War, were poor. And, being poor, they leaned irresistibly toward a *sklavmoral*,[34] for all their surface contentment. That is to say, they were spiritually humble. Their eyes were fixed, not upon the abyss behind and below them, but upon the long and rocky road ahead of them. Their moral passion was limitless, but it had a habit of turning into self-accusing, self-denial, self-scourging. They began by howling their sins from the mourner's bench; they came to their end, many of them, in the supreme immolation of battle. But out of the war came prosperity, and out of prosperity came a new and more assertive morality, to wit, the *herrenmoral*. Many great fortunes were made in the war itself; an uncounted number got started during the two decades following. What is more, this material prosperity, so soothing to the troubled soul, was generally dispersed through all classes: it affected the common workman and the remote farmer quite as much as the actual merchant and manufacturer. Its first effect, as we all know, was a universal cockiness, a rise in pretentions, a comfortable feeling that the republic was a success, and with it its every citizen. This change made itself quickly obvious, and even odious, in all the secular relations of life. The American became a sort of braggart playboy of the Western world, enormously sure of himself and ludicrously contemptuous of all other men, including his own countrymen. Kipling, coming later, embalmed him in an unforgettable stanza:

> Enslaved, illogical, elate,
> He greets th' embarrassed Gods, nor fears
> To shake the iron hand of Fate
> Or match with Destiny for beers.[35]

And on the ghostly side there appeared the same accession of confidence, the same sure assumption of authority, though at first less self-evidently and offensively. The religion of the American began to lose its old inward direction; it became less and less a scheme of personal salvation and more and more a scheme of pious derring-do. The revivals of the seventies had all the bounce and fervor of those of half a century before, but the mourner's bench began to lose its old standing as their symbol, and in its place arose the collection basket, the endowment, the *kriegskasse*.[36] Instead of reviling and damning himself, the tear-soaked convert now volunteered to track down and bring in the other fellow. His enthusiasm was not for repentance, expiation, atonement, but for what he began to call service. In brief, the national sense of energy and fitness gradually superimposed itself upon the Puritanism, and from that marriage sprang a keen *wille zur macht*, a lusty will to power.[37] The Puritan began to feel his oats. He had the men, he had the guns and he had the money, too. All that was needed was organization. The rescue of the unsaved could be converted into a wholesale business, unsentimentally and economically conducted, and with all the usual aids to efficiency, from skillful sales management to seductive advertising, and from rigid accounting to the ruthless shutting off of competition.

Out of this new will to power, founded upon the old Christian idea that even the devil may be bought off, there came many brobdingnagian and wind-filled enterprises, with the so-called "institutional" church at their head. Piety, once so simple and so lowly, became bumptious and protean. It was cunningly rolled in sugar and rammed down unsuspecting throats. It became basketball, billiards, bowling alleys, gymnasia. The sinner was lured to grace with Turkish baths, lectures on Gothic architecture and free instruction in stenography, rhetoric and double entry bookkeeping, The prevailing Christianity lost all its old contemplative and esoteric character and became a frankly worldly venture, a thing of balance sheets and ponderable profits, magnificently capitalized and astutely manned. Naturally enough, there was no place in this new scheme of things for the spiritual type of leader, the fledgling archangel, the master devotee, with his white chokers, his affecting austerities and his interminable "fourthlies." He was displaced by a brisk gentleman in a "business suit," who looked, talked and thought like a seller of Mexican mining stock.

Plan after plan for the swift evangelization of the nation was launched, some of them of truly astonishing sweep and daring. They kept pace, step by step, with the mushroom growth of enterprise in the commercial field. The Y. M. C. A. swelled to the porportions of a Standard Oil Company, a United States Steel Corporation. Its huge buildings began to rise in every city; it developed a swarm of specialists in now and fantastic moral and social sciences; it enlisted the same gargantuan talent which managed the railroads, the big banks and the larger national industries. And beside it rose the Young People's Society of Christian Endeavor, the Sunday school associations and a score of other such grandiose organizations, each with its millions of adherents and its fathomless treasury. No new device of rapid fire conquest was too ridiculous to bring forth volunteers and money. Even the undertakings that had come down from an older and less expansive day were pumped up and put upon a Wall Street basis: the American Bible Society, for example, began to give away Bibles by the million instead of by the thousand, and to invent new languages to print them in, and the venerable Tract Society took on the feverish activity of a daily newspaper, even of a yellow journal.[38] Down into our own day this trustification (to coin a bad word) of pious endeavor has gone on. The Men and Religion Forward Movement[39] proposes to convert the whole country, including the insular possessions, by twelve o'clock noon of such and such a day; the Student Volunteer Movement[40] announces that, given so many more millions, the whole mainland of Asia will be as good as saved; the Order of Gideons[41] announces that it will make every traveler read the Bible (American Revised Version!), whether he will or not;

in a score of cities there are committees of opulent *hadjis* who take half-pages in the newspapers and advertise the Decalogue and the Beatitudes as if they were commodities of trade.

Thus the national energy which created the Beef Trust and the Oil Trust has achieved equal marvels in the field of religious organization, and by the same methods. One need be no very subtle psychologist to perceive in all this a good deal less actual religious zeal than mere lust for staggering accomplishment, for empty bigness, for the unprecedented and the prodigious. Many of these great evangelical enterprises, indeed, lost all save the faintest flavor of devotion soon after they were set up—for example, the Y. M. C. A., which is now no more than a sort of national club system, with its doors open to anyone not palpably felonious.

But while the war upon godlessness thus degenerated into a purely secular sport in one direction, it maintained all its pristine quality, and even took on a new ferocity, in another direction. Here it was that the lamp of American Puritanism kept on burning. Here it was, indeed, that the lamp became converted into a huge bonfire, or rather a blast furnace, with flames mounting to the very heavens, and sinners stacked like cordwood at the hand of an eager black gang. In brief, the new will to power, working in the true Puritan as in the mere religious sportsman, stimulated him to a campaign of repression and punishment perhaps unequalled since the Middle Ages, and developed an art of militant morality as complex in technique and as rich in professors as the more ancient art of iniquity.

If we take the passage of the Comstock Postal Act, on March 3, 1873, as a starting point, the legislative stakes of this new Puritan movement sweep upward in a grand curve to the passage of the Mann[42] and Webb acts, in 1911 and 1913, the first of which ratifies and re-enacts the Seventh Commandment with a salvo of artillery, and the second of which puts the overwhelming power of the Federal Government behind the enforcement of the prohibition laws in the so-called "dry" States. The mind at once recalls the salient campaigns of this war of a generation: first the attack upon "vicious" literature (*i.e.*, upon Tolstoi's *The Kreutzer Sonata*, Hauptmann's *Hannele* and the whole canon of Zola!) begun by Comstock and the New York Society for the Suppression of Vice, but quickly extending to every city in the land; then the long fight upon the open gambling houses, culminating in its retreat behind the skirts of a corrupted constabulary; then the revival of prohibition, abandoned at the outbreak of the Civil War, and the grotesque attempt to enforce it in a growing list of States; then the successful onslaught upon the Louisiana lottery, and upon its swarm of rivals and successors; then the gradual stamping out of horse racing, and the ensuing attack upon the poolroom; then the rise of a theater censorship in all of the large cities, and of a moving picture censorship following; then the renaissance of Sabbatarianism, with the Lord's Day Alliance, a Canadian invention, in the van; then the attack upon the army canteen; then the gradual tightening of the laws against polygamy, with the Roberts and Smoot cases and the unenforceable New York Adultery Act as typical products;[43] and lastly, the general plowing up and emotional discussion of sexual matters, chiefly by man haters male and female, with compulsory instruction in "sex hygiene" as its mildest manifestation and the medieval fury of the vice crusade as its worst.

Differing widely in their targets and working methods, these various Puritan enterprises have had one character in common: they are all efforts to combat immorality with the weapons designed for crime. In each of them there is a visible effort to erect the individual's offense against himself into an offense against society. Beneath all of them there is the dubious principle—the very determining principle, indeed, of Puritanism—that it is competent for the community to limit and condition the most private acts of its members, and with it the inevitable corollary that there are some members of the community who have a special talent for such legislation, and that their arbitrary fiats are, and of a right ought to be, binding upon all. This is the essential fact of Puritanism, new or old: its recognition of the moral expert, the professional sinhound, the virtuoso of virtue. The difference between the old and the new is merely a difference in organization, in magnitude and in virulence.

Under the theocracy, of course, the chase and punishment of sinners was a purely ecclesiastical function, and almost of a sacramental character. The laity might lend a hand, but only under sacerdotal direction. Even the sworn officers of the law, when they took to the trail of heretics, did so as mere agents of the higher power. But with the disintegration of the theocracy, there came a gradual augmentation of lay authority, and by the time the new Puritanism dawned, the secular arm was triumphant. That is to say, the special business of pursuing and flaying the erring was taken away from the preachers and put into the hands of laymen diligently trained in its technique and mystery, and there it remains today. The new Puritanism has created an army of inquisitors and headmen who are not only distinct from the hierarchy, but who, in many instances, actually command and intimidate the hierarchy. This is conspicuously evident in the case of the Anti-Saloon League, a nationwide and enormously effective fighting organization, with a large staff of highly accomplished experts in its service. These experts do not wait for ecclesiastical support, nor even ask for it: they force it. Any clergyman who presumes to protest against their furious war upon the saloon, even upon the quite virtuous ground that its excesses make it ineffective, runs a risk of condign and merciless punishment. So plainly is this understood, indeed, that in more than one State the clergy of the Puritan denominations openly take orders from the lay specialists, and court their favors without shame. It is in that direction that all ecclesiastical preferment lies, and by that route more than one bishop has been manufactured. Here a single Puritan enterprise, heavily capitalized and superbly officered, has engulfed the entire Puritan movement, and a part has become more than the whole.

In a dozen other sanguinary fields of moral combat this tendency to transform a religious business into a purely secular business, with lay backers and lay commanders, is plainly visible. The increasing wealth of Puritanism has not only augmented its scope and audacity, but it has also had the effect of attracting clever men, of no particular spiritual enthusiasm, to its service. Moral endeavor, in other words, has become a recognized trade, or rather a profession, and there have appeared men who pretend to an expert and enormous knowledge of it, and who show enough truth in their pretension to gain the unlimited support of Puritan capitalists. The vice crusade, to mention but one example, has produced a large crop of such experts, and some of them are in such demand that they are overwhelmed with engagements. The majority of these men come from the social settlements and freshwater colleges, with a sprinkling of unsuccessful physicians and second-rate lawyers to lighten the mass, and they seldom show the slightest flavor of sacerdotalism. They are not pastors, nor even lay preachers, but detectives, press agents, statisticians and mob orators, and not infrequently their secularity is distressingly evident. Their aim, as they say, is to do things. Their success is measured by the turmoil they can stir up and the number of scalps they can take. And so, with "moral sentiment" behind them, they override all criticism and opposition without argument, and proceed to the business of dispersing prostitutes, of browbeating and terrorizing weak officials, and of forcing extravagant legislation through city councils and State legislatures.

The very cocksureness of these self-constituted authorities is their chief source of strength. They combat objections with such violence and with such devastating cynicism that all objectors are quickly driven to flight. The more astute politicians, in the face of so ruthless a fire, commonly profess conversion and join the colors, just as their brethren go over to prohibition in the "dry" States, and the newspapers seldom hold out much longer. The result is that the "investigation" of the social evil, a business demanding the highest prudence and sagacity, becomes an orgy of quacks and mountebanks, and that the ensuing "report" of the inevitable "vice commission" is made up of two parts pornographic fiction and three parts pious platitude. Of all the vice commissions that have held the stage in the United States of late, not one has done its work without the help of these singularly vociferous rabble-rousers, and not one has contributed a single new idea, nor even an old idea of undoubted value, to the solution of the problem.

But it is not only in the twin wars upon the brothel and the saloon that the new Puritan specialist has usurped the old office of the clergy, nor does he here best reveal his growing potency. These wars, after all, are quite as much secular as religious: an atheist might conceivably be as strongly in favor of closing dramshops and hounding prostitutes as the most orthodox pietist. But what of the campaign for Sabbath observance, and, in particular, for the drastic enforcement of draconian

Blue Laws? The call here would seem to be upon the gentlemen of the cloth: the whole argument against recreation on Sunday is essentially a theological one, whatever may be the character of the argument against work. And yet the direction of the campaign has been gradually taken over by lay bravos, and the general staff is now a purely secular organization, with trained sub-staffs for handling definite portions of the work—for example, the collection of contributions and informers' fees, the preparation and circulation of literature, the gathering of evidence against offenders, and last but far from least, the operation of legislative lobbies. So successful has this business become, indeed, that a good many clergymen have actually abandoned the pulpit in order to engage in it. It is interesting, it is lucrative, and in view of the nine lives of the devil, it promises to be permanent. In nearly every State there is now a strong central organization with a multitude of branches, all living upon the country, all adding local embellishments to the main jehad. And in Washington there is a national bureau with its guns trained upon Congress—and more than once of late the lawmakers have performed wild mazurkas to its whistling.

But I need not go on piling up examples of this new form of Puritan snouting and rowelling, with its radical departure from a religious foundation and its elaborate development as an everyday business. The impulse behind it I have called a *wille zur macht*, a will to power. In terms more homely, it was described by John Fiske as "the disposition to domineer," and in his unerring way he lays its dependence upon the gratuitous assumption of infallibility, an immemorial characteristic of the Puritan mind. Every Puritan is a one-horse Pope, a Sheik ul Islam, an amateur Messiah: to dissent from his private revelation is to be nominated for his hell. He cannot imagine honesty in an opponent, nor even ordinary decency. But still stronger than his superstitious reverence for his own inspiration is his hot yearning to make someone jump. He has an ineradicable taste for cruelty in him; he is a sportsman even before he is an exegete and moralist, and very often his blood lust leads him into lamentable excesses. The various vice crusades offer innumerable cases in point. In one city, if the press dispatches are to be believed, the proscribed women of the Tenderloin were pursued with such ferocity that seven of them were driven to suicide.[44] And in another city, after a campaign of repression so unfortunate in its effects that it was actually denounced by clergymen elsewhere, a distinguished (and very friendly) connoisseur of such affairs referred to it ingenuously as "more fun than a fleet of airships."[45]

Such disorderly and pharisaical combats with evil, of course, produce nothing but more evil. It is a commonplace, indeed, that a city is always in worse condition after it has been "cleaned up" by Puritans than it was before. New York, Los Angeles, Chicago and Des Moines offer evidence as to the social evil, and Savannah, Atlanta and Charleston, S. C., as to the saloon. Four or five years after Los Angeles had been made chemically pure by policewomen, searchlights and an incomparable spy system, it was discovered that the city harbored houses of vice so unutterably vile that even Port Said would have been ashamed of them. And in Des Moines, to take but one other example, the enforcement of the so-called Iowa Red Light Law led to such a saturnalia of sex that even the army surgeon at Fort Des Moines was staggered. But the Puritans who finance these enterprises are not daunted by untoward results. They get their thrills, not out of any possible obliteration of vice, but out of the galloping pursuit of the vicious. There is fair reason for assuming, indeed, that they would oppose any scheme of hunting which promised to exterminate the game. In all the "dry" States they have left loopholes for the speakeasy, and when the Webb Law stopped those loopholes, they promptly made new ones. The thing that gives them pleasure is to spy out, track down and apply the switch to a sinner—preferably an attractive *fille de joie*, but failing that, a gambler, a bootlegger, a Sabbath breaker or a turkey trotter. Their ideal quarry is the white slave trader, who is four-fifths a myth and hence not permanently crippled by their artillery. They can kill him all over again once a week.

Naturally enough, this organization of Puritanism upon the scale and basis of baseball, racing and vaudeville has tended to attract and create a type of "expert" crusader whose determination to give his employers a good run for their money is uncontaminated by any consideration for the public welfare. The result has been a steady increase of scandals, a constant collapse of moral organization, a frequent unveiling of whited sepulchres. Various observers have sought, of late, to direct the public attention to this significant and inevitable corruption of the new Puritanism. On May 8 last the New York *Sun*, in the course of a protest against the appointment of a vice commission for New York, denounced the paid agents of private Puritan organizations as "notoriously corrupt, undependable and dishonest," and three days later the Rev. W. S. Rainsford, in a letter to the same paper, bore testimony, out of his abundant experience, to their lawlessness, their absurd pretensions to special knowledge, their questionable methods of gathering evidence and their devious devices for forestalling honest criticism. A few months later the Baltimore grand jury made somewhat similar accusations against certain agents of the local vice society—a society chiefly managed, curiously enough, by a former Attorney General of the United States.[46] Proofs have been added to such accusations more than once. In fully a score of cities the agents of vice societies have come to grief for violating the very laws they profess to enforce. And the other Puritan brotherhoods, notably the Anti-Saloon League, have nourished plentiful tribes of bogus Puritans, some of whom have gone over to the opposition, and are now serving the hosts of darkness as gallantly as they once served the angels.

But does all this raise a public row? Do the American people show any sign of putting down this debauch of sham virtue, this orgy of snouting and quackery? Alas, I am unable to report that they do. A few courageous critics mount the rostrum to protest—Rainsford, Brand Whitlock, Carter Harrison, the late Mayor Gaynor, Father Russell in Washington. But the majority of Americans get too much fun out of the show to spoil it. It costs them nothing: all of the bills are paid by a small group of opulent saints. The average vice society is supported by half a dozen men. And say what you will against these bondholders of Heaven, they at least offer good sport to the populace here on earth. They keep the newspapers supplied with hot stuff. They dramatize the dullness of everyday.

two

The American Landscape

Good Old Baltimore

In the life of every Baltimorean not to the manner born—that is to say, of every Baltimorean recruited from the outer darkness—there are three sharply defined stages. The first, lasting about a week, is one of surprise and delight—delight with the simple courtesy of the people, with the pink cheeks and honest hips of the girls, with the range and cheapness of the victualry, with the varied loveliness of the surrounding land and water, with the touch of Southern laziness in the air. Thus the week of introduction, of discovery, of soft sitting in the strangers' pew.

Follows now a sudden reaction—and six months of discontent. Baltimore, compared to New York or Chicago, even to Atlanta or Kalamazoo, is indubitably slow. No passion for novelty, no hot yearning for tomorrow, is in her burghers. They change their shirts but once a day—flattery!—flattery!—and their prejudices but once a generation. It is not easy to sell them new goods; it is not easy to make them sell their own goods in a new way. They show, collectively, communally, the somewhat touchy *intransigeance* of their ancient banks, their medieval public offices. Mount a soapbox and bawl your liver pills—and they will set their catchpolls on you. Give them a taste of New York brass, of Western wind music—and their smile of courtesy will freeze into a smile of amused contempt, if not into a downright sneer. Naturally enough, the confident newcomer, bounding full tilt into this barbed psychic barrier, feels that he is grossly ill used. The Baltimoreans—think of it!—actually laugh at his pedagogy, revile his high flights of commercial sapience, fling back at him his offers to lift them up! Boors, blockheads, fossils! And so the victim, leaking blood from his metaphysical wounds, sees himself a martyr, pines for home and mother, and issues a proclamation of damnation. Whence arises, beloved, the perennial news that the cobblestones of Baltimore are rough, that the harbor of Baltimore is no compote of roses, that the oysters of Baltimore are going off, that the folk of Baltimore suffer the slings and arrows of *arterio-sclerosis*.

Six months of that scorn, that fever, that rebellion. And then, one day, if the gods be kind enough to keep him so long, the rebel finds himself walking down Charles Street hill, from the Cardinal's house toward Lexington Street. It is five o'clock of a fine afternoon—an afternoon, let us say, in Indian summer. A caressing softness is in the air; the dusk is stealing down; lights begin to show discreetly, far back in prim, dim shops. Suddenly a sense of the snugness, the coziness, the delightful intimacy of it all strikes and fills the wayfarer. Suddenly he glows and mellows. Suddenly his heart opens, like a clam reached by the tide. Where else in all Christendom is there another town with so familiar and alluring a promenade? Where else are there so many pretty girls to the square yard? Where else do they bowl along so boldly and yet so properly, halting here to gabble with acquaintances and block the narrow sidewalk, and there to hail other acquaintances across the narrow driveway?

Baltimoreans, filled with strange juices at Merchants' and Manufacturers' Association banquets, talk magnificently of widening Charles Street, of making it a Fifth Avenue, a Boulevard des Italiens, a Piccadilly. But so far they have never actually come to it—and let us all send up a prayer that they never will! To widen Charles Street would be like giving Serpolotte the waist of Brünnhilde—an act of defilement and indecency. The whole enchantment of that incomparable lane lies in its very narrowness, its check-by-jowlness, its insidious friendliness.

And in the same elements lies the appeal of Baltimore. The old town will not give you the time of your life; it is not a brazen hussy among cities, blinding you with its xanthous curls, kicking up its legs, inviting you to exquisite deviltries. Not at all. It is, if the truth must come out, a Perfect Lady. But for all its resultant narrowness, its niceness, its air of merely playing at being a city, it has, at bottom, the one quality which, in cities as in women, shames and survives all the rest. And that is the impalpable, indefinable, irresistible quality of charm.

Here, of course, I whisper no secret; some news of this has got about. Even the fellow who denounces Baltimore most bitterly—the baffled seller of green goods, the scorned and rail-ridden ballyhoo man—is willing, once his torn cartilages have begun to knit, to grant the old town some measure of that bewitchment, or at least to admit that others feel it and justly praise it. He will tell you that, whatever the hunkerousness, the archaic conservatism of the Baltimoreans, they know, at all events, how to cook victuals—in particular, how to cook terrapin à la Maryland. Again, he will admit the subtle allurement, almost as powerful as the lure of money, of a city with an ancient cathedral upon its central hill—the only North American city in which it was possible, until very lately, to see a prince of the Holy Church, red-hatted, lean and other-worldly, walking among his people.[1]

So far, indeed, the preëminence of Baltimore is an axiom, a part of the American tradition. It is, by unanimous consent, the gastronomical capital of the New World, and it is also, by unanimous consent, the one genuine cathedral city of our fair republic. Other cities, of course, have cathedrals, too—out in the West, I believe, they are run up by the half-dozen—but only in Baltimore is there the authentic cathedral atmosphere. Only in Baltimore is there any reflection of that ecclesiastical efflorescence which gives enchantment to such Old World towns as Seville and Padua, Moscow and Milan. Only in Baltimore is it possible to imagine a procession of monks winding down a main-traveled road, holding up the taxicabs and the trolley cars, and striking newsboys dumb with reverence.

Such is the Baltimore picture that fills the public eye—a scene of banqueting and devotion. Unluckily for romance, there is not much truth in either part of it. The diamond back terrapin, true enough, is native to the Chesapeake marshes, and the see of Baltimore, true enough, is to Catholic America what the see of Rome is to all Christendom; but when you have said that you have said your say. The fact is that the terrapin, once so plentiful that it was fed to the hogs and blackamoors, has long since faded into a golden mist. It is a fowl consumed in Baltimore, as elsewhere, only at long intervals, and as an act of extraordinary debauchery. I have heard tales of ancient gourmets at the Maryland Club, obese, opulent and baggy under the eyes, who eat it daily, or, at any rate, four times a week.

But such virtuosi, in the very nature of things, must be rare. The average Baltimorean is held back from that licentiousness by what the Socialists call economic pressure. He eschews the terrapin for the same reason that he eschews yachting, polygamy and the collection of ceramics. Of the six hundred thousand folk in the town, I venture to say that three hundred thousand have never even seen a genuine diamond back, that four hundred thousand haven't the slightest notion how the reptile is cooked, and that five hundred thousand have never tasted it, nor even smelled it. Conservative figures, indeed. Let other figures support them. *Imprimis*, it is an unimaginable indecorum, if not a downright impossibility, to eat a rasher of terrapin without using champagne to wash the little bones out of the tonsils—and champagne costs four dollars a bottle. *Zum zweiten*, an ordinary helping of terrapin—not a whole *meal* of terrapin, understand, nor a whole terrapin, but an ordinary, six-ounce helping, made up, let us say, of two schnitzels from the flank, a hip, a neck, two claws and three yellow eggs—costs three dollars in the kitchen and from three fifty to four dollars on the table! So an eminent Baltimore chef told me once, dining with me, off duty, in a spaghetti joint.

"But I have eaten diamond back at two fifty," I protested.

"Aha!" said he, and lifted his diabolic brows.

"Then it wasn't genuine terrapin?" I asked in surprise.

"The good God knows!"

"But isn't it just possible that it *was?*"

"Everything is possible."

More red wine loosed his tongue, and the tale that he told was of hair raising effect upon a passionate eater—a tale of vulgar mud turtles with diamonds photographed upon their backs, of boiled squirrel helping the sophistication, of terrapin eggs manufactured in the laboratory.

"But certainly not at the —— Hotel!"

A shrug of the shoulders.

"Or at the —— !"

Two shrugs—and the faintest ghost of a snicker.

"But the possibility of detection—the scandal—the riot!"

A frank chuckle, and then:

"In Baltimore there are eighteen men only who know terrapin from—not terrapin. In the United States, thirty-seven."

Alas, the story of the diamond back is not the whole story! Baltimore victualry is afflicted in these days, not merely by a malady of the heart, but by a general paralysis and decay of the entire organism—a sort of progressive coma, working inward from the extremities. That it was once unique, ineffable, almost heavenly—so much we must assume unless we assume alternatively that all the old-time travelers were liars. For you can't open a dusty *Journal of a Tour in the United States of North America, circa* 1820, without finding a glowing chapter upon the romantic eating to be had in Baltimore taverns. From the beginning of the century down to the Civil War each successive tourist grew lyric in its praises. That was the Golden Age of Maryland cookery. Then it was that the black mammy of sweet memory, turbaned and oleose, reared her culinary Taj Mahals and attained to her immortality. Then it was that cornbread soared the interstellar spaces and the corn flitter (*not* fritter) was born.

But the black mammy of that arcadian day was too exquisite, too sensitive an artist to last. (The rose is a fragile flower. The sunset flames—and is gone.) Her daughter, squeezed into corsets, failed of her technique and her imagination. The seventies saw the rise of false ideals, of spurious tools and materials—saleratus, self-rising buckwheat, oleomargarine, Chicago lard, the embalmed egg, the carbolated ham, the gas stove. Today the destruction is complete. The native Baltimore cook, granddaughter to kitchen Sapphos and Angelica Kauffmanns, is now a frank mechanic, almost bad enough to belong to a union—a frowzy, scented houri in the more preposterous gauds of yesteryear, her veins full of wood alcohol and cocaine, her mind addled by the intrigues of Moorish high society, her supreme achievement a passable boiled egg, a fairish kidney stew or a wholly third rate pot of sprouts.

And if cooking in the home thus goes to the devil in Baltimore, cooking in the public inns departs even further from its old high character and particularity. In sober truth, it has almost ceased to exist—that is to say, as a native art. The Baltimore hotel chef of today shows his honorable discharges from the Waldorf-Astoria, the Auditorium Annex, the Ponce de Leon. He is simply a journeyman cook, a single member of the undistinguished world brotherhood; and the things he dishes up in Baltimore are exactly the same things he was taught to dish up in New York, or Chicago, or wherever it was that he escaped from the scullery. Good food, I do not deny, but not of Baltimore, Baltimorean. Demand of him a plate of lye hominy in the Talbot County manner, with honest hog meat at its core—and he will fall in a swoon. Ask him for soft crabs—and he will send them to the table in cracker dust! Talk to him of chitlings—and you will talk to a corpse. The largest oyster he has ever heard of is about the size of a watch. The largest genuine Maryland oyster— the veritable bivalve of the Chesapeake, still to be had at oyster roasts down the river and at street stands along the wharves—is as large as your open hand. A magnificent, matchless reptile! Hard to swallow? Dangerous? Perhaps to the novice, the dastard. But to the veteran of the raw bar, the man of trained and lusty esophagus, a thing of prolonged and kaleidoscopic flavors, a slow slipping saturnalia, a delirium of joy!

Here, it may be, I go too far. Not, of course, in celebrating the Chesapeake oyster, but in denouncing the Baltimore hotels. Let me at once ameliorate the indictment by admitting exceptions. There are hotel cooks in Baltimore, I freely grant, who have absorbed a lingering secret or two from the native air—not many, but still a few. At one hotel, for example, you will find, amid a welter of *à la's*, the authentic soft crab of Maryland, cooked at the open fire, pronged to a sliver of country bacon—and *without* cracker dust! At another, perhaps, a very decent plate of jowl and sprouts. At a third, pawnhoss in season, fresh from the woodland sausage vats of Frederick County—and fried properly in slender shingles. At a fourth, Ann' 'Ran'el strawberries with their arteries still pulsing. At a fifth, genuine Patuxent sweet potatoes, candied in their own sugar. And always, in the background, there is that last truly Baltimore hotel—sole survivor of the glorious dynasty of Guy's and Barnum's—wherein, at the lunch bar down in the cellar, the oyster potpie is still a poem and a passion, a dream and an intoxication, a burst of sunlight and a concord of sweet sounds.

Oh, the mellowness of it! Oh, the yellowness of it! A rich, a nourishing, an exquisite dish! A pearl of victualry, believe me, and not for swine. The man who appreciates and understands it, who penetrates to the depths of its perfection, who feels and is moved by those nuances which transfigure it and sublimate it and so lift it above all other potpies under the sun—that man is of the lineage of Brillat-Savarin, and no mere footman of metabolism. But the oyster pie, however ravishing, is yet but transitory—here today and gone tomorrow, a mirage as much as a miracle—for no cultured Baltimorean will eat an oyster, dead or alive, if the mercury in the tube be above thirty-two degrees Fahrenheit.

Thus experience speaks. A thawed oyster is, at best, a dubious oyster, and may be a downright homicidal oyster. Visitors gobble the bivalve far into May and June, and then bulge the hospitals and morgues; the native, save drink masters him, is more cautious. But even if the oyster pie is thus a fleeting guest, there yet remains crab soup, its cousin and rival. I mean here, of course, not the vulgar crab soup of the barrooms, full of claws and tomato skins and with a shinbone as its base, but crab bisque, of white meat, country butter and rich cream all compact. You can find it, from May to October, just where the oyster pie blooms and glows from November to March, and that is, to give away the secret at last, in the lower eating room of the Rennert Hotel. There Maryland cookery lives out the palsied evening of its days. There the oyster pie, crab soup, boiled tongue and spinach, turkey wings with oyster sauce, early York cabbage, Charles County ham and a few other such doddering thoroughbreds make their last gallant stand against the filet mignon, the Wiener schnitzel and all the rest of the exotic *à la's*. When the old Carrollton went up in smoke, in 1904, the planked shad, as planks and shad were known to Lord Fairfax and Charles Carroll, vanished from the earth. And when, in the course of human events, the Rennert gives way to some obscene skyscraper, the last genuine oyster potpie will say good-bye.

Sic transit gloria—and whatever the bad Latin is for eating with the heart. Baltimore, of course, yet offers decent food to the stranger within her gates, but it is food he knows at home and is tired of. The native idiocrasy, the local color, save as I have indicated, are gone. One must have a guide to find a plate of indubitable hog and hominy; even so noble a dish as crab Creole, a Louisiana invention raised to the stars by Maryland crabs and Maryland genius, now hides at Joyce's, an eating house remote from the white lights of the town. And for Chesapeake oysters of adult growth, the visitor must go, as I have said, down the river, a hazardous journey in winter, or brave the stenches and shanghaiers of the docks.

So, too, with the legendary processions of monks, to which we now come back after a long excursion into victualry. One looks for them in the American Rome—and finds them only after a hard search. Go out to Paca Street and peep through the portcullis of St. Mary's Seminary, *alma mater* of unnumbered bishops (and perhaps of some pope of day after tomorrow), and one may see sedate scholastics treading the shady walks, digesting their Angelic Doctor and their fast day mackerel; go out to St. Joseph's, on the Frederick Road, and one may see paunchy Passionists pottering about their grapevines—learned and venerable men; drop down Maiden Choice Lane to St. Mary's Industrial School, and one may happen upon half a dozen young Xaverians, their cassocks flapping about their legs, helping their boys at market gardening or baseball. But of ecclesiasticism in any genuine and general sense, Baltimore is bare. No Neapolitan love of processions and ceremonials, no liking for following the crozier and bowing low to the passing holy image, no feeling for the poetry and beauty of religious show seems to be left in her people. Those of them who cling to the old faith have taken away from it, I think, much that is of its essence and more that is of its spell. They go to church on Sundays; they are faithful, they are reverent, they are pious. But the old romance has gone out of their piety.

Thus the effect of the American air, of a diverse and enticing life, of the so-called enlightenment. But is that really an enlightenment which reduces gilt and scarlet to drab and gray? Alas, I am pagan enough, if not Catholic enough, to doubt it—pagan enough to lament that the pomp and circumstance visible in the ancient cathedral on a high day have so little echo in the town on all days. But whatever the pity, there is the fact. The American Rome sets no feast of crosses and banners for the pilgrim's eye; he may wander its streets for days, and yet fall upon no single hint that Holy Church has here her Western sentry post. The truth is, in brief, that the Romanism of Baltimore has a lot more of tradition in it than of reality. To speak of it, to assume it, to posit it with delight or with horror, has become a sort of convention, like the habit of calling Broadway gay. But go behind that convention to things as they are, and you will make the rather startling discovery that Baltimore, for all its primacy, is scarcely a Catholic town at all, but a stronghold of dour and dismal Puritanism—a town in which faith has lost inner beauty as well as outer ceremonial, and joy has gone with beauty. I mean, of course, joy in the Greek sense, the joy rooted in innocence, the joy of a Neapolitan procession. The Baltimore of today is not innocent. Its curse, indeed, is its conscience, an extraordinarily alert and sensitive organ. And to attend and poke that conscience, to keep alive the notion that all that is joyful must be sinful and all that is good must give pain, there are hordes of male vestals in chokers and white cravats, virtuosi of virtue, moralists clerical and moralists lay, hounds of happiness, specialists in constructive and esoteric sin.

Few things that stir the blood of man and lift him out of his wallow of lost hopes are permitted by the laws of Maryland. It is unlawful in Baltimore to throw confetti on New Year's Eve; it is unlawful, without elaborate permissive process, for a harpist to accompany flute music on the public street; it is a crime to sell chewing gum on Sunday, or to play tennis, or to have one's chin shaved, or to give a concert—or to go hawking! Fact! The Blue Laws were passed in 1723, and go back to the hell fire harangues of Cotton Mather, but every effort to mitigate and modernize them is opposed with truly savage violence. Under them, the impresario who had an orchestra play the nine symphonies of Beethoven on nine successive Sunday afternoons would be liable to a minimum fine of $25,550 and 220 days in jail.

Remember, I said "minimum." The maximum would be $127,600 and fifteen months—and Baltimore judges, being elected officers, sometimes woo the parsons in their sentences. No wonder the festive drummer, finding himself in Baltimore on a Saturday night, flees in hot haste. Even if Washington, but forty miles away, be his furthest bourne, he may at least divert himself there, on the ensuing Sunday, with moving pictures. But not in Baltimore. Baltimore fears such Babylonish lecheries. Baltimore sees the flickering film as something unspeakably secular and demoniacal. On week days it may be tolerated, as a concession to Adam's fall. But on the Sabbath it must rest.

Yet, for all that brummagem goodygoodiness, that bogus virtue, that elaborate hocus-pocus of chemical purity, that grotesque conspiracy against beauty and festivity and joy, there remains the indubitable charm of the old town. Stay there only long enough and it will infallibly descend upon you and consume you, and you will remain a Baltimorean, in spirit if not in bodily presence, to the end of your days. And it is not merely the charm of the picturesque, nor of the South, nor of the ancient, nor of the celebrated and honorable—though Baltimore delights the painter, and stands sentry for the South, and looks back to the seventeenth century, and has given the nation not only heroes but also poets to sing them. The roots and sources of that charm, in truth, go deeper than that.

Trace them down and you will come at last, I believe, to certain genuine peculiarities, to certain qualities which may not be so conveniently ticketed, to certain traits and combinations of traits which, shading into one another, give the net effect of uncommon and attractive individuality, of something not remote from true distinction. The authentic Baltimorean, the Baltimorean of Baltimoreans born and ever filled with that fact, the Baltimorean lifted above all brute contact and combat with the native blacks and the invading Goths and Huns—in brief, the Baltimorean whose home you must enter if you would really know Baltimore—is a fellow who touches civilization at more places, perhaps, than any other American. There is a simplicity about him which speaks of long habituation to his own opinions, his own dignities, his own class. In a country so largely dynamic and so little static that few of its people ever seem (or are) quite at home in their own homes, he represents a more settled and a more stately order. There yet hangs about him some of the repose, the air, the fine superiority of the Colonial planter, despite the pianola in his parlor and his daily journey to a skyscraper. One sees as the setting of his ultimate dream, not a gilded palace and a regiment of servitors, not the bent necks of multitudes and a brass band playing "Hail to the Chief!" but only his own vine and fig tree, and the good red sun of Maryland beating down.

I speak, of course, of the civilized, the cultured, the mellowed, the well rooted Baltimorean, not of the mere mob man living in Baltimore. This Baltimorean makes up, putting the test as low as you will, but a small minority of Baltimore's people, and yet no long acquaintance with him is necessary to show you that whatever is essentially Baltimorean in the town is the reflection of his philosophy and his personality. The black, nearly a hundred thousand strong, is a mere cipher. Indirectly, as I shall presently show, he has greatly influenced the communal life, but directly he is as little to be considered as the cab horses. And the swarming foreigner, with his outlandish customs and his remoteness from the stream of tradition, is almost as negligible. Go down into Albemarle or President streets, and you are as far from Mt. Vernon Place or Peabody Heights or Harlem Park or Walbrook or Roland Park or any other genuine part of Baltimore as you are from the North Pole.

And yet it is precisely this vast body of *servi* and *ignobiles*,[2] once all black, but of late grown disconcertingly yellow and white, that must be blamed for most of the austerity of Baltimore, and by secondary effect, for that peculiar hominess which is always marked as the distinguishing quality of the town. It was the darkey who inspired, in the years long past, many of the draconian statutes which yet linger upon the books, and many of the stern habits and self-restraints which reinforce them. Even today it is common to hear a Baltimorean say in defense of a given prohibition, not that he himself is opposed to the antithetical privilege, or thinks it, in itself, immoral or demoralizing, but that it would be unwise to let the nigger taste it. And if not the nigger, then the foreigner newly come. So, for example, with the Blue Laws above mentioned. The Baltimorean's fear of a more humane Sunday is not a fear that it would imperil his own soul, but a fear that the Lithuanian and the Sicilian, aided and abetted by the native Ethiop, would make of it a debauch. And so he clings to his ancient rigors.

To what has all of this brought us? To the fact, in brief, that the conditions of the Baltimorean's life have thrown him upon himself, that they have forced him to cultivate those social qualities which center particularly about the home and are inseparable from the home. It is a New Yorker's tendency, once he attains to ease, to make his home merely one of the hotels at which he stops. In the end, perhaps, it becomes the least of these hotels: desiring to show special favor to a guest, he will hesitate between his club, a favorite grillroom and his own hearth. The training and traditions of the Baltimorean all pull in a different direction. He cannot quite rid himself of the notion that, until a newcomer has stretched comfortably in his dining room, and admired the children and the family portraits, and examined the old water pitcher brought from England in 1735, and petted the cat, and fingered the old books in the library upstairs, and praised the bad biscuits of black Gwendolyn in the kitchen, with her high heel shoes, her eminence in the Grand United Order of Nazarenes and her fond hopes of wedding a *colorado maduro*[3] barrister—that, until all this ceremonial has been gone through, he and the newcomer are yet strangers. Down to ten or twelve years ago, I believe, it was still considered a bit indecent for a Baltimore gentleman to take his own wife to a hotel for supper after the theater. That was not asceticism, but mere habit. The social tradition of the town had no concern with public places. The Baltimoreans had so devised their chief joys, for years and years, that the home was the background of every one. And something of that old disposition still lingers.

A quaint town! A singular people! And yet the charm is there! You will miss the prodigal gaiety of New York—the multitude of theaters, the lavishness of entertaining, the elaborate organization of the business of pleasure. Baltimore has, between November and April, but ten performances of grand opera on a metropolitan scale. For her six hundred thousand people there are but three first class theaters. In the whole town there is not a single restaurant, not merely a hotel dining room, worth mentioning to your friends. And yet—and yet—it is not dull, it is not a prison—at least not to the Baltimoreans—at least not to those who get the Baltimore point of view.

What if the Carusos and Farrars pipe their lays but ten times a year? So much greater the joy in hearing them when they come! What if the theaters be but three? Washington, down the trolley line, has but two. And three are sufficient to house all the plays really worth seeing. Baltimore misses, perhaps, a few that Broadway enjoys—but more that Broadway suffers. And who wants to gobble the à la's in a gilded and public hell when a Smithfield ham is on the sideboard at home, with beer on ice to wash it down, and a box of smuggled cigars in the lower drawer of the old secretary—and the hour invites to a neighborly palaver with Smith and Benson and Old Taylor, while the ladies exchange fashions and scandals, novel plots and obstetrics in the parlor? What fool would be in New York tonight, dodging the taxicabs, blinded by the whiskey signs, robbed by the waiters? Who would leave Baltimore, once Baltimore has taken him to her arms?

Maryland: Apex of Normalcy

In all tables of statistics Maryland seems to gravitate toward a safe middle place, neither alarming nor depressing. The colony was settled after Massachusetts and Virginia, but before Pennsylvania and the Carolinas; the State lies today about half-way down the list of American commonwealths, in population, in the value of its manufactures, and in its production of natural wealth. I thumb all sorts of strange volumes of figures and find this median quality holding out. The percentage of native-born whites of native parentage in the country as a whole is somewhere between 55 and 60; in Maryland it is also between 55 and 60; below lie the very low percentages of such States as New York, and above lie the very high percentages of such States as Arkansas. In the whole United States the percentage of illiteracy is 7.7; in Maryland it is 7.2. In the whole country the blind number 62.3 in every 100,000 of population; in Maryland they number 61.9. Ranging the States in the order of the average salary paid to a high-school principal, Maryland is twenty-third among the 48; ranging them in the order of automobile licenses issued it is twenty-ninth; ranging them in the order of the ratio of Roman Catholics to all Christian communicants it is twenty-second. The chief city of Maryland, Baltimore, lies half-way down the list of great American cities; the State's average temperature, winter and summer, is half-way between the American maximum and minimum. It is in the middle of the road in its annual average of murders, suicides and divorces, in the average date of its first killing frost, in the number of its moving-picture parlors per 100,000 of population, in the circulation of its newspapers, in the ratio between its street railway mileage and its population, in the number of its people converted annually at religious revivals, and in the percentage of its lawyers sent to prison yearly for felony.

Popular opinion holds the Mason and Dixon line to be the division between the North and the South; this is untrue geographically, culturally and historically. The real frontier leaps out of the West Virginia wilderness somewhere near Harper's Ferry, runs down the Potomac to Washington, and then proceeds irregularly east-ward, cutting off three counties of the Maryland Western Shore and four of the Eastern Shore. Washington is as much a Northern town as Buffalo, despite the summer temperature and the swarms of Negroes; Alexandria, Va., across the river, is as thoroughly Southern as Macon, Ga. In Maryland the division is just as no-ticeable. The vegetation changes, the mode of life changes, the very people change. A Marylander from St. Mary's County or from the lower reaches of the Eastern Shore is as much a stranger to a Marylander from along the Pennsylvania bound-ary, or even from Baltimore, as he would be to a man from Maine or Wisconsin. He thinks differently; he has different prejudices, superstitions and enthusiasms; he actually looks different. During the Civil War the State was even more sharply di-vided than Kentucky or Missouri, and that division still persists. It results in con-stant compromises—an almost Swiss need to reconcile divergent traditions and instincts. Virginia to the southward is always Democratic and Pennsylvania to the northward is always Republican, but Maryland is sometimes one and sometimes the other, and when Baltimore is one the counties are commonly the other. The influence of this single big city, housing nearly half the population of the State, is thrown toward maintaining the balance. It has *nearly* half the population, but not *quite* half; thus the rural Marylanders must always pay heed to it, but need never submit to it slavishly. The result is a curious moderation in politics. Mary-land is liberal and swiftly punishes political corruption, but it is suspicious of all the new sure-cures that come out of the South and Middle West—the recall of judges, the city manager system, prohibition, the initiative, government ownership, and so on. That moderation extends to all the social and economic relationships. Though there are large minorities of Negroes in every political division, there is seldom any trouble between the races, and even in the darkest counties every well-behaved Negro is now allowed to vote. Though Baltimore, in some parts, is alive with foreigners, they are not harassed and persecuted by the usual 100 per cent poltroons, and even during the war and at the height of the ensuing alarm about radicals they were reasonably protected in their rights. And though the typical Marylander, once a farmer, is now a hand in a factory, industrial disputes of any seriousness are relatively rare, and even the Maryland miner, though his brothers to both sides, in Pennsylvania and West Virginia, are constantly in difficulties, is but seldom butchered by the State militia.

In brief, Maryland bulges with normalcy. Freed, by the providence of God, from the droughts and dervishes, the cyclones and circular insanities of the Middle West, and from the moldering doctrinairism and appalling bugaboos of the South, and from the biological decay of New England, and from the incurable corruption and menacing unrest of the other industrial States, it represents, in a sense, the ideal toward which the rest of the Republic is striving. It is safe, fat, and unconcerned. It can feed itself, and have plenty to spare. It drives a good trade, foreign and domestic; makes a good profit; banks a fair share of it. It seldom freezes in winter, and it stops short of actual roasting in summer. It is bathed in a singular and various beauty, from the stately estuaries of the Chesapeake to the peaks of the Blue Ridge. It is unthreatened by floods, Tulsa riots, Nonpartisan Leagues, Bolshevism or Ku Klux Klans. It is bare of Len Smalls, Mayor Thompsons, Lusks, Hylans, A. Mitchell Palmers, Bryans, Vardamans, Volsteads, Upton Sinclairs, Parkhursts, Margaret Sangers, Mrs. Carrie Chapman Catts, Monk Eastmans, Debses, Hearsts, Mrs. Kate O'Hares, Prof. Scott Nearings, John D. Rockefellers, Stillmans, Harry Thaws, Jack Johnsons, La Follettes, Affinity Earles, Judge Cohalans, W. E. Burghardt Du Boises, Percy Stickney Grants, Dreisers, Cabells, Amy Lowells, Mrs. Eddys, Ornsteins, General Woods, William Z. Fosters, Theodore Roosevelt, Jrs., Cal Coolidges. Its Federal judge believes in and upholds the Constitution. Its Governor is the handsomest man in public life west of Cherbourg.[4] The Mayor of its chief city is a former Grand Supreme Dictator of the Loyal Order of Moose.[5] It has its own national hymn, and a flag older than the Stars and Stripes. It is the home of the oyster, of the deviled crab, of hog and hominy, of fried chicken *à la* Maryland. It has never gone dry.

I depict, you may say, Utopia, Elysium, the New Jerusalem. My own words, in fact, make me reel with State pride; another *Lis'l* of that capital moonshine *Löwenbräu*, and I'll mount the keg and begin bawling "Maryland, My Maryland." Here, it appears, is the dream paradise of every true Americano, the heaven imagined by the Rotary Club, the Knights of Pythias and the American Legion. Here is the goal whither all the rest of the Republic is striving and pining to drift. Here, as I have said, is normalcy made real and visible. Well, what is life like in arcadian Maryland? How does it feel to live amid scenes so idyllic, among a people so virtuous and so happy, on the hooks of statistics so magnificently meridional? I answer frankly and firstly: it is dull. I answer secondly: it is depressing. I answer thirdly: it steadily grows worse. Everywhere in the United States, indeed, there is that encroaching shadow of gloom. Regimentation in morals, in political theory, in every department of thought has brought with it a stiffening, almost a deadening in manners, so that the old goatishness of the free democrat—how all the English authors of American travel-books denounced it two or three generations ago!—has got itself exchanged for a timorous reserve, a curious psychical flabbiness, an almost complete incapacity for innocent joy. To be happy takes on the character of the illicit: it is jazz, spooning on the back seat, the Follies, dancing without corsets, wood alcohol. It tends to be an adventure reserved for special castes of antinomians, or, at all events, for special occasions. On all ordinary days, for all ordinary Americans, the standard carnality has come to be going into a silent and stuffy hall, and there, in the dark, gaping stupidly at idiotic pictures in monochrome. No light, no color, no sound!

So everywhere in the Republic, from Oregon's icy mountains to Florida's coral strand. But in Maryland there is a special darkening, due to an historical contrast. Save only Louisiana, and, for very brief spaces, Kentucky and California, Maryland is the only American State that ever had a name for gaiety. Even in the earliest days it knew nothing of the religious bigotry that racked New England, nor of the Indian wars that ravaged Georgia and New York, nor of the class conflicts that menaced Virginia. Established on the shores of its incomparably rich waters, its early planters led a life of peace, tolerance and ease, and out of their happy estate there grew a civilization that, in its best days, must have been even more charming than that of Virginia. That civilization was aristocratic in character, and under it the bonds of all classes were loose. Even the slaves had easy work, and plenty of time for jamborees, when work was done, and perhaps a good deal more to eat than was good for them. The upper classes founded their life upon that of the English country gentry, but they had more money, and, I incline to think, showed a better average of intelligence. They developed their lands to a superb productiveness, they opened mines and built wharves, they lined the Chesapeake with stately mansions—and in the hours of their leisure they chased the fox, fished the rivers, visited their neighbors, danced, flirted, ate and drank. It was then that the foundation of Maryland's fame as a gastronomical paradise was laid; it was those ancients who penetrated to the last secrets of the oyster, the crab and the barnyard fowl. Nor were they mere guzzlers and tipplers. Annapolis, down to Washington's presidency, was perhaps the most civilized town in America. It had the best theater, it had the best inns, and it also had the best society. To this day a faint trace of its old charm survives; it is sleepy, but it is lovely.

What overturned the squirearchy, of course, and with it Maryland civilization, was the rise of the industrial system. It shifted the center of gravity from the great estates to the rushing, pushing, dirty, and, after awhile, turbulent and hoggish town of Baltimore, and so, bit by bit, the old social organization fell to pieces, and the very landscape itself began to lose its old beauty. Wherever there was a manor house along the Bay in the eighteenth century there is now a squalid town, and wherever there is a town there is a stinking cannery, or an even more odoriferous factory for making fish guano. For years there was a more or less fair and equal struggle between town and country. Baltimore grew and grew, but the old landed gentry hung on to their immemorial leadership, in politics if not in trade. Even so recently as a generation ago, half of the counties were still dominated by their old land-owning families; out of them came the supply of judges, State senators, governors, congressmen. Even into our own day they retain tenaciously a disproportionate share of seats in the State Assembly. But it was a losing fight, and as year followed year the advantages of the new industrial magnates grew more visible. As in so many other States, it was a railroad—the Baltimore & Ohio—that gave mere money the final victory over race. The Baltimore & Ohio, for more than fifty years, steadily debauched the State. Then it was overthrown, and the political system that it had created went with it, but by that time it was too late to revive the aristocratic system of a more spacious day. Today the State is run by the men who pay the wages of its people. They do it, it must be said for them, with reasonable decency, but they do it absolutely without imagination, and all links with the past are broken forever. Maryland was once a state of mind; now it is a machine.

The tightening of the screws goes on unbrokenly; the end, I suppose, as everywhere else in These States, will be a complete obliteration of distinction, a wiping out of all the old traditions, a massive triumph of regimentation. It is curious to note some of the current symptoms of the process. There is, for example, the Fordization of the Johns Hopkins University. The Johns Hopkins was founded upon a plan that was quite novel in the United States: it was to be, not a mere college for the propagation of the humanities among the upper classes, but a genuine university in the Continental sense, devoted almost wholly to research. To that end it set up shop in a few plain buildings in a back street—and within twenty years its fame was world-wide, and its influence upon all other American universities of the first rank was marked. It had no campus, no dormitories, no clubs of college snobs, no college yells, but if you go through the roster of its students during its first two or three decades you will go through a roster of the principal American scholars and men of science of today. The death of Daniel Coit Gilman was a calamity to the university, and following it came demoralization. Today the Johns Hopkins is reorganized, but upon a new plan. It has a large and beautiful campus; its buildings begin to rise in huge groups; it challenges Harvard and Princeton. Interiorly it turns to the new efficiency, the multitudinous manufacture of sharp, competent, $10,000 a year men. There is a summer-school for country schoolmarms eager for six weeks of applied psychology, official history and folk-singing. There is instruction for young men eager to be managers of street railways, automobile engineers and city editors of newspapers. There is patriotic drilling on the campus. There is a growing college spirit. Gifts and endowments increase. Everything is booming. But the old Johns Hopkins is dead.

Turn now to Baltimore society. In the old days it was extraordinarily exclusive — not in the sense of stupid snobbishness, but in the sense of prudent reserve. The aristocracy of the State was a sound one, for it was firmly rooted in the land, and it looked with proper misgivings upon all newcomers who lacked that foundation. It had friendly relations with the aristocracy of Virginia, but with the industrial magnates of the North and their wives and daughters it was inclined to be a bit stand-offish. When it gave a party in Baltimore or in one of the county towns, the display of clothes was perhaps not startling, but there was at least a show of very pretty girls, and their pa's and ma's were indubitably gentlemen and ladies. I am still almost too young, as the saying is, to know my own mind, but I well remember the scandal that arose when the first millionaire bounders tried to horn in by *force majeure*. Even the proletariat was against them, as it would have been against a corporation lawyer who presumed to climb upon the bench with the judge. But today—God save the mark! The old landed aristocracy, put beside the new magnates and their women, seems shabby and unimportant; it has lost its old social leadership, and it has even begun to lose its land, its traditions and its *amour propre*. The munitions millionaires of the war years entered to the tune of loud wind music; a fashionable ball today is an amazing collection of gilded nobodies; all eyes are turned, not toward the South, but toward New York. There are leaders of fashion in Baltimore today whose mothers were far from unfamiliar with the washtub; there are others whose grandmothers could not speak English. The whole show descends to a fatuous and tedious burlesque. It has the brilliance of a circus parade, and the cultural significance of an annual convention of the Elks.

The decay of the Johns Hopkins is accompanied by a general eclipse of intellectualism. Music becomes a mere fashionable diversion; it is good medicine for pushers to go to opera and symphony concert and suffer there for an hour or two. As for intellectual society, it simply doesn't exist. If some archaic bluestocking were to set up a *salon*, it would be mistaken for a saloon, and raided by some snouting cleric. In Baltimore lives Lizette Woodworth Reese, perhaps the finest poet of her generation yet alive in America. Some time ago a waggish newspaper man there had the thought to find out how Baltimore itself regarded her. Accordingly, he called up all of the town magnificoes, from the president of the Johns Hopkins down to the presidents of the principal women's clubs. He found that more than half of the persons he thus disturbed had never so much as heard of Miss Reese, and that all save two or three of the remainder had never read a line of her poetry! Edgar Allan Poe is buried in the town, in the yard of a decrepit Presbyterian church, on the edge of the old red-light district. It took sixteen years to raise enough money to pay for a modest tombstone to his memory; it took seventy-two years to provide even an inadequate monument. During that time Baltimore has erected elaborate memorials to two founders of tin- pot fraternal orders, to a former Mayor whose long service left the city in the physical state of a hog-pen, and to the president of an obscure and bankrupt railroad. These memorials are on main streets. That to Poe is hidden in a park that half the people of Baltimore have never so much as visited. And on the pedestal there is a thumping misquotation from his poetry!

Such is Maryland in this hundred-and-forty-sixth year of the Republic—a great, a rich, and a puissant State, but somehow flabby underneath, somehow dead-looking in the eyes. It has all the great boons and usufructs of current American civilization: steel-works along the bay, movies in every town, schools to teach the young how to read and write, high-schools to ground them in a safe and sane Americanism, colleges for their final training, jails to keep them in order, a State police, a judiciary not wholly imbecile, great newspapers, good roads. It has vice crusaders, charity operators, drive managers, chambers of commerce, police-women, Y.M.C.A.'s, women's clubs, Chautauquas, Carnegie libraries, laws against barking dogs, the budget system, an active clergy, uplifters of all models and gauges. It is orderly, industrious, virtuous, normal, free from Bolshevism and atheism. . . . Still, there is something wrong. At the moment, thousands seem to be out of work. Wages fall. Men are ironed out. Ideas are suspect. No one appears to be happy. Life is dull.

The City of Seven Sundays

Traveling some ninety-odd miles in a sou'westerly direction from the city of New York, the voyager, if winds be fair, comes upon a settlement of homogeneous red brick houses attached to white marble steps and inhabited by a curious hibernating race of the general appearance of human beings (save that in wet weather it is given to adorning itself with overshoes)—but, contradictorily enough, of the general manner of Bostonians. This singular race subsists largely on an exotic, colorless, tasteless drink called water and a queer food compound known as scrapple. Its leading species of diversion takes the form of regular attendance at illustrated lectures on "The Swiss Alps" in a building named the Academy of Music (so-called because, like all Academies of Music, it isn't one) and its religion takes the form of worshiping a strange god known as universityofpennsylvania. Its social system is so exclusive that when a dance is given there are not enough men to go 'round. It has

THE AMERICAN LANDSCAPE

two distinct political parties. One believes and stoutly maintains that Market street should be paved all over again on Tuesdays, while the other believes and stoutly maintains that Market street should be paved all over again on Fridays. Both parties are usually successful at the elections. The trade in safe-deposit boxes, incidentally, is very great in the settlement.

The settlement, the name of which is Philadelphia (which means "city of brotherly love" just as Terre Haute, Indiana, means "high land" or as Old Point Comfort means what it says), is known chiefly to the rest of the country through the circumstance that it is in its northern section that one changes cars for Atlantic City and through the further circumstance that its tribe includes the celestial-digited Dr. Munyon, John Wanamaker and one smaller branch of the United States Mint, Cyrus K. Curtis, the man who devised masses for the literature, Rudolph Blankenburg (celebrated as the only man in national public life with a name that sounds like Max Rogers in footlight action), to say nothing of a couple of Drexels, a couple of Biddles, a couple of Drexel-Biddles and Biddles-Drexels. However, to say nothing of the Drexels and the Biddles and the Drexel-Biddles is to say nothing of Philadelphia. And to say nothing of Philadelphia is to say everything. (G. K. Chesterton might sell that last sentence for at least twenty-five cents a word.) Nevertheless, it has some sense. Just as it would be a well-nigh Sisyphean labor to describe on paper the taste of celery, just as it would have been a task of uniform difficulty for Berlioz, as Huneker points out, to solve to his own satisfaction the prelude to *Tristan*,[6] just so would it be an infinite toil to persuade my editor that the best and most acute way in which to describe Philadelphia would be to say nothing about it. But, of course, a mere title with my name under it—although I will, in order to stop any heated argument over the matter, readily admit the value of the latter—would still scarcely be worth the handsome emolument that the editor has set aside in return for my five thousand Philadelphic oracle parts of speech.

Philadelphia gives one the impression of a xylophone duet of "Hearts and Flowers" rendered in a cold-storage plant on Washington's Birthday morning by Anthony Comstock and Elizabeth Robins, with a whistling obligato by Richard Harding Davis. Philadelphia still shudders and believes that plump and tender virgins are waylaid on the dark highways by unshaved Italians and spirited away to mysterious houses with barred windows, there to be impressed into the harrowing life of "white slaves." Philadelphia still believes that the huddled knot of fugitive castaways that spewed and kecked its way across the Atlantic in the *Mayflower* is the *stammvater* of American aristocracy. Philadelphia still catches its breath and inhales with awe the scenery of David Belasco, the high notes of Mary Garden, the drama of *Ben Hur*,[7] the literature of Pierre de Coulevain, the India love lyrics of Laurence Hope, the transcendental meanings of Omar Khayyam, the humor of John Kendrick Bangs and the wickedness of Gaby Deslys. Philadelphia still believes that from that moment in 1776 when John Hancock, in Independence Hall, placed his name at the bottom of a piece of paper with some writing on it, the United States has been a free, independent and democratic country. Philadelphia still believes that Broadway at night is gay and sinful, that to drink a cocktail in the St. James Hotel and then ask the manicure if she's married is the next thing to being a very devil of a fellow, and that its City Hall is a fine piece of architecture. Philadelphia still believes, indeed, even in Philadelphia.

Lest, however, my attitude toward Philadelphia be translated faultily, lest I be deemed a prejudiced party (as is ever the case when a writer takes the other side of any argument)—allow me to explain my "youthful cynicism." Unquestionably this latter phrase has already been bestowed by you upon me. It always is. Yet am I neither youthful nor cynical. True, I still refrain from eating an apple before I retire for the night, and true, I regard Julia Sanderson as a more valuable server of humanity than Inez Milholland; yet am I, I repeat, neither youthful nor cynical. On the contrary, I am merely young and, consequently, observing. I realize that the properly impressive manner in which to write of Philadelphia or any other city is to criticize the city spicily and ironically—and, on the whole, adversely—for some four thousand, eight hundred and fifty-odd words and then wind up with a brief recanting flourish of wind instruments and cymbals in something after the following magniloquent fashion: "But, despite all I have said, despite its many deficiencies, crudities and bourgeoisies, the splendor of its future is the splendor of the rising sun's; its star beckons brilliantly to the flowering generation, and the call of its voice is beginning to sound across the nation; here is the city of tomorrow, throbbing with a million hearts, breathing with a million aspirations and ambitions"—or with some such similar untrue but pacifying rubbish. Unfortunately, I do not believe in writing such perfumed buncombe; which goes to explain why I am a poor man.

Contrary to the strict technique of an article of the sort I am here composing, I shall place my last paragraph up here near the beginning. This paragraph will elucidate any confusion over my attitude. Comes the paragraph:

Although there is no genuinely typical American city in the United States, Philadelphia—were there such a city—would be it. Philadelphia, in other words, is the least un-American city in the nation. Its people, its people's processes of thought, private lives, philosophy and general ideas of physical activity are less un-American than the peoples and their ways of the other large native commonwealths.

There is the simple paragraph. It is neither a poetic flight nor a retraction. It is simply the truth simply told as the truth has presented itself to the eyes of simple truth teller. Were I a crystal gazer I might predict a purpler future for Philadelphia; but, alas, I am only a person with a pencil and a pad of paper. It is given me only to report Philadelphia as Philadelphia today reports itself to me.

Just as it is not beyond the bounds of possibility to imagine that New York City may in time be populated to some extent by Americans and thus eventually become part of the United States, so is it not entirely beyond the bounds of possibility to imagine that Philadelphia may in time be populated by a few individuals who will not wear heavy underwear in summer and who may eventually bring to Philadelphia a less frigid sense of morals than now obfuscates the vision of both settler and visitor. A city is to be judged always by its sense of morals; not by its morals—have you a care!—but by its *sense*, its *idea*, of morals. Its sense of morals is to be judged from its Sundays. Philadelphia is the City of Seven Sundays. In art and letters, in alcohol and gentlemanly carnality, in foods properly cooked and personal liberty, in municipal viewpoint and national viewpoint (if, in all conscience, there be such a thing), the daily hymn of Philadelphia is "Backward, Christian Soldiers." The spirit of the Quaker, albeit adorned now with a nobby Kuppenheimer, is abroad in the land. The spirit of the Quaker tugs at Philadelphia's coattails, and if, at times, the coattail is stronger than the tug, the tug is yet there.

I speak now of the coattail. And, speaking of the coattail, I tell you that Philadelphia, while posing virtue and hiding its glance 'neath its velvet lids, is still the most immoral-minded city of all the man's-sized cities of the combined States. Its thoughts are lewd if its physical expressions of those thoughts are not. In action, the Quaker; in mind, the Quacker. Such a lecherous, concupiscent theatrical exhibition as *The Girl with the Whooping Cough*,[8] suppressed even in New York, crowds the playhouse to the exits in Philadelphia. Suggestive entertainment, in the vernacular, "goes big" along the Schuylkill. Here is no idle word—here is box-office fact. Pornography in literature induces an imperial sale in Philadelphia. For Philadelphia talks Weir Mitchell and reads Victoria Cross; for it babbles Maeterlinck and covertly glues its eyes to Paul de Kock. To Philadelphia George Moore exists primarily in terms of Doris (or had I better say "upon terms with Doris"?); to Philadelphia Greuze exists primarily in terms of broken pitchers. Philadelphia, when D'Annunzio is mentioned, thinks first and foremost of a beautiful snaky brunette of voice of melted and honeyed platinum with whom he had an affair; when Robert Burns is spoken, Jane Armour is the connotation; when Aaron Burr, the little grave at Princeton.

Gorky suggests a writer who was barred from an American hotel because he had with him a woman who was not his wife. Napoleon, to Philadelphia, was that general about whose exploits "you just ought to read in Joseph Turquan's *Napoléon Amoureux*." Flaubert—"ah, the story of that Bovaryan cab ride!" Shaw—*Mrs. Warren's Profession*. Wagner—"Abendstern."[9] Wilde—*Dorian Gray*. Paris suggests the stage Maxim's and the Rue de Berlin and the little postcard shops in the Rue de Rivoli; London, the "clubs" shrinking back in long shadows of the Empire and the smelly furnished flats that blink through the damp night, a couple of shillings' taxi journey eastward from Trafalgar Square. Havelock Ellis—"racy reading!" (Is there one of my Philadelphia readers who knows, for testing instance, that Ellis has written other works than those dealing with sex—a study of Nietzsche, for example?) Plato—"platonic love" (mental laughter). I recommend Plato's *De Republica* to Philadelphia. Strindberg—Julia and the valet.[10] Kipling—"Judy O'Grady and the Colonel's lady are sisters under their skins."[11] Thus the Philadelphia mind: "I believe that anyone who takes a drink on the Lord's Day is doomed to the Eternal Fires." Thus the Philadelphia pose: "Sadie Thomas, I sentence you to pay a fine of five hundred dollars for maintaining a disorderly house." Thus the Philadelphia action.

From the 1910–1914 statistics gathered by *The Bookman*, one is enabled to prove the Philadelphia appetite for the suggestive in literature. The suggestiveness of Robert W. Chambers and the suggestion of Hermann Sudermann are one and the same to the Philadelphia understanding. There is no distinction. (Of course, I am speaking of Philadelphia as a whole. There are, patently, a number of intelligent residents, for not *all* Philadelphia residents were born in Philadelphia.)

Let us glance at a few haphazard and casually chosen statistical tables of book sales. What come we upon? September, 1911, showed Chambers's *The Common Law* at the head of the Philadelphia list. June, 1912 (when the Steinheil scandal jabber was being echoed in the daily journals), finds *My Memoirs*, by Madame Steinheil, heading the sale of non-fiction books.[12] What disappointment was there here for the buyers by title! April, 1912, showed *To M. L. G.*[13] at the top of the selling list—and in this month, as in the one preceding and half a dozen before and after, the book of Eugène Brieux's plays, including *Damaged Goods*, occupied a hefty position in the so-called non-fiction tables. Sudermann's *Song of Songs* loomed large in the statistics for March, 1910, and November, 1909, revealed *Bella Donna*[14] in the first selling position. October, 1911, disclosed the erotic Hichens again atop the table with another of his odoriferous fables. And thus the figures went and still go— and do not lie. Oh, Philadelphia, cradle of liberty! Oh, Philadelphia, cradle of mental libertinism! What sins are committed in thy—pericranium!

* * * *

I shift my baton. My verbal orchestra follows my lead. The bass drum is silent henceforth; the cymbals are no more. Hark, the bass viol and the lute! With your eyes soothed into sepia mood and your mind caressed into ready yielding by the mellifluous tones of my musicianly pencil, come you with me in spirit to Philadelphia. It is early spring. It is of a Sunday. Across the asphalt moor of Broad street a lonely and tearful sparrow makes his way to a more hospitable clime. The carriage starter of the Ritz and the carriage starter of the Bellevue, as inactive as two Henry

James verbs, are foregathered a block away with the carriage starter of the Walton, wondering if Woodrow Wilson was elected President and wishing there were some carriages around to start. Having nothing more tangible to start, these worthies start an argument. This argument, like almost all Philadelphia arguments no matter what their prefatory nature, concludes in the unanimous agreement that Fairmount Park is the finest in the world and that it must be awful to have to live in Camden. An unkempt, lopsided-heeled girl, yellow in the cheeks, with dirty pink flowers on her hat and soup spots on her blue serge skirt, furtively tracks her path homeward. Last night was Saturday night. With two other little shopgirls, a blonde manicure and an Eleventh street dressmaker with a good shape, this pitiful rag constitutes the rank and file of the unprofessional Philadelphia demi-monde. And this demi-monde—five strong—extrudes itself weekly in a devilish revel of domestic Wurzburger and Sweet Caporals in one of two rancid restaurants to the east of Broad street, or, if the patron of the hour be of funds more ample, in a westward café of somewhat gaudier countenance. Far to the north, in the park, a stray couple is whispering the harmless battledore and shuttlecock of *amour*. He is young. She is young. A Philadelphia policeman scowls upon them. One hears a child laughing. One hears another child laughing. And as the laughter leaves the little lips, the fugitive thought is born that God is sending down wireless messages in protest against the adult laughlessness of this great, humorless city. A modish dogcart wheels by. A puffy stockbroker holds the reins in chamois-covered hands. A feeling of awe permeates the breasts of the onlookers. Another child laughs. Its governess slaps it across the mouth. One must be taught good manners when one is young.

Back in the empty belly of the city, stiff, stark, set-featured folk are making their way to the churches. Some carry Bibles. Others carry nothing. But none carries a novel or a magazine. These folk, churchgoers from tradition, take their churchgoing seriously. And, consequently, unintelligently. The average Philadelphia churchgoer's idea of religion is paying pew rent, inviting the minister to dinner, being able to recite the Ten Commandments without a slip and disapproving violently of women who smoke cigarettes in public. A street car limps its way westward. . . . An hour passes. . . . A street car limps its way eastward.

One becomes sick at heart. One seeks a potion of strong liquor. It being another Philadelphian conception of virtue not to vend alcoholic refreshment on Sunday, the accomplishment of such a feat is no facile matter. But he who knows Philadelphia never leaves himself unprepared; he gleans from some good spirit a visitor's card to one of the local clubs, where, in the hour of his dire need, his unholy palate may freely bathe itself in nepenthe. Thus the restless pilgrim in the course of time—which is usually a matter of two minutes—hies himself thitherward. Tables are black with Philadelphians whose wives have been told they have to go downtown to meet a man from New York on important business. Before each there reposes an alcoholic cadenza or a malt roulade. Everything is pianissimo; but on the face of each hypocrite—for each believes in public that the preservation of the sanctity of the Philadelphia home can be secured only by stopping the sale of liquor on the Lord's Day, the day set aside by the Lord beginning, by the Lord's watch, at 12:01 A.M. precisely—on the face of each hypocrite there is a fortissimo grin. One bides with one's ears. What the intellectual degree, what the conversational interest of these folk? Municipal problems, literature, music, art, metaphysics, theology, sociology, pathology? Words take form. Words, phrases, clauses, whole sentences presently become audible.

"Met a fella from Chicago on the train last week. He kidded me about living in Philadelphia, but you bet your life before I got through I put it all over him!"

"Go on, Gus; tell us how you did it."

And thus Gus: "Well, he said on Sunday in Chicago you could see a lot o' people on the streets, but that on Sunday in Philadelphia you couldn't see anyone on the streets unless you had a magnifying glass. And say, do you know what I said to him? I said: 'Do you know why you don't see anybody on the streets in Philadelphia on Sunday? Well, I'll tell you. It's because everybody in this here town has got a home!' You should have seen him dry up. Then I said to him: 'Do you know why you see a lot of people on the streets of Chicago on Sunday? I'll tell you. It's because nobody in Chicago has got a home!'"

"Good boy, Gus! That's the way to hand it to those rubes, Gus!! Yes, sir; Philadelphia is a city of homes. Every workingman has his house here. Nobody wants to hang around the streets!!"

Gurgle, gurgle, gurgle. Garson, some more drinks.

"I see by the papers that Germany has built fifty more airships that'll hold fifty soldiers apiece and twenty Gatling guns. The ships can stay up in the air ten whole hours, too."

"Gee, a fine chance we'd stand against all those airships!"

"Fine chance, nothing! Why our army can lick Germany with one hand tied behind its back and its eyes blindfolded!"

Gurgle, gurgle. Garson, more drinks.

* * * *

Again my fingers clasp the baton; and the baton calls now to the piccolo and the hautboy.

Philadelphia society—I employ the latter word in the sense that it is conventionally employed by the mentally vulgar—has as its backbone a small group of descendants from traders and politicians who conspicuously capitalized their cunning at the time when the smell of revolutionary gunpowder streaked the Colonies and confused a fighting people's senses. I grant, and I grant freely, that this society, even such as it is, is of firmer grade and keener blood authenticity than what passes muster for society in any other large American municipality; its component parts have less the odor of the money sesame to them, less the scent of Newport real estate, less the nostril-plugging musk of the ticker tape. There is something of tradition to the society of the Schuylkill brand, albeit that tradition, when hounded to the death, discloses itself to be grounded—after the manner of the bulk of native social traditions—upon what is intrinsically bladdered pretense. In Philadelphia the boast is that Philadelphia society is born in the cradle, that it is blue blood deduced from blue blood, and that it holds out naught of welcome for blood of any other shade. So be it; so be it. And yet the deobstruent fact persists that Philadelphia society patterns its every act, its every manner, its every little step after a species of society that, far from being born in the cradle, is born in the double bed. In another phrase, the society born of marriages—in another phrase, the society of New York.

Cherishing at its breast its whim of the aristocracy of birth in itself (by the way, not wholly the preposterous thing our form of government makes a pretense of believing), the social stratum of this Pennsylvania settlement on every possible occasion flaunts a tracing of its lineage back to Independence Hall. This is one of Philadelphia's little unconscious jokes. Curiously enough, where in other American cities there is in the air a skeptical and somewhat pugnacious attitude toward the claims of the society elements in those communities, in Philadelphia the proletariat regards its society's exclusiveness with a feeling of ponderous awe and veneration. In New York, society is looked upon with a spirit of pity blended with condescending humor by everyone possessed of taste, education and normal intelligence. Naturally enough, this does not include society editors or persons who live on the upper West Side and who follow avidly what the society editors write. In Chicago, society is looked upon with a spirit of good-natured raillery—by itself. It alone in the States seems to realize its own intrinsic jest, and, consequently, to a considerable extent, it justifies itself. In Boston, society is regarded by all the respectable people of Boston as being too dull a coterie of ancestor-worshipers for words. But in Philadelphia!

I have seen the King and Queen of Britain coaching 'mid wild trumpet blare past ten thousand bareheaded Englishmen lined along the winding drives of Hyde Park; I have seen the President of monarchic-blooded France move to his box at Longchamps through a lane of drawn sabres while thousands of his people gave him verbal veneration; I have heard from the Kaiser's cousin and the bodyguard of the Tsar of all the Russians how these rulers once clattered on their way together under the Linden trees while the populace of Berlin with wet and humbled eyes gave mute testimony of its loyalty and affection. All this have I seen with my eyes, have I heard with my ears. But none of these ocular spectacles, none of these aural pageantries is invested with the air of humility and veneration that confronts one in the instance of the Philadelphia middle class viewing Philadelphia's society. Let a grande dame sweep through the narrow corridor of the Bellevue toward the Walnut street entrance, and a hundred women's hearts crouched on the border of carmine benches jell in self-submissiveness, in self-abasement. Let a blue-blood take a seat at a Ritz table and a dozen saucers fill with tea from nervous, excited, humiliated cups. In short, as I have already said, Philadelphia is the least un-American city in the United States.

For many years there has persisted an hallucination, said hallucination having blown its thistledown across the counties to the cities near and far, that Philadelphia's *puellae* composed a lovelier crew than any other commonwealth could boast. Chestnut street of an afternoon, so it has been published, discloses trimmer ankles, smarter figures, prettier faces than this or that vaunting thoroughfare further along the railroad. Rittenhouse Square of a spring Sunday morning and upper Walnut street, so the wires have currented, show visages the like of which might not be matched this side of the Woods of Boulogne. In brief, Philadelphia girls were so many pulse-quickening symphonies, so many intoxicating tears wrung from golden grapes along the Loire, so many chords of b flat, g, b flat, so many little sisters of Circe. I myself, by way of confessing, have assisted in the dissemination of the phantasm. But the moon was saffron in the coast sky that night and the stars were dreaming in the silent sea when I saw her. And she wore, I remember, something of very soft dark green, and the spun sable silk that mere prose writers would have called her hair caught in orange chiffon. The band was playing that wonderful wailing heart-cry out of *Samson and Delilah*.[15] The air was gentle and warm as eiderdown. "I beg your pardon," I remember I said, catching up with her; "haven't I met you somewhere before?" (I am always strikingly original.) "No," she returned decisively, *"you have not!"* Several hours later, when the breeze from overseas puckered its lips in a chill whistling and all the world was still, she told me—and her voice had the sound of Crème Yvette and all the fragrance of a Chopin nocturne—that she lived in Philadelphia.

✳ ✳ ✳ ✳ ✳

The next afternoon I sat down and composed a poem eulogizing the homeric virtues and enlarging upon the staggeringly angelic fairness of Philadelphia girls *in toto*. In due time, my poem was copied in all the Philadelphia newspapers. In due time, my poem was reprinted in the journals of the outlands—the fame of Philadelphia's fair women the while spreading and spreading and still spreading. And in due time, I discovered that my gorgeous midnight maiden whose pale olive cheeks had been kissed by the rising suns and in whose eyes the souls of two amethysts lay sleeping—I discovered that this ravishing wench had lied me. Her home was in Egg Harbor, New Jersey.

Well, well, such is the mutability of human affairs, whatever that means. No, the girls of Philadelphia are not made of such divine stuff as miladi of the starry adventure. Here and there, on my nomad saunters along the boulevards and byways of the city of Penn, have I espied a creature whose mien has flicked my passing fancy, who has gratified my lonely, wayfaring eye. Likely baggages, by me faith, but not a whit more likely than such as I have observed in my pilgrimages adown the highways of less boastful municipalities. The Philadelphia girl, be she however beautiful, fails in provoking a complete enravishment of the connoisseur because she one and all lacks that signal quality without which beauty is but corked perfume. I speak of that quality known to Americans by the sound "shick." There is to the Philadelphia girl no sense of the trig, no air of the sartorially, mentally, physically alert, no feeling of the straight and even heel, of the glycerine and rose-water bathed pupil, of the invisibility of all hooks and eyes. To a very considerable degree, these deficiencies are chargeable to upbringing. The average Philadelphia girl of average home and average means and position is coached into adolescence after what is believed in Philadelphia to be a manner obtaining in the case of New York girls, but what in reality is the case of Harlem girls. The typical New York girl is brought up by her mother to look, act and use the manner (if not the content) of speech of the higher class *demi-mondaine*. The Harlem girl (or the Brooklyn girl, for the two classes are much the same) is brought up to imitate the Philadelphia girl who has been brought up in imitation of the New York girl. Thus filtered and crossed, the Philadelphia girl, as a complete product, is neither fresh, flash, foul nor well-bred herring.

Mentally, the tutelage of the Philadelphia maiden is upon the dark principle of the nineteenth century: "My mother told me no more," as Wedekind has it.[16] The principle of hush is here. What the result? Schoolgirl minds in women's bodies; bashful blushes in place of clean and fearless complexions; shock in place of chic. Beauty, to be sure, is not a matter of mind, as certain thick-blocks have wished at times to impress us; the most beautiful girl in America today has the vilest mind to the hitherward side of the Rue Vivienne. Beauty is a matter of physical courage— and physical courage and the mind are bound by the remotest of blood ties. The Philadelphia girl is (I trust I am not too ungentlemanly)—afraid. She is afraid of her mother, afraid of her father, afraid of her girl friends, afraid of her men friends, afraid of herself. Her fear makes her consistently self-conscious. Her consistent self-consciousness gives her the air of vanity. And this seeming—if mayhap intrinsically absent—vanity disannuls what other impressions of beauty her externals may bequeath. The Parisienne is beautiful because she is courageous; the maid of London town is unbeautiful because she is fearful. There is courage in Egg Harbor!

* * * *

The key of C natural, gentlemen. Picture to yourselves a man whose days are passed in a quaint old garden walled off from a throbbing, horizon-stretching land, a garden whose spiked stone fences interpose themselves between it and the thinking, quivering world and whose lazy quadrillian air is unawake to the echoes of the great thitherward mazurka. Picture to yourselves this man translating the resonant cannonading of life's contending armies as a mere passing summer thunder shower. Picture him the faded-blooded, hiccoughing son of a race that once, when hearts were young, threw the banner of an admirably impudent people to the winds of the world and carved its way into the world's nations. Picture him groping with eyes that will not see for a dusty family album, while close at his hand lies the Book of National Life. Picture him peering through his spectacles at the pages of a mythical and puny aristocracy, while from the pages of the other book at his elbow there look up at him the photographs of erstwhile newsboys now become great financiers, of erstwhile printers' devils now become great leaders of public opinion, of erstwhile horse-car drivers now become great statesmen. Picture to yourselves this man, his arms large, but fibreless, sinewless, muscleless from inactivity; his thoughts concerned with nourishing a small bed of pansies within his little enclosed garden while from beyond the garden walls there comes to his ears the laughing promise of a new generation.

The key of C natural, gentlemen. Through the veil of your eloquent Laranaga, see you this man nettled under the pinpricks of unwritten blue laws; see you him trying to urge melody to his lips, but halting, blanch at the thought of what his neighbors may think of him. See you him creep his way to the garden wall. See you him stand at its base hopeless, longingly. Oh, for a ladder to climb to its top, there to view the other world and profit by its breathing panorama. Oh, for such a ladder, the ladder that men call courage!

Picture to yourselves this man.

For *He* is Philadelphia.

Along the Potomac

I

Washington, Tuesday.

Emerging from the grandiose Union Station, the eye of the visitor to this capital of a great republic falls upon a frowsy sand-lot, then upon a couple of glorified cigar-box hotels, and then upon all that is mortal of the Billy Sunday tabernacle. Beyond, to the right, is a whole village of harsh and graceless concrete boarding-houses for government clerks—a sprawling monument to the incomparable rapacity of Washington landlords. They were finished just in time to go to the scrap heap; as the painters and plumbers left, the war clerks were all passing on their way to the

Union Station and their far-flung homes. Beyond them, like some trivial afterthought, rises the fine dome of the Capitol, with the marble flood of the Senate Office Building just before it.

The scene is typical and searchingly revelatory of this least self-respecting of capitals. Up to a year ago—and maybe yet: I forgot to notice on my way in—the entrance to the Senate Office Building on the Delaware avenue side, was by a pair of wooden stairs suggesting the Odd Fellows' Hall above the Niagara Hose-House in an eighth-rate country town. And all along Pennsylvania avenue, between Capitol Hill and the White House, there is a double row of Greek fruit stores, dead-and-alive groceries, fly-blown book stalls and Chinese yokami joints.

Horror succeeds horror from end to end of this grandiloquent thoroughfare, the Nevsky Prospect, Unter den Linden and Calle Mayor of the nation. Beginning superbly with the mountainous pile of the Capitol, perhaps the finest legislative building in the world, and ending decently upon the harmonious note of the Treasury and the White House, it runs the whole gamut of architectural cacophony between. What barbarian, one wonders, conceived and erected that frightful building for the Postoffice at Eleventh street? And who then topped it with the District Building? And who topped the District Building with the Southern Railway Building?—a brick stable set beside an overgrown tombstone.

II

Wednesday.

Everywhere the same disharmony, the same almost incredible lack of elementary taste. In front of the Capitol, across the fine plaza on its east side, is a fountain in red granite, surely the most hideous stone ever quarried by man. Directly beyond, set like a boil between the Capitol and the House Office Building, is the florid excrescence of the Library of Congress, the most overestimated public building, I daresay, in all Christendom.

I say overestimated because there seems to be a general conspiracy to call it lovely, and that conspiracy has apparently bagged the yokelry of the republic. One never approaches it without encountering groups of backwoods tourists outside, painfully admiring its dirty yellow-gray color, its flashes of absurd pink, its tinselly and imbecile dome. And one never enters without finding the same docile patriots, stockstill and spell-bound before the paltry chromos on the walls. A series of bathrooms with insurance calendars made into friezes. Nothing worse is in the Vatican.

What a conscientious architect might say of the corn-fed Corinthian of the Capitol I don't know; it was built by engineers, military men, amateurs, not by professors of the orders. But the proof of the pudding, after all, is in the eating. Theory forgotten, the thing fills the eye and the imagination. It is dignified, impressive, unmistakably grand. It dominates Washington as clearly as the Acropolis dominated

Athens. And there, directly in front of it, stands its exquisite burlesque. What could be more cunningly chosen than all that pseudo-Italian Renaissance gingerbread to poke fun at its honest county-courthouse Corinthian? What could flout it, and upset it, and spit into its eye more effectively?

III

Thursday.

But if I revile the Library of Congress (perhaps ignorantly) let me make haste to add that I stop at the building, and do not extend my mirth to the actual collection of books. That collection, on the contrary, fills me with a degree of respect verging upon downright awe: it is one of the most underestimated possessions of the American people, as the library building is one of the most overestimated. I find in books, almost every day, kind words for this library or that—the libraries of the universities, that of the Surgeon-General of the Army, the Chicago and Boston libraries, the New York Public Library—but seldom a word for the Library of Congress. Scholars seem to use it very little; the majority of persons I meet in its reading-room are plainly mere idlers—lovers whispering behind folios, ancient wrecks of office-seekers, blackamoors grandly conscious of their rights and dignities.

And yet it is one of the largest and most comprehensive libraries in the world, and is fast overhauling and surpassing all others. Give a glance to its card catalogue and you will be surprised; in a hundred useful ways it is already the full peer of the British Museum; in a dozen ways it is already far ahead. Moreover, it is more usable. The books in it are easy to locate; they are brought promptly; the personnel is polite and helpful. The long waits of the New York Public Library are unheard of. The imbecile system of watching for a number to flash on a dial—there is none of this. Instead the reader finds his books on his desk and is treated as a guest.

I recommend this great collection to all persons seeking wisdom. It is a pleasant work-place. True enough, the man accustomed to civilized surroundings could not possibly stay long in Washington, even to gain wisdom, but there is no actual need to do so. Live in Baltimore, forty miles away, and commute daily—by fast expresses, forty-five minutes; at most, an hour. From the station to the library is but five minutes' walk; one need not enter Washington at all.

IV

Friday.

Always cheap, tawdry, vulgar, frowsy and disgusting, prohibition has made Washington virtually impossible; only the money they are wallowing in holds the crowds now here. Years ago there was capital eating; some of the old-time restaurants, in fact, were famous from end to end of the land. But I can't recall a first-rate meal in the town for fifteen years past. Up to the time it went dry, of course, one could wash down bad victuals with what came out of bottles. At one small restaurant there was very good draft ale; at another there was a bartender, Mike by name, who made decent cocktails when wind and tide were favorable; on a hotel roof there was quasi-Pilsner that greeted the pylorus with a heavenly buss.

But no more. Imagine the capital of a great nation on the rations of diabetics, chautauqua orators and prisoners in the penitentiaries! What must the diplomats here interned think of it—the Latin-Americans, the French and Russians, the Spanish ambassador? I should like to hear the last-named on the subject, behind closed doors in his sub-cellar. Or the young bucks of the British Embassy.

V

Saturday.

Behind the door, of course, drinks are to be had—chiefly very bad whiskey at a dollar a half-pint. Until the lid was clamped down, a few months ago, every train from Baltimore was loaded with darkies running jugs, and every black kitchen wench in town had a lover who brought in the family supply. When the police began searching train passengers, the darkies took to automobiles, and for months the Baltimore road was crowded with jug-laden Fords all day. Innumerable and incredible accidents marked this traffic. Every bootlegger, before leaving Baltimore, would sample his cargo, and so it was not uncommon for him to smash his Ford into a telegraph pole on the way, or to run up a bank, or go over a bridge-rail, or run down a yokel. But now the traffic diminishes, and the caravan of Fords is no more. Day by day, one pays more for a drink, and gets worse liquor. Trade goods that even a New York policeman would sniff at are here sold to millionaires and great officers of state at the normal cost of 100-year-old brandy. Everyone is full of synthetic red-eye. The town reeks of bad whisky.

Nowhere in America, indeed, is the swinishness of prohibition more apparent. Washington has become an eighth-rate country town, hoggish and hypocritical. One is nauseated by the atmosphere. It is as if one were sent back to school again, and caned for shooting spit-balls by a chalky Pecksniff in a long-tailed coat. The man who cherishes his self-respect sends for a time-table and packs his valise. It is not a place to linger in, but to get out of.

VI

Sunday.

Five or six years ago the town enjoyed another and worse uplifting. That time it was the vice crusaders who performed the purification—with the usual effects. Theoretically the town is one vast Christian Endeavor meeting; actually it is the most libidinous that I know. Nowhere else within my knowledge, in truth, is there a more ardent pursuit of the poor working girl. Go into the eating-rooms of any hotel in town and you will find fifty oldish fellows making heavy love to fifty cuties. Or, if you can't stand the food, you must eat to pay rent, go to the Speedway after dark. Or into Rock Creek Park. Or out into Maryland.

Alas, most of the fair ones thus wooed to their foul disaster are anything but fair in actuality. Not even Philadelphia has more ugly women. I walk along the streets for blocks, searching in vain for a pretty face. The war-work seems to have brought in the hopeless and embittered old maids of the whole country; one sees thousands of faded frumps in the lunchrooms. They have worked very hard and the climate is atrocious—no wonder they look yellow and anemic. But even in the wealthy neighborhoods, where war work was surely not burdensome, female pulchritude is rare.

Nay, the seeker after beauty had better not come here. It is the wrong address. The town itself will torture him with nightmares. The gals will send him leaping to a monastery. Be warned! Stay away!

San Francisco: A Memory

I

What fetched me instantly (and thousands of other newcomers with me) was the subtle but unmistakable sense of escape from the United States—the feeling that here, at last, was an American city that somehow managed to hold itself above pollution by the national philistinism and craze for standardization, the appalling progress of 100% Americanism, the sordid and pathetic dreams of unimaginative, timorous and inferior men.

The East, it seems to me, is gone, and perhaps for good. All the towns along the seaboard are now as like as so many soldiers in a row. They think alike. They act alike. They hope and fear alike. They smell alike. They begin to look alike. What one says all the others say. What one does all the others do. It is as if some gigantic and relentless force labored to crush all personality, all distinction, all tang and savor out of them. They sink to the spiritual and intellectual level of villages, fat, lethargic and degraded. Their aspirations are the aspirations of curb brokers, green grocers and honorary pallbearers. The living hope of their typical citizen is to die respected by bank cashiers, Young Men's Christian Association secretaries and policemen. They are ironed out, disemboweled, denaturized, dephlogisticated, salted down, boiled, baked, dried in a kiln.

Think of Washington: a hundred thousand miserable botches of ninth-rate clerks, all groveling at the feet of such puerile caricatures as Daniels, Burleson and Palmer. Baltimore: mile after mile of identical houses, all inhabited by persons who regard Douglas Fairbanks as a greater man than Beethoven. (What zoologist, without a blood count and a lumbar picture, could distinguish one Baltimorean from another?) Philadelphia: an intellectual and cultural slum. Newark: a worse one. New York: a wholesale district with an annex for entertaining the visiting trade. New Haven and Hartford: blanks. Boston: a potter's field, a dissecting room. Mental decay in all its forms, but one symptom there is in common: the uneasy fear of ideas, the hot yearning to be correct at all costs, the thirst to be well esteemed by cads.

II

What is it that lifts San Francisco out of that wallow? I am not at all sure. It may be something intrinsic—specifically, something ethnological. The stock out there differs visibly from any Eastern stock that I know. It is not that half of the people are actual foreigners, for that is also true of New York and nearly true of Baltimore; it is that the native born belong to a distinct strain, mentally and physically—that the independence and enterprise of the pioneers are still in them—that their blood is still running hot and clear. Above all, remember the recentness of this heritage. They are not the children of men who were bold and daring in the seventeenth century, but the children of men who were bold and daring in the mid-nineteenth.

I met a man in the Bohemian Club who began to tell me casually of his grandmother. This lady, an Irishwoman of good birth, came to California from Ireland in 1849, by way of Panama. Imagine the journey: the long sea voyage, the infernal struggle across the Isthmus, the worse trip up the coast, the trek inland. Well, she brought a piano with her!—got it aboard ship in Ireland, guarded it all the way to Panama, dragged it through the jungle, then shipped it again, and finally packed it to her home in the hills! I daresay many of us could find such grandmothers, going back far enough. But in 1849—70 years ago? Our Baltimore grandmothers, in 1849, were sitting snugly by the new Latrobe stoves, reading *Dombey and Son* and knitting socks.

III

Mere geography helps, with a polite bow to meteorology. The climate, to an Easterner, is almost too invigorating. The heat of the Sacramento Valley sucks in such cold breezes through the Golden Gate that they over-stimulate like raw alcohol. An Arctic current comes down the coast, and the Pacific is so chilly that sea bathing is almost impossible, even in midsummer. Coming off this vast desert of ice water, the San Francisco winds tickle and sting. One arises in the morning with a gigantic sense of fitness—a feeling of superb well-being. Looking out at the clear yellow sunlight, one is almost tempted to crow like a rooster. It is a land of magnificent mornings.

But of somewhat less magnificent nights, at least to one from the East. The thrill of it leads to over-estimates. One suffers from the optimism of a man full of champagne. Toward evening, perhaps, a clammy fog rolls in, and one begins to feel a sudden letting down. The San Franciscans have learned how to bear it. They are stupendously alive while they are in motion, but they knock off betimes. The town is rich in loafing places—restaurants, theaters, parks. No one seems to work very hard. The desperate, consuming industry of the East is quite unknown. One could not imagine a sweatshop in the town. Puffs of Oriental air come with the fog. There is nothing European about the way life is lived; the color is all Asiatic.

IV

Now imagine the scene. A peninsula with the Pacific on one side of it and the huge bay on the other—a peninsula bumpy with bold, precipitous hills, some of them nearly a thousand feet high. The San Franciscans work in the valleys and live on the hills. Cable cars haul them up in a few minutes, or they make the voyage in astonishing taxicabs—taxicabs that seem capable of running up the side of a house. Monument street, east of the monument, is nothing;[17] here are hills that are genuinely steep. Coming down on foot one hugs the houses. Going up on foot—but I had better confine myself to what I know.

Once up, the scene almost staggers. It is incomparably more beautiful than any view along the Grand Corniche; from the Twin Peaks San Francisco makes Monaco seem tawdry and trivial. Ahead is the wide sweep of the bay, with the two great shoulders of the Golden Gate running down. Behind is the long curtain of California mountains. And below is the town itself—great splashes of white, pink and yellow houses climbing the lesser hills—houses half concealed in brilliant green—houses often sprawling and ramshackle, but nevertheless grouping themselves into lovely pictures, strange and charming. No other American town looks like that. It is a picture out of the East—dazzling, exotic and curiously romantic.

V

The foreign and half barbaric color gets into everything. One notices it at once without being able precisely to define it. There is the thing that no Atlantic town has ever been able to manage—gayety without grossness. In a sense, the place is wide open, but not in the way that New York and Baltimore and Washington used to be wide open—vulgarly, garishly, hoggishly. The business is achieved with an air, almost a grand manner. It is good-humored, engaging, innocent. There is no heavy attitude of raising the devil. One may guzzle as one will, but one may also drink decently and in order, and shake a leg in the style of Haydn, and lift an eye to a pretty girl without getting knocked in the head or having one's pocket picked. It is a friendly place, a spacious and tolerant place, a place heavy with strangeness and charm. It is no more American, in the sense that American has come to carry, than a wine festival in Spain or the carnival at Nice. It is cut off sharply from all the rest of this dun and dour republic.

But how securely? I have my uneasy doubts. Down a side street I saw a Gospel joint and heard its grisly drum. An Italian, while I was there, was jailed for selling grappo, a native brandy fit for embalming heroes. (The judge, true enough, protested against the raid from the bench, but the poor wop had confessed.) During the war the commercial bounders of the town swindled the Government out of millions, and are now organized in the usual booming clubs, anti-Red vereins, and chambers of illicit commerce. Chinatown is now as respectable as Guilford, and a good deal less naughty under cover. Sailors touring the Barbary Coast drink sarsaparilla. There is a movement by earnest Christian men to prohibit kissing in the parks. Forward-lookers turn their eyes to the East, and sniff its brummagem evangels. . . .

I advise you to lose no time. In two years San Francisco, too, may be 100% American. Go while the going is good.

San Francisco

A Washington bootlegger who knows everything tells me that it is now a moral certainty that one of the national conventions of next summer will be held at San Francisco.[18] The news is too pleasant to be doubted for an instant. I accept it at once, giving humble thanks to God, and prepare myself to view once more the only genuinely civilized city in the United States. It is such occasional escapes from Moronia that make journalism an agreeable profession. The same bootlegger—who knows more United States senators than Dr. Dawes himself, and is vastly more respected by them—tells me that the other convention is to go to Detroit. I rejoice again, and flap my wings.

I have been reporting national conventions for the great organs of patriotic opinion ever since the year 1900, but the only decent one that I have ever seen was the one held in San Francisco in 1920. I use the word decent in its narrowest sense. A national convention is usually not only grossly offensive to the higher cerebral centers; it is also immensely painful to the eye, the ear and the nose. Not to put too fine a point upon the matter, it stinks. But there was no stink in San Francisco. On the contrary, there were lovely zephyrs from the south seas, and on them came the scent of flowers. The eye was caressed by charming decorations. The ear was caressed by sound music. The esophagus was caressed by pre-war bourbon.

The effect upon the delegates was almost miraculous. Whole platoons of them were converted from politicians into gentlemen. They refrained from bawling, fighting and rolling in the gutter. They changed their collars daily, and their shirts twice a week. They learned how to drink without coughing, batting their eyes and slapping their tummies. They gave up spitting on the floor. They abandoned hot dogs in favor of ripe figs, pomegranates and the steaks of the abalone. Having descended upon the town with the dreadful snorts and bellows of sailors home from the Horn, they departed two weeks later in the delicate, pizzicato manner of ambassadors.

I believe that that convention did more to foster true refinement in these states than anything else since the launching of my friend Gerard Lambert's historic war upon halitosis, the curse of great business executives. The thousand-odd delegates and the thousand-odd alternates [not to mention the five hundred newspaper correspondents] were exposed for two weeks to the mellowing influences of a really civilized town. They learned how to drink; they learned table manners; they learned how to love. Returning anon to such sinks as Boston, Cincinnati, Harrisburg, Pa., Jackson, Miss., and La Crosse, Wis., they carried their new elegance with them, and spread it gently. All those places, save perhaps Boston, show the effects today.

It was simple cleanliness, I believe, that moved them most profoundly. Most of them had been to national conventions before and knew what to expect, to wit, a barnlike, hideous and filthy hall, double prices at all the hotels, the incessant blare of bands, liquor fit only for southern congressmen, and food fit only for hogs. Above all, they expected dirt—dirty places to eat, dirty washrooms, dirt and smells everywhere. In San Francisco, to their astonishment, they found none of these things. The hall was beautiful and spotlessly clean. The food everywhere was appetizing and cheap. The hotels did no profiteering. The decorations were in good taste. There was good music. The wines of the country were superb.

For a day or two the delegates and alternates staggered around like men emerging from anæsthetics. It seemed somehow fabulous. Drinking, they expected to fall to the ground and pass into fits. Eating, they expected to be doubled up by ptomaines. Attending at the hall, they expected to be deafened by noises and asphyxiated by stenches. Returning to their hotels, they expected to be blackjacked. When none of these things happened, they were as men in a dream. Then, suddenly, they began to rejoice. And then they began to leap and shout hosannas.

I confess to a great weakness for San Francisco. It is my favorite American town, as it is of almost every one else who has ever visited it. It looks out, not upon Europe, like New York, nor upon the Bible belt, like Chicago, but upon Asia, the ancient land, and the changeless. There is an Asiatic touch in its daily life, as there is a touch of Europe [and especially of the slums and bagnios of Europe] in the life of New York. No doubt it has its go-getters; if so, they are humanely invisible. Its people take the time to live, and they are aided in that laudable enterprise by the best climate in the world.

The earthquake of April 18, 1906 [To San Francisco editors: All right, call it a fire if you want to], gave San Francisco a dreadful wallop, and for a decade or more thereafter it seemed in peril of succumbing to the standardization that prevails everywhere else in America. Many of its most picturesque quarters were wiped out, and in the rebuilding there was little effort to reproduce them. Worse, the work of reconstruction attracted a great many strangers, and some of them came from the evangelical wilds of the middle west.

The result was a long effort to convert San Francisco into a sort of Asbury Park. Wowsers arose with the demand that the town be made safe for Sunday school superintendents. Anon came prohibition, and a fresh effort to iron it out. But though its peril, for a while, was anything but inconsiderable, it managed to survive this onslaught, and today it seems to be out of danger. Most of the wowsers have moved to Los Angeles, where the populace welcomes and admires them. San Francisco has returned to its more spacious and urban life. It is agreeably wet, sinful and happy. A civilized traveler may visit it today without running any risk of being thrown into jail or ducked in a baptismal tank.

The rise of Los Angeles, indeed, has been a godsend to the whole San Francisco region, though the San Franciscans once viewed it with alarm. It has drawn off the middle western morons who flock to the coast, and concentrated them in the south. The weather down there is warmer—an important consideration to farmers who have been chilblained and petrified by the long, harsh winters of Iowa. And more attention is paid to the perils of the soul—always an important matter to agronomists. In San Francisco there seems to be very little active fear of hell. The unpleasantness of roasting forever is sometimes politely discussed, but no one seems to get into a lather about it.

In Los Angeles the hell question is always to the fore, and so the yokels find the place more to their taste. There are more than 10,000 evangelists in the town, all of them in constant eruption. They preach every brand of theology ever heard of in the world, and many that are quite unknown elsewhere. When two eminent pastors engage in a slanging match, which is very frequently, the combat attracts as much attention as another set piece by Dempsey and Tunney. There are Iowans in Los Angeles who go to church three times a day, and to a different basilica every time. It is a paradise of Bible-searchers.

No such frenzy to unearth and embrace the truth is visible in San Francisco. As I have said, the influence of Asia is upon the town, and Asia got through all the theological riddles that now engage Los Angeles a thousand years ago. San Francisco takes such things lightly. It consecrates its chief energies to the far more pleasant and important business of living comfortably on this earth. It is one of the most agreeable great cities in the world—mild and balmy in its climate, beautiful in its situation and tolerant and civilized in its point of view. I sincerely hope that the Washington bootlegger is right, and that one of the conventions will be held there next year. The Democrats had the last; let the Republicans now take their turn. Their 1924 convention was held in Cleveland, and their 1920 convention in a huge hot frame at Chicago. They, too, are God's creatures, and deserve a little decent comfort. And something better than needle beer to wet their whistles.

New York

I

The most interesting book that I have explored since our last service is Fremont Rider's *New York City: A Guide to Travelers,* lately reissued in a second and revised edition. I have been plowing through it, in fact, for days, and the end is yet far off. It presents a colossal mass of information about the new capital of Christendom, and that information is admirably sorted out upon the plan invented by Karl Baedeker, to whom Mr. Rider makes graceful acknowledgment in his preface. Almost every conceivable fact about New York is here got into one volume of 670 pages—the origin of all the principal street names, the names of the sculptors who designed the hideous statuary of the town, the exact size and history of the parks, the traffic rules in Fifth avenue, the principal contents of the public museums, the hours when God is wooed and flattered in the churches, and lists of the theaters, concert halls, clubs, restaurants, hotels and office buildings. I can find nothing about bootlegging, a very important matter to strangers who, with provincial shyness, hesitate to apply to the police; perhaps Mr. Rider will add a section upon the subject to his next edition. Meanwhile, I hope, he will be polite to purchasers of the book who call him up at the office of his publishers. He makes up for the lack by bespattering his pages with strange odds and ends—that the Pennsylvania Hotel telephone switchboard has room for 22 operators; that the Woolworth Building weighs 206,000,000 pounds; that St. Bartholomew's Church in Park avenue "replaces one of the largest breweries on Manhattan Island"; that Irving place was named after Washington Irving; that the Hotel Commodore contains 412,000 feet of plumbing pipe; that President Chester A. Arthur took the oath of office at 123 Lexington avenue on September 19, 1881.

Such information, of course, is useless, but so is practically all other information. Nevertheless, human beings always take great delight in amassing it. As for me, reading Mr. Rider's most instructive tome makes my conscience toss and grunt a bit, for the fact is borne upon me that, despite my long familiarity with New York, I really know nothing about the town. The truth is that, like most other persons who visit it regularly and like many who live in it, I confine my habitual travels in it to a very limited area.[19] The region between Forty-second street on the south, Forty-fifth street on the north, Fifth avenue on the east and Sixth avenue on the west I know pretty well—well enough, indeed, to navigate it day or night without lights. It is within that rectangle that I sleep when I am in New York, and there I have my office and eat most of my meals. What lies outside is, in the main, mysterious to me, though I have been making trips around the town for twenty-five years. My glimpses of it, in fact, have never greatly tempted me to explore it more diligently. New York, it seems to me, is a city strangely lacking in physical charm. If it were actually beautiful, as, say, London is beautiful, then New Yorkers would not be so childishly enthusiastic about the few so-called beauty spots that it has—for example, Washington Square, Gramercy Park, Riverside drive and Fifth avenue. Washington Square, save for the one short row of old houses on the north side, is actually very shabby and ugly. The trees have a mangy appearance; the grass is like stable litter; the tall tower on the south side is ungraceful; the memorial arch is dirty; the whole place looks dingy. As for Gramercy Park, it is celebrated only because it is in New York; if it were in Washington it would not attract a glance. Fifth avenue, to me, seems to be gaudy rather than beautiful. What gives it distinction is simply its spick and span air of wealth; it is the only New York street that is clean. Riverside drive lacks even that; it looks second-rate from end to end. New York is the only great Eastern city that has never developed a characteristic domestic architecture—that is, of any merit. There are neighborhoods in Boston, in Philadelphia, in Baltimore and in many of the lesser cities that have all the charm of London, but in New York the brownstone mania brought down all the side streets to one horrible level of ugliness, and in Fifth avenue there has never been any development of indigenous design, but only a naïve copying of foreign models, most of them bad and all of them inappropriate.

Mr. Rider prints a long bibliography of books about New York, including novels, and says that they are innumerable. Nevertheless, it is a curious fact that relatively few American novelists of any distinction have devoted themselves to it, and that nearly all the serious novels dealing with it are bad, for example, Ernest Poole's *The Harbor*, Dreiser's *The "Genius"* and James Lane Allen's *A Cathedral Singer*. Chicago, Boston and San Francisco have offered far greater temptations and opportunities to the novelists; there is no novel about New York that is so good as Frank Norris's *McTeague* or Dreiser's *Jennie Gerhardt*. Perhaps Abraham Cahan's *The Rise of David Levinsky* ought to be remembered here, but in that very excellent tale there is very little New Yorkish flavor; the scene might be shifted to Chicago without changing a single episode. Nine-tenths of the more serious novelists of today seem eager to avoid the city altogether, for example, Cabell, Herrick and Willa Cather; the rest, dealing with it, do so very gingerly, for example, Hergesheimer. What a chance wasted! The fact is that the life of the city is as interesting as its physical aspect is dull. It is, even more than London, Paris or Berlin, the modern Babylon, and since 1914 it has entered upon a period of luxuriousness that far surpasses anything seen in the Paris of the Second Empire. I daresay that, during many a single week, more money is spent upon useless things in New York than would suffice to run the kingdom of Denmark for a year. All the colossal accumulated wealth of the United States, the greatest robber nation in history, tends to force itself at least once a year through the narrow neck of the Manhattan funnel. To that bald, harsh island come all the thieves of the Republic with their loot—bankers from the fat lands of the Middle West, lumbermen from the Northwestern coasts, mine owners from the mountains, oil speculators from Texas and Oklahoma, cotton-mill sweaters from the South, steel magnates and manufacturers from the Black Country, blacklegs and exploiters without end—all laden with cash, all eager to spend it, all easy marks for the town rogues and panders.

The result is a social organization that ought to be enormously attractive to novelists—a society founded upon the prodigious wealth of Monte Cristo and upon the tastes of sailors home from a long voyage. At no time and place since the fall of the Eastern Empire has harlotry reached so delicate and yet so effusive a develop-ment; it becomes, in one form or another, one of the leading industries of the town. New York, indeed, is the heaven of every variety of man with something useless and expensive to sell. There come the merchants with their bales, of Persian prayer-rugs, of silk pajamas, of yellow girls, of strange jugs and carboys, of hand-painted oil-paintings, of old books, of gimcracks and tinsel from all the four corners of the world, and there they find customers waiting in swarms, their check-books open and ready. What town in Christendom has ever supported so many houses of en-tertainment, so many mimes and mountebanks, so many sharpers and cony-catchers, so many bawds and pimps, so many hat-holders and door-openers, so many mis-cellaneous servants to idleness and debauchery? The bootlegging industry in the town takes on proportions that are almost unbelievable; there are thousands of New Yorkers, resident and transient, who pay more for alcohol every year than they pay for anything else save women. It is astonishing that no Zola has arisen to describe this engrossing and incomparable dance of death. Upton Sinclair once attempted it in *The Metropolis*, but Sinclair, of course, was too indignant for the job. More-over, the era he dealt with was mild and amateurish; today the pursuit of sensation has been brought to a far higher degree of perfection. One must go back to the ori-ental capitals of antiquity to find anything even remotely resembling it. Compared to the revels that go on in New York every night, the carnalities of the West End of Berlin are trivial and childish, and those of Paris and the Côte d'Azure take on the harmless aspect of a Sunday-school picnic.

II

What will be the end of the carnival? If historical precedent counts for anything, it will go on to catastrophe. But what sort of catastrophe? I refuse to venture upon a prophecy. Manhattan Island, with deep rivers all around it, seems an almost ideal scene for a great city revolution, but I doubt very much that there is any revolu-tionary spirit in its proletariat. Some mysterious enchantment holds its workers to their extraordinarily uncomfortable life; they apparently get a vague sort of delight out of the great spectacle that they are no part of. The low-browed New Yorker pa-tronizes fellow low-brows from the provinces even more heavily than the Wall street magnate patronizes country mortgage-sharks. He is excessively proud of his citizenship in the great metropolis, though all it brings him is an upper berth in a dog kennel. Riding along the elevated on the East Side and gaping into the windows of the so-called human habitations that stretch on either side, I often wonder what process of reasoning impels, say, a bricklayer or a truckdriver to spend his days in such vile hutches. True enough, he is paid a few dollars more a week in New York than he would receive anywhere else, but he gets little more use out of them than an honest bank teller. In almost any other large American city he would have a much better house to live in, and better food; in the smaller towns his advantage would be very considerable. Moreover, his chance of lifting himself out of slavery to some measure of economic independence and autonomy would be greater anywhere else; if it is hard for the American workmen everywhere to establish a business of his own, it is triply hard in New York, where rents are killingly high and so much capital is required to launch a business that only Jews can raise it. Nevertheless, the poor idiot hangs on to his coop, dazzled by the wealth and splendor on display all around him. His susceptibility to this lure makes me question his capacity for revolution. He is too stupid and poltroonish for it, and he has too much respect for money. It is this respect for money in the proletariat, in fact, that chiefly safeguards and buttresses capitalism in America. It is secure among us because Americans venerate it too much to attack it.

What will finish New York in the end, I suppose, will be an onslaught from without, not from within. The city is the least defensible of great capitals. Give an enemy command of the sea, and he will be able to take it almost as easily as he could take Copenhagen. It has never been attacked in the past, indeed, without being taken. The strategists of the General Staff at Washington seem to be well aware of this fact, for their preparations to defend the city from a foe afloat have always been half-hearted and lacking in confidence. Capt. Stuart Godfrey, U. S. A., who contributes the note on the fortifications of the port to Mr. Rider's book, is at pains to warn his lay readers that the existing forts protect only the narrow spaces in front of them — that "they cannot be expected to prevent the enemy from landing elsewhere," e.g., anywhere along the long reaches of the Long Island coast. Once such a landing were effected, the fact that the city stands upon an island, with deep water behind it, would be a handicap rather than a benefit. If it could not be taken and held, it could at least be battered to pieces, and so made untenable. The guns of its own forts, indeed, might be turned upon it, once those forts were open to attack from the rear. After that, the best the defenders could do would be to retire to the natural bomb-proofs in the cellars of the Union Hill, N. J., breweries, and there wait for God to deliver them. They might, of course, be able to throw down enough metal from the Jersey heights to prevent the enemy occupying the city and reopening its theatres and bordellos, but the more successful they were in this enterprise the more cruelly

Manhattan would be ill used. Altogether, an assault from the sea promises to give the New Yorkers something to think about.

That it will be attempted before many years have come and gone seems to me to be very likely. The Anglo-American *entente*, despite the vast energy expended upon pumping it up, shows very few signs of healthy development. The truth is that the fundamental interests of England and the United States are antagonistic, and must always remain so—that at least 50 cents of every dollar that drops into an American pocket has to come out of an English pocket. The English have got on in the world, not by outwitting their rivals in trade, for they lack the commercial skill for that, but by beating them in war. The German bugaboo having been laid, at least temporarily, they are now obviously greatly perturbed by the American bugaboo. The fact that the United States is bursting with riches, that all the money in the world tends to flow in this direction, is a matter that the English newspapers never tire of discussing, usually with ill-concealed disquiet. There is never any hint in these discussions that the prosperity of Uncle Sam is due to sound sense and capacity, or that it is deserved in any other way; always the theory is thrown out that it is due to sharp practises. Thus the moral foundation is laid for a struggle to the death, and I am convinced that it will come as soon as the running-amuck of the French is halted and Europe comes to a safe equilibrium. At the moment the English rear is too insecure to permit of operations on the front, but soon or late the old balance of power on the Continent will be restored, and its hereditary enemies will efficiently police each other. Then the time will come to give attention to the Yankee pickpocket, bully, bluenose and foe to democracy and Christianity.

As a veteran of five wars and a lifelong student of military science, I am often made uneasy by the almost universal American assumption that no conceivable enemy could inflict serious wounds upon the Republic—that the Atlantic Ocean alone, not to mention the stupendous prowess of the *Boobo americanus*, makes it eternally safe from aggression. This notion has just enough truth in it to make it dangerous. That the *whole* country could not be conquered and occupied I grant you, but no intelligent enemy would think for a moment of trying to conquer it. All that would be necessary to bring even the most intransigeant patriots to terms would be to take and hold a small part of it—say the part lying to the east and north of the general line of the Potomac river. Early in the late war, when efforts were under weigh to scare the American *booboisie* with the German bugaboo, one of the Allied propagandists printed a book setting forth plans alleged to have been made by the German General Staff to land an army at the Virginia capes, march on Pittsburgh, and so separate the head of the country from its liver, kidneys, gizzard, heart, spleen, bladder, lungs and other lights. The plan was persuasive, but I doubt that it originated in Potsdam; there was a smell of Whitehall upon it. One of the things most essential to its execution, in fact, was left out as it was set forth, to wit, a thrust southward from Canada to meet and support the thrust northwestward. But even this is not necessary. Any invader who emptied New York and took the line of the Hudson would have Uncle Sam by the tail, and could enter upon peace negotiations with every prospect of getting very polite attention. The American people, of course, could go on living without New York, but they could not go on living as a great and puissant nation. Steadily, year by year, they have made New York more and more essential to the orderly functioning of the American state. If it were cut off from the rest of the country, the United States would be in the hopeless position of a man relieved of his medulla oblongata—that is to say, of a man without even enough equipment left to be a father, a patriot and a Christian.

Nevertheless, it is highly probable that the predestined enemy, when he comes at last, will direct his first and hardest efforts to cutting off New York, and then make some attempt to keep it detached afterward. This, in fact, is an essential part of the new higher strategy, which is based upon economic considerations, as the old strategy was based upon dynastic considerations. In the middle ages, the object of war was to capture and hamstring a king; at present it is to dismember a great state, and so make it impotent. The Germans, had they won, would have broken up the British Empire, and probably detached important territories from France, Italy and Russia, beside gobbling Belgium *in toto*. The French, tantalized by a precarious and incomplete victory, now attempt to break up Germany, as they have already broken up Austria. The chances are that an enemy capable of taking and holding New York would never give it back wholly—that is, would never consent to its restoration to the Union on the old terms. What would be proposed, I venture, would be its conversion into a sort of free state—a new Dantzig, perhaps functioning, as now, as the financial and commercial capital of the country, but nevertheless lying outside the bounds politically. This would solve the problem of the city's subsistence, and still enable the conqueror to keep his hold upon it. It is my belief that the New Yorkers, after the first blush of horror, would agree to the new arrangement and even welcome it. Their patriotism, as things stand, is next to nothing. There is, indeed, not a single honest patriot in the whole town; every last man who even pretends to kiss the flag is simply a swindler with something to sell. This indifference to the great heart-throbs of the hinterland is not to be dismissed as mere criminality; it is founded upon the plain and harsh fact that New York is alien to the rest of the country, not only in blood and tastes, but also in fundamental interests—that the sort of life that New Yorkers lead differs radically from the sort of life that the rest of the American people lead, and that their deepest instincts vary with it. The city, in truth, already constitutes an independent free state in all save the name. The ordinary American law does not run there, save when it has been specifically ratified, and the ordinary American *mores* are quite unknown there. What passes as virtue in Kansas is regarded as intolerable vice in New York, and *vice versa*.

The town is already powerful enough to swing the whole country when it wants to, as it did on the war issue in 1917, but the country is quite impotent to swing the town. Every great wave of popular passion that rolls up on the prairies is dashed to spray when it strikes the hard rocks of Manhattan.

As a free state, licensed to prey upon the hinterland but unharassed by its Crô-Magnon prejudices and delusions, New York would probably rise to heights of very genuine greatness, and perhaps become the most splendid city known to history. For one thing, it would be able, once it had cut the painter, to erect barriers and conditions around the privilege of citizenship, and so save itself from the double flood that now swamps it—first, of broken-down peasants from Europe, and secondly and more important, of fugitive rogues from all the land west and south of the Hudson. Citizenship in New York is now worth no more than citizenship in Arkansas, for it is open to any applicant from the marshes of Bessarabia, and, still worse, to any applicant from Arkansas. The great city-states of history have been far more fastidious. Venice, Antwerp, London, the Hansa towns, Carthage, Tyre, Cnossus, Alexandria—they were all very sniffish. Rome began to wobble when the Roman franchise was extended to immigrants from the Italian hill country, *i.e.*, the Arkansas of that time. The Hansa towns, under the democracy that has been forced upon them, are rapidly sinking to the level of Chicago and Philadelphia. New York, free to put an end to this invasion, and to drive out thousands of the gorillas who now infest it—more, free from the eternal blackmail of laws made at Albany and the Methodist tyranny of laws made at Washington—it could face the future with resolution and security, and in the course of a few generations it might conceivably become genuinely civilized. It would still stand as toll-taker on the chief highway of American commerce; it would still remain the premier banker and insurer of the Republic. But it would be loosed from the bonds which now tend so strenuously to drag it down to the level of the rest of the country. Free at last, it could cease to be the auction-room and bawdy-house that it is now, and so devote its brains and energy to the building up of a civilization.

# three

American Politics, Morality, and Religion

Meditation in E Minor

I

I seem to be the only sort of man who is never heard of in politics in the Republic, either as candidate or as voter. *Also*, I must write my own platform, make my own speeches, point with my own pride, view with my own alarm, pump with my own hopes and ideals, invent my own lies, posture and grimace upon my own front porch. . . .

II

Politically I am absolutely honest, which is to say, as honest as possible; which, is to say, honest more or less; which is to say, far more honest than the general. My politics are based frankly and wholly upon what, in the dim light now shining in the world, I take to be my self-interest. I do not pretend to any pressing interest in the welfare of any other man, whether material or spiritual; in particular, I do not pretend to any interest in the welfare of any man who belongs to a class that differs clearly from my own. In other words, I am intensely class-conscious—almost the ideal citizen of the radical vision. Virtually all of the men that I know and like and respect belong to my own class, or to some class very closely allied to it. I can't imagine having any active good-will toward a man of a widely differing class—say the class of professional politicians and bureaucrats, or that of wealthy manufacturers, or that of schoolmasters, or that of policemen, ordained and lay. Such men simply do not interest me, save as convenient targets for the malevolence that is in all of us. I like to vex them; beyond that, as old Friedrich used to say, I hand them over to statistics and the devil. If all the members of such a class were deported by Dr. Palmer and his blacklegs tomorrow, my indignation would be transient and theoretical; if I yelled, it would be as I yell occasionally about the massacres in Ireland, Haiti, Armenia and India, hoping all the while that the show doesn't stop.

Here, of course, I wallow in platitudes; I, too, am an American, God save us all! The blather of politics is made up almost wholly of violent and disingenuous attempts to sophisticate and obfuscate those platitudes. Often, of course, the boshmonger succumbs to his own bosh. The late Major-General Roosevelt, I have no doubt, convinced himself eventually that he was actually the valiant and aseptic Bayard of Service that he pretended to be—that he was a Lafayette sweating unselfishly and agonizingly to protect, instruct, inspire, guide and lift up the great masses of the plain people, his inferiors. He was, perhaps, honest, but he was wrong. What moved him was simply a craving for facile and meaningless banzais, for the gaudy eminence and power of the leader of a band of lynchers, for the mean admiration of mean men. His autobiography gives him away;[1] what he left out of it he babbled to the deacon of his mass, Leary, and to the sub-deacon, Abbott. Had Roosevelt been the aristocrat that legend made him, his career would have presented a truly astonishing spectacle: Brahms seeking the applause of organ grinders, piano tuners and union cornetists. But he was no such aristocrat, either by birth or by training. He was simply a professional politician of the democratic kidney, by Harvard out of the Rotary Club bourgeoisie, and his good was always the good of the well-fed, bombastic and extremely shallow class. Immediately his usual victims became class-conscious on their own hook, he was their enemy, and showed all the horror of them that one would look for in John D. Rockefeller, Jr., Judge Gary or Frank A. Munsey.

III

The class that I belong to is an inferior sub-class of the order of capitalists. I am not rich, but my ease and welfare depends very largely upon the security of wealth. If stocks and bonds became valueless tomorrow, I'd be forced to supplement my present agreeable work with a good deal of intensely disagreeable work. Hence I am in favor of laws protecting property, and am an admirer of the Constitution of the United States in its original form. If such laws can be enforced peacefully, *i.e.*, by deluding and hornswoggling the classes whose interests they stand against, then I am in favor of so enforcing them; if not, then I am in favor of employing professional bullies, *e.g.*, policemen, soldiers and Department of Justice thugs, to enforce them with the sword. Here I borrow the morality of the the radicals, who are my enemies; their arguments in favor of an alert class-consciousness convince me, but I stick to my own class. I borrow even more from the liberals, who are also my enemies. In particular, I borrow the doctrine that peace in such matters is better than war—that it is foolish to hire gunmen when it is so much simpler and easier to bamboozle the boobs with phrases. Here, of course, a trade interest helps out my class-consciousness; I am a professional maker of phrases and delight in displays of virtuosity. The liberals feed me with that delight. This explains why I like them and encourage them, though their politics usually depress me.

But though I am thus in favor of property and would be quite content to see one mob of poor men (in uniform) set to gouging and ham-stringing another mob of poor men (in overalls) in order to protect it, it by no means follows that I am in favor of the wealthy bounders who now run the United States, or of the politics that they preach in their kept press. On the contrary, I am even more violently against them than I am against the radicals with their sticks of dynamite and the liberals with their jugs of Peruna.[2] And for a plain reason. On the one one hand, these swine oppress me excessively and unnecessarily—by putting up prices, by loading me with inordinate taxes, by setting hordes of bureaucrats to looting me, by demanding that I give my assent to all their imbecile and dishonest ideas, and by threatening me with the cost of endless wars, to them extremely profitable. On the other hand, and even more importantly, their intolerable hoggishness threatens to raise the boobery in revolt and bring about a reign of terror from which only the strongest will emerge. That revolt would ruin me. I am not large enough, as a capitalist, to make a profit out of wars and turmoils. I believe that the rising of the proletariat, if it ever comes in this country, will end in a colossal victory for capitalism—that capitalism, as at present and in the past, will play off one mob against another, and pick the pockets of both. But it will also pick my pockets. It will also force me, who had nothing to do with the row, and protested against it bitterly, to pay a tremendous price for getting out alive. I'll have my naked hide, but everything else will be lost, including honor.

Ah, that my vision were a mere nightmare, the child of encroaching senility and bad beer! Unluckily, the late lamentable war showed its terrible reality. That war was fought against my advice and consent, and I took no part in it whatever, save as spectator. In particular, I made no profit out of it—not a cent, directly or indirectly. Well, what is my situation today? In brief, I find that my property is worth, roughly speaking, no more than half of what it was worth at the end of 1916, and that, considering its ratio to the total national wealth, and the difference between the national debt then and now, I owe, as a citizen of the United States, something between $8,000 and $10,000. To whom? Who got it, and how, for what? . . . Let us not go into the question too particularly. I find my class-consciousness wobbling!

IV

Meanwhile, however, I still manage to eat without too much labor, and so I incline to the Right, and am a Tory in politics, and trust in God. It would give me great pleasure to vote for a Tory candidate for the Presidency—not a hollow ass like General Wood, but an honest and unashamed Tory, one voicing the sincere views of the more civilized section of the propertied class, not a mere puppet for usurers. Unfortunately, no such candidate ever offers himself. The men put up by these usurers are always such transparent frauds that it is impossible, without anæsthetics, to vote for them. I admire liars, but surely not liars so clumsy that they cannot fool even themselves. I am an old hand at political shows, and witnessed both the nomination of Harding at Chicago and that of Cox at San Francisco. It would be difficult to imagine more obscene spectacles. Who, being privy to their disgusting trimming, their mean courting of mean men, their absolute lack of any sense of dignity, honor or self-respect, could vote for either? It will take me all the time between now and November, abandoning all other concerns, to work up the necessary cynicism—and no doubt I'll fail even then. But could I vote for Christiansen?[3] He is a Knight of Pythias; allow me my prejudices! Debs? Please don't suggest it in plain words. It would be anguish unspeakable; I am probably the only man in Christendom who has never been a Socialist even for an instant. An idiot, this Debs, but honest, and he says plainly that he is against me. I'd be a worse idiot if I voted for him.

My dilemma, alas, is not unique. Thousands of other men must face it—men of my class, men of related classes, perhaps even men of classes far removed. It visualizes one of the penalties that democracy, the damnedest of frauds, inflicts upon every man who violates all its principles by trying to be honest.

What Ails the Republic

I

The Hon. William Allen White, the Kansas *doctor famosissimus*, states the case against the Puritan hegemony very frankly and effectively in the current issue of the eminent *Nation*.[4] This Dr. White, it should be remembered, is no scoundrelly foe to the Puritan revelation, as I am, but a Puritan by birth and conviction. He regards it as offensive to God to guzzle a bottle of Clos Vougeot 1906. He never works on Sunday. It gives him as much pain to see a pretty girl smoking a cigarette as it would give me to see her shoeing a horse. He is both too fat and too *fromm* to shimmy. When he is in New York (which is far too seldom!) he avoids the cabarets and the aphrodisiac shows of Broadway, and remits his savings to the receivers of the Men and Religion Forward Movement. At Atlantic City, unlike all other Americans of his wealth, he goes under his own name.

Nevertheless, this Kansas virtuoso of virtue is no common bluenose, but a fellow with some humor in him, and, what is more, some sense. He has traveled, he has observed sharply, and he has meditated to no little effect upon the basic woes of Christendom. Some of the fruits of that meditation are visible in the article I have mentioned. Superficially, it is a treatise extolling the deights of human existence under Puritanism, and specifically the republic of Kansas. But underneath the exultation there is something scarcely to be distinguished from a groan, and that groan, it seems to me, is of the utmost significance. In brief, Dr. White has begun to have doubts. First, he views his fellow-Kansans proudly and even a bit challengingly: they go to church, they avoid the wine-cup, they keep out of jail, they abhor the cigarette, they pursue the scarlet woman with staghounds, they are patriots, they have cement sidewalks in front of their houses, their children go to high school, they have money in the bank. But then it suddenly occurs to him that, at bottom, they are mere blobs—that they are blind to beauty and bare of charm, that they are an ignorant and ignoble people, that they don't know what joy is, that all their fundamental ideas are pathetically narrow, trivial and sordid.

II

Here Dr. White stops, very dramatically and eloquently—upon a shivery chord in C minor. But there is an implication in his discourse that he neglects to state, and so I presume to state it for him. It may be put succinctly in the following terms: that what ails the United States primarily is that the sort of folks whom he describes as typical of Kansas are the sort who run the country, against the advice and consent of their betters—that the American who is *not* blind to beauty, who is *not* ignorant and ignoble, who is *not* incapable of civilized joy, and who is *not* a victim to ideas that are narrow, trivial and sordid—that this American must submit steadily to the mandates and rages of the American who *is*.

In other words, the curse of Puritanism is the general curse of democracy. No matter how romantically democracy may be described, it always resolves itself, in the end, into a scheme for enabling weak and inferior men to force their notions and desires, by mass action, upon strong and superior men. Its essence is this substitution of mere numbers for every other sort of superiority—this fundamental assumption that a group of idiots, if only its numbers be large enough, is wiser and more virtuous than any conceivable individual who is not an idiot. That is the essence of the thing, and it is also the immovable objection to the thing. For there is actually no truth in the fundamental assumption. On the contrary, it is one of the most obvious imbecilities ever stated by mortal man. The multiplication of idiocy does not produce wisdom; it produces worse idiocy. The crowd is even more stupid and degraded than any of its constituent members. And when this multiplied and augmented idiocy has irresistible power behind it—when it is free not only to cherish its debased and caduceous delusions, but also to impose them harshly upon men who stand above them—then the orderly processes of human progress are arrested, and we behold the flatulent barbarism that Dr. White observes in Kansas, and that is gradually engulfing the whole United States.

III

On the political side democracy usually proceeds by the direct method of creating a fictitious virtue. That is to say, it first sets up the grotesque doctrine that any man, as a citizen, as a voter, as a judge in matters of government and state, is the full equal of any other man, and then assumes that the opinion of the majority of men represents the highest imaginable wisdom. But on the cultural side it works by indirection, and rather more subtly. Instead of accentuating the virtue of the majority it now devotes itself to establishing the sinfulness of the minority. Whatever is preferred or done by a man patently different from the general is *ipso facto* sinful. Does he work on Sunday and rest on some other day? Then it is against God. Does he delight in certain books? Then they must be forbidden the mails. Does he drink wine? Then it is a crime. Does he permit his wife to smoke cigarettes? Then she must be rescued by law from his rascality.

What chiefly lies under all this, of course, is lack of comprehension, and what chiefly converts lack of comprehension into hostility is envy. The inferior man is congenitally incapable of many very charming forms of joy, including practically all of those that depend upon an active imagination and a tradition of ease. When he thinks of alcohol, he thinks of revolting decoctions swigged from a jug behind the door—of drunkenness that puts him at a disadvantage, of money and time wasted, of an intolerable *Katzenjammer*. When he thinks of a Sabbath purged of Blue Laws, he is palsied by a fear that it will force him to work seven days a week. When he remembers certain books, peeped into *in camera*, he recalls the extremely disagreeable visions of sin, the flabbergasting emotions that they aroused in him. When he contemplates his wife with a cigarette, he thinks of the effect that the spectacle is likely to have on his fellow-slaves—their embarrassing interpretation of it—the probable correctness of the interpretation.

So all such things, as Dr. White says, become "wrongs," and must be put down. The inferior man is incapable of them without gross risk and damage. He cannot enjoy them decently; in many cases he cannot enjoy them at all. *Ergo*, they are forbidden by Divine Revelation, and must be prohibited by the secular arm.

IV

No educated man, I believe, is opposed to Puritanism as a personal ethic. He may not like the immediate presence of Puritans, but he has no objection to the private practice of their rococo asceticism on their remote farms or in the galvanized-iron tabernacles that they erect on suburban dumps. He may even have a certain academic admiration for its practitioners—for unhappy men who voluntarily renounce what little joy they have. If they annoy him it is only as the bass drum of the Salvation Army annoys him, vaguely and transiently. He is willing to suffer so much for the general good of the community, and to give practical effect to his theory of toleration. I have never heard of any civilized man proposing to put down by force any of the bizarre abnegations that honest blue-noses practise. He may pity the theological teetotaler, but he certainly does not compel him to drink.

If Puritanism stopped here, no one would be at war with it. But it never stops here; it has never stopped here in the whole history of the world. The Puritan not only believes that the non-Puritan is wrong; he also hates him actively and has an overmastering desire to dragoon and punish him. This desire, under democracy, is given satisfaction. It is perfectly possible, under cover of a Government organized as ours is, for men who are thus incapable of joy and envious of it in others to batter it out of those others by force. The machinery is lying to their hand, and they have learned how to use it. The Salvation Army not only beats its drum; it also hoofs its way into the house of the polite sufferer and proceeds to apply the drumstick vigorously to his knuckles, his occiput and the seat of his pantaloons. If he yells, there is a cop at hand to reinforce the drumstick with an espantoon.

This, in brief, is the pass that we have come to in the United States. The Puritans, deprived by their singularly savage God of the capacity for anything properly describable as civilization, now undertake to penalize that capacity when it appears in their betters. The ideal they have in mind is an ideal already realized in the Kansas so frankly limned by Dr. White. The attack is in full swing, and every day another citadel falls. So far the counter-attack has confined itself to remonstrance, reasoning, appeals to sense and decency. As well assault an hyena with the works of Benedetto Croce. There will be no relief, I am convinced, until the drumstick is met with lead.

The American Politician

> No person shall be a Representative who . . . shall not, when elected, be an inhabitant of that State in which he shall be chosen. . . . No person shall be a Senator who . . . shall not, when elected, be an inhabitant of that State for which he shall be chosen.

Specialists in political archaeology will recognize these sentences: they are from Article I, Sections 2 and 3, of the constitution of the United States. I have heard and forgotten how they got there; no doubt the cause lay in the fierce jealousy of the States. But whatever the fact, I have a notion that there are few provisions of the constitution that have had a more profound effect upon the character of practical politics in the Republic, or, indirectly, upon the general color of American thinking in the political department. They have made steadily for parochialism in legislation, for the security and prosperity of petty local bosses and machines, for the multiplication of pocket and rotten boroughs of the worst sort and, above all, for the progressive degeneration of the honesty and honor of representatives. They have greased the ways for the trashy and ignoble fellow who aspires to get into Congress, and they have blocked them for the man of sense, dignity and self-respect. More, perhaps, than any other single influence they have been responsible for the present debauched and degraded condition of the two houses, and particularly of the lower one. Find me the worst ass in Congress, and I'll show you a man they have helped to get there and to stay there. Find me the most shameless scoundrel, and I'll show you another.

No such centripedal mandate, as far as I have been able to discover, is in the fundamental law of any other country practising the representative system. An Englishman, if ambition heads him toward St. Stephen's, may go hunting for a willing constituency wherever the hunting looks best, and if he fails in the Midlands he may try again in the South, or in the North, or in Scotland or Wales. A Frenchman of like dreams has the same privilege; the only condition, added after nineteen years of the Third Republic, is that he may not be a candidate in two or more *arrondissements* at once. And so with a German, an Italian or a Spaniard. But not so with an American. He must be an actual inhabitant of the State he aspires to represent at Washington. More, he must be, in all save extraordinary cases, an actual inhabitant of the congressional district—for here, by a characteristic American process, the fundamental law is sharpened by custom. True enough, this last requirement is not laid down by the constitution. It would be perfectly legal for the thirty-fifth New York district, centering at Syracuse, to seek its congressman in Manhattan, or even at Sing Sing. In various iconoclastic States, in fact, the thing has been occasionally done. But not often; not often enough to produce any appreciable effect. The typical congressman remains a purely local magnifico, the gaudy cock of some small and usually far from appetizing barnyard. His rank and dignity as a man are measured by provincial standards of the most puerile sort, and his capacity to discharge the various and onerous duties of his office is reckoned almost exclusively in terms of his ability to hold his grip upon the local party machine.

If he has genuine ability, it is a sort of accident. If he is thoroughly honest, it is next door to a miracle. Of the 430-odd representatives who carry on so diligently and obscenely at Washington, making laws and determining policies for the largest free nation ever seen in the world, there are not two dozen whose views upon any subject under the sun carry any weight whatsoever outside their own bailiwicks, and there are not a dozen who rise to anything approaching unmistakable force and originality. They are, in the overwhelming main, shallow fellows, ignorant of the grave matters they deal with and too stupid to learn. If, as is often proposed, the United States should adopt the plan of parliamentary responsibility and the ministry should be recruited from the lower house, then it would be difficult, without a radical change in election methods, to fetch up even such pale talents and modest decencies as were assembled for their cabinets by Messrs. Wilson and Harding. The better sort of congressmen, to be sure, acquire after long service a good deal of technical proficiency. They know the traditions and precedents of the two houses; they can find their way in and out of every rathole in the Capitol; they may be trusted to carry on the legislative routine in a more or less shipshape manner. Of such sort are the specialists paraded in the newspapers—on the tariff, on military affairs, on foreign relations, and so on. They come to know, in time, almost as much as a Washington correspondent, or one of their own committee clerks. But the average congressman lifts himself to no such heights of sagacity. He is content to be led by the fugelmen and bellwethers. Examine him at leisure, and you will find that he is incompetent and imbecile, and not only incompetent and imbecile, but also incurably dishonest. The first principles of civilized law-making are quite beyond him; he ends, as he began, a local politician, interested only in jobs. His knowledge is that of a third-rate country lawyer—which he often is in fact. His intelligence is that of a country newspaper editor, or evangelical divine. His standards of honor are those of a country banker—which he also often is. To demand sense of such a man, or wide and accurate information, or a delicate feeling for the public and private proprieties, is to strain his parts beyond endurance.

The constitution, of course, stops with Congress, but its influence is naturally powerful within the States, and one finds proofs of the fact on all sides. It is taking an herculean effort everywhere to break down even the worst effects of this influence; the prevailing tendency is still to discover a mysterious virtue in the office-holder who was born and raised in the State, or county, or city, or ward. The judge must come from the bar of the court he is to adorn; the mayor must be part and parcel of the local machine; even technical officers, such as engineers and health commissioners, lie under the constitutional blight. The thing began as a belief in local self-government, the oldest of all the sure cures for despotism. But it has gradually taken on the character of government by local politicians, which is to say, by persons quite unable to comprehend the most elemental problems of State and nation, and unfitted by nature to deal with them honestly and patriotically, even if they could comprehend them. Just as prohibition was forced upon the civilized minorities collected in the great cities against their most vigorous and persistent opposition, so the same minorities, when it comes to intra-state affairs, are constantly at the mercy of predatory bands of rural politicians. If there is any large American city whose peculiar problems are dealt with competently and justly by its State legislature, then I must confess that twenty years in journalism have left me ignorant of it. An unending struggle for fairer dealing goes on in every State that has large cities, and every concession to their welfare is won only at the cost of gigantic effort. The State legislature is never intelligent; it represents only the average mind of the county bosses, whose sole concern is with jobs. The machines that they represent are wholly political, but they have no political principles in any rational sense. Their one purpose and function is to maintain their adherents in the public offices, or to obtain for them in some other way a share of the State funds. They are quite willing to embrace any new doctrine, however fantastic, or to abandon any old one, however long supported, if only the business will promote their trade and so secure their power.

This concentration of the ultimate governmental authority in the hands of small groups of narrow, ignorant and unconscionable manipulators tends inevitably to degrade the actual office-holder, or, what is the same thing, to make office-holding prohibitive to all men not already degraded. It is almost impossible to imagine a man of genuine self-respect and dignity offering himself as a candidate for the lower house—or, since the direct primary and direct elections brought it down to the common level, for the upper house—in the average American constituency. His necessary dealings with the electors themselves, and with the idiots who try more or less honestly to lead them, would be revolting enough, but even worse would be his need of making terms with the professional politicians of his party—the bosses of the local machine. These bosses naturally make the most of the constitutional limitation; it works powerfully in their favor. A local notable, in open revolt against them, may occasionally beat them by appealing directly to the voters, but nine times out of ten, when there is any sign of such a catastrophe, they are prompt to perfume the ticket by bringing forth another local notable who is safe and sane, which is to say, subservient and reliable. The thing is done constantly; it is a matter of routine; it accounts for most of the country bankers, newspaper owners, railroad lawyers, proprietors of cement works and other such village bigwigs in the lower house. Here everything runs to the advantage of the bosses. It is not often that the notable in rebellion is gaudy enough to blind the plain people to the high merits of his more docile opponent. They see him too closely and know him too well. He shows none of that exotic charm which accounts, on a different plane, for exogamy. There is no strangeness, no mysteriousness, above all, no novelty about him.

It is my contention that this strangle-hold of the local machines would be vastly less firm if it could be challenged, not only by rebels within the constituency, but also by salient men from outside. The presidential campaigns, indeed, offer plenty of direct proof of it. In these campaigns it is a commonplace for strange doctrines and strange men to force themselves upon the practical politicians in whole sections of the country, despite their constant effort to keep their followers faithful to the known. All changes, of whatever sort, whether in leaders or in ideas, are opposed by such politicians at the start, but time after time they are compelled to acquiesce and to hurrah. Bryan, as every one knows, forced himself upon the Democratic party by appealing directly to the people; the politicians, in the main, were bitterly against him until further resistance was seen to be useless, and they attacked him again the moment he began to weaken, and finally disposed of him. So with Wilson. It would be absurd to say that the politicians of his party—and especially the bosses of the old machines in the congressional districts—were in favor of him in 1912. They were actually against him almost unanimously. He got past their guard and broke down their resolution to nominate some more trustworthy candidate by operating directly upon the emotions of the voters. For some reason never sufficiently explained he became the heir of the spirit of rebellion raised by Bryan sixteen years before, and was given direct and very effective aid by Bryan himself. Roosevelt saddled himself upon the Republican party in exactly the same way. The bosses made heroic efforts to sidetrack him, to shelve him, to get rid of him by any means short of homicide, but his bold enterprises and picturesque personality enchanted the people, and if it had not been for the extravagant liberties that he took with his popularity in later years he might have retained it until his death.

The same possibility of unhorsing the machine politicians, I believe, exists in even the smallest electoral unit. All that is needed is the chance to bring in the man. Podunk cannot produce him herself, save by a sort of miracle. If she has actually hatched him, he is far away by the time he has come to his full stature and glitter—in the nearest big city, in Chicago or New York. Podunk is proud of him, and many other Podunks, perhaps, are stirred by his ideas, his attitudes, his fine phrases—but he lives, say, in some Manhattan congressional district which has the Hon. Patrick Googan as its representative by divine right, and so there is no way to get him into the halls of Congress. In his place goes the Hon. John P. Balderdash, State's attorney for five years, State senator for two terms, and county judge for a brief space—and always a snide and petty fellow, always on the best of terms with the local bosses, always eager for a job on any terms they lay down. The yokels vote for the Hon. Mr. Balderdash, not because they admire him, but because their only choice is between him and the Hon. James Bosh. If anything even remotely resembling a first-rate man could come into the contest, if it were lawful for them to rid themselves of their recurrent dilemma by soliciting the interest of such a man, then they would often enough rise in their might and compel their parish overlords, as the English put it, to adopt him. But the constitution protects these overlords in their business, and in the long run the voters resign all thought of deliverance. Thus the combat remains one between small men, and interest in it dies out. Most of the men who go to the lower house are third-raters, even in their own narrow bailiwicks. In my own congressional district, part of a large city, there has never been a candidate of any party, during the twenty years that I have voted, who was above the intellectual level of a corner grocer. No successful candidate of that district has ever made a speech in Congress (or out of it) worth hearing, or contributed a single sound idea otherwise to the solution of any public problem. One and all, they have confined themselves exclusively to the trade in jobs. One and all, they have been ciphers in the house and before the country.

Well, perhaps I labor my point too much. It is, after all, not important. The main thing is the simple fact that the average representative from my district is typical of Congress—that, if anything, he is superior to the normal congressman of these, our days. That normal congressman, as year chases year, tends to descend to such depths of puerility, to such abysses of petty shysterism, that he becomes offensive alike to the intelligence and to the nose. His outlook, when it is honest, is commonly childish—and it is very seldom honest. The product of a political system which puts all stress upon the rewards of public office, he is willing to make any sacrifice, of dignity, of principle, of honor, to hold and have those rewards. He has no courage, no intellectual *amour propre*, no ardent belief in anything save his job, and the jobs of his friends. It was easy for Wilson to beat him into line on the war issue; it was easy for the prohibitionists to intimidate and stampede him; it is easy for any resolute man or group of men to do likewise. I read the *Congressional Record* faithfully, and have done so for years. In the Senate debates, amid oceans of tosh, I occasionally encounter a flash of wit or a gleam of sense; direct elections have not yet done their work. But in the lower house there is seldom anything save a garrulous and intolerable imbecility. The discussion of measures of the utmost importance—bills upon which the security and prosperity of the whole nation depend—is carried on in the manner of the chautauqua and the rural stump. Entire days go by without a single congressman saying anything as intelligent, say, as the gleams that one sometimes finds in the New York *Herald*, or even in the New York *Times*. The newspapers, unfortunately, give no adequate picture of the business. No American journal reports the daily debates comprehensively, as the debates in the House of Commons are reported by the London *Times*, *Daily Telegraph*, and *Morning Post*. All one hears of, as a rule, is the action taken, and only too often the action taken, even when it is reported fairly, is unintelligible without the antecedent discussion. If any one who reads this wants to know what such a discussion is like, then I counsel him to go to the nearest public library, ask for the *Record* for 1918 and read the debate in the lower house on the Volstead Act. It was, I believe, an average debate, and on a subject of capital importance. It was, from first to last, almost fabulous in its evasion of the plain issue, its incredible timorousness and stupidity, its gross mountebankery and dishonesty. Not twenty men spoke in it as men of honor and self-respect. Not ten brought any idea into it that was not a silly idea and a stale one.

That debate deserves a great deal more study than it will ever get from the historians of American politics, nearly all of whom, whether they lean to the right or to the left, are bedazzled by the economic interpretation of history, and so seek to account for all political phenomena in terms of crop movements, wage scales and panics in Wall Street. It seems to me that that obsession blinds them to a fact of the first importance, to wit, the fact that political ideas, under a democracy as under a monarchy, originate above quite as often as they originate below, and that their popularity depends quite as much upon the special class interests of professional politicians as it depends upon the underlying economic interests of the actual voters. It is, of course, true, as I have argued, that the people can force ideas upon the politicians, given powerful leaders of a non-political (or, at all events, non-machine) sort, but it is equally true that there are serious impediments to the process, and that it is not successful very often. As a matter of everyday practise the rise and fall of political notions is determined by the self-interest of the practical politicians of the country, and though they naturally try to bring the business into harmony with any great popular movements that may be in progress spontaneously, they by no means wait and beg for mandates when none are vociferously forthcoming, but go ahead bravely on their own account, hoping to drag public opinion with them and so safeguard their jobs. Such is the origin of many affecting issues, later held dear by millions of the plain people. Such was the process whereby prohibition was foisted upon the nation by constitutional amendment, to the dismay of the solid majority opposed to it and to the surprise of the minority in favor of it.

What lay under the sudden and melodramatic success of the prohibitionist agitators was simply their discovery of the incurable cowardice and venality of the normal American politician—their shrewd abandonment of logical and evidential propaganda for direct political action. For years their cause had languished. Now and then a State or part of a State went dry, but often it went wet again a few years later. Those were the placid days of white-ribbon rallies, of wholesale pledge-signings, of lectures by converted drunkards, of orgiastic meetings in remote Baptist and Methodist churches, of a childish reliance upon arguments that fetched only drunken men and their wives, and so grew progressively feebler as the country became more sober. The thing was scarcely even a nuisance; it tended steadily to descend to the level of a joke. The prohibitionist vote for President hung around a quarter of a million; it seemed impossible to pull it up to a formidable figure, despite the stupendous labors of thousands of eloquent dervishes, lay and clerical, male and female. But then, out of nowhere, came the Anti-Saloon League, and—sis! boom! ah! Then came the sudden shift of the fire from the people to the politicians—and at once there was rapid progress. The people could only be wooed and bamboozled, but the politicians could be threatened; their hold upon their jobs could be shaken; they could be converted at wholesale and by *force majeure*. The old prohibition weepers and gurglers were quite incapable of this enterprise, but the new janissaries of the Anti-Saloon League—sharp lawyers, ecclesiastics too ambitious to pound mere pulpits, outlaw politicians seeking a way back to the trough—were experts at every trick and dodge it demanded. They understood the soul of the American politician. To him they applied the economic interpretation of history, resolutely and with a great deal of genial humor. They knew that his whole politics, his whole philosophy, his whole concept of honesty and honor, was embraced in his single and insatiable yearning for a job, and they showed him how, by playing with them, he could get it and keep it, and how, by standing against them, he could lose it. Prohibition was rammed into the constitution by conquering the politicians; the people in general were amazed when the thing was accomplished; it may take years to reconcile them to it.

It was the party system that gave the Anti-Saloon League manipulators their chance, and they took advantage of it with great boldness and cleverness. The two great parties divide the country almost equally; it is difficult to predict, in a given year, whether the one or the other musters the most votes. This division goes down into the lowest electoral units; even in those backward areas where one party has divine grace and the other is of the devil there are factional differences that amount to the same thing. In other words, the average American politician is never quite sure of his job. An election (and, if not an election, then a primary) always exposes him to a definite hazard, and he is eager to diminish it by getting help from outside his own following, at whatever cost to the principles he commonly professes. Here lies the opportunity for minorities willing to trade on a realistic political basis. In the old days the prohibitionists refused to trade, and in consequence they were disregarded, for their fidelity to their own grotesque candidates protected the candidates of both the regular parties. But with the coming of the Anti-Saloon League they abandoned this fidelity and began to dicker in a forthright and unashamed manner, quickly comprehensible to all professional politicians. That is, they asked for a pledge on one specific issue, and were willing to swallow any commitment on other issues. If Beelzebub, running on one ticket, agreed to support prohibition, and the Archangel Gabriel, running on another, found himself entertaining conscientious doubts, they were instantly and solidly for Beelzebub, and they not only gave him the votes that they directly controlled, but they also gave him the benefit of a campaign support that was ruthless, pertinacious, extraordinarily ingenious and overwhelmingly effective. Beelzebub, whatever his swinishness otherwise, was bathed in holy oils; Gabriel's name became a thing to scare children.

Obviously, the support thus offered was particularly tempting to a politician who found himself facing public suspicion for his general political practises—in brief, to the worst type of machine professional. Such a politician is always acutely aware that it is not positive merit that commonly gets a man into public office in the United States, but simply disvulnerability. Even when they come to nominate a

President, the qualities the two great parties seek are chiefly the negative ones; they want, not a candidate of forceful and immovable ideas, but one whose ideas are vague and not too tenaciously held, and in whose personality there is nothing to alarm or affront the populace. Of two candidates, that one usually wins who least arouses the distrusts and suspicions of the great masses of undifferentiated men. This advantage of the safe and sane, the colorless and unprovocative, the apparently stodgy and commonplace man extends to the most trivial contests, and politicians are keen to make use of it. Thus the job-seeker with an aura of past political misdemeanor about him was eager to get the Christian immunity bath that the prohibitionists offered him so generously, and in the first years of their fight they dealt almost exclusively with such fellows. He, on his side, promised simply to vote for prohibition—not even, in most cases, to pretend to any personal belief in it. The prohibitionists, on their side, promised to deliver the votes of their followers to him on election day, to cry him up as one saved by a shining light, and, most important of all, to denounce his opponent as an agent of hell. He was free, by this agreement, to carry on his regular political business as usual. The prohibitionists asked no patronage of him. They didn't afflict him with projects for other reforms. All they demanded was that he cast his vote as agreed upon when the signal was given to him.

At the start, of course, such scoundrels frequently violated their agreements. In the South, in particular, dry legislature after dry legislature sold out to the liquor lobby, which, in those days, still had plenty of money. An assemblyman would be elected with the aid of the prohibitionists, make a few maudlin speeches against the curse of drink, and then, at the last minute, vote wet for some thin and specious reason, or for no avowed reason at all. But the prohibition manipulators, as I have said, were excellent politicians, and so they knew how to put down that sort of treason. At the next election they transferred their favor to the opposition candidate, and inasmuch as he had seen the traitor elected at the last election he was commonly very eager to do business. The punishment for the treason was condign and merciless. The dry rabble-rousers, lay and clerical, trumpeted news of it from end to end of the constituency. What was a new and gratifying disvulnerability was transformed into a vulnerability of the worst sort; the recreant one became the county Harry Thaw, Oscar Wilde, Captain Boy-Ed, and Debs. A few such salutary examples, and treason became rare. The prohibitionists, indeed, came to prefer dealing with such victims of their reprisals. They could trust them perfectly, once the lesson had been learned; they were actually more trustworthy than honest believers, for the latter usually had ideas of their own and interfered with the official plans of campaign. Thus, in the end, the professional politicians of both parties came under the yoke. The final battle in Congress transcended all party lines; Democrats and Republicans fought alike for places on the bandwagon. The spectacle offered a searching and not unhumorous commentary on the party system, and on the honor of American politicians no less. Two-thirds, at least, of the votes for the amendment were cast by men who did not believe in it, and who cherished a hearty hope, to the last moment, that some act of God would bring about its defeat.

Such holocausts of frankness and decency are certainly not rare in American politics; on the contrary, they glow with normalcy. The typical legislative situation among us—and the typical administrative situation as well—is one in which men wholly devoid of inner integrity, facing a minority that is resolutely determined to get its will, yield up their ideas, their freedom, and their honor in order to save their jobs. I say administrative situation as well; what I mean is that in these later days the pusillanimity of the actual law-maker is fully matched by the pusillanimity of the enforcing officer, whether humble assistant district attorney or powerful judge. The war, with its obliteration of customary pretenses and loosening of fundamental forces, threw up the whole process into high relief. For nearly two long years there was a complete abandonment of sense and self-respect. Rowelled and intimidated by minorities that finally coalesced into a frantic majority, legislators allowed themselves to be forced into imbecility after imbecility, and administrative officers, including some of the highest judges in the land, followed them helter-skelter. In the lower house of Congress there was one man—already forgotten—who showed the stature of a man. He resigned his seat and went home to his self-respect. The rest had no self-respect to go home to. Eager beyond all to hold their places, at whatever cost to principle, and uneasily conscious of their vulnerability to attack, however frenzied and unjust, they surrendered abjectly and repeatedly—to the White House, to the newspapers, to any group enterprising enough to issue orders to them and resolute enough to flourish weapons before them. It was a spectacle full of indecency—there are even congressmen who blush when they think of it to-day—but it was nevertheless a spectacle that was typical. The fortunes of politics, as they now run, make it overwhelmingly probable that every new recruit to public office will be just such a poltroon. The odds are enormously in favor of him, and enormously against the man of honor. Such a man of honor may occasionally drift in, taken almost unawares by some political accident, but it is the pushing, bumptious, unconscionable bounder who is constantly *fighting* to get in, and only too often he succeeds. The rules of the game are made to fit his taste and his talents. He can survive as a hog can survive in the swill-yard.

Go to the Congressional Directory and investigate the origins and past performances of the present members of the lower house—our typical assemblage of typical politicians, the cornerstone of our whole representative system, the symbol of our democracy. You will find that well over half of them are obscure lawyers, school-teachers, and mortgage-sharks out of almost anonymous towns—men of common traditions, sordid aspirations and no attainments at all. One and all, the members of this majority—and it is constant, no matter what party is in power—

are plastered with the brass ornaments of the more brummagem fraternal orders. One and all, they are devoid of any contact with what passes for culture, even in their remote bailiwicks. One and all their careers are bare of civilizing influences. . . . Such is the American *Witenagemot*[5] in this 146th year of the Republic. Such are the men who make the laws that all of us must obey, and who carry on our dealings with the world. Go to their debates, and you will discover what equipment they bring to their high business. What they know of sound literature is what one may get out of McGuffey's Fifth Reader. What they know of political science is the nonsense preached in the chautauquas and on the stump. What they know of history is the childish stuff taught in grammar-schools. What they know of the arts and sciences — of all the great body of knowledge that is the chief intellectual baggage of modern man — is absolutely nothing.

Religion in America

1. *Evangelical Pastors*

Under Prohibition, Fundamentalism and the complex ideals of the Klan there runs a common stream of bilge: it issues from the ghostly glands of the evangelical pastors of the land. The influence of these consecrated men upon the so-called thinking of the American people has been greatly underestimated by fanciers; in fact, most of the principal professors of such forms of metabolism overlook it altogether. Yet it must be obvious that their power is immense, and that they exert it steadily and with great gusto. It was not primarily the Christian faithful of the backwoods who fastened Prohibition upon us; it was the rustic *curés* working upon the Christian faithful, whose heat, in turn, ran the State legislators amok. If the *curés*, clinging to 1 Timothy, v. 23,[6] had resolved to spare light wines and beer, we'd have them today, not behind the arras but in the full glare of rectitude. Here, as always in our moral Republic, scriptural exegesis preceded the uplift, and gave it its punch. While the agents of the brewers and distillers were fatuously bribing legislators, and paying higher and higher prices as session succeeded session, the Prohibitionists were out in the Bryan Belt organizing the country ecclesiastics. Once the latter had steam up the rest was only a matter of choosing the time. It came conveniently in the midst of war's alarms, at a moment of mystical exaltation. If history says that William H. Anderson, Wayne B. Wheeler and company turned the trick then history will err once more. It was really turned by a hundred thousand Methodist and Baptist pastors.

As I say, the doings of these gentlemen of God have been investigated but imperfectly, and so too little is known about them. Even the sources of their power, so far as I know, have not been looked into. My suspicion is that it has developed as the influence of the old-time country-town newspapers has declined. These news-papers, in large areas of the land, once genuinely molded public opinion. They at-tracted to their service a shrewd and salty class of rustic philosophers; they were outspoken in their views and responded only slightly to prevailing crazes. In the midst of the Bryan uproar, a quarter of a century ago, scores of little weeklies in the South and Middle West kept up a gallant battle for sound money and the Hanna idealism. There were red-hot Democratic papers in Pennsylvania, and others in Ohio; there were Republican sheets in rural Maryland, and even in Virginia. The growth of the big city dailies is what chiefly reduced them to puerility. As communications improved every yokel got dragged into the glittering orbits of Brisbane, Dr. Frank Crane, and Mutt and Jeff. The rural mail carrier began leaving a 24-page yellow in every second box. The hinds distrusted and detested the politics of these great or-gans, but enjoyed their imbecilities. The country weekly could not match the latter, and so it began to decline. It is now in a low state everywhere in America. Half of it is boiler-plate and the other half is cross-roads gossip. The editor is no longer the leading thinker of his dunghill; instead, he is commonly a broken and despairing man, cadging for advertisements and hoping for a third-rate political job.

His place has been taken by the village pastor. The pastor got into public affairs by the route of Prohibition. The shrewd shysters who developed the Anti-Saloon League made a politician of him, and once he had got a taste of power he was eager for more. It came very quickly. As industry penetrated the rural regions the new-blown Babbitts began to sense his capacity for safeguarding the established order, and so he was given the job: he became a local Billy Sunday. The old-line politi-cians, taught a lesson by the Anti-Saloon League, began to defer to him in general, as they had yielded to him in particular. He was consulted about candidacies; he had his say about policies. The local school-board soon became his private pre-serve. The wandering cony-catchers of the tin-pot fraternal orders found him a useful man. He was, by now, a specialist in all forms of public rectitude, from tee-totalism to patriotism. He was put up on days of ceremony to sob for the flag, vice the county judge, retired. When the Klan burst upon the peasants all of his new du-ties were synthesized. He was obviously the chief local repository of its sublime principles, theological, social, ethnological and patriotic. In every country town in America today the chief engine of the Klan is a clerk in holy orders. If the Baptists are strong, their pastor is that engine. Failing Baptists, the heroic work is assumed by the Methodist parson, or the Presbyterian, or the Campbellite.[7] Take away these sacerdotal props and the Invisible Empire would fade like that of Constantine.

II

What one mainly notices about these ambassadors of Christ, observing them in the mass, is their colossal ignorance. They constitute, perhaps, the most ignorant class of teachers ever set up to lead a civilized people; they are even more ignorant than the county superintendents of schools. Learning, indeed, is not esteemed in the evangelical denominations, and any literate plowhand, if the Holy Spirit inflames him, is thought to be fit to preach. Is he commonly sent, as a preliminary, to a training-camp, to college? But what a college! You will find one in every mountain valley of the land, with its single building in its bare pasture lot, and its faculty of half-idiot pedagogues and broken-down preachers. One man, in such a college, teaches oratory, ancient history, arithmetic and Old Testament exegesis. The aspirant comes in from the barnyard, and goes back in a year or two to the village. His body of knowledge is that of a street-car motorman or a movie actor. But he has learned the *clichés* of his craft, and he has got him a long-tailed coat, and so he has made his escape from the harsh labors of his ancestors, and is set up as a fountain of light and learning.

It is from such ignoramuses that the American peasantry gets its view of the cosmos. Certainly Fundamentalism should not be hard to understand when its sources are inspected. How can the teacher teach when his own head is empty? Of all that constitutes the sum of human knowledge he is as innocent as an Eskimo. Of the arts he knows absolutely nothing; of the sciences he has never so much as heard. No good book ever penetrates to those remote "colleges," nor does any graduate ever take away a desire to read one. He has been warned, indeed, against their blandishments; what is not addressed solely to the paramount business of saving souls is of the devil. So when he hears by chance of the battle of ideas beyond the sky-rim, he quite naturally puts it down to Beelzebub. What comes to him, vaguely and distorted, is unintelligible to him. He is suspicious of it, afraid of it—and he quickly communicates his fears to his dupes. The common man, in many ways, is hard to arouse. It is a terrific job to ram even the most elemental ideas into him. But it is always easy to scare him.

That is the daily business of the evangelical pastors of the Republic. They are specialists in alarms and bugaboos. The rum demon, atheists, Bolsheviki, the Pope, bootleggers, Leopold and Loeb[8]—all these have served them in turn, and in the demonology of the Ku Klux Klan all have been conveniently brought together. The old stock company of devils has been retired, and with it the old repertoire of sins. The American peasant of today finds it vastly easier to claw into heaven than he used to. Private holiness has now been handed over to the Holy Rollers and other such survivors from a harsher day. It is sufficient now to hate the Pope, to hate the Jews, to hate the scientists, to hate all foreigners, to hate whatever the cities yield to. These hatreds have been spread in the land by rev. pastors, chiefly Baptists and Methodists. They constitute, with their attendant fears, the basic religion of the American clod-hopper today. They are the essence of the new Christianity, American style.

III

Their public effects are constantly underestimated until it is too late. I ask no indulgence for calling attention again to the case of Prohibition. Fundamentalism, in its various forms, sneaks upon the nation in the same disarming way. The cities laugh at the yokels, but meanwhile the politicians take careful notice; such mountebanks as Peay of Tennessee and Blease of South Carolina have already issued their preliminary whoops. As the tide rolls up the pastors will attain to greater and greater consequence. Already, indeed, they swell visibly, in power and pretension. The Klan, in its early days, kept them discreetly under cover; they labored valiantly in the hold, but only lay go-getters were seen upon the bridge. But now they are everywhere on public display, leading the anthropoid host. At the great outpouring in Washington a few months ago[9]—which alarmed the absentee Dr. Coolidge so vastly that he at once gave a high Klan dignitary a federal office of trust and profit— there were Baptist mullahs all over the lot, and actually more in line, I daresay, than bootleggers or insurance solicitors.

The curious and amusing thing is that the ant-like activity of these holy men has so far got little if any attention from our established publicists. Let a lone Red arise to annoy a barroom full of Michigan lumber-jacks, and at once the fire alarm sounds and the full military and naval power of the nation is summoned to put down the outrage. But how many Americanos would the Reds convert to their rubbish, even supposing them free to spout it on every street-corner? Probably not enough, all told, to make a day's hunting for a regiment of militia. The American moron's mind simply does not run in that direction; he wants to keep his Ford, even at the cost of losing the Bill of Rights. But the stuff that the Baptist and Methodist dervishes have on tap is very much to his taste; he gulps it eagerly and rubs his tummy. I suggest that it might be well to make a scientific inquiry into the nature of it. The existing agencies of sociological snooting seem to be busy in other direction. There are elaborate surveys of some of the large cities, showing how much it costs to teach a child the principles of Americanism, how often the average citizen falls into the hands of the cops, how many detective stories are taken out of the city library daily, and how many children a normal Polish woman has every year. Why not a survey of the rustic areas, where men are he and God still reigns? Why not an attempt to find out just what the Baptist dominies have drilled into the heads of the Tennesseeans, Arkansans and Nebraskans? It would be amusing—and instructive.

And useful. For it is well, in such matters, to see clearly what is ahead. The United States grows increasingly urban, but its ideas are still hatched in the little towns. What the swineherds credit today is whooped tomorrow by their agents and attorneys in Congress, and then comes upon the cities suddenly with all the force of law. Where do the swineherds get it? Mainly from the only publicists and metaphysicians they know: the gentlemen of the sacred faculty. It was not the bawling of the mountebank Bryan, but the sermon of a mountain Bossuet that laid the train of the Scopes case and made a whole State forever ridiculous. I suggest looking more carefully into the notions that such divine ignoramuses spout.

2. Church and State

Congress shall make no law respecting an establishment of religion, or prohibiting . . . But you know the rest of the First Amendment—that is, if you are not a Methodist bishop or a Federal judge—quite as well as I do. The purport, though not the letter, of its first two strophes is that every free-born Americano shall stand clear of ecclesiastical domination, and be at liberty to serve, dodge or bamboozle Omnipotence by whatever devices appeal to his taste, or his lack of it. As the common phrase has it, church and state are separate in the Federal Union, with the province of each plainly marked out, and each forbidden to invade the province of the other. But in the common phrase, as usual, there is only wind.

The fact is that the United States, save for a short while in its infancy, while the primal infidels survived, has always diluted democracy with theocracy. Practically all our political campaigns have resolved themselves into witch-hunts by the consecrated, and all our wars have been fought to hymn tunes. It remains so to this day, despite the murrain of jazz and gin. The event of November 6[10] will be determined, not on political grounds, nor even on economic grounds, but mainly if not solely on theological grounds. The chief figures in the combat, for all the roaring of politicians in the foreground, are bishops and presbyters, and they have at their opponents with all the traditional ferocity of ambassadors of Christ. The thing to be decided by the plebiscite, as the typical American voter is taught to see it, is whether one gang of these holy men shall continue to run the country, or whether they shall be unhorsed and another gang put in their place.

All this, it appears, is deplored by the judicious. There are many demands that the chief sacerdotal whoopers lie down and be still. Even in the Hookworm Belt, where skeptics are as rare as monogamists on Long Island, the Baptist pastors are being urged to abate their fury, and consider the nigger question and the Beatitudes. And on the other side, unless circumstantial evidence is worthless, there is a powerful effort to hold hot-blooded young priests in check, and so prevent them making a bad situation worse. But why should it be considered bad? What is the objection to religious men taking religion seriously? I can find none in the books. Why should they not prefer, when a free choice is before them, to be governed by men holding to their own peculiar comforts and certainties, and doomed to sweat with them forever in the same Hell?

Is it a trivial matter? An irrelevant matter? Surely not to true believers. Surely not to earnest Christians. Myself completely neutral in theology, and long ago resigned to damnation, I can afford to treat it with easy philosophy. I'd as lief vote for a Catholic as for a Presbyterian; I'd as lief vote for a Quaker as for an Episcopalian—though Quakers, I confess, are almost too much for me: it takes nine Jews, six Armenians or two Greeks to undo one. I'd call it a red-letter day if the chance ever offered to vote for a Moslem, a Holy Roller, a Spiritualist, or a worm-feed, caterpiller-tread, chigger-proof, poppet-valved Lutheran of the Missouri Synod. Even my objection to Baptists is not theological. They have John the Baptist on their side when they duck their customers: the thing I object to is their doctrine that what is good enough to purge the soul is good enough to drink. (What a sect they would be if they abandoned creeks and cow-ponds and set up vats of Pilsner!) But though I am thus happily neutral and lost, it seems to me to be quite clear that the average American remains a partisan. The theological inclinations of his forebears linger in him, though they may be buried in his unconscious. He distrusts all revelations save one. Even when, debauched by reading Tom Paine, Ingersoll and Haldeman-Julius, he comes out boldly for evolution and boasts that his grandfather was a chimpanzee, it is with reservations. Hating all the warring sects, he always hates one of them more than the rest. And to the extent of that superior hatred he remains a faithful and orthodox Christian.

Four Americans out of every five fall under this heading—perhaps even nine out of ten. The proof of it lies in the fact that every American community, large or small, continues to have its local *shaman*, admired, deferred to and revered. His pronunciamentoes are heard with grave respect. The town newspapers treat him politely. He is to the fore in all public orgies. His moral ideas, though they may be challenged, prevail. In the South he is the Baptist parson; in the Middle West he is the Methodist or some other. Coming to big towns, he is commonly a bishop, and hence able to bind and loose. Nowhere in this great land is he missing. Do I forget such Babylons as New York? Specifically, I include New York. Where else (save maybe in Boston) do all the high dignitaries of the local government drop to their knees to kiss an archepiscopal ring?

II

Thus it must be plain that the United States remains a realm of faith, and that religious questions belong properly to its public life. If they are discussed hotly, then it is only proof that Americans hold them to be important. If they smother and shut off the discussion of other questions, then it only shows that no other question is so well worth discussing.

I can see no possible objection to estimating a man by his religion, or by his lack of it. We all do it every day, and experience supports the soundness of the test. There is in all Jews, despite a great play of variation, a common quality, universally recognized. There is a like common quality in all Catholics, in all Presbyterians, in all Methodists and Baptists, in all Lutherans, and in all skeptics. Relying upon its existence, we are seldom disappointed. It would be as shocking for a Catholic to react like a Methodist as it would be for a Jew to react like a Holy Roller. When, as happens rarely, God sends the marvel, it always draws a full house. I point to the case of my old friend, Col. Patrick H. Callahan, of Louisville, Ky., a Catholic Prohibitionist, *i.e.*, a Catholic with a Methodist liver. More than once, encountering him in palaver with his fellow drys, I have observed their uneasiness. They welcome his support, and that of his 234 followers, but they feel that there is something unnatural, and hence something a bit sinister about it. They half expect him to produce a bowie knife and begin slitting their throats in the name of the Pope. If, suddenly turning Methodist altogether, he were to loose a hallelujah, nine-tenths of them would run.

The religious label, in truth, tells more about a given man than any other label, and what it tells is more apposite and momentous. All the other classifications that the art of politics attempts are artificial and unsound. The difference between honest politicians and those who have been caught is no more than a difference in bookkeping. Plutocrats and proletarians are brothers, pursuing with equal frenzy the same dollar. Even the gap separating city men from yokels is easily bridged, at least in one direction: half the bootleggers of New York, like half the bank presidents, were born on farms. But it takes a tremendous rubbing to get the theological label off, and even then its mark remains. Convert a High Church Episcopalian to baptism by total immersion, and he still revolts queasily against going into the tank with his fellow Baptists. Turn a Jew into an Episcopalian, and he becomes five times as Jewish as he was before. Make a Catholic of a Methodist, and he has a dreadful time keeping quiet at mass.

These differences ought to be acknowledged, taken account of, and even encouraged, not denied and concealed. They help to make life various and amusing. If Al and Lord Hoover were both sound Presbyterians, the present campaign would be as dull and witless as a love affair between a deaf girl and a blind man. It is their irreconcilable differentiation that now makes the Republic roar, and entertains a candid world. For religious disparities and enmities, being real, cannot be disposed of by weasel words. They crash through the thickest ramparts of politeness, and set off lovely sky-rockets. They have caused all the bloodiest wars of the past, and, properly encouraged in America, they will make for bigger and better campaigns. I protest formally against every effort to dispose of them.

III

Even those idealists who conscientiously deplore them—and for such opponents I have all due respect, as I have for psychic researchers, theosophists and believers in international peace—even sincere lamenters of the current fuming and fury must admit that the combat between the Ku Klux clergy and Holy Church may well achieve some salubrious effects. Each side indulges in arguments that have a pleasing persuasiveness to neutrals. On the one hand the Baptist and Methodist brethren seek to prove that a church pretending to secular authority is dangerous to free government; on the other hand the spokesmen of Holy Church argue that intolerance is a villainous pox, and discreditable to civilized man.

I can only say that I hope both sides prevail, up to and including the hilt. If they convince everybody, then there will be an uprising the next time a Catholic archbishop orders the police to put down birth-controllers, and another and greater uprising the next time a Methodist bishop attempts to blackjack a State Legislature. The antagonists argue well, and especially the Ku Kluxers. Their proofs that it would be impolitic to let the College of Cardinals run the United States are logically unanswerable. But the more they prove their case against the College of Cardinals, the more they raise up doubts about the Anti-Saloon League, the Methodist Board of Temperance, Prohibition and Public Morals, and all the other bands of prehensile theologians who now impose their superstitions upon the rest of us.

Thus good may flow out of what is deplored as evil. I insist, however, that it is really good. In a country so hag-ridden by fraud and bombast as this one, *anything* is good that makes for an honest and unfettered exchange of opinion. Men are surely not at their worst when they say what they actually think, even when it is shocking to their neighbors. Our basic trouble in the United States is that nearly all our public discussion is carried on in terms of humbug, and by professional hypocrites. The typical American statesman for a decade past has been a Prohibitionist with a red nose. Certainly it can do no harm to go behind that obscene imposture to the fundamental realities, and trot them out for an airing. So I rejoice to see men deciding against Al on the frank ground that he is a Catholic, and I rejoice even more to see other men preparing to vote for him on the frank ground that they are tired of being ruled by a rabble of Baptist and Methodist witch-burners.

3. *The American Religion*

As every schoolboy knows, the course of biological evolution is marked by a steady increase of functional differentiation among the cells. In the lowest organisms, though they may consist of immense aggregations of cells, all are substantially alike, and if one could hear one of them speak one would hear all of them. But in the highest organisms there are wide differences, and in man they are not only wide but also very numerous. How many separate and distinct kinds of cells make up the human body I don't know, and neither does anyone else, but certainly it must be many thousands. In the liver alone there are hundreds, each as unlike its fellows as a Congressman is unlike a holy Christian martyr. The neurons which make up the nerves are so different from the cells which float in the blood plasm that it is hard to believe that they descend from a single zygote. Nor is it easy to think of the cells of the *lens crystallina* and those of a wart as the offspring of the same fertilized ovum. Here nature pants and sweats for specialization, and very often it is carried to astonishing lengths.

So in the social organism. Human society simply repeats the history of the living creature. It begins with all individuals acting pretty much alike. There are males and females, but that is about all. Every man practises all the arts that any man knows, and every woman can do what all her sisters do. But as culture develops so does differentiation. There come to be kings and subjects, philosophers and laborers, traders and artists, farmers and priests, doctors and lawyers, and so on almost *ad infinitum.* In the most advanced societies such differences are as wide and dramatic as those between the different classes of cells in the body. If there is any likeness between, say, a Huxley on the one hand and a Mississippi Baptist on the other, it is a likeness mainly of gross anatomy; functionally, and especially psychologically, they differ almost as much as a whale and a June-bug. Not only is the Baptist incapable of doing any of the things that make a Huxley what he is; he is also incapable of imagining Huxley doing them, just as a June-bug is incapable of imagining a whale swallowing Jonah.

But neither in the physical organism or in the social organism does this specialization go unchallenged. Now and then, in a human body otherwise apparently healthy, certain lowly varieties of cells run amuck and begin assaulting their betters: their aim is to bring the whole body down to their own vulgar and incompetent level. The result is what is called a cancer. In the social organism the parallel phenomenon is called democracy. The aim of democracy is to destroy if possible, and if not, then to make ineffective, the genetic differences between man and man. It begins in the political domain—by setting up the doctrine that one man's opinion about the common affairs of all is as good as any other man's—but it always tries to extend itself to other and higher domains. In a democratic society it is more hazardous than elsewhere to show any oddity in conduct or opinion. Whoever differs from the general is held to be inferior, though it may be obvious, by any rational standard, that he is really superior. People who live under democracy tend to wear the same kind of hats, to eat the same food, to laugh at the same jokes, and to admire the same mountebanks. They become, as the phrase has it, standardized. Their laws lay heavy penalties on any man whose taste in reading, in drinking or in any other private avocation differs from that of his neighbors. Life tends to be regimented and unpleasant, and everyone is more or less uneasy.

In the United States, where democracy has gone further than anywhere else, this levelling tendency is frequently remarked. There was a time, for example, when the Americans spent a lot of time debating political theories, and developed a great many new ones, but of late they are so much of the same mind that the difference between the two chief parties is scarcely discernible. A Democrat in Georgia believes precisely what a Republican in Kansas believes; if they continue to vote against one another it is only because they are too stupid to notice their complete agreement. And as in politics, so in every every other field of thought and action. There is no longer any substantial difference between man and man. All decent Americans believe that it is better to boost than to knock, that the radio is a wonderful invention, that all communists come from Russia and ought to be sent back there, that the public schools do a great work, and that the best cure for anything that happens to ail one is a dose of aspirin. On all such matters there is a steady approach to unanimity. It becomes a grave indecorum to question anything that is generally believed.

Of late this movement has begun to show itself even in the field of religion, where for centuries past there has been nothing but quarrel and turmoil. Theoretically, to be sure, the old animosity between sect and sect is still alive, and now and then, as in the national campaign of 1928, it takes on a melodramatic reality; nevertheless, I believe that it is slowly dying, and that in another century or so it will be pretty well forgotten. Not only will the various varieties of Protestants then lie down together in relative amity; there will also be a truce between the Protestants as a whole and the Catholics. The result, I believe, will be a common American religion, based mainly upon Wesleyan ideas but borrowing a great deal from Latin practises. Two influences will bring it in. On the one hand the Protestants of the land, as they gradually grow civilized, will tire of the vulgarity of evangelism and turn to something more dignified and self-respecting. And on the other hand, the Catholics will tire of their allegiance to Rome, and set up shop on their own, as the faithful of the Near East did in the year 1054, and as the French came near doing toward the close of the Seventeenth Century. Once these revolutions are permitted by God, actual union will become possible.

The learned ex-Jesuit, Dr. E. Boyd Barrett, believes that the Catholics of the United States are already drifting away from Rome, though most of them are probably still unaware of it. He points out that the Roman theory of government and the American theory are hopelessly at odds, and that American Catholics are outraged in some of their dearest beliefs every time the former is stated, say in one of the recurrent papal encyclicals. The contention scarcely needs argument. During the Smith-Hoover combat various Catholic theologians tried to reconcile the two theories, but they never got far enough to make even Al himself understand them. The obvious fact is that the American theory is incurably repugnant to Rome, and that on some near tomorrow it may be categorically condemned. When that time comes the way will be open for a new schism.

But there is something more. A good many American Catholics, even now, may be unpleasantly conscious of the conflict in this department, and eager to throw off Rome, but such a wish is surely not common in the American hierarchy. Its members are faithful to Rome, and they will probably remain faithful to the last ditch. Nevertheless, they also, at least by residence, are Americans, and if they do not succumb to the American theory of government, they plainly succumb to a multitude of other American notions. There was a time when, if a bishop spoke, one could tell at once from what he said whether he was a Catholic or a Protestant. But that time is no more. With one cardinal archbishop damning Einstein as a corruptor of youth and another entering into an alliance with the Methodists and Presbyterians to drive all ideas out of the theater, it becomes increasingly difficult to mark the point where John Wesley ceases to be a heretic and becomes a saint.

This Methodization of Holy Church in the Republic has gone a good deal further than most people seem to think. It has, within the space of two generations, changed the whole character of the Roman hierarchy. Once it was made up chiefly of pious and courtly souls of the general character of Cardinal Gibbons, but today it is full of go-getters who are almost indistinguishable from their Wesleyan brethren. They carry on the enterprises of the church by mass production methods, and do not hesitate to bulge out into secular affairs. One hears from them increasingly in the halls of legislation, and many of them cherish schemes to improve and save non-Catholics at wholesale and even by force. It is, I think, a significant change, and I can only ascribe it to the effects of living in a Methodist land and breathing evangelical air. Many of these right rev. brethren, no doubt, are quite unaware of their own transformation, but there it is all the same.

But if they thus yield to the Wesleyan heretics, then the Wesleyan heretics respond by a mad shinning up the slopes of Canossa. Here, again, what is going on is too little observed. With Bishop Cannon constantly in the limelight, such men as Bishop O'Connell are overlooked. But even Bishop Cannon offers plenty of evidence of the change going on. On the one hand, he has not held a revival for years, and on the other hand he has boldly proposed a revision of the traditional Methodist code of ethics. Sitting in Washington, with one eye on the White House and the other on Capitol Hill, he moves further and further from the circuit rider of yesterday and more and more toward the Roman cardinal. Nor is he alone in that progress, nor is it confined to such novelties as he himself has introduced. Even more significant is the abandonment of conversion by orgy among Methodists generally, and the increasing popularity of ritual. There was a time when a Methodist service was almost indistinguishable from an auction sale, but today 16,000 of the brethren in holy orders pine publicly for the Book of Common Prayer as it was revised by Wesley in 1784, and in many of their tabernacles they go through ceremonies almost as stately as a hanging, and some of them have even taken to burning candles.

As a neutral in theology, I express no formal opinion about these changes. Naturally enough, I incline toward those which make for decorum rather than for those which make for unpleasantness, and so, if I took a side, it would probably be what now seems to be the Wesleyan side. But fortunately there is no need to do so, for the process cannot be influenced by either praise or blame. It is a function of the general standardization now going on in the United States. Fifty years ago, or even thirty years ago, anyone who predicted that Democrats and Republicans would ever be brought together on a common plarform would have been set down a lunatic, but the thing has actually happened, and the country seems little the worse for it. It will take longer to bring on amity among Christians, for it is God's will that they should hate one another with a blistering and implacable hatred. Nevertheless, that will may be changed at any time, and, as I have tried to set forth, I suspect that it is being changed even now. Children born today may see the beginnings of a genuine state church in the Republic, with a hierarchy of live wires and a purely American theology. I regret that I am too old to wait for it, for if it comes it will be a lulu.

The Burden of Credulity

The Negroes of the United States, taking one with another, probably constitute the poorest racial group in the country. Even the Indians, despite expropriation and oppression, show a higher average wealth, for not a few of them, in late years, have got rich from oil lands, and white philanthropists have not yet managed to pick them clean. Maybe the Mexicans are as poor as the Negroes, but I doubt it. Many of them have worked their way into high positions, both private and public. There is prejudice against them so long as they are in poverty, but as soon as they get money they may aspire to anything. But the overwhelming majority of Negroes are still doomed to dull and profitless toil. Not many of them do well in business, and even fewer succeed in the professions. A really successful Negro lawyer, physician, banker, engineer or man of science is still a sort of miracle. Nor are Negro artists much better off. The more meretricious sort often make money, but not the good ones. I can think of no Negro painter or writer who makes $10,000 a year. A few musicians perhaps—but that is about all.

Part of this lack of success is due, plainly enough, to the prejudice of the dominant white. He still thinks of the Negro as congenitally inferior, and is thus loath to employ him in situations calling for unusual skill. Not many white men, even in New England, go to Negro doctors when they are ill, or seek the advice of Negro lawyers when they are in trouble, or engage Negro teachers to teach their children. Even when a Negro does manifestly superior work there is a disposition to decry it. Every time I print an article by a Negro in *The American Mercury* certain readers send me word that it is bad, and ought not to have been printed. Similarly, when I sat lately to a Negro portrait painter, a number of friends assured me that the painting would be a botch, though they had not seen it and did not know the artist. Along with this hostility, of course, there goes, at least in certain quarters, a disposition to excessive friendliness. It is enough to give the Negro writer or painter his chance, but it is seldom enough to make him really secure. The common run of whites do not share it. They suspect everything that is black, whether it be free verse or pathology.

This burden is matched by another: there is little apparent tendency among Negroes themselves to support and encourage their genuinely salient men. Normally, they seem to follow only two kinds of leaders: those who try to make them satisfactory to white people and those who try to make monkeys of them. In the former class (along with many palpable frauds), are a number of honest men, and some of them are my friends. But I believe they are all on the wrong track. No matter how much Negroes come to be like white men, they will still be Negroes, and white men will continue to notice the fact. Perhaps the problem thus presented is intrinsically insoluble. I do not pretend to answer. But I am sure that very little is accomplished for the race by following leaders who associate so much with whites that they have come to think white themselves. Once they got social equality for all Negroes of their own class, as they have got it for themselves, they would apparently be content. But great races are never satisfied with equality. What they always try to demonstrate is superiority.

That Negroes, in more than one way, are superior to most American whites is something that I have long believed. I pass over their gift for music (which is largely imaginary) and their greater dignity (which Dr. Eleanor R. Wembridge has described more eloquently than I could do it), and point to their better behavior as members of our common society. Are they, on the lower levels, somewhat turbulent and inclined to petty crime? Perhaps. But that crime is seldom anti-social. It gets a lot of advertising when it is, but that is not often. Professional criminals are rare among Negroes, and, what is more important, professional reformers are still rarer. The horrible appetite of the low-caste Anglo-Saxon to police and harass his fellow-men is practically non-existent among them. No one ever hears of Negro wowsers inventing new categories of crime, and proposing to jail thousands of their own people for committing them. Negro Prohibitionists are almost as rare as Catholic Prohibitionists. No Negro has ever got a name by pretending to be more virtuous than the rest of us. In brief, the race is marked by extraordinary decency. Even the hog-wallow Christianity that it commonly patronizes has not sufficed to degrade it to the cannibalistic level of the white cracker.

I wish I could add that this Christianity is otherwise worthy of a self-respecting people, but I fear that I cannot. As a matter of fact, it is extraordinarily stupid, ignorant, barbaric and preposterous. Almost I am tempted to add that it is down-right simian. Borrowed at the start from the lowest class of Southern whites, it has been so further debased by moron Negro theologians that, on its nether levels, it is now a disgrace to the human race. These theologians constitute a body of bold and insatiable parasites, and getting rid of them is a problem that will daunt all save the bravest of the future leaders of black America. They fill their victims with ideas fit only for the jungle, and for that office they take a toll that is cruel and debilitating. What it amounts to annually I don't know, but it undoubtedly makes up the heaviest expenditure of the Negro people. All they get for it is continued subjugation to the superstitions of the slave quarters. They are kept in a bondage to credulity and fear that is ten times as degrading as any political bondage could ever be.

Some time ago an eminent Baptist ecclesiastic was boasting that, among all the Negro Baptists in America, there was not one who was not a Fundamentalist. I daresay that the Methodists might plausibly echo that boast. It is a shameful thing to say of any people who aspire to advance in the world. Fundamentalism is not a body of doctrine that rational men may take or leave; it is a body of doctrine for ignoramuses exclusively; it is the negation of every intellectual decency. To spread it among simple folk is as immoral as it would be to teach them that a horse-hair put into a bottle will turn into a snake. It may be that many of the black racketeers who preach it believe in it themselves. If so, that only proves that they should be chased out of their pulpits as public nuisances, and put to useful work.

I see no reason why Negroes should be such heavy patrons of these dunghill varieties of Christianity. If their nature demands the consolations of religion, then there is plenty of room for them on more decorous levels. In Baltimore my friend, Dr. George F. Bragg, Jr., shepherds a flock of Episcopalians: they are intelligent and civilized people, and he himself is respected as a scholar and as a man. There are in the same town many Negro Catholics—quiet, devoted, self-respecting men and women, to whom a Methodist revival would be as horrifying as it would be to the president of Harvard. But four-fifths of the more pious Negroes of Baltimore are still under the hooves of evangelical theologians, and it is these gentry who get their hard-earned money and keep them dumb and hopeless. Within half a mile of my home in the town there are dozens of grotesque chapels, each radiating anthropoid superstitions, each supporting an oily go-getter, and each pumping dollars out of poor people. Further on are huge churches almost without number—most of them foisted on the ignorant by whites eager to clear out, and each with its mortgage. Meanwhile, the 150,000 Negroes of Baltimore are unable to support their one small hospital, and when they are ill most of them have to turn to the whites.

The curse of this barnyard theology lies over the whole of America. It is responsible for the worst corruptions of our politics, and the generally uneasy and uncomfortable tone of American life. It gave us Prohibition. It put Hoover into the

White House. In the South it is solidly behind Ku Kluxery, and is hence mainly to blame for the exploitation and ill-usage of the Negro. Yet there are so-called Negro leaders who argue gravely that it is a boon to their own people—that there is something mysteriously refining and uplifting about it—in other words, that it is a merit to keep Negroes ignorant. I only hope that this appalling doctrine finds no customers among the young Negroes who now pour out of the colleges, eager to find some way to help their own. If they come out Methodists and Baptists, then the situation of the Negro in America is indeed hopeless. But if they emerge with some share of sound knowledge and a decent respect for their own minds, then they will apply themselves to combatting this last and worst vestige of slavery. There can be no real and general progress in the race until it is disposed of. So long as Negroes believe in rubbish they will never get beyond the level of the Southern poor whites. In other words, they will never get beyond the level of the most ignorant and degraded white men now known on earth.

Notes on Negro Strategy

Of all the peoples in captivity in the United States it seems to me that the Negroes are the frankest in discussing their own situation. Reading the magazines and newspapers of the race, I am constantly amazed (and I may add, delighted) by the candor with which such men as Dr. Kelly Miller and George S. Schuyler discourse on Negro weaknesses and Negro illusions. Certainly nothing of the sort is visible in any other quarter. One seldom finds an article against a Jew in a Jewish paper, and never a word against Jews in general. Anti-Semitism, as it is depicted therein, is a purely satanic phenomenon, without the faintest color of excuse in Jewish torts. The Irish, when they contemplate themselves, are just as cocksure and humorless, and so are the Germans, the Italians, the Poles, the Swedes and the rest. But the dark brethren, though they have their romantics too, also have a band of realists, and these realists are surely not given to weasel words.

At one point, however, their libido for the bald and blistering fact seems to slacken a bit, and they join the romantics in embracing a theory that is probably far from sound. This is the theory that the Negro, under the American system of government, has certain inalienable rights, both political and social, and that when he is deprived of them by wicked men he can get them back by making an uproar. On what does he ground his confidence here? On a reading, I suppose, of the Bill of Rights, and of its three supplements, the Thirteenth, Fourteenth and Fifteenth Amendments. But what is this sonorous charter of liberties really worth? It is worth to the Negro precisely what it is worth to the American white man. That is to say, it is worth whatever courts and legislatures choose to make it from time to time. And what they choose to make it is no more and no less than what the consensus of opinion—not of enlightened opinion, mind you, but of general opinion, of mass opinion, of mob opinion—wants to see it made.

They may go counter to this mass opinion on occasion, but it is only by a kind of inadvertence; taking one day with another they heed it very sedulously. In fact, they seldom move at all until it has made itself known, and then they commonly move with great alacrity, leaping over every impediment, whether in the Bill of Rights or in common decency, with the lightness of a gazelle. Thus it must always be vain, in the long run, to ask them to protect any rights that are denied by the popular will. The Constitution, in theory, would give them support if they stood fast for those rights, but they are realists not theorists, and as realists they are well aware that the Constitution, at any given moment and as a practical matter, is no more than what the majority conceives it to be and wants it to be.

That the majority will has been running against rights in late years is a notorious fact. It is so all over Europe, from the North Cape to the Bosphorus, and it is only too plainly so in the United States. There is a kind of revulsion against liberty everywhere, and against everything that goes with it. Now and then it may recover some lost ground or make a trifling gain, but the general movement is overwhelmingly in the other direction. In every country the people are losing rights that they had yesterday, and in most countries they are losing them willingly. The chief heroes everywhere are persons who have discovered new forms of subjugation, and in many cases what they ordain to loud applause is hard to distinguish from downright slavery.

In the face of this tendency the American Negro is certainly not likely, at least in the near future, to realize the dreams of those who propose with so much confidence to deliver him. Even if his rights could be recovered by a purely legal process, disregarding the popular will, they could not be enjoyed against the popular will. And the popular will, only too manifestly, is opposed to granting them. The general feeling in the country, unless I misjudge it sadly, is that the Negro has gone far enough, that he already has as much as he deserves, and should be content for a while. But whether I am right or wrong here, it is surely plain enough that the public mood is against granting any more rights to anyone, whether deserved or not. There is some crying up of new privileges, but none of new rights. The majority of the American people are hunting for cover, not for freedom.

Well, what is to be done about it? It may be, for all I know, that nothing can be done about it. Many people seem to believe, as a cardinal article of faith, that what *ought* to be cured *can* be cured, but I have never been able to find any evidence of it in history. Some of the most pressing of human problems remain as far from solution today as they were in the days of Hammurabi. The problem of sex is an obvious example. How are we to reconcile the impulses let loose in every human being at puberty with the restraints necessary to an orderly society? There have been ten thousand answers, but not one has really answered. Nor has there ever been a satisfactory solution of the problem of government. Some governments, of course, are better than others, but every one is almost intolerably bad at bottom, and not all the wiseacres the world has seen in forty centuries have been able to devise a good one.

Thus it may well be that the problem facing the American Negro is insoluble too. In tackling it he has his choice of following dreamers of a gaudy fancy or realists with serpents' tongues, but perhaps they are alike impotent in the premises. It is possible that he may have to get whatever consolation he can out of the idea that lost rights, like unrequited love, have their high psychical uses. Indeed, it would not be hard to argue that the Negro, if he had gained full and real equality in 1865, might have gone a great deal less further along the road than he has got today, tripped and haltered at every step. He might have sunk into the complacency of a stupid and half-forgotten peasantry: It is oppression that has brought out his best qualities, and bred his most intelligent leaders. The Jews, who have always had grievances a-plenty, have nevertheless managed to do pretty well in the world, taking one country with another, and not a few of their philosophers believe that they do worst where their rights are largest. The meaning of complete equality, to a minority race, is only too often annihilation.

Here it may be well to remember that it is only a little while, as history goes, that such minorities have had any rights at all, and that their rights are nowhere unqualified, even today. When the League of Nations was formed after the war an effort was made to define and secure them, but that effort, as everyone knows, has failed. The Jew, once persecuted more barbarously in Russia than the Negro has ever been persecuted anywhere, has made himself safe there by acquiring a large share in the control of the state, and in England and France he has achieved the same end by throwing off much of his racial character and submitting to a high degree of assimilation. But he may lose his hegemony in Russia at any moment and find himself precisely where he was under the Czars, and late events in Germany prove that even a high degree of assimilation, so long as it falls short of complete obliteration, is not enough in itself to safeguard a minority.

For all these reasons I find myself full of doubt that the American Negro will recover his constitutional rights on any near tomorrow. His politicians promise him that he will, but they are only politicians. Some of his white friends tell him the same, but they have fooled him in the past. My private hope is that he will get them all soon or late, for the only future I can endure to think of is one in which no man will lack what he reasonably wants, and can show that he deserves. But before any such Utopia dawns there must be a considerable change in the thinking of the human race. It must cease believing in quacks, and transfer its confidence to facts. Above all, it must pump up more courage than it has now, for freedom is impossible without it. In order to be really free men must be ready and able to face the universe. Today most of them tremble in fear, and ask only to be herded into some safe pen.

Is the change I imagine possible? Perhaps. But it will take a long while. What can be done now? Much can be done. The Negro, like the rest of us, has his choice and his chance. If he floats with the prevailing tide such rights as he still has will follow those that he has already lost, and he will end with none at all. But if he throws himself wholeheartedly into the battle for the recovery of liberties in general, then he will be in a fair way, soon or late, to get back those rights that he craves and esteems especially. It is impossible to separate the one group from the other. They rise or fall together.

four

American Art, Literature, and Culture

Puritanism as a Literary Force

I

"Calvinism," says Dr. Leon Kellner, in his excellent little history of American literature,[1] "is the natural theology of the disinherited; it never flourished, therefore, anywhere as it did in the barren hills of Scotland and in the wilds of North America." The learned doctor is here speaking of theology in what may be called its narrow technical sense—that is, as a theory of God. Under Calvinism, in the New World as well as the Old, it became no more than a luxuriant demonology; even God himself was transformed into a superior sort of devil, ever wary and wholly merciless. That primitive demonology still survives in the barbaric doctrines of the Methodists and Baptists, particularly in the South; but it has been ameliorated, even there, by a growing sense of the divine grace, and so the old God of Plymouth Rock, as practically conceived, is now scarcely worse than the average jail warden or Italian padrone. On the ethical side, however, Calvinism is dying a much harder death, and we are still a long way from the enlightenment. Save where Continental influences have measurably corrupted the Puritan idea—e.g., in such cities as New York, St. Louis and New Orleans,—the prevailing American view of the world and its mysteries is still a purely moral one, and no other human concern gets half the attention that is endlessly lavished upon the problem of conduct, particularly of the other fellow. It needed no announcement of a President of the United States to define the function and office of the republic as that of an international expert in morals, and the mentor and exemplar of the less righteous nations. Within, as

147

well as without, the eternal rapping of knuckles and proclaiming of new austerities goes on. The American, save in moments of conscious and swiftly lamented deviltry, casts up all ponderable values, including even the values of beauty, in terms of right and wrong. He is, beyond all things else, a judge and a policeman; he believes firmly that there is a mysterious power in law; he supports and embellishes its operation with a fanatical vigilance.

Naturally enough, this moral obsession has given a strong color to American literature. In truth, it has colored it so brilliantly that American literature is set off sharply from all other literatures. In none other will you find so wholesale and ecstatic a sacrifice of æsthetic ideas, of all the fine gusto of passion and beauty, to notions of what is meet, proper and nice. From the books of grisly sermons that were the first American contribution to letters down to that amazing literature of "inspiration" which now flowers so prodigiously, with two literary ex-Presidents among its chief virtuosi,[2] one observes no relaxation of the moral pressure. In the history of every other literature there have been periods of what might be called moral innocence—periods in which a naïve *joie de vivre* has broken through all concepts of duty and responsibility, and the wonder and glory of the universe have been hymned with unashamed zest. The age of Shakespeare comes to mind at once: the violence of the Puritan reaction offers a measure of the pendulum's wild swing. But in America no such general rising of the blood has ever been seen. The literature of the nation, even the literature of the enlightened minority, has been under harsh Puritan restraints from the beginning, and despite a few stealthy efforts at revolt— usually quite without artistic value or even common honesty, as in the case of the cheap fiction magazines and that of smutty plays on Broadway, and always very short-lived—it shows not the slightest sign of emancipating itself today. The American, try as he will, can never imagine any work of the imagination as wholly devoid of moral content. It must either tend toward the promotion of virtue, or be suspect and abominable.

If any doubt of this is in your mind, turn to the critical articles in the newspapers and literary weeklies; you will encounter enough proofs in a month's explorations to convince you forever. A novel or a play is judged among us, not by its dignity of conception, its artistic honesty, its perfection of workmanship, but almost entirely by its orthodoxy of doctrine, its platitudinousness, its usefulness as a moral tract. A digest of the reviews of such a book as David Graham Phillips' *Susan Lenox* or such a play as Ibsen's *Hedda Gabler* would make astounding reading for a Continental European. Not only the childish incompetents who write for the daily press, but also most of our critics of experience and reputation, seem quite unable to estimate a piece of writing as a piece of writing, a work of art as a work of art; they almost inevitably drag in irrelevant gabble as to whether this or that personage in it is respectable, or this or that situation in accordance with the national notions of what is edifying and nice. Fully nine-tenths of the reviews of Dreiser's *The Titan*, without question the best American novel of its year, were devoted chiefly to indignant denunciations of the morals of Frank Cowperwood, its central character. That the man was superbly imagined and magnificently depicted, that he stood out from the book in all the flashing vigor of life, that his creation was an artistic achievement of a very high and difficult order—these facts seem to have made no impression upon the reviewers whatever. They were Puritans writing for Puritans, and all they could see in Cowperwood was an anti-Puritan, and in his creator another. It will remain for Europeans, I daresay, to discover the true stature of *The Titan*, as it remained for Europeans to discover the true stature of *Sister Carrie*.

Just how deeply this corrective knife has cut you may find plainly displayed in Dr. Kellner's little book. He sees the throttling influence of an ever alert and bellicose Puritanism, not only in our grand literature, but also in our petit literature, our minor poetry, even in our humor. The Puritan's utter lack of æsthetic sense, his distrust of all romantic emotion, his unmatchable intolerance of opposition, his unbreakable belief in his own bleak and narrow views, his savage cruelty of attack, his lust for relentless and barbarous persecution—these things have put an almost unbearable burden upon the exchange of ideas in the United States, and particularly upon that form of it which involves playing with them for the mere game's sake. On the one hand, the writer who would deal seriously and honestly with the larger problems of life, particularly in the rigidly-partitioned ethical field, is restrained by laws that would have kept a Balzac or a Zola in prison from year's end to year's end; and on the other hand the writer who would proceed against the reigning superstitions by mockery has been silenced by taboos that are quite as stringent, and by an indifference that is even worse. For all our professed delight in and capacity for jocosity, we have produced so far but one genuine wit—Ambrose Bierce—and, save to a small circle, he remains unknown today. Our great humorists, including even Mark Twain, have to take protective coloration, whether willingly or unwillingly, from the prevailing ethical foliage, and so one finds them levelling their darts, not at the stupidities of the Puritan majority, but at the evidences of lessening stupidity in the anti-Puritan minority. In other words, they have done battle, not against, but *for* Philistinism—and Philistinism is no more than another name for Puritanism. Both wage a ceaseless warfare upon beauty in its every form, from painting to religious ritual, and from the drama to the dance—the first because it holds beauty to be a mean and stupid thing, and the second because it holds beauty to be distracting and corrupting.

Mark Twain, without question, was a great artist; there was in him something of that prodigality of imagination, that aloof engrossment in the human comedy, that penetrating cynicism, which one associates with the great artists of the Renaissance. But his nationality hung around his neck like a millstone; he could never throw off his native Philistinism. One plows through *The Innocents Abroad* and through parts of *A Tramp Abroad* with incredulous amazement. Is such coarse and ignorant clowning to be accepted as humor, as great humor, as the best humor that the most humorous of peoples has produced? Is it really the mark of a smart fellow to lift a peasant's cackle over *Lohengrin?* Is Titian's chromo of Moses in the bullrushes seriously to be regarded as the noblest picture in Europe? Is there nothing in Latin Christianity, after all, save petty grafting, monastic scandals and the worship of the knuckles and shin-bones of dubious saints? May not a civilized man, disbelieving in it, still find himself profoundly moved by its dazzling history, the lingering remnants of its old magnificence, the charm of its gorgeous and melancholy loveliness? In the presence of all beauty of man's creation — in brief, of what we roughly call art, whatever its form — the voice of Mark Twain was the voice of the Philistine. A literary artist of very high rank himself, with instinctive gifts that lifted him, in *Huckleberry Finn*, to kinship with Cervantes and Aristophanes, he was yet so far the victim of his nationality that he seems to have had no capacity for distinguishing between the good and the bad in the work of other men of his own craft. The literary criticism that one occasionally finds in his writings is chiefly trivial and ignorant; his private inclination appears to have been toward such romantic sentimentality as entrances school-boys; the thing that interested him in Shakespeare was not the man's colossal genius, but the absurd theory that Bacon wrote his plays.[3] Had he been born in France (the country of his chief abomination!) instead of in a Puritan village of the American hinterland, I venture that he would have conquered the world. But try as he would, being what he was, he could not get rid of the Puritan smugness and cocksureness, the Puritan distrust of new ideas, the Puritan incapacity for seeing beauty as a thing in itself, and the full peer of the true and the good.

It is, indeed, precisely in the works of such men as Mark Twain that one finds the best proofs of the Puritan influence in American letters, for it is there that it is least expected and hence most significant. Our native critics, unanimously Puritans themselves, are anæsthetic to the flavor, but to Dr. Kellner, with his half-European, half-Oriental culture, it is always distinctly perceptible. He senses it, not only in the harsh Calvinistic fables of Hawthorne and the pious gurglings of Longfellow, but also in the poetry of Bryant, the tea-party niceness of Howells, the "maiden-like reserve" of James Lane Allen, and even in the work of Joel Chandler Harris. What! A Southern Puritan? Well, why not? What could be more erroneous than the common assumption that Puritanism is exclusively a Northern, a New England, madness? The truth is that it is as thoroughly national as the kindred belief in the devil, and runs almost unobstructed from Portland to Portland and from the Lakes to the Gulf. It is in the South, indeed, and not in the North, that it takes on its most bellicose and extravagant forms. Between the upper tier of New England and the Potomac river there is not a single prohibition state — but thereafter, alas, they come in huge blocks! And behind that infinitely prosperous Puritanism there is a long and unbroken tradition. Berkeley, the last of the Cavaliers, was kicked out of power in Virginia so long ago as 1650. Lord Baltimore, the Proprietor of Maryland, was brought to terms by the Puritans of the Severn in 1657. The Scotch Covenanter, the most uncompromising and unenlightened of all Puritans, flourished in the Carolinas from the start, and in 1698, or thereabout, he was reinforced from New England.[4] In 1757 a band of Puritans invaded what is now Georgia—and Georgia has been a Puritan barbarism ever since. Even while the early (and half-mythical) Cavaliers were still in nominal control of all these Southern plantations, they clung to the sea-coast. The population that moved down the chain of the Appalachians during the latter part of the eighteenth century, and then swept over them into the Mississippi valley, was composed almost entirely of Puritans—chiefly intransigeants from New England (where Unitarianism was getting on its legs), kirk-crazy Scotch and that plupious and beauty-hating folk, the Scotch-Irish. "In the South today," said John Fiske a generation ago, "there is more Puritanism surviving than in New England." In that whole region, an area three times as large as France or Germany, there is not a single orchestra capable of playing Beethoven's C minor symphony, or a single painting worth looking at, or a single public building or monument of any genuine distinction, or a single factory devoted to the making of beautiful things, or a single poet, novelist, historian, musician, painter or sculptor whose reputation extends beyond his own country. Between the Mason and Dixon line and the mouth of the Mississippi there is but one opera-house, and that was built by a Frenchman, and is now, I believe, closed. The only domestic art this huge and opulent empire knows is in the hands of Mexican greasers; its only native music it owes to the despised negro; its only genuine poet was permitted to die up an alley like a stray dog.[5]

II

In studying the anatomy and physiology of American Puritanism, and its effects upon the national literature, one quickly discerns two main streams of influence. On the one hand, there is the influence of the original Puritans—whether of New England or of the South—, who came to the New World with a ready-made philosophy of the utmost clarity, positiveness and inclusiveness of scope, and who attained to such a position of political and intellectual leadership that they were able to force it almost unchanged upon the whole population, and to endow it with such vitality that it successfully resisted alien opposition later on. And on the other hand, one sees a complex of social and economic conditions which worked in countless irresistible ways against the rise of that dionysian spirit, that joyful acquiescence in life, that philosophy of the *Ja-sager*,[6] which offers to Puritanism, today as in times past, its chief and perhaps only effective antagonism. In other words, the American of the days since the Revolution has had Puritanism diligently pressed upon him from without, and at the same time he has led, in the main, a life that has engendered a chronic hospitality to it, or at all events to its salient principles, within.

Dr. Kellner accurately describes the process whereby the æsthetic spirit, and its concomitant spirit of joy, were squeezed out of the original New Englanders, so that no trace of it showed in their literature, or even in their lives, for a century and a half after the first settlements. "Absorption in God," he says, "seems incompatible with the presentation (*i.e.*, æsthetically) of mankind. The God of the Puritans was in this respect a jealous God who brooked no sort of creative rivalry. The inspired moments of the loftiest souls were filled with the thought of God and His designs; spiritual life was wholly dominated by solicitude regarding salvation, the hereafter, grace; how could such petty concerns as personal experience of a lyric nature, the transports or the pangs of love, find utterance? What did a lyric occurrence like the first call of the cuckoo, elsewhere so welcome, or the first sight of the snowdrop, signify compared with the last Sunday's sermon and the new interpretation of the old riddle of evil in the world? And apart from the fact that everything of a personal nature must have appeared so trivial, all the sources of secular lyric poetry were offensive and impious to Puritan theology. . . . One thing is an established fact: up to the close of the eighteenth century America had no belletristic literature."

This Puritan bedevilment by the idea of personal sin, this reign of the God-crazy, gave way in later years, as we shall see, to other and somewhat milder forms of pious enthusiasm. At the time of the Revolution, indeed, the importation of French political ideas was accompanied by an importation of French theological ideas, and such men as Franklin and Jefferson dallied with what, in those days at least, was regarded as downright atheism. Even in New England this influence made itself felt; there was a gradual letting down of Calvinism to the softness of Unitarianism, and that change was presently to flower in the vague temporizing of Transcendentalism. But as Puritanism, in the strict sense, declined in virulence and took deceptive new forms, there was a compensating growth of its brother, Philistinism, and by the first quarter of the nineteenth century, the distrust of beauty, and of the joy that is its object, was as firmly established throughout the land as it had ever been in New England. The original Puritans had at least been men of a certain education, and even of a certain austere culture. They were inordinately hostile to beauty in all its forms, but one somehow suspects that much of their hostility was due to a sense of their weakness before it, a realization of its disarming psychical pull. But the American of the new republic was of a different kidney. He was not so much hostile to beauty as devoid of any consciousness of it; he stood as unmoved before its phenomena as a savage before a table of logarithms. What he had set up on this continent, in brief, was a commonwealth of peasants and small traders, a paradise of the third-rate, and its national philosophy, almost wholly unchecked by the more sophisticated and civilized ideas of an aristocracy, was precisely the philosophy that one finds among peasants and small traders at all times and everywhere. The difference between the United States and any other nation did not lie in any essential difference between American peasants and other peasants, but simply in the fact that here, alone, the voice of the peasant was the single voice of the nation—that here, alone, the only way to eminence and public influence was the way of acquiescence in the opinions and prejudices of the stupid and Philistine mob. Jackson was the *Stammvater* of the new statesmen and philosophers; he carried the mob's distrust of good taste even into the field of conduct; he was the first to put the rewards of conformity above the dictates of common decency; he founded a whole hierarchy of Philistine messiahs, the roaring of which still belabors the ear.

Once established, this culture of the intellectually disinherited tended to defend and perpetuate itself. On the one hand, there was no appearance of a challenge from within, for the exigent problems of existence in a country that was yet but half settled and organized left its people with no energy for questioning what at least met their grosser needs, and so met the pragmatic test. And on the other hand, there was no critical pressure from without, for the English culture which alone reached over the sea was itself entering upon its Victorian decline, and the influence of the native aristocracy—the degenerating *Junkers* of the great estates and the boorish magnates of the city *bourgeoisie*—was quite without any cultural direction at all. The chief concern of the American people, even above the bread-and-butter question, was politics. They were incessantly hag-ridden by political difficulties, both internal and external, of an inordinate complexity, and these occupied all the leisure they could steal from the sordid work of everyday. More, their new and troubled political ideas tended to absorb all the rancorous certainty of their fading religious ideas, so that devotion to a theory or a candidate became translated into devotion to a revelation, and the game of politics turned itself into a holy war. The custom of connecting purely political doctrines with pietistic concepts of an inflammable nature, then firmly set up by skillful persuaders of the mob, has never quite died out in the United States. There has not been a presidential contest since Jackson's day without its Armageddons, its marching of Christian soldiers, its crosses of gold, its crowns of thorns. The most successful American politicians, beginning with the anti-slavery agitators, have been those most adept at twisting the ancient gauds and shibboleths of Puritanism to partisan uses. Every campaign that we have seen for eighty years has been, on each side, a pursuit of bugaboos, a denunciation of heresies, a snouting up of immoralities.

But it was during the long contest against slavery, beginning with the appearance of William Lloyd Garrison's *Liberator* in 1831 and ending at Appomattox, that this gigantic supernaturalization of politics reached its most astounding heights. In those days, indeed, politics and religion coalesced in a manner not seen in the world since the Middle Ages, and the combined pull of the two was so powerful that none could quite resist it. All men of any ability and ambition turned to political activity for self-expression. It engaged the press to the exclusion of everything else; it conquered the pulpit; it even laid its hand upon industry and trade. Drawing the best imaginative talent into its service—Jefferson and Lincoln may well stand as examples—it left the cultivation of belles lettres, and of all the other arts no less, to women and admittedly second-rate men. And when, breaking through this taboo, some chance first-rate man gave himself over to purely æsthetic expression, his reward was not only neglect, but even a sort of ignominy, as if such enterprises were not fitting for males with hair on their chests. I need not point to Poe and Whitman, both disdained as dreamers and wasters, and both proceeded against with the utmost rigors of outraged Philistinism.

In brief, the literature of that whole period, as Algernon Tassin shows in *The Magazine in America*,[7] was almost completely disassociated from life as men were then living it. Save one counts in such crude politico-puritan tracts as *Uncle Tom's Cabin*, it is difficult to find a single contemporaneous work that interprets the culture of the time, or even accurately represents it. Later on, it found historians and anatomists, and in one work, at least, to wit, *Huckleberry Finn*, it was studied and projected with the highest art, but no such impulse to make imaginative use of it showed itself contemporaneously, and there was not even the crude sentimentalization of here and now that one finds in the popular novels of today. Fenimore Cooper filled his romances, not with the people about him, but with the Indians beyond the sky-line, and made them half-fabulous to boot. Irving told fairy tales about the forgotten Knickerbockers; Hawthorne turned backward to the Puritans of Plymouth Rock; Longfellow to the Acadians and the prehistoric Indians; Emerson took flight from earth altogether; even Poe sought refuge in a land of fantasy. It was only the frank second-raters—e.g., Whittier and Lowell—who ventured to turn to the life around them, and the banality of the result is a sufficient indication of the crudeness of the current taste, and the mean position assigned to the art of letters. This was pre-eminently the era of the moral tale, the Sunday-school book. Literature was conceived, not as a thing in itself, but merely as a hand-maiden to politics or religion. The great celebrity of Emerson in New England was not the celebrity of a literary artist, but that of theologian and metaphysician; he was esteemed in much the same way that Jonathan Edwards had been esteemed. Even down to our own time, indeed, his vague and empty philosophizing has been put above his undeniable capacity for graceful utterance, and it remained for Dr. Kellner to consider him purely as a literary artist, and to give him due praise for his skill.

The Civil War brought that era of sterility to an end. As I shall show later on, the shock of it completely reorganized the American scheme of things, and even made certain important changes in the national Puritanism, or, at all events, in its machinery. Whitman, whose career straddled, so to speak, the four years of the war, was the leader—and for a long while, the only trooper—of a double revolt. On the one hand he offered a courageous challenge to the intolerable prudishness and dirty-mindedness of Puritanism, and on the other hand he boldly sought the themes and even the modes of expression of his poetry in the arduous, contentious and highly melodramatic life that lay all about him. Whitman, however, was clearly before his time. His countrymen could see him only as immoralist; save for a pitiful few of them, they were dead to any understanding of his stature as artist, and even unaware that such a category of men existed. He was put down as an invader of the public decencies, a disturber of the public peace; even his eloquent war poems, surely the best of all his work, were insufficient to get him a hearing; the sentimental rubbish of "The Blue and the Gray" and the ecstatic supernaturalism of "The Battle Hymn of the Republic" were far more to the public taste.[8] Where Whitman failed, indeed, all subsequent explorers of the same field have failed with him, and the great war has left no more mark upon American letters than if it had never been fought. Nothing remotely approaching the bulk and beam of Tolstoi's *War and Peace*, or, to descend to a smaller scale, Zola's *The Attack on the Mill*, has come out of it. Its appeal to the national imagination was undoubtedly of the most profound character; it colored politics for fifty years, and is today a dominating influence in the thought of whole sections of the American people. But in all that stirring up there was no upheaval of artistic consciousness, for the plain reason that there was no artistic consciousness there to heave up, and all we have in the way of Civil War literature is a few conventional melodramas, a few half-forgotten short stories by Ambrose Bierce and Stephen Crane, and a half dozen idiotic popular songs in the manner of Randall's "Maryland, My Maryland."

In the seventies and eighties, with the appearance of such men as Henry James, William Dean Howells, Mark Twain and Bret Harte, a better day seemed to be dawning. Here, after a full century of infantile romanticizing, were four writers who at least deserved respectful consideration as literary artists, and what is more, three of them turned from the conventionalized themes of the past to the teeming and colorful life that lay under their noses. But this promise of better things was soon found to be no more than a promise. Mark Twain, after *The Gilded Age*, slipped back into romanticism tempered by Philistinism, and was presently in the era before the Civil War, and finally in the Middle Ages, and even beyond. Harte, a brilliant technician, had displayed his whole stock when he had displayed his technique: his stories were not even superficially true to the life they presumed to depict; one searched in vain for an interpretation of it; they were simply idle tales. As for Howells and James, both quickly showed that timorousness and reticence which are the distinguishing marks of the Puritan, even in his most intellectual incarnations. The American scene that they depicted with such meticulous care was chiefly peopled with marionettes. They shrunk, characteristically, from those larger, harsher clashes of will and purpose which one finds in all truly first-rate literature. In particular, they shrunk from any interpretation of life which grounded itself upon an acknowledgment of its inexorable and inexplicable tragedy. In the vast combat of instincts and aspirations about them they saw only a feeble jousting of comedians, unserious and insignificant. Of the great questions that have agitated the minds of men in Howells' time one gets no more than a faint and far-away echo in his novels. His investigations, one may say, are carried on *in vacuo*; his discoveries are not expressed in terms of passion, but in terms of giggles.

In the followers of Howells and James one finds little save an empty imitation of their emptiness, a somewhat puerile parodying of their highly artful but essentially personal technique. To wade through the books of such characteristic American fictioneers as Frances Hodgson Burnett, Mary E. Wilkins Freeman, F. Hopkinson Smith, Alice Brown, James Lane Allen, Winston Churchill, Ellen Glasgow, Gertrude Atherton and Sarah Orne Jewett is to undergo an experience that is almost terrible. The flow of words is completely purged of ideas; in place of them one finds no more than a romantic restatement of all the old platitudes and formulæ. To call such an emission of graceful poppycock a literature, of course, is to mouth an absurdity, and yet, if the college professors who write treatises on letters are to be believed, it is the best we have to show. Turn, for example, to A *History of American Literature Since 1870*, by Prof. Fred Lewis Pattee, one of the latest and undoubtedly one of the least unintelligent of these books. In it the gifted pedagogue gives extended notice to no less than six of the nine writers I have mentioned, and upon all of them his verdicts are flattering. He bestows high praises, direct and indirect, upon Mrs. Freeman's "grim and austere" manner, her "repression," her entire lack of poetical illumination. He compares Miss Jewett to both Howells and Hawthorne, not to mention Mrs. Gaskell—and Addison! He grows enthusiastic over a hollow piece of fine writing by Miss Brown. And he forgets altogether to mention Dreiser, or Sinclair, or Medill Patterson, or Harry Leon Wilson, or George Ade! . . .

So much for the best. The worst is beyond description. France has her Brieux and her Henry Bordeaux; Germany has her Mühlbach, her stars of the *Gartenlaube*;[9] England contributes Caine, Corelli, Oppenheim and company. But it is in our country alone that banality in letters takes on the proportions of a national movement; it is only here that a work of the imagination is habitually judged by its sheer emptiness of ideas, its fundamental platitudinousness, its correspondence with the imbecility of mob thinking; it is only here that "glad" books run up sales of hundreds of thousands. Richard Harding Davis, with his ideals of a floor-walker; Gene Stratton-Porter, with her snuffling sentimentality; Robert W. Chambers, with his "society" romances for shop-girls; Irvin Cobb, with his labored, *Ayers' Almanac* jocosity; the authors of the *Saturday Evening Post* school, with their heroic drummers and stockbrokers, their ecstatic celebration of the stupid, the sordid, the ignoble — these, after all, are our typical *literati*. The Puritan fear of ideas is the master of them all. Some of them, in truth, most of them, have undeniable talent; in a more favorable environment not a few of them might be doing sound work. But they see how small the ring is, and they make their tricks small to fit it. Not many of them ever venture a leg outside. The lash of the ringmaster is swift, and it stings damnably. . . .

I say not many; I surely do not mean none at all. As a matter of fact, there have been intermittent rebellions against the prevailing pecksniffery and sentimentality ever since the days of Irving and Hawthorne. Poe led one of them — as critic more than as creative artist. His scathing attacks upon the Gerald Stanley Lees, the Hamilton Wright Mabies and the George E. Woodberrys of his time keep a liveliness and appositeness that the years have not staled; his criticism deserves to be better remembered. Poe sensed the Philistine pull of a Puritan civilization as none had before him, and combated it with his whole artillery of rhetoric. Another rebel, of course, was Whitman; how he came to grief is too well known to need recalling. What is less familiar is the fact that both the *Atlantic Monthly* and the *Century* (first called *Scribner's*) were set up by men in revolt against the reign of mush, as *Putnam's* and the *Dial* had been before them. The salutatory of the *Dial*, dated 1840, stated the case against the national mugginess clearly. The aim of the magazine, it said, was to oppose "that rigor of our conventions of religion and education which is turning us to stone" and to give expression to "new views and the dreams of youth."[10] Alas, for these brave *révoltés*! *Putnam's* succumbed to the circumambient rigors and duly turned to stone, and is now no more. The *Atlantic*, once so heretical, has become as respectable as the New York *Evening Post*. As for the *Dial*,[11] it was until lately the very pope of orthodoxy and jealously guarded the college professors who read it from the pollution of ideas. Only the *Century* has kept the faith unbrokenly. It is, indeed, the one first-class American magazine that has always welcomed newcomers, and that maintains an intelligent contact with the literature that is in being, and that consistently tries to make the best terms possible with the dominant Philistinism. It cannot go the whole way without running into danger; let it be said to the credit of its editors that they have more than once braved that danger.

The tale might be lengthened. Mark Twain, in his day, felt the stirrings of revolt, and not all his Philistinism was sufficient to hold him altogether in check. If you want to find out about the struggle that went on within him, read the biography by Albert Bigelow Paine, or, better still, *The Mysterious Stranger* and *What Is Man?* Alive, he had his position to consider; dead, he now speaks out. In the preface to *What Is Man?* dated 1905, there is a curious confession of his incapacity for defying the taboos which surrounded him. The studies for the book, he says, were begun "twenty-five or twenty-seven years ago"—the period of A *Tramp Abroad* and *The Prince and the Pauper*. It was actually written "seven years ago"—that is, just after *Following the Equator* and *Personal Recollections of Joan of Arc*. And why did it lie so long in manuscript, and finally go out stealthily, under a private imprint?[12] Simply because, as Mark frankly confesses, he "dreaded (*and could not bear*) the disapproval of the people around" him. He knew how hard his fight for recognition had been; he knew what direful penalties outraged orthodoxy could inflict; he had in him the somewhat pathetic discretion of a respectable family man. But, dead, he is safely beyond reprisal, and so, after a prudent interval, the faithful Paine begins printing books in which, writing knowingly behind six feet of earth, he could set down his true ideas without fear. Some day, perhaps, we shall have his microbe story, and maybe even his picture of the court of Elizabeth.[13]

A sneer in Prof. Pattee's history, before mentioned, recalls the fact that Hamlin Garland was also a rebel in his day and bawled for the Truth with a capital T. That was in 1893. Two years later the guardians of the national rectitude fell afoul of *Rose of Dutcher's Coolly* and Garland began to think it over; today he devotes himself to the safer enterprise of chasing spooks; his name is conspicuously absent from the Dreiser Protest.[14] Nine years before his brief offending John Hay had set off a discreet bomb in *The Bread-Winners*—anonymously because "my standing would be seriously compromised" by an avowal. Six years later Frank Norris shook up the Phelpses and Mores of the time with *McTeague*. Since then there have been assaults timorous and assaults head-long—by Bierce, by Dreiser, by Phillips, by Fuller—by Mary MacLanes and by Upton Sinclairs—by ploughboy poets from the Middle West and by jitney geniuses in Greenwich Village—assaults gradually tapering off to a mere sophomoric brashness and deviltry. And all of them like snowballings of Verdun. All of them petered out and ineffectual. The normal, the typical American book of today is as fully a remouthing of old husks as the normal book of Griswold's day. The whole atmosphere of our literature, in William James' phrase, is "mawkish and dishwatery." Books are still judged among us, not by their form and organization as works of art, their accuracy and vividness as representations of life, their validity and perspicacity as interpretations of it, but by their conformity to the national prejudices, their accordance with set standards of nicensss and propriety. The thing irrevocably demanded is a "sane" book: the ideal is a "clean," an "inspiring," a "glad" book. [. . .][15]

V

I have gone into the anatomy and physiology of militant Puritanism because, so far as I know, the inquiry has not been attempted before, and because a somewhat detailed acquaintance with the forces behind so grotesque a manifestation as Comstockery, the particular business of the present essay, is necessary to an understanding of its workings, and of its prosperity, and of its influence upon the arts. Save one turn to England or to the British colonies, it is impossible to find a parallel for the astounding absolutism of Comstock and his imitators in any civilized country. No other nation has laws which oppress the arts so ignorantly and so abominably as ours do, nor has any other nation handed over the enforcement of the statutes which exist to agencies so openly pledged to reduce all æsthetic expression to the service of a stupid and unworkable scheme of rectitude. I have before me as I write a pamphlet in explanation of his aims and principles, prepared by Comstock himself and presented to me by his successor. Its very title is a sufficient statement of the Puritan position: MORALS, Not Art or Literature.[16] The capitals are in the original. And within, as a sort of general text, the idea is amplified: "It is a question of peace, good order and morals, and not art, literature or science." Here we have a statement of principle that, at all events, is at least quite frank. There is not the slightest effort to beg the question; there is no hypocritical pretension to a desire to purify or safeguard the arts; they are dismissed at once as trivial and degrading. And jury after jury has acquiesced in this; it was old Anthony's boast, in his last days, that his percentage of convictions, in 40 years, had run to 98.5.[17]

Comstockery is thus grounded firmly upon that profound national suspicion of the arts, that truculent and almost unanimous Philistinism, which I have described. It would be absurd to dismiss it as an excrescence, and untypical of the American mind. But it is typical, too, in the manner in which it has gone beyond that mere partiality to the accumulation of a definite power, and made that power irresponsible and almost irresistible. It was Comstock himself, in fact, who invented the process whereby his followers in other fields of moral endeavor have forced laws into the statute books upon the pretense of putting down John Doe, an acknowledged malefactor, and then turned them savagely upon Richard Roe, a peaceable, well-meaning and hitherto law-abiding man. And it was Comstock who first capitalized moral endeavor like baseball or the soap business, and made himself the first of its kept professors, and erected about himself a rampart of legal and financial immunity which rid him of all fear of mistakes and their consequences, and so enabled him to pursue his jihad with all the advantages in his favor. He was, in brief, more than the greatest Puritan gladiator of his time; he was the Copernicus of a quite new art and science, and he devised a technique and handed down a professional ethic that no rival has been able to better.

The whole story is naïvely told in Anthony Comstock, Fighter,[18] a work which passed under the approving eye of the old war horse himself and is full of his characteristic pecksniffery.[19] His beginnings, it appears, were very modest. When he arrived in New York from the Connecticut hinterland, he was a penniless and uneducated clodhopper, just out of the Union army, and his first job was that of a porter in a wholesale dry-goods house. But he had in him several qualities of the traditional Yankee which almost always insure success, and it was not long before he began to make his way. One of these qualities was a talent for bold and ingratiating address; another was a vast appetite for thrusting himself into affairs, a yearning to run things—what the Puritan calls public spirit. The two constituted his fortune. The second brought him into intimate relations with the newly-organized Young Men's Christian Association, and led him to the discovery of a form of moral endeavor that was at once novel and fascinating—the unearthing and denunciation of "immoral" literature. The first, once he had attracted attention thereby, got him the favourable notice, and finally the unlimited support, of the late Morris K. Jesup, one of the earliest and perhaps the greatest of the moral *entrepreneurs* that I have described. Jesup was very rich, and very eager to bring the whole nation up to grace by *force majeure*. He was the banker of at least a dozen grandiose programs of purification in the seventies and eighties. In Comstock he found precisely the sort of field agent that he was looking for, and the two presently constituted the most formidable team of professional reformers that the country had ever seen.

The story of the passage of the Act of Congress of March 3, 1873,[20] under cover of which the Comstock Society still carries on its campaigns of snouting and suppression, is a classical tale of Puritan impudence and chicanery. Comstock, with Jesup and other rich men backing him financially and politically,[21] managed the business. First, a number of spectacular raids were made on the publishers of such pornographic books as *The Memoirs of Fanny Hill* and *Only a Boy*.[22] Then the newspapers were filled with inflammatory matter about the wide dispersal of such stuff, and its demoralizing effects upon the youth of the republic. Then a committee of self-advertising clergymen and "Christian millionaires" was organized to launch a definite "movement." And then a direct attack was made upon Congress, and, to the tune of fiery moral indignation, the bill prepared by Comstock himself was forced through both houses. All opposition, if only the opposition of inquiry, was overborne in the usual manner. That is to say, every Congressman who presumed to ask what it was all about, or to point out obvious defects in the bill, was disposed of the insinuation, or even the direct charge, that he was a covert defender of obscene books, and, by inference, of the carnal recreations described in them. We have grown familiar of late with this process: it was displayed at full length in the passage of the Mann Act, and again when the Webb Act and other such prohibition measures were before Congress. In 1873 its effectiveness was helped out by its novelty, and so the Comstock bill was rushed through both houses in the closing days of a busy session, and President Grant accommodatingly signed it.

Once it was upon the books, Comstock made further use of the prevailing uproar to have himself appointed a special agent of the Postoffice Department to enforce it, and with characteristic cunning refused to take any salary. Had his job carried a salary, it would have excited the acquisitiveness of other virtuosi; as it was, he was secure. As for the necessary sinews of war, he knew well that he could get them from Jesup. Within a few weeks, indeed, the latter had perfected a special organization for the enforcement of the new statute, and it still flourishes as the New York Society for the Suppression of Vice; or, as it is better known, the Comstock Society. The new Federal Act, dealing only with the mails, left certain loopholes; they were plugged up by fastening drastic amendments upon the New York Code of Criminal Procedure—amendments forced through the legislature precisely as the Federal Act had been forced through Congress.[23] With these laws in his hands Comstock was ready for his career. It was his part of the arrangement to supply the thrills of the chase; it was Jesup's to find the money. The partnership kept up until the death of Jesup, in 1908, and after that Comstock readily found new backers. Even his own death, in 1915, did not materially alter a scheme of things which offered such admirable opportunities for the exercise of the Puritan love of spectacular and relentless pursuit, the Puritan delusion of moral grandeur and infallibility, the Puritan will to power.

Ostensibly, as I have said, the new laws were designed to put down the traffic in frankly pornographic books and pictures—a traffic which, of course, found no defenders—but Comstock had so drawn them their actual sweep was vastly wider, and once he was firmly in the saddle his enterprises scarcely knew limits. Having disposed of *The Confessions of Maria Monk* and *Night Life in Paris*,[24] he turned to Rabelais and the Decameron, and having driven these ancients under the book-counters, he pounced upon Zola, Balzac and Daudet, and having disposed of these too, he began a *pogrom* which, in other hands, eventually brought down such astounding victims as Thomas Hardy's *Jude the Obscure* and Harold Frederic's *The Damnation of Theron Ware*. All through the eighties and nineties this ecstatic campaign continued, always increasing in violence and effectiveness. Comstock became a national celebrity; his doings were as copiously reported by the newspapers as those of P. T. Barnum or John L. Sullivan. Imitators spring up in all the larger cities: there was hardly a public library in the land that did not begin feverishly expurgating its shelves; the publication of fiction, and particularly of foreign fiction, took on the character of an extra hazardous enterprise. Not, of course, that the reign of terror was not challenged, and Comstock himself denounced. So early as 1876 a national organization demanding a reasonable amendment of the postal laws got on its legs; in the late eighties "Citizen" George Francis Train defied the whirlwind by printing the Old Testament as a serial; many indignant victims, acquitted by some chance in the courts, brought suit against Comstock for damages. Moreover, an occasional judge, standing out boldly against the usual intimidation, denounced him from the bench; one of them, Judge Jenkins, accused him specifically of "fraud and lying" and other "dishonest practices."[25] But the spirit of American Puritanism was on his side. His very extravagances at once stimulated and satisfied the national yearning for a hot chase, a good show—and in the complaints of his victims, that the art of letters was being degraded, that the country was made ridiculous, the newspaper-reading populace could see no more than an affectation. The reform organization of 1876 lasted but five years, and then disbanded without having accomplished anything; Train was duly jailed for "debauching the young" with an "obscene" serial;[26] juries refused to being in punitive verdicts against the master showman.

In carrying on this war of extermination upon all ideas that violated their private notions of virtue and decorum, Comstock and his followers were very greatly aided by the vagueness of the law. It prohibited the use of the mails for transporting all matter of an "obscene, lewd, lascivious . . . or filthy" character, but conveniently failed to define these adjectives. As a result, of course, it was possible to bring an accusation against practically *any* publication that aroused the Comstockian bloodlust, however innocently, and to subject the persons responsible for it to costly, embarrassing and often dangerous persecution. No man, said Dr. Johnson, would care to go on trial for his life once a week, even if possessed of absolute proofs of his innocence. By the same token, no man wants to be arraigned in a criminal court, and displayed in the sensational newspapers, as a purveyor of indecency, however strong his assurance of innocence. Comstock made use of this fact in an adroit and characteristically unconscionable manner. He held the menace of prosecution over all who presumed to dispute his tyranny, and when he could not prevail by a mere threat, he did not hesitate to begin proceedings, and to carry them forward with the aid of florid proclamations to the newspapers and ill concealed intimidations of judges and juries.

The last-named business succeeded as it always does in this country, where the judiciary is quite as sensitive to the suspicion of sinfulness as the legislative arm. A glance at the decisions handed down during the forty years of Comstock's chief activity shows a truly amazing willingness to accommodate him in his pious enterprises. On the one hand, there was gradually built up a court-made definition of obscenity which eventually embraced almost every conceivable violation of Puritan prudery, and on the other hand the victim's means of defense were steadily restricted and conditioned, until in the end he had scarcely any at all. This is the state of the law today. It is held in the leading cases that anything is obscene which may excite "impure thoughts" in "the minds . . . of persons that are susceptible to impure thoughts,"[27] or which "tends to deprave the minds" of any who, because they are "young and inexperienced," are "open to such influences"[28]—in brief, that anything is obscene that is not fit to be handed to a child just learning to read, or that may imaginably stimulate the lubricity of the most foul-minded. It is held further that words that are perfectly innocent in themselves—"words, abstractly considered, [that] may be free from vulgarism"—may yet be assumed, by a friendly jury, to be likely to "arouse a libidinous passion . . . in the mind of a modest woman." (I quote exactly! The court failed to define "modest woman.")[29] Yet further, it is held that any book is obscene "which is unbecoming, immodest. . . ."[30] Obviously, this last decision throws open the door to endless imbecilities, for its definition merely begs the question, and so makes a reasonable solution ten times harder. It is in such mazes that the Comstocks safely lurk. Almost any printed allusion to sex may be argued against as unbecoming in a moral republic, and once it is unbecoming it is also obscene.

In meeting such attacks the defendant must do his fighting without weapons. He cannot allege in his defense that the offending work was put forth for a legitimate, necessary and decent purpose;[31] he cannot allege that a passage complained of is from a standard work, itself in general circulation;[32] he cannot offer evidence that the person to whom a book or picture was sold or exhibited was not actually depraved by it, or likely to be depraved by it;[33] he cannot rest his defense on its lack of such effect upon the jurymen themselves;[34] he cannot plead that the alleged obscenity, in point of fact, is couched in decent and unobjectionable language;[35] he cannot plead that the same or a similar work has gone unchallenged elsewhere;[36] he cannot argue that the circulation of works of the same class has set up a presumption of toleration, and a tacit limitation of the definition of obscenity.[37] The general character of a book is not a defense of a particular passage, however unimportant; if there is the slightest descent to what is "unbecoming," the whole may be ruthlessly condemned.[38] Nor is it an admissible defense to argue that the book was not generally circulated, and that the copy in evidence was obtained by an *agent provocateur*, and by false representations.[39] Finally, all the decisions deny the defendant the right to introduce any testimony, whether expert or otherwise, that a book is of artistic value and not pornographic, and that its effect upon normal persons is not pernicious. Upon this point the jury is the sole judge, and it cannot be helped to its decision by taking other opinions, or by hearing evidence as to what is the general opinion.

Occasionally, as I have said, a judge has revolted against this intolerable state of the court-and Comstock-made law, and directed a jury to disregard these astounding decisions.[40] In a recent New York case Judge Samuel Seabury actually ruled that "it is no part of the duty of courts to exercise a censorship over literary productions."[41] But in general the judiciary has been curiously complaisant, and more than once a Puritan on the bench has delighted the Comstocks by prosecuting their case for them.[42] With such decisions in their hands and such aid from the other side of the bar, it is no wonder that they enter upon their campaigns with impudence and assurance. All the odds are in their favor from the start. They have statutes deliberately designed to make the defense onerous; they are familiar by long experience with all the tricks and surprises of the game; they are sheltered behind organizations, incorporated without capital and liberally chartered by trembling legislatures, which make reprisals impossible in case of failure; above all, they have perfected the business of playing upon the cowardice and vanity of judges and prosecuting officers. The newspapers, with very few exceptions, give them ready aid. Theoretically, perhaps, many newspaper editors are opposed to Comstockery, and sometimes they denounce it with great eloquence, but when a good show is offered they are always in favor of the showman[43]—and the Comstocks are showmen of undoubted skill. They know how to make a victim jump and writhe in the ring; they have a talent for finding victims who are prominent enough to arrest attention; they shrewdly capitalize the fact that the pursuer appears more heroic than the prey, and the further fact that the newspaper reader is impatient of artistic pretensions and glad to see an artist made ridiculous. And behind them there is always the steady pressure of Puritan prejudice—the Puritan feeling that "immorality" is the blackest of crimes, and that its practitioner has no rights. It was by making use of these elements that Comstock achieved his prodigies, and it is by making use of them that his heirs and assigns keep up the sport today. Their livelihood depends upon the money they can raise among the righteous, and the amount they can raise depends upon the quality of the entertainment they offer. Hence their adept search for shining marks. Hence, for example, the spectacular raid upon the Art Students' League, on August 2, 1906. Hence an artful turning to their own use of the vogue of such sensational dramatists as Eugène Brieux and George Bernard Shaw, and of such isolated plays as *Trilby* and *Sapho*.[44] Hence the barring from the mails of the inflammatory report of the Chicago Vice Commission—a strange, strange case of dog eating dog.

But here we have humor. There is, however, no humor in the case of a serious author who sees his work damaged and perhaps ruined by a malicious and unintelligent attack, and himself held up to public obloquy as one with the vendors of pamphlets of flagellation and filthy "marriage guides." He finds opposing him a flat denial of his decent purpose as an artist, and a stupid and ill-natured logic that baffles sober answer.[45] He finds on his side only the half-hearted support of a publisher whose interest in a single book is limited to his profits from it, and who desires above all things to evade a nuisance and an expense. Not a few publishers, knowing the constant possibility of sudden and arbitrary attack, insert a clause in their contracts whereby an author must secure them against damage from any "immoral" matter in his book. They read and approve the manuscript, they print the book and sell it—but if it is unlucky enough to attract the Comstockian lightning, the author has the whole burden to bear,[46] and if they seek safety and economy by yielding, as often happens, he must consent to the mutilation or even the suppression of his work. The result is that a writer, in such a situation, is practically beaten before he can offer a defense. The professional book-baiters have laws to their liking, and courts pliant to their exactions; they fill the newspapers with inflammatory charges before the accused gets his day in court; they have the aid of prosecuting officers who fear the political damage of their enmity, and of the enmity of their wealthy and influential backers; above all, they have the command of far more money than any author can hope to muster. Finally, they derive an advantage from two of the most widespread of human weaknesses, the first being envy and the second being fear. When an author is attacked, a good many of his rivals see only a personal benefit in his difficulties, and not a menace to the whole order, and a good many others are afraid to go to his aid because of the danger of bringing down the moralists' rage upon themselves. Both of these weaknesses revealed themselves very amusingly in the Dreiser case, and I hope to detail their operations at some length later on, when I describe that *cause célèbre* in a separate work.[47]

Now add to the unfairness and malignancy of the attack its no less disconcerting arbitrariness and fortuitousness, and the path of the American author is seen to be strewn with formidable entanglements indeed. With the law what it is, he is quite unable to decide *a priori* what is permitted by the national delicacy and what is not, nor can he get any light from the recorded campaigns of the moralists. They seem to strike blindly, unintelligently, without any coherent theory or plan. *Trilby* is assaulted by the united Comstockery of a dozen cities, and *The Yoke* somehow escapes.[48] *Hagar Revelly* is made the subject of a double prosecution in the State and Federal courts, and *Love's Pilgrimage* and *One Man* go unmolested.[49] The publisher of Przybyszewski's *Homo Sapiens* is forced to withdraw it; the publisher of Artzibashef's *Sanine* follows it with *The Breaking Point*.[50] The serious work of a Forel is brought into court as pornography, and the books of Havelock Ellis are barred from the mails; the innumerable volumes on "sex hygiene" by tawdry clergymen and smutty old maids are circulated by the million and without challenge. Frank Harris is deprived of a publisher for his *Oscar Wilde: His Life and Confession* by threats of immediate prosecution; the newspapers meanwhile dedicate thousands of columns to the filthy amusements of Harry Thaw. George Moore's *Memoirs of My Dead Life* are bowdlerized, James Lane Allen's *A Summer in Arcady* is barred from libraries, and a book by D. H. Lawrence is forbidden publication altogether; at the same time half a dozen cheap magazines devoted to sensational sex stories attain to hundreds of thousands of circulation. A serious book by David Graham Phillips, published serially in a popular monthly, is raided the moment it appears between covers; a trashy piece of nastiness by Elinor Glyn goes unmolested.[51] Worse, books are sold for months and even years without protest, and then suddenly attacked; Dreiser's *The "Genius,"* Kreymborg's *Edna* and Forel's *The Sexual Question* are examples. Still worse, what is held to be unobjectionable in one State is forbidden in another as *contra bonas mores*.[52] Altogether, there is madness, and no method in it. The livelihoods and good names of hard-striving and decent men are at the mercy of the whims of a horde of fanatics and mountebanks, and they have no way of securing themselves against attack, and no redress for their loss when it comes.

VI

So beset, it is no wonder that the typical American maker of books becomes a timorous and ineffective fellow, whose work tends inevitably toward a feeble superficiality. Sucking in the Puritan spirit with the very air he breathes, and perhaps burdened inwardly with an inheritance of the actual Puritan stupidity, he is further kept upon the straight path of chemical purity by the very real perils that I have just rehearsed. The result is a literature full of the mawkishness that the late Henry James so often roared against—a literature almost wholly detached from life as men are living it in the world—in George Moore's phrase, a literature still at nurse. It is on the side of sex that the appointed virtuosi of virtue exercise their chief repressions, for it is sex that especially fascinates the lubricious Puritan mind; but the conventional reticence that thus becomes the enforced fashion in one field extends itself to all others. Our fiction, in general, is marked by an artificiality as marked as that of Eighteenth Century poetry or the later Georgian drama. The romance in it runs to set forms and stale situations; the revelation, by such a book as *The Titan*, that there may be a glamor as entrancing in the way of a conqueror of men as in the way of a youth with a maid, remains isolated and exotic. We have no first-rate political or religious novel; we have no first-rate war story; despite all our national engrossment in commercial enterprise, we have few second-rate tales of business. Romance, in American fiction, still means only a somewhat childish amorousness and sentimentality—the love affairs of Paul and Virginia,[53] or the pale adulteries of their elders. And on the side of realism there is an almost equal vacuity and lack of veracity. The action of the novels of the Howells school goes on within four walls of painted canvas; they begin to shock once they describe an attack of asthma or a steak burning below stairs; they never penetrate beneath the flow of social concealments and urbanities to the passions that actually move men and women to their acts, and the great forces that circumscribe and condition personality. So obvious a piece of reporting as Upton Sinclair's *The Jungle* or Robert Herrick's *Together* makes a sensation; the appearance of a *Jennie Gerhardt* or a *Hagar Revelly* brings forth a growl of astonishment and rage.

In all this dread of free inquiry, this childish skittishness in both writers and public, this dearth of courage and even of curiosity, the influence of Comstockery is undoubtedly to be detected. It constitutes a sinister and ever-present menace to all men of ideas; it affrights the publisher and paralyzes the author; no one on the outside can imagine its burden as a practical concern. I am, in moments borrowed from more palatable business, the editor of an American magazine, and I thus know at first hand what the burden is. That magazine is anything but a popular one, in the current sense. It sells at a relatively high price; it contains no pictures or other baits for the childish; it is frankly addressed to a sophisticated minority. I may thus assume reasonably, I believe, that its readers are not sex-curious and itching adolescents, just as my colleague of the *Atlantic Monthly* may assume reasonably that his readers are not Italian immigrants. Nevertheless, as a practical editor, I find that the Comstocks, near and far, are oftener in my mind's eye than my actual patrons. The thing I always have to decide about a manuscript offered for publication, before ever I give any thought to its artistic merit and suitability, is the question whether its publication will be permitted—not even whether it is intrinsically good or evil, moral or immoral, but whether some roving Methodist preacher, self-commissioned to keep watch on letters, will read indecency into it. Not a week passes that I do not decline some sound and honest piece of work for no other reason. I have a long list of such things by American authors, well-devised, well-imagined, well-executed, respectable as human documents and as works of art— but never to be printed in mine or any other American magazine. It includes four or five short stories of the very first rank, and the best one-act play yet done, to my knowledge, by an American. All of these pieces would go into type at once on the Continent; no sane man would think of objecting to them; they are no more obscene, to a normal adult, than his own bare legs. But they simply cannot be printed in the United States, with the law what it is and the courts what they are.

I know many other editors. All of them are in the same boat. Some of them try to get around the difficulty by pecksniffery more or less open—for example, by fastening a moral purpose upon works of art, and hawking them as uplifting.[54] Others, facing the intolerable fact, yield to it with resignation. And if they didn't? Well, if one of them didn't, any professional moralist could go before a police magistrate, get a warrant upon a simple affidavit, raid the office of the offending editor, seize all the magazines in sight, and keep them impounded until after the disposition of the case. Editors cannot afford to take this risk. Magazines are perishable goods. Even if, after a trial has been had, they are returned, they are worthless save as waste paper. And what may be done with copies found in the actual office of publication may be done too with copies found on news-stands, and not only in one city, but in two, six, a dozen, a hundred. All the costs and burdens of the contest are on the defendant. Let him be acquitted with honor, and invited to dinner by the judge, he has yet lost his property, and the Comstock hiding behind the warrant cannot be made to pay. In this concealment, indeed, lurk many sinister things—not forgetting personal enmity and business rivalry. The actual complainant is seldom uncovered; Comstockery, taking on a semi-judicial character, throws its chartered immunity around the whole process. A hypothetical outrage? By no means. It has been perpetrated, in one American city or another, upon fully half of the magazines of general circulation published today. Its possibility sticks in the consciousness of every editor and publisher like a recurrent glycosuria.[55]

But though the effects of Comstockery are thus abominably insane and irritating, the fact is not to be forgotten that, after all, the thing is no more than an effect itself. The fundamental causes of all the grotesque (and often half-fabulous) phenomena flowing out of it are to be sought in the habits of mind of the American people. They are, as I have shown, besotted by moral concepts, a moral engrossment, a delusion of moral infallibility. In their view of the arts they are still unable to shake off the naïve suspicion of the Fathers.[56] A work of the imagination can justify itself, in their sight, only if it show a moral purpose, and that purpose must be obvious and unmistakable. Even in their slow progress toward a revolt against the ancestral Philistinism, they cling to this ethical bemusement: a new gallery of pictures is welcomed as "improving," to hear Beethoven "makes one better." Any questioning of the moral ideas that prevail—the principal business, it must be plain, of the novelist, the serious dramatist, the professed inquirer into human motives and acts—is received with the utmost hostility. To attempt such an enterprise is to disturb the peace—and the disturber of the peace, in the national view, quickly passes over into the downright criminal.

These symptoms, it seems to me, are only partly racial, despite the persistent survival of that third-rate English strain which shows itself so ingenuously in the colonial spirit, the sense of inferiority, the frank craving for praise from home. The race, in truth, grows mongrel, and the protest against that mongrelism only serves to drive in the fact. But a mongrel race is necessarily a race still in the stage of reaching out for culture; it has not yet formulated defensible standards; it must needs rest heavily on the superstitions that go with inferiority. The Reformation brought Scotland among the civilized nations, but it took Scotland a century and a half to live down the Reformation.[57] Dogmatism, conformity, Philistinism, the fear of rebels, the crusading spirit; these are the marks of an upstart people, uncertain of their rank in the world and even of their direction.[58] A cultured European, reading a typical American critical journal, must needs conceive the United States, says H. G. Wells, as "a vain, garrulous and prosperous female of uncertain age and still more uncertain temper, with unfounded pretensions to intellectuality and an ideal of refinement of the most negative description . . . the Aunt Errant of Christendom."[59] There is always that blushful shyness, that timorous uncertainty, broken by sudden rages, sudden enunciations of impeccable doctrines, sudden runnings amuck. Formalism is the hall-mark of the national culture, and sins against the one are sins against the other. The American is school-mastered out of gusto, out of joy, out of innocence. He can never fathom William Blake's notion that "the lust of the goat is also to the glory of God." He must be correct, or, in his own phrase, he must bust.

Via trita est tutissima.[60] The new generation, urged to curiosity and rebellion by its mounting sap, is rigorously restrained, regimented, policed. The ideal is vacuity, guilelessness, imbecility. "We are looking at this particular book," said Comstock's successor[61] of The *"Genius,"* "from the standpoint of its harmful effect on female readers of immature mind."[62] To be curious is to be lewd; to know is to yield to fornication. Here we have the medieval doctrine still on its legs: a chance word may arouse "a libidinous passion" in the mind of a "modest" woman. Not only youth must be safeguarded, but also the "female," the untrustworthy one, the temptress. "Modest" is a euphemism; it takes laws to keep her "pure." The "locks of chastity" rust in the Cluny Museum; in place of them we have Comstockery. . . .

But, as I have said in hymning Huneker, there is yet the munyonic consolation. Time is a great legalizer, even in the field of morals. We have yet no delivery, but we have at least the beginnings of a revolt, or, at all events, of a protest. We have already reached, in Howells, our Hannah More; in Clemens, our Swift; in Henry James, our Horace Walpole; in Woodberry, Robinson *et al.*, our Cowpers, Southeys and Crabbes; perhaps we might even make a composite and call it our Johnson. We are sweating through our Eighteenth Century, our era of sentiment, our spiritual measles. Maybe a new day is not quite so far off as it seems to be, and with it we may get our Hardy, our Conrad, our Swinburne, our Thoma, our Moore, our Meredith and our Synge.

The American Tradition

Ever since Professor Brownell published his little volume *Standards*, in 1917, a great clatter has been going on among the university *Gelehrten*, particularly West and South, in favor of what they call the American tradition in letters. Perhaps I libel Brownell by hinting that he started this nonsense; it may be that its actual papa was George Creel, A. Mitchell Palmer, James M. Beck, Otto H. Kahn or some other such master-mind of that critical and intelligent era. Whatever its parentage, it was at least born in the holiest sort of wedlock, and if I pull its ear today I surely hope that no one will suspect that I thereby question its legitimacy. It is, in fact, absolutely and irrefragably American from snout to *os calcis*, not only in outward seeming and tendency, but also in inner essence, and any one who flouts it also flouts all that is most sacred in the spirit of Americanism. To this business I now address myself briefly.

What, then, is the spirit of Americanism? I precipitate it into the doctrine that the way to ascertain the truth about anything is to take a vote upon it, and that the way to propagate that truth, once it has been ascertained, is with a club. This doctrine, it seems to me, explains everything peculiarly American and particularly everything American that is most puzzling to men of older and finer cultures—

from American politics to American learning, and from the astounding American code of morals to the still more astounding American concept of honor. At one end it explains the archetypical buffooneries of the Ku Klux Klan, the American Legion, the Lusk Committee, the Anti-Saloon League, the Department of Justice and all the other great national engines of cultural propaganda, and at the other end it explains the amusing theory that the limits of the nation's æsthetic adventures are to be fixed by a vague and self-elected committee of rustic Ph.D.'s, and that any artist, native or imported, who dares to pass them is not only a bungler but also a traitor to the flag, and ought, shall and must be put down by the secular arm.

How far this last notion goes is best shown, not in the *pianissimo* pronunciamentos of such relatively suave and cautious dons as Brownell—who are themselves often sadly polluted by foreign ideas, despite their gallant efforts to be pure—but in the far more frank and passionate bulls of their followers in the swarming seminaries of the cow States, where every visible male of *Homo sapiens* has hair on his chest, and horn on his hands, and is a red-blooded, go-getting, up-and-coming 100 per cent American he-man. I turn at once to Professor Dr. Leonard Doughty of the University of Texas—so far unknown to the diabetic East, but eminent, I hope, henceforth. Unlike Professor Beers of Yale, who was lately saying that he had read none of the new books he was denouncing, Professor Doughty has plowed into a whole stack of them—into all the new poetry from Carl Sandburg to *The Spoon River Anthology*, and all the novels from Dreiser to Waldo Frank, and all the vast mass of subversive criticism that has accompanied them, from that in the *Dial* to that in the *Little Review, The Literary Review* and *Broom*.

> For many months now (he says) there has passed before me the whole ghastly array. . . . I have read the "books," the "fiction" and the "verse"; the "drama," the "articles" and the "essays"; the "sketches" and the "criticisms," and whatever else is squealed and gibbered by these unburied and not-to-be-handled dead. . . . It is this unnamable by-product of congenital deficiency, perverted dissipation and adulterated narcotics . . . which I refer to as "modern literature."[63]

And what is the Texas Sainte-Beuve's verdict upon this modern literature? The verdict, in brief, of all the other alarmed professors—the necessary and inevitable verdict of every red-blooded 100 per cent Americano. He not only finds that it is in itself nothing but "swept-up rottenness and garbage—the dilute sewage of the sordid mental slums of New York and Chicago"; he also finds that the ladies and gentlemen who compose it are "a horde of chancre-laden rats," that they constitute a "devil's crew of perverted drug addicts," that they are engaged unanimously in a "flabby and feeble assault . . . upon that ancient decency that for unnumbered generations of the white Northern races of mankind, at least, has grown and strengthened as a seed cast upon kindly soil," and, finally, that "no one of the 'writers' of this unhappy array was in the service of the United States in the great war"— in brief, that the whole movement is no more than a foul conspiracy to insult the flag, uproot the Republic and exterminate the unparalleled Nordic blond, and that, in consequence, it is the duty of every American who is a member "of a white Nordic race—save the Teutonic"—to come sliding down the pole, grab the tarpot and go galloping to the rescue. So concluding and stating, the professor proceeds to rend a typical book by one of these hellish foes to "the heritage of American and English men." The one he chooses is *Jurgen*, by James Branch Cabell of Virginia!

This long-horn *savant*, I admit, is more exuberant than most. There are no soothing elms on the campus at Austin; instead there is the great open space demanded by meetings of the Ku Klux Klan. But his doctrine, in its essence, is precisely the doctrine of his more urbane colleagues—of Brander Matthews, of Boynton, of Sherman, of Beers, of Erskine, of all the rest. It is a doctrine, as I have said, that is thoroughly American—as American, indeed, as prohibition, correspondence schools, the Knights of Pythias or the Mann act. But by the same token it is a doctrine that has no more fundamental sense or dignity in it than the politics of a Harding or the theology of a Billy Sunday. It is, in fact, almost inconceivably ignorant, childish and ridiculous. It is the product of men who, educated beyond their capacity for taking in ideas, have borrowed the patriotic philosophy of suburban pastors, ice-wagon drivers and country schoolmarms and now seek to apply it in the consideration of phenomena that are quite beyond their comprehension.

The simple truth is, of course, that the standards and traditions these sublimated prohibition enforcement officers argue for so shrilly have no actual existence in the first-line literature of the American people—that what they demand is no more and no less than an artificial and absurd subservience to ideas and traditions that were regarded with contempt by every American of the civilized minority even when they prevailed. In other words, what they argue for is not a tradition that would take in Poe, Hawthorne, Emerson, Whitman and Mark Twain, but a tradition that would pass over all these men to embrace Cooper, Bryant, Donald G. Mitchell, N. P. Willis, Mrs. Sigourney and the Sweet Singer of Michigan.[64] Even Longfellow, I dare say, must be left out, for didn't he drink of green and terrible waters in Paris as a youth and didn't Poe accuse him of stealing from the Spanish and the German? Certainly even Longfellow, to go back to Professor Doughty's interdict, "simmered in the devil's cauldron of Central Europe" and was "spewed out of Italy and France." Could Bryant himself qualify? Didn't he trifle with strange tongues and admire enemy aliens? And what of Lowell? His Dante studies surely had a sinister smack; one can't imagine Professor Doughty approving them. Bayard Taylor I refrain from mentioning at all. His translation of *Faust* came to a just judgment at last when it was hurled from the shelves of every American university patronized by red-blooded, 100 per cent Americans. Its incineration on a hundred far-flung campuses, indeed, was the second great patriotic event of the *annus mirabilis* which saw the launching of Brownell's *Standards* and the entrance of the Ku Klux into literary criticism.

How little the patriot-pedagogues know of the veriest elements of American literary history was shown very amusingly a few months ago, when one of them, a specialist in the Emerson tradition, got himself into a lather denouncing some Greenwich Village Brandes for arguing that beauty was independent of morals and its own sufficient justification—only to be confronted by the disconcerting fact that Emerson himself had argued the same thing. Can it be that even pedagogues are unaware that Emerson came to fame by advocating a general deliverance from the stupid and flabby tradition his name is now evoked to support—that his whole system of ideas was an unqualified protest against hampering traditions of every sort—that if he were alive today he would not be with the professors, but unalterably against them? And Emerson was surely not alone. Go through the list of genuinely first-rate men: Poe, Hawthorne, Whitman, Mark Twain. One and all they stood outside the so-called tradition of their time; one and all they remain outside the tradition that fools try so vainly to impose upon a literature in active being. Poe's poems and tales not only seemed strange to the respectable dolts of his time; they seemed downright horrible. His criticism, which tells us even more about him, was still worse; it impinged upon such dull fellows as Griswold exactly as *Jennie Gerhardt* impinged upon the appalled tutors in the alfalfa colleges. And what of Hawthorne? Hawthorne's onslaught upon the Puritan ethic was the most formidable and effective ever delivered save only Emerson's. And Whitman? Whitman so staggered the professors that it is only within the last few years that they have begun to teach him at all; those who flourished in 1870 avoided all mention of him as carefully as their successors of today avoid mention of Dreiser or Cabell. And Mark Twain? I put a professor on the stand—to wit, my Christian friend, Phelps of Yale. Go to Phelps's *Essays on Modern Novelists* and you will find a long and humorous account of the efforts of unintelligent pedagogues to read Mark out of the national letters altogether—and go to Van Wyck Brooks's *The Ordeal of Mark Twain* and you will discover what great damage this imbecility did to the man himself. Phelps printed his book in 1910. It was the first book by a *Doctor Philosophiæ* in beautiful letters to admit categorically that Mark was an artist at all! All the other professors, even in 1910, were still teaching that Washington Irving was a great humorist and Mark a mere clown, just as they are teaching now that the criticism of Howells was superior to the criticism of Huneker and that Henry van Dyke is a great artist and Cabell a bad one.

Historically there is thus nothing but folly and ignorance in all the current prattle about a restoration of the ancient American tradition. The ancient American tradition, in so far as it was vital and productive, was obviously a tradition of individualism and revolt, not of herd-morality and conformity. If one argues otherwise one must inevitably argue that the great men of the Golden Age were not Emerson, Hawthorne, Poe and Whitman, but Cooper, Irving, Longfellow and Whittier. This nonsense no doubt is actually argued in the prairie seminaries; it even has its prophets, perhaps, in backwaters of the East; certainly one finds little in controversion of it in the prevailing text-books. But it remains nonsense all the same. The fact that it has been accepted for years explains the three great disgraces of American letters: the long neglect of Whitman, Melville and Mark Twain. And the fact that it is now challenged actively—that practically all young Americans of any appreciable intelligence now rebel against it—that the most significant sign of the times in many ways is the open revolt of the new generation against the teaching of their elders—this fact explains the new vigor that has got into American literature and its constant running amok. That running amok, to be sure, is leading to excesses, but so did the running amok of Whitman lead to excesses; so did the timorous running amok of Mark Twain. In order to get the rest of *Leaves of Grass* we must somehow manage to survive "A Woman Waits for Me"; in order to get *Huckleberry Finn* we must swallow the dreadful buffooneries of *The Innocents Abroad*. In brief, we must be willing to pay a price for freedom, for no price that is ever asked for it is half the cost of doing without it.

It so happens that many of the men and women who have sought to exercise this freedom in our time have been of stocks other than the so-called Anglo-Saxon, either wholly or in part. The fact, in a day of intense racial animosities, has greatly colored the whole controversy and made it extraordinarily acrimonious. I have already quoted some typical snarls from the Texas Nordic blond, Professor Dr. Doughty—the gentleman who seems quite as content to take his anthropology from Madison Grant and Gertrude Atherton as he is to take his manners from the Methodist sorcerers of his native steppes. Even more ludicrous attempts to set up an Invisible Empire in letters might be dredged from the writings of Sherman and Brander Matthews. Ernest Boyd, viewing the combat from his Irish crag, has given the whole body of such puerile stuff the waggish name of Ku Klux Kriticism. Its effect, I suspect, has differed greatly from that intended by those who discharged it. Far from alarming the non-Anglo-Saxons at whom it has been aimed, it has actually forced them, despite their differences, into some sort of alliance, and so made them much more formidable than they were at the start. And far from establishing any intellectual superiority in the Anglo-Saxon, it has only spread the suspicion that, for all his pretensions, he must be at bottom a very inferior fellow, else he would not be so eager to call in the mob to help him in a purely literary feud. For one, I believe in this inferiority thoroughly, and it constitutes for me one of the best of reasons for opposing the upholders of the alleged American tradition. What they ask all the rest of us to do, in brief, is to come down to their own cultural level—the level, that is to say, of the Anglo-Saxons (usually with a large Celtic admixture) who still make up the majority of the American population. The rest of us naturally refuse, and they thereupon try to make acquiescence a patriotic matter and to alarm the refractory with all sorts of fantastic threats and penalties. But it must be obvious that they fail—and their failure is a melancholy proof of their intrinsic inferiority. With overwhelming numbers on their side and every form of authority and all the prevailing shibboleths, they come to grief every time they tackle the minority, and at no time do they come to grief more dramatically than when (as during the late war) they prepare for the fight by first tying their opponents' hands.

As I say, the so-called Anglo-Saxon of the American majority seems to me to be a very inferior man, and as he comes into sharper and sharper conflict with men of other stocks his inferiority only grows the more patent. He is, to a large extent, quite incapable of education. His political ideas are crude and shallow. He is almost wholly devoid of æsthetic sense. Train him, make a teacher of him, and he still remains ninth-rate. His fundamental defects are two: first, his congenital fear of ideas, and, second, his incapacity for fair and honorable combat—his incurable tendency to seek apparently easy victims. Ku Kluxery is nothing new to him; he is a born Ku Kluxer; his whole history is a history of gallant attempts, at odds of 100 to 1, to put down dissent. I speak here, of course, of the general stock, not of the small and despairing superior minority. That general stock is full of very bad blood—blood worn out and running thin; perhaps not much at the start. In order to produce men capable of any functions above those of a Kansas mortgage shark or a Chautauqua orator it needs the stimulus of other strains. Poe, Whitman, Mark Twain—all of them were the products of such crosses. The fact that they increase is the best hope of the fine arts in America today. They shake the race out of its intellectual and spiritual lethargy and introduce it to disquiet and experiment. In opposing the process, whether in letters or any other field, the prophets of Anglo-Saxon purity only make themselves ridiculous. Under the absurd and pathetic *Kultur* that they advocate Agassiz would have been deported and Whitman would have been hanged and the most eminent men of letters flourishing in the Republic today would be Edgar Guest and Dr. Frank Crane.

The Low-Down on Hollywood

Having completed your æsthetic researches at Hollywood, what is your view of the film art now?

I made no researches at Hollywood, and was within the corporate bounds of the town, in fact, only on a few occasions, and then for only a few hours. I spent my time in Los Angeles, studying the Christian pathology of that great city. When not so engaged I mainly devoted myself to quiet guzzling with Joe Hergesheimer, Jim Quirk, Johnny Hemphill, Walter Wanger and other such literati. For the rest, I visited friends in the adjacent deserts, some of them employed in the pictures and some not. They treated me with immense politeness. Nothing would have been easier than to have had me killed, but they let me go.

Did you meet any of the eminent stars? If so, what reflections did they inspire in you?

Simply that they were all most wonderfully nice. I had known some of them for a long while; others I met for the first time. They were all charming.

Did any of them introduce you to the wild night-life of the town?

The wildest night-life I encountered was at Aimee McPherson's tabernacle. I saw no wildness among the movie-folk. They seemed to me, in the main, to be very serious and even sombre people. And no wonder, for they are worked like Pullman porters or magazine editors. When they finish their day's labors they are far too tired for any recreation requiring stamina.

I encountered but two authentic souses in three weeks. One was a cowboy and the other was an author. I heard of a lady getting tight at a party, but I was not present. The news was a sensation in the town. Such are the sorrows of poor mummers: their most banal peccadilloes are magnified into horrors.

Regard the unfortunate Chaplin. If he were a lime and cement dealer his divorce case would not get two lines in the newspapers. But now he is placarded all over the front pages because he has had a banal disagreement with his wife. I don't know him, but he has my prayers.

The world hears of such wild, frenzied fellows as Jim Tully, and puts them down as typical of Hollywood. But Jim is not an actor; he eats actors. I saw him devour half a dozen of them on the half-shell in an hour. He wears a No. 30 collar and has a colossal capacity for wine-bibbing; I had to call up my last reserves to keep up with him. But the typical actor is a slim and tender fellow. What would be a mere *apéritif* for Tully or me would put him under the table, yelling for his pastor.

So you caught no glimpses of immorality?

Immorality? Oh, my God! Hollywood seemed to me to be one of the most respectable towns in America. Even Baltimore can't beat it. The notion that actors are immoral fellows is a delusion that comes down to us from Puritan days, just as the delusion that rum is a viper will go down to posterity from our days. There is no truth in it whatsoever.

The typical actor, at least in America, is the most upright of men: he always marries the girl. It is his incurable sentimentality that makes him do it. He is a born romantic, and sweats only the most refined emotions. Worse, his profession supports his natural weakness for decency. In plays and movies he almost invariably marries the girl in the end, and so he finds it only natural to do so in real life.

I heard, of course, a great deal of gossip in Los Angeles, but all save a trivial part of it was excessively romantic. Nearly every great female star, it appeared, was desperately in love with either her husband or some pretty and worthy fellow, usually not an actor. And every male star was mooning over some coy and lovely miss.

I heard more sweet love stories in three weeks than I had heard in New York in the previous thirty years. The whole place was perfumed with orange-blossoms. Is honest love conducive to vice? Then one may argue that it is conducive to boozing to be a Presbyterian elder. One of the largest industries in Hollywood is that of the florists. Next comes that of the traffickers in wedding presents. One beautiful lady star told me that buying such presents cost her $11,000 last year.

But the tales go 'round. Is there no truth in them at all?

To the best of my knowledge and belief, none. They are believed because the great masses of the plain people, though they admire movie actors, also envy them, and hence hate them. It is the old human story. Why am I hated by theologians? It is because I am an almost unparalleled expert in all branches of theology. Whenever they tackle me, my superior knowledge and talent floor them.

In precisely the same way I hate such fellows as Jack Gilbert. Gilbert is in amiable and tactful young man, and treats me with the politeness properly due to my years and learning. But I heard in Culver City that no less that two thousand head of women, many of them rich, were mashed on him. Well, I can recall but fifteen or twenty women who show any sign of being flustered by me, and not one of them, at a forced sale, would realize $200. Hence I hate Gilbert, and would rejoice unaffectedly to see him taken in some scandal that would stagger humanity. If he is accused of anything less than murdering his wife and eight children I shall be disappointed.

Then why do you speak for Mr. Chaplin?

Simply because he is not a handsome dog, as Gilbert is. The people who hate him do so because he is rich. It is the thought that his troubles will bust him that gives them delight. But I have no desire for money and so his prosperity does not offend me. I always have too much money; it is easy to get in New York, provided one is not a Christian. Gilbert, I suppose, is rich too; he wears very natty clothes. But it is not his wealth that bothers me: it is those two thousand head of women.

Did you see any movies in the Western country?

Exactly three, and one of them was three years old and another I had seen before. The remaining one was *What Price Glory*.[65] I saw it the first night, and the vast herd of morons that stormed the theater interested me, I fear, somewhat more than the picture. I was the guest of King Vidor and Eleanor Boardman, and was hauled to the theater by Aileen Pringle.

When I got out of the motor-car with Miss Pringle the proletariat on the sidelines gave us a rousing cheer. But though they knew her, of course, they didn't know who I was, and so they began to speculate after we had gone into the theater. A private agent later informed me that they had come to the conclusion that I was Tom Mix. This somehow flattered me.

Then you continue quite ignorant of the film art in all its phases?

Ignorant? How could a man continue ignorant of the movies after three weeks in Los Angeles? As well continue ignorant of laparotomy after three weeks on a hospital veranda. No, I am full of information about them, for I heard them talked day and night, and by people who actually knew something about them. Moreover, I have hatched some ideas of my own.

As for example?

That the movie folks are on the hooks of a sad dilemma. In order to meet the immense cost of making a gaudy modern film they have to make it appeal to a gigantic audience. And in order to make it appeal to a gigantic audience they have to keep it within a narrow range of ideas and emotions, fatal to genuine ingenuity. Soon or late the movies will have to split into two halves. There will be movies for the mob, and there will be movies for the relatively civilized minority. The former will continue idiotic; the latter, if competent men to make them are unearthed, will show sense and beauty.

Have you caught the scent of any such men?

Not yet. There are some highly skillful craftsmen in Hollywood. (I judge them by their talk: I have not seen their actual pictures.) They tackle the problems of their business in a very intelligent manner. They know what they are trying to do. They are, in the main, very modest fellows, and despite the legend to the contrary, are quite willing to listen to advice, even when it is ignorant. They have learned a lot from the Germans. But I think it would be stetching a point to say that there are any first-rate artists among them—as yet. They are adept, but not inspired.

The movies need a Shakespeare. If he is in Hollywood today, he is probably bootlegging, running a pants pressing parlor or grinding a camera crank. The movie magnates seek him in literary directions. They pin their faith to novelists and playwrights. I presume to beleve that this is bad medicine.

The fact that a man can write a competent novel is absolutely no reason for assuming that he can write a competent film. The two things are as utterly unlike as Pilsner and Coca-Cola. Even a sound dramatist is not necessarily a competent scenario-writer.

What the movies need is a school of authors who will forget all dialogue and description, and try to set forth their ideas in terms of pure motion. It can be done, and it will be done. The German, Dr. Murnau, showed the way in certain scenes of *The Last Laugh*. But the American magnates continue to buy bad novels and worse plays, and then put over-worked professionals to the sorry job of translating them into movies. It is like hiring men to translate college yells into riddles. Aeschylus himself would be stumped by such a task.

Have you ever thought of venturing into the art yourself?

Why should I? Have I ever ventured into architecture? Or viola playing? Let every man stick to his natural trade. Mine is that of dogmatic theology. I hope to write a new Ten Commandments before I die. Moses has kept his monopoly too long. Walter Wanger offered me $100,000 to write the titles for a new Zane Grey picture, but I had to decline, for my old gift for epigram has begun to leave me. Irving Thalberg and Louis B. Mayer proposed to star me in a picture called *The Aphrodisiac*, but I incline to think that they were spoofing. When Lionel Barrymore heard of it, he threatened to burn down the Metro studio.

When do you think the Shakespeare of the movies will appear? And where will he come from?

God knows. He may even be an American, as strange as it may seem. One thing, only, I am sure of: he will not get much for his masterpieces. He will have to give them away. But the first manager who puts them on will lose money. The movies today are too rich to have any room for genuine artists. They produce superb craftsmen, but no artists. Can you imagine a Beethoven making $100,000 a year? If so, then you have a better imagination than Beethoven himself. No, the present movie folk, I fear, will never quite solve the problem, save by some act of God. They think too much about money. They have allowed it to become too important to them, and believe they couldn't get along without it. This is an unfortunate delusion.

Money is important to mountebanks, but not to artists. The first really great movie, when it comes at last, will probably cost less than $1,000. A true artist is always a romantic. He doesn't ask what the job will pay; he asks if it will be interesting. In this way all the loveliest treasures of the human race have been fashioned—by careless and perhaps somewhat foolish men. The late Johann Sebastian Bach, compared to a movie star with nine automobiles, was simply a damned fool. But I cherish the feeling that a scientific inquiry would also develop other differences between them.

What do you think, Herr Mencken, of the acting in the movies?

A delicate question, for I have seen none. But let me add hastily that I have a low opinion of acting and hence rejoice. The professional actor, as he reveals himself on the speaking stage, is simply a walking artificiality. The better he acts, the worse his acting. What he represents is not human beings, but stuffed dummies out of the immemorial storehouse of the stage.

I used to be a professional dramatic critic, and had a considerable knack for the science. But I gave it up because looking at acting was damaging my health. In the few movies that I have seen I saw nothing properly describable as acting. I simply saw groups of more or less charming people trying to appear natural. It was often very attractive, as the acting of little girls is attractive. But it would have made the late Richard Mansfield yell. He was a true actor. He staggered his audiences with his technical virtuosity, but so far as I can recall he never produced any illusion. No one ever believed that his *Baron Chevrial* was real. But the people who appear in the movies often achieve something very close to reality. Are they at times *gauche* and preposterous? Then so are you, and so is your old man. Then so am I.

You propose, then, that professional actors be kept out of the films?

There is no need to propose it: the public is doing it. Very few professional actors of any skill and experience have ever succeeded on the screen. I am surely no admirer of the public, but in this case it seems to show a sound instinct.

The movies began by trying to represent, not the artificialities that prevail on the stage, but life itself. Thus a taste for realism was implanted in their audience, and to this day that audience remains impatient of the factitious strutting and posturing that is professional acting. It prefers a charming woman, engaged only upon being charming, to all the most accomplished face-pullers and eye-poppers in the world. So do I.

In the course of my few visits to the movie parlors I have seen gals so lovely that I rushed home to write them fan letters. True enough, I always signed such letters with false names, and so avoided scandal; nevertheless, I wrote them. Perhaps many a worthy and beautiful girl at Hollywood cherishes such a letter today, wondering all the while how Seth Burkhardt, of Red Lion, Pa., ever achieved so delicate and eloquent a prose style. I was too bashful to inquire when I was there. I assume that the male stars of the screen get many similar letters from female literati. Very few of these stars, thank God, are actors. The great films of the future, like the good films of today, will be mainly done by amateurs.

But certainly you except such superb actors as Emil Jannings?

I do not. Jannings is unquestionably a competent actor. He has mastered the technique of the craft. But put him beside an earnest amateur, and at once the hollowness of acting becomes manifest. Turn to *The Last Laugh.* Jannings gave a very good performance in that film. He was full of tricks and ingenuities. He played every scene in a highly dexterous manner. But he was never real for an instant. No one actually mistook him for the old fellow he was playing.

Well, in the same play there was another performer who achieved the effect of reality almost perfectly. He played the ancient who is Jannings' successor as keeper of the hotel wash-room. I went to the trouble of inquiring about him of secret agents in Berlin. They reported that he was an amateur—an old goat who yearned to appear in the films, and was given his chance because Jannings happened to know him. He was a waiter by profession. One of the most eminent of American lady stars, I have heard, was once a waitress. Why not? There is too much prejudice in such matters. I put waiters far above golf players.

Are you against the star system?

I am neither for it nor against it. A star is simply a performer who pleases better than the average. Certainly I see no reason why such a performer should not be paid a large salary. The objection to swollen salaries should come from the stars themselves—that is, assuming them to be artists. The system diverts them from their proper business of trying to produce charming and amusing movies, and converts them into bogus society folk. What could be more ridiculous? And pathetic? I go further: it is tragic. Nothing, indeed, is more tragic in this world than for otherwise decent people to meanly admire and imitate mean things. One may have some respect for the movie lady who buys books and sets up as an intellectual, for it is a worthy thing to want to be (or even simply to want to appear) well-informed and intelligent. But I can see nothing worthy in wanting to be mistaken for the president of a bank.

Artists should sniff at such dull drudges, not imitate them. The movies will leap ahead the day some star in Hollywood organizes a string quartette and begins to study Mozart. One blast of Mozart makes a cleaner air than all the Rolls-Royces ever built.

Have you anything more to say upon the fascinating subject?

Not a word. I have said a great deal too much already. I shall catch hell from many kind friends, and no doubt justly. They will accuse me of making free with their confidences. But all their real confidences I reserve *in petto*: to violate them would be to shock the country.

Hollywood, I believe, is full of unhappy people. Many of its notables are successful and rich, but I don't think that many of them are satisfied. The sort of attention that falls upon a movie personage is irksome, and, in most of its aspects, insulting. There may be men and women out there who enjoy being pawed and applauded by millions of idiots, but if so I am not acquainted with them.

I recall a conversation with the late Valentino. He was precisely as happy as a small boy being kissed by two hundred fat aunts. Venetian palaces and one hundred pairs of pantaloons are not for artists—and Valentino, within his limits, tried to be one, and thought of himself as one. He was, under the surface, a sad young man. He has, in the movies, plenty of brothers—and sisters.

Palmy Days for Authors

These are palmy days for the authors of the Republic. There was never a time when they had wider or more eager markets, or got larger honoraria. Nor was there ever a time when the reading public demanded an ampler range of goods. The writer of fiction used to have a sort of monopoly: he was the only American author treated politely by bankers, lawyers, bishops and other such clients of the Golden Calf. But now there is a steady and immense sale for so-called serious books, and some of the fattest fortunes made in the scrivening trade of late have been made by historians, psychologists, biologists and even philosophers. A new book of metaphysics, catching the public fancy, is apt to run to a sale of 150,000. In such a sale, counting in the by-products, there is more money for the metaphysician than the total professional takings of all his predecessors from Thales to Kant. I hear of historians, after a couple of lucky strikes, buying country estates with swimming pools; of psychologists acquiring cellars; of biologists getting so rich that hopeful one-building "universities" begin plastering them with LL.D.'s. The by-products that I have mentioned come from the lecture platform and the train-boy magazines. The latter, with their gigantic circulations, pay such prices for safe but lively manuscripts as would have staggered the opulent collaborators in the *Edinburgh Review*. There must be nothing in these manuscripts against the Hon. Andy Mellon, but otherwise the field is wide and luscious. On the platform there is more easy money, for with the decay of the chautauqua the old-time lyceum seems to be reviving, even in the big cities, and the fees that it offers are often extremely generous. Let a professor write a book that sells beyond 5,000, and at once he is flooded with offers of lecture engagements. Nor is his thumping fee the whole of it: his expenses are also paid, and he is lured with dark hints about trustworthy gin and sightly gals. This resuscitation of the lyceum deserves to be investigated. It was once a struggling pansy; now it is a gaudy and exuberant dahlia, dripping genuine Scotch. No doubt the collapse of the theater on the road has had something to do with the change. Mrs. Babbitt used to give theatre parties, and vent her libido for the intellectual by going back stage to meet James K. Hackett or Mrs. Leslie Carter. But now the show-houses in the provinces are almost unanimously given over to dismal horrors out of Hollywood, and so she turns to the literary historians, psychologists, biologists and metaphysicians. The wise one throttles his lecture at the end of an hour.

Those literati who devote themselves to fiction prosper quite as heavily as their brethren of the enlightenment. One reads anon in the public prints that the day of the best-seller is over, and in a sense it is so: there are not many novels today that match the sales of such champions of yesteryear as *David Harum, Ben Hur* and *Three Weeks*.[66] But there are still plenty that sell above 50,000, and more than a few that cross 100,000, and with the standard trade price lifted from 98 cents to $2 or even $2.50, the author now derives more actual revenue from a sale of 100,000 than he used to get from one of 250,000. Moreover, his serial rights, when he can dispose of them, bring four to five times as much as they used to bring. Yet more, the brisk trade in short stories that follows a success yields him even greater usufructs: he used to brag about it in the saloons when he got $200 for a story; now the *Saturday Evening Post* and its rivals pay him $2,000, $3,000 or even more. Finally, there is Hollywood. It has failed, so far, to make anything save botches of best-sellers, but that failure has surely not been due to parsimony. It pays truly colossal prices for screen rights—and then scraps them in favor of the well-tried trade goods of its resident Nick Carters[67] and Ethel M. Dells. A price of $25,000 for a bad novel is a commonplace. Some time ago it gave an eminent American fictioneer $90,000 for the film rights to a novel weighing four pounds, and of moral treachery and Freudian psychology all compact—and then discovered, after he had departed rapidly with the money, that the work, if actually filmed, would make 125 reels.[68]

II

On the lower levels the corn-fed Balzacs and Turgenievs wallow in the same fat. There are more cheap fiction magazines on the stands today than ever before, and the sharp competition among them works for a steady increase in their scale of prices. The lowly hack who used to get $35 or $30 for a short story now gets $100 or even $150. And when he runs short of ideas he can always turn to writing "confessions" for the scandal magazines, and so keep his Cadillac in gas. The demand for such "confessions"—of reformed night-club hostesses, of almost-seduced secreraries, of Ruth Snyders who think of God in time—is tremendous: there is never enough on the literary wharves. More than one ingenious newspaper reporter, turning to their confection, has delivered his bones from wage-slavery, and lifted himself to the opulence of a Prohibition agent, a movie actor or a nose and throat specialist.

Thus the Republic, in this great year 1927, rewards its literary artists. They used to lurk in the cellars of Greenwich Village, gnawing petrified spaghetti; now they take villas at Pasadena or St. Jean de Luz, and dress their wives like Follies girls. It is a spectacle that somehow caresses the gills. As a critic I hail and welcome it, just as a policeman welcomes a wave of crime: it augments, in a way, the public importance of my job. I wish I could add that the labors so heavily rewarded are also intrinsically meritorious, but here, alas, I run into inconvenient facts. There is, indeed, not the slightest sign that the art of letters in the United States has kept pace with the prosperity of the literary trade. On the contrary, there is every evidence that the thing runs the other way. It has become so easy to sell second-rate work, and at vast prices, that the old incentive to do first-rate work has slackened, and, in some quarters, quite vanished. Why try to write a *Revolt of the Angels* or a *Lord Jim*?[69] The magazines for Babbitts will have none of it, and Hollywood will have none of it. There is in it, at best, a sale of 25,000 copies—with no serial rights, no stage rights, no movie rights. In other words, there is in it, at best, a second-hand Ford. But in the safe and easy stuff there is a Packard, and maybe, if the winds are really fair, a Rolls-Royce.

So the safe and easy stuff is being manufactured *en gros*, and the life of a book reviewer begins to have its pains. The new novels show a vast facility, but one must be romantic, indeed, to argue that they show anything else. The thing vaguely called creative passion is simply not in them; they are plausible and workmanlike, but they are never moving. The best fiction of today is being written by authors who were already beginning to oxidize ten years ago; the youngsters, debauched by the experiments of such men as James Joyce, wander into glittering futilities. One hears every day that a new genius has been unearthed, but it always turns out, on investigation, that he is no more than a clever sophomore. No first book as solid and memorable as *McTeague* or *Sister Carrie* has come out since the annunciation of Coolidge. Nor is any progress visible in the short story. Delivered at last from the blight of the O. Henry influence, it has settled down into banality, and becomes formalized anew. The aim of every short story writer, apparently, is to horn into the popular magazines: it is as if the aim of every painter were to do their covers. The annual collections of "best" stories make very sad reading.[70] They meet, no doubt, the specifications of the dreadful pedagogues who teach the craft of fiction by correspondence, but as works of art they are as hollow as jugs. Who remembers them? Who, indeed, remembers *any* American short story published during the past five years? I recall a few fine pieces by Miss Suckow, and a few others by lesser performers, but that is all. The heroes whose names glare at one from the covers of the magazines have simply covered so much paper, got their princely honoraria, and then departed—no doubt for Hollywood.

III

If they have done anything out there save collect more honoraria, there is as yet no sign of it. The movies sweat and pant for help, but it does not seem to be forthcoming. If they show any improvement at all, it is only on the technical side: the transactions they depict remain indistinguishable from the maudlin melodrama of the "confessions" magazines. All the American novelists save a lonely half dozen or so have tried their fists at the movies. Why have they produced nothing above the level of the serials in the tabloids? The common answer is that the movie magnates will have none of it—that they insist upon bilge, and only bilge. But that answer, it seems to me, is rather too easy. In point of fact, they waste millions trying to unearth better stuff. If they encountered a scenario as instantly and overwhelmingly moving, *as* a scenario, as *Kim* and *Lord Jim* were moving as novels, would they take it or leave it? I suspect that they would take it. They may be fools, but they are also gamblers.

These later years, indeed, have been too fat to prosper the fine arts, which tend to languish, as everyone knows, when the artist is overfed. It is now possible for a young composer in America to make an excellent income writing for the orchestra—but he must write jazz. Some of that jazz, to be sure, has its moments, but I doubt that any critic, save perhaps in New York, would range it seriously beside the music of, say, Johannes Brahms. What it lacks is sober dignity; if it arouses emotions, they are transient and superficial emotions; it warms without burning and leaving scars. That is what also ails the thousands of novels and tens of thousand of short stories now issuing from the American presses—and the so-called poetry that follows after them. They are competent, but they do not reach below the diaphragm; reading them is a diversion, not an experience. There is no moving passion in them; they leave the withers unwrung. When, from that placid and brackish stream there leaps anon an *Elmer Gantry*, it seems a sort of indecorum. All the scrivening boys and gals, it appears, can do better than that. They have better manners; they know how to entertain without shocking. But the works of art that last are those that shock.

I remain, as a sound 100% American, optimistic. We have been through such doldrums before, and survived them. They simply cannot last: one day a sharp, stinging wind blows up, and that is the end of the transient palmy days. The magazines that everybody reads, especially those who read nothing else, do not run to longevity. One *Atlantic Monthly* has outlived a dozen *Godey's*, New York *Ledgers* and *Fireside Companions*. On a higher level the public turns from flabby fiction to the compositions of the hortatory historians, psychologists, biologists and metaphysicians. And the movie men, tired of being stung, abandon the literary Mellons and Charlie Schwabs for bright youngsters—untried, but at all events not hopeless. The days were dark enough, God knows, in the 90's. But with the last gasps of the century came *McTeague*.

Epilogue: Testament

In three years I'll be fifty years old—a great age for an active journalist, as it would be for a June bug. Coming of a short-lived and somewhat impatient race—my grandfather was married at nineteen, my father was in business on his own at twenty, and I was the city editor of a big daily at twenty-three—I naturally doubt the actuarial promise that I still have a quarter of a century to go. Instead, I look backward and take stock, marveling at the futility which is human life, and trying to disentangle a few fundamental and abiding superstitions from the vast mass of notions that I have been throwing into space since the dawn of the century—many of them borrowed, and the rest largely mere rhetoric. What do I believe, at bottom and immovably? I believe (and preach) three main doctrines, to wit:

1. That it is better to tell the truth than to lie.
2. That is is better to be free than to be a slave.
3. That it is better to have knowledge than to be ignorant.

These notions are banal enough, God knows, and it is hard (in theory) to imagine any rational man challenging them. But it is my experience that, for some occult reason or other, they are inordinately offensive to the overwhelming majority of Americans, and that anyone who essays to whoop them up among us is sure to acquire a considerable unpopularity.

In so far as I am heard of at all in the Republic—and I doubt that 1 per cent. of its people has ever heard of me, save maybe in the vague and uneasy way that they have heard of Confucius, Louis XIV and Allen G. Thurman—I now appear to enjoy that unpopularity. The clipping-bureaux profit by it immensely, to the damage of my heirs and assigns. Every week they send me huge packets of denunciations, remonstrances, expostulations. The master-minds of Rotary seldom unsheath their idealistic Excaliburs without taking a hack at me (usually in company with Sinclair Lewis), and I seem to be one of the favorite hobgoblins of Fundamentalists and Prohibitionists, not to mention Christian Scientists and chiropractors.

I have been denounced on the floor of Congress by statesmen from the Bible Belt, and in blistering terms. The wowsers dislike me and have tried to jail me. I have been barred from the mails. During the late War for Human Freedom I was on the suspect list of the celebrated Department of Justice, along with Sacco and Vanzetti,[1] and one of my own partners was put to watching me. The evangelical Protestant papers charge me with favoring the Pope's scheme to put a Catholic in the White House, and the Catholic papers damn me for atheism and antinomianism. The Red-hunters put me among the Radicals, and the Radicals belabor me as an intransigeant Tory. In Greenwich Village I am thwacked as medieval, and among college professors I am regarded as an anarchist. During the twelve months of 1926 more than five hundred separate newspaper editorials upon my heresies were printed in the United States, and at least four hundred of them were hostile.

Yet so far as I can recall, I have not printed a single sober line in the past twenty-five years—I bar, of course, some obvious buffooneries—that did not fit snugly into one or another of the three platitudes I have recited.

All of this seems strange to me, though I have got used to it; my marveling over the fact is often mistaken for indignation, a weakness that I permit myself very seldom, and never against ideas. It is, curiously enough, the second of my axioms that arouses the greatest repugnance and opposition. The whole swing of things among us is against every substantial form of freedom; it has been going that way ever since the Civil War, and especially since 1914.

This swing I object to, not on doctrinaire grounds, but as a matter of the baldest expediency. It seems to me that if anything is plain in this confusing world it is that human progress, in the highest and soundest sense, depends upon liberty—that men cannot function effectively when their functioning is conditioned. I am thus wholly in favor of the Bill of Rights, and only wish that it were wider in scope. I believe that its guarantee should be enforced jealously and to the letter, even at the cost of a considerable amount of folly and turmoil, even if a certain proportion of guilty men go free. I'd rather see a thousand bootleggers at large than one peaceable and honest man molested in his inalienable rights. I'd rather, with Thomas Jefferson, see a revolution every fifty years than a government strong enough to ill-use even the humblest and most foolish of citizens.

But such notions are now unpopular in the Federal Union, and any man who merchants them must expect to be denounced as a public enemy. The Americano, once so proud of his liberty, now becomes a docile goose-stepper. He no longer has any private business, as he no longer has any castle; both may be invaded at will by any scoundrel wearing a badge. Worse, he is so far gone in pusillanimity that he makes a virtue of his ignominy, and is against any man who comes to his succor. Mention the Bill of Rights today, and you are at once suspect; in some States it becomes a downright crime.

This spectacle disquiets me, but I should add at once that it also amuses me. To find its equal in human history one must rise from the actual to the purely hypothetical. That is, one must try to imagine Bismarck jailing men for being in favor of the Prussian monarchy, and the Bolsheviki hanging men as Reds. If the Bill of Rights is not the foundation-stone of the American scheme of things, then the Sermon on the Mount is not the foundation-stone of Christianity. But both, in the United States, have succumbed to a perverse and paradoxical rabbinism. The chief Christians of the land—I take them at their own valuation—would be compelled, by their appalling logic, to jail Christ at sight, and the chief patriots, official and unofficial, make it a cardinal article that to talk of freedom is to talk of treason.

Here is the essence of comedy, and I enjoy it pleasantly, and do what I can to point up its salient humors. The American show, in fact, is precisely to my taste, and so nothing is ever heard from me about departing for fairer scenes. When I was younger and full of hormones it used to irritate me to observe the thing known throughout the world as American hypocrisy; I thought it a discredit to an otherwise worthy people. But as I slowly oxidized I began to see that this hypocrisy was necessary, lest life among us become impossible.

The American is no realist, but a soaring romantic; he cannot bear the harsh facts. So in order to escape them he must gild them and disguise them. Badgered by Prohibition blacklegs, he invents the doctrine that it is the good citizen's duty to obey the law, however insane and oppressive it may be. Confronted by a Sacco-Vanzetti case, he swallows a gross and palpable injustice in order to get rid of a fear and be able to sleep of nights. Governed by a camorra of obvious rogues and mountebanks, with a vacuum at the head of the state, he consoles himself by converting them into imaginary supermen, and by making it heresy to laugh at them.

All this, as I say, entertains me in a way befitting my tastes and station in life. The efforts of the Rotarians and Kiwanians to prove that a realtor is an idealist and the investment securities business a form of Service—these efforts delight me, and so do the attempts of the American Legion to enforce the dogma that the United States engaged in the late war for altruistic purposes. I am charmed by the Klan, and feel a glow in my heart for the Anti-Saloon League: both have served me as bootleggers serve Federal judges. The Methodist Board of Temperance, Prohibition and Public Morals is one of my favorites, and if it were put down by the common hangman tomorrow I'd imagine it, and keep on enjoying it. I go further: I am a partisan of the D.A.R., the W.C.T.U.,[2] the Y.M.C.A., the National Civic Federation, and the Comstock Society. All of these great organizations, in their several ways, have lightened the burdens of my journey through this sorry vale.

But to enjoy them is one thing, and to say that they are useful, or necessary, or honest is quite another. I don't believe that they are, and much of my time is devoted to announcing that doubt. There have been times, I suppose, when I have announced it with gratuitous harshness, but there has never been a time, I am convinced, when I have gone beyond the plain letter of the record. In brief, my conscience is clear, if a man long resigned to Hell may be said to have one. So far as I am aware, I have never uttered a single word, in serious controversy, that was not safely true. My sin, indeed, has not been a yielding to exaggeration but a weakness for platitude. I have labored the obvious cruelly, after the manner of controversialists at all times and everywhere.

But a forthright manner, however sound its grounding in platitude, is not popular in a land of compromise and euphemism, and so I am frequently denounced for intolerance. This charge, it seems to me, flows out of a conflict of opinion regarding the nature of liberty, and especially of free speech. I am myself in favor of liberty absolute and unrestrained, up to the extreme limit of human endurance. If any proposal were made to put down the Anti-Saloon League by law I'd be against it, and if the power were in my hands I'd certainly stop its execution. But it is my belief that the inalienable right of the Anti-Saloon League to exist and function gives me an equally inalienable right to challenge and denounce its acts, so long as I keep within the bounds of common decency.

The American doctrine, I believe, is quite different. It does not admit that the Anti-Saloon League has any inalienable right to exist. It holds, on the contrary, that the existence of any such organization or institution is a mere matter of grace—that any transient majority, or any minority come to transient power, may put it down at any time, for any reason or no reason at all. But it holds further that so long as any such organization or institution exists by grace its *bona fides* should be accepted as a matter of course—that challenging it is a grave indecorum, and ought to be discouraged.

Here I cannot follow the orthodox American. It seems to me that his definition of liberty is too narrow. All the thing amounts to, as he sees it, is a sort of license— not infrequently, in practise, a license to perform anti-social acts, but still only a license. I dispute that view, and with loud bawls. Liberty is something in itself, a *Ding an sich*. Neither Government nor public opinion has any right to condition it. If I am not free to say precisely what I think, in any seemly terms that occur to me, then I am not free at all.

All this seems so obvious to me that I can scarcely imagine a rational man disputing it, yet it is disputed every time a 100 per cent. American addresses his fellows. Such societies as the American Legion, the National Security League and the various organizations of Babbitts seem to be devoted almost wholly to denying it, and to trying to put it down as treason. The fact often subjects me to excessive inconvenience and greatly diminishes my value as a citizen of the Republic.

I collide with it every time I venture upon the pleasant business of refuting and denouncing Radicals. These Radicals, though they amuse me, also fatigue me: their reasoning seems to me to be full of holes, and I have grave doubts about the honesty of many of them. Thus it is an agreeable business to belabor them, and to it I have given over hundreds of articles and no less than two complete books.[3] But every time I undertake it I am diverted by the endless raids upon their plain rights.

How can I aim my blunderbuss at them while some American Legion blackleg or ambitious chief of police or knavish agent of the Department of justice is trying to silence them by force? I not only want to hear them myself, in order to get material against them; I believe that they have an inalienable right to be heard. Thus much of the time that I'd like to devote to defending capitalism against them has to be wasted in defending them against the assaults of the gunmen of capitalism.

The consequences are often extremely humorous. I am, in the easy American manner, assailed as a Radical myself. My name, in fact, is on all the lists of suspects that executive secretaries of enlightened self-interest prepare for alarmed bank directors and Ford agents. Even some of the Radicals, unable to think save in American terms, begin to embrace me as one of them—but not, I am glad to say, many of them. My prejudices here are very sharp. I enjoy all sorts of uplifters, but contact with them is not to my taste.

What I argue for is simply the abandonment of the whole imposture of 100 per cent. Americanism, which gathers within its fold every variety of fear, cowardice, imbecility and false pretense. It is cheap, nonsensical and dangerous to civilization. Its advocates are immensely stupid, else they would see that dragooning men is a sorry way to win their hearts, and that even the truth ceases to be true when it is propagated by force. I am in favor of capital punishment, as I am in favor of capitalism, but it seems clear to me that butchering Sacco and Vanzetti was a colossal folly. It was the act of men in a panic of fear; the motive behind it was obviously a desire to put down heresy. But its sole effect is to give heresy the glamor of the heroic, and to make the executioners ignominious and ridiculous.

No man can be dignified so long as he is afraid, nor can any people. We have in this country too much trembling. We are, as Wendell Phillips once said, too horribly afraid of one another. Millions fear the banalities of Darwinism; more millions fear the Rum Demon; yet more shake whenever they think of the Bolsheviks, those tragic comedians. The organization of such fears becomes a leading American industry; the Government itself engages in the business wholesale. How many policemen do we support? Count in the hordes of Federal spies and *agents provocateurs*, the great gangs of Chamber of Commerce Red-hunters, the marching hosts of W.C.T.U. smellers and snouters, the watchers at the ports, the censors of books, plays and movies, the endless brigades of Klan regulators, the Methodist prowlers, the Baptist guardians of the sacred vessels—certainly it must run to a corps unmatched in any civilized country, ancient or modern.

The national mentality becomes that of a police lieutenant, with overtones of a fugitive from justice. Liberty retires endlessly to new Hindenburg lines, and abandons them as soon as they are occupied. It becomes the official dogma that a good citizen does nothing without permission, and thinks nothing that is not thought unanimously. The old categories of true and false disappear from the American metaphysic, and in place of them there are only categories of right and wrong. It is right, it appears, to spy upon a neighbor; it is wrong to take a bottle of wine to a sick friend. It is right to support palpably prejudiced and incompetent judges; it is wrong to argue that men accused of capital crimes should have fair trials. It is right to applaud the buncombe of donkeys in high office; it is wrong to deride their donkeyism. It is right to be respectful to a theology that was stale two thousand years ago; it is wrong to believe in the Bill of Rights.

Let us face the plain fact that all this is evil. The easier it seems now, the more bitter will be its fruits hereafter. No good, in the long run, can come out of forbidding men to state their honest opinions, fully and even foolishly. No good can come out of harassing them with oppressive and extravagant laws, against their peace and consciences. No good can come out of supporting biased judges, cowardly and dishonest law-makers, numskull Presidents. It is an evil thing to believe in nonsense, however virtuously. It is an evil thing to honor ignoramuses and mountebanks. It is an evil thing to be always afraid. I confess that I do not like cowards; perhaps that is why 100 per cent. Americanism lies outside my reach. I observed the American people in 1917 and 1918, reduced to a frenzy of fear by a public enemy three thousand miles away, and obviously quite unable to deal them a blow. I have watched whole sections of them trembling at thought of the Pope.

Today I see the men of money among them, entrenched and buttressed as no men of money ever were in this world, stampeded and run amok by the mouthings of half-witted soap-boxers. It is, in its way, a comic spectacle, but it has its unpleasant elements. Venturing to have at it with mocking, I have got the usual reward. But I think I may say without affectation that I desire no other. My weakness, like that of all other literati, is a vast self-sufficiency. I have no appetite for the good-will of those I don't respect.

Notes

Introduction

1. A substantial number of them have been reprinted in *The Impossible H. L. Mencken*, ed. Marion Elizabeth Rodgers (New York: Doubleday, 1991). HLM himself, at the urging of his publisher, gathered his reports of the 1932 conventions in the volume *Making a President* (New York: Alfred A. Knopf, 1932), although he later stated that the book was among his least successful in terms of sales.

2. HLM, "The Monthly Feuilleton," *SS* 59, no. 4 (December 1922): 140.

3. Ambrose Bierce, "Ashes of the Beacon: An Historical Monograph Written in 4930" (1909), in *The Fall of the Republic and Other Political Satires*, ed. S. T. Joshi and David E. Schultz (Knoxville: University of Tennessee Press, 2000), p. 21.

4. HLM, "The Fringes of Lovely Letters," *Prejudices: Fifth Series* (New York: Alfred A. Knopf, 1926), p. 202.

5. An extensive selection of HLM's writings on religion can now be found in *H. L. Mencken on Religion*, ed. S. T. Joshi (Amherst, N.Y.: Prometheus Books, 2002).

6. HLM, *My Life as Author and Editor*, ed. Jonathan Yardley (New York: Alfred A. Knopf, 1993), p. 49.

7. *The American Language*, 4th ed. (New York: Alfred A. Knopf, 1936), p. 421.

8. For a selection of HLM's reviews of the American literature of his time, see *H. L. Mencken on American Literature*, ed. S. T. Joshi (Athens: Ohio University Press, 2002).

9. See *The Editor, the Bluenose, and the Prostitute: H. L. Mencken's History of the "Hatrack" Censorship Case*, ed. Carl Bode (Boulder, Colo.: Roberts Rinehart, 1988).

10. Elizabeth Drew, *The Corruption of American Politics: What Went Wrong and Why* (Secaucus, N.J.: Carol Publishing, 1999).

Prologue: On Living in the United States

1. The Ku Klux Klan, originally established in 1866 by Southern whites to combat the effects of Prohibition, was reconstituted by William J. Simmons in 1915 and for the next decade attracted a wide following in its hostility to Catholics, Jews, and African Americans. Many Klan members also supported Prohibition. The Anti-Saloon League was founded in Ohio in 1893 by the Rev. H. H. Russell; it became a national organization in 1895 and led the campaign for enactment of a prohibition amendment. It was chiefly supported by evangelical Protestant churches, and used various forms of propaganda and

pressure politics to persuade state and national politicians to support prohibition. It was one of HLM's longtime *bêtes noires*.

2. "Genuine privy councillor."

3. HLM may be referring to either William Lyon Phelps or Brander Matthews.

4. HLM refers to General John J. Pershing (1860–1948), leader of the American Expeditionary Forces in Europe during World War I.

5. Probably a reference to William James (1842–1910). For HLM's cynical view of James's celebrity as an American philosopher, see "Prof. Veblen and the Cow," *SS* 59, no. 1 (May 1919): 138–39.

6. The reference is to President Woodrow Wilson. Shortly after Wilson's declaration of war against Germany in April 1917, the British foreign secretary Arthur James Balfour visited Washington; evidently HLM believed that Balfour managed to persuade Wilson to give private assurances of greater U.S. support to the Allies than Wilson had publicly stated. In the election of 1920, Wilson's prestige as a statesman suffered significantly when his chosen successor, the Democratic candidate James M. Cox, lost by more than 7 million votes to the Republican Warren G. Harding.

7. In the election of 1921, John F. Hylan (1868–1936), of the Tammany organization, was easily re-elected to a second term as mayor of New York City, defeating Henry Curran.

8. HLM refers to the Naval Arms Conference held in Washington, D.C. (1921–22), which resulted in significant reductions of naval weapons by major European and Asian powers. HLM covered the conference (see various articles in *BES*, 14 November 1921–16 January 1922).

1. The American: A Treatise

1. The chandala are the lowest ("untouchable") caste in Hindu society. HLM often used the term metaphorically to denote lower-class individuals.

2. The Christian Endeavor Society was an evangelical and interdenominational youth ministry founded in 1881 by Francis E. Clark, a Congregational minister, to encourage young people to take an active role in their local church and to prepare them for future leadership.

3. HLM frequently and whimsically proposed the establishment of an American monarchy; see, e.g., "Why Not an American Monarchy?" *Vanity Fair* 43, no. 3 (November 1934): 21–22.

4. "Divine law" and "natural law." HLM should have written *jus divinum*.

5. The Lord's Day Alliance was an organization founded in 1888 by the leaders of several Protestant churches to promote Sunday as a day of rest and to urge state and national governments to pass laws criminalizing a variety of activities if performed on Sundays. A Canadian branch of the Alliance was a leading force behind the Lord's Day Act (1906; repealed 1985), and in the United States the Alliance was successful in pressuring state legislatures to ban many activities (including baseball, golf, and the delivery of the mail) on Sunday.

6. HLM refers to the Mormon church.

7. "Wild beasts."

8. The Mormons of Utah were compelled to outlaw the practice of polygamy (sanctioned by the *Book of Mormon*) in 1890, preparatory to Utah's being admitted as a state in 1896.

9. The report of the Chicago Vice Commission, issued in the spring of 1911, was subsequently banned as obscene because of its frank discussion of the city's difficulties with prostitution. Some years later HLM wrote about the report of the Baltimore Vice Commission: "The Report of the Vice Commission" (*BES*, 28 December 1915, 30 December 1915, 1 January 1916).

10. Thomas Jefferson, letter to John Waldo (16 August 1813), in *Writings*, ed. Merrill D. Peterson (New York: Library of America, 1984), pp. 1295–96.

11. John Stephen Farmer (1845?–1915?) and W. E. Henley (1849–1903), *A Dictionary of Slang and Colloquial English* (1905), an abridgment of *Slang and Its Analogues* (1890–1904; 7 vols.).

12. For a still longer list, see HLM's "Contributions to a Thesaurus of American Synonyms for 'Whiskers,'" *SS* 45, no. 2 (February 1915): 29–30 (as by "James P. Ratcliffe, Ph.D.").

13. Shakespeare, *Hamlet* 3.1.64.

14. On this matter see further the section "Edgar Allan Poe" in the article "Three American Immortals" (*P1*).

15. *The Merry Widow* (1905) is an opera by Franz Léhar (1870–1948). The dance referred to is the celebrated "Merry Widow Waltz" in Act II. *Floradora* (1899) is a popular musical of the period (book by Owen Hall, lyrics by E. Boyd Jones and Paul Rubens, music by Leslie Stuart). It created a sensation with a double sextet, "Tell Me, Pretty Maiden," the most famous show number of its time. *Lohengrin* (1850) is an opera by Richard Wagner (1813–1883).

16. The references are to a celebrated tenor aria in the opera *Aïda* (1871) by Giuseppe Verdi (1813–1901) and to the operas *I Pagliacci* (1892) by Ruggiero Leoncavallo (1857–1919) and *Rigoletto* (1851) by Verdi.

17. The references are to the opera *Tannhäuser* (1845) by Richard Wagner and the "Light Cavalry" overture (1866; in the operetta *Leichte Kavallerie*) by Franz von Suppé (1819–1895).

18. The references are to the operas *Il Trovatore* (1853) by Verdi and *Lucia di Lammermoor* (1835) by Gaetano Donizetti (1797–1848).

19. See "The Schooling of a Theologian" (*New Yorker*, 8 July 1939; rpt. in *Happy Days* [1940], ch. 11) for HLM's own singing of Methodist hymns during his early attendance of Sunday school.

20. "Spring Song" is the informal title for *Lied ohne Worte* (Song without words) no. 30 (1843) by Felix Mendelssohn (1809–1847).

21. On this subject see further the section "The Libido for the Ugly" in the essay "Five Little Excursions" (*P6*).

22. *The Easiest Way* (1909), by American playwright Eugene Walter (1874–1941), a bold play about a kept woman. It had 157 performances on Broadway.

23. HLM alludes to the annexation of Cuba in 1898 and the Philippines in 1899 in

the course of the Spanish-American War, conducted during the administration of the Republican president William McKinley.

24. Prior to the Civil War, Southern Democrats defended slavery on the principle of states' rights.

25. Theodore Roosevelt left the Republican party in 1912 over disputes with President William Howard Taft and ran as a third-party candidate for the Bull Moose party. As a result of their splitting the Republican vote, both Roosevelt and Taft lost to the Democrat Woodrow Wilson.

26. HLM probably refers to Daniel Coit Gilman, president of Johns Hopkins University in Baltimore.

27. The Millerites were followers of William Miller (1782–1849), a Baptist lay preacher who believed that the Second Coming would occur around 1843. At one time his followers numbered approximately 100,000.

28. Dwight L. Moody (1837–1899) and Ira David Sankey (1840–1908) were evangelists who preached to immense audiences in many of the major cities of the United States and United Kingdom during the 1870s and 1880s, culminating in a large gathering at the Chicago World's Fair in 1893. See HLM's review of a biography of Moody, William Revell Moody's *D. L. Moody* (AM, September 1930).

29. The YMCA was founded in England in 1844; U.S. and Canadian branches were opened in 1851.

30. The Salvation Army was founded in England by William Booth in 1865; branches in the United States were opened in 1880. Loosely connected with the Methodist church, the Salvation Army initially stressed the energetic performance of charitable works for the saving of souls. In 1890 Thomas Henry Huxley wrote a series of letters to the *London Times* (gathered in the pamphlet *Social Diseases and Worse Remedies*, 1891) accusing Booth of self-aggrandizement in his schemes for social reform.

31. The reference is to the depression caused by the panic of 1873, a result of overspeculation in land and securities. Thousands of businesses failed, and the economy did not fully recover until 1879.

32. W. C. P. Breckinridge (1837–1904), a Kentucky congressman, and Madeline Pollard were involved in a much-publicized breach of promise suit in 1894. The suit spelled the end of Breckinridge's political career.

33. The Webb-Kenyon Interstate Liquor Act of 1913, sponsored by Representative E. Y. Webb of North Carolina and Senator William Squire Kenyon of Iowa, prohibited the transportation of liquor into those states where its sale was illegal.

34. "Slave morality," Nietzsche's term for the morality of the common people, as opposed to the *Herrenmoral* ("master morality") of the aristocracy.

35. Rudyard Kipling, "An American" (1894), lines 49–52.

36. "War-cash," i.e., money to be used for warfare.

37. The conception is Nietzsche's. The volume entitled *Der Wille zur Macht* (1901) is, however, an unauthorized posthumous assemblage of notes and aphorisms.

38. The American Bible Society, a nondenominational organization devoted to distributing the Bible throughout the world, was founded in 1816. The American Tract So-

ciety, a leading publisher of religious material during the nineteenth century, was founded in 1825.

39. The Men and Religion Forward Movement was an interdenominational campaign conceived by Harry B. Arnold and promoted by Fred B. Smith in the late nineteenth century for the purpose of making churches "efficient" in advocating personal acceptance of Jesus Christ and in making religion a central and practical aspect of life.

40. The Student Volunteer Movement for Foreign Missions was organized by Dwight L. Moody and others as a conduit for foreign missionary work. Popular in the late nineteenth century, it began to decline in the 1920s.

41. The Gideons organization was conceived by John Nicholson and other businessmen in 1899 to foster the worldwide distribution of Scripture by placing Bibles in hotel rooms, hospitals, prisons, etc.

42. The Mann Act, passed by Congress in 1910, prohibited the interstate transportation of women for "immoral" purposes.

43. Brigham H. Roberts (1857–1933), a Mormon and a polygamist, was elected to Congress as U.S. representative from Utah in 1898. Popular hostility to his polygamous practices resulted in the House of Representatives voting not to admit him, and in a special election in 1900 William H. King was elected in his stead. Reed Smoot (1862–1941), a polygamist, was elected to the U.S. Senate in 1903; after four years of fighting for his seat he prevailed and remained in the Senate until 1932.

44. In "The Free Lance" (*BES*, 3 June 1913), HLM recounts this anecdote, giving the *Philadelphia Press* as his source.

45. In "The Free Lance" (*BES*, 15 May 1913), HLM attributes the remark to a Baltimore clergyman, the Reverend William T. Ellis.

46. The reference is to Charles J. Bonaparte (1851–1921), secretary of the navy (1905–6) and attorney general of the United States (1906–9). He was secretary of the Baltimore chapter of the Society for the Suppression of Vice in the 1910s. Early in his career HLM wrote a flattering article on him, "Charles J. Bonaparte: A Useful Citizen," *Frank Leslie's Popular Monthly* 57, no. 2 (December 1903): 166–69 (as by "John F. Brownell").

2. The American Landscape

1. HLM refers to James, Cardinal Gibbons.

2. "Slaves" and "commoners."

3. A "mature colored [man]."

4. The governor of Maryland in 1922 was Albert C. Ritchie (governor from 1920 to 1935).

5. HLM alludes to William Broening, mayor of Baltimore (1919–23, 1927–31).

6. The reference is to Richard Wagner's music drama *Tristan und Isolde* (1865); the celebrated prelude to Act I is frequently performed as a concert piece.

7. *Ben Hur: A Tale of the Christ* (1880), a best-selling novel by Lew Wallace (1827–1905), was turned into a highly successful stage play in 1899 by William Young.

8. *The Girl with the Whooping Cough* (1910), a somewhat risqué vaudeville farce starring Valeska Surratt, in fact opened in New York on 25 April 1910.

9. HLM refers to the aria "O du mein holder Abendstern" in Richard Wagner's opera *Tannhäuser* (1845), a song to the evening star (Venus).

10. HLM refers to Strindberg's *Countess Julie* (1888), in which the daughter of a nobleman has an affair with a valet.

11. From Kipling's poem "The Ladies" (lines 63–64), in *Barrack-Room Ballads* (1892).

12. In 1912 Madame Marguerite Steinheil (b. 1869) sued a London publisher, T. Werner Laurie, for issuing a book, *Woman and Crime* (1912) by Hargrave L. Adam, asserting that she had conspired to kill her husband and stepmother. (In 1908 she had been tried for murder but acquitted.) The publisher settled the lawsuit and withdrew the book from distribution. Steinheil wrote *Mes Mémoires* (1912; Eng. tr. as *My Memoirs*, 1912).

13. *To M. L. G.* (1912), an anonymous account (whether real or fictional is unclear) of an American actress's progress from youth to adulthood, with discussions of the sordidness of theatrical life.

14. *Bella Donna* (1909) is a best-selling novel by British novelist Robert Hichens (1864–1950) about a loose woman who, when taken to Egypt by her husband, unsuccessfully conspires with an Egyptian man to poison him. HLM reviewed the novel dismissively in SS, January 1910.

15. *Samson et Dalila* (1877) is an opera by Camille Saint-Saëns (1835–1921).

16. Possibly a reference to a line, "O Mother, why didn't you tell me everything!" spoken by a young woman, Wendla Bergmann, in *Frühlings Erwachen* (1891; Eng. tr. as *The Awakening of Spring*, 1910) by Frank Wedekind, a play about Wendla's sexual awakening. Wedekind (1864–1918) was a German playwright who pioneered the treatment of sexual issues in drama.

17. HLM refers to Monument Street in Baltimore, the street leading to the Washington Monument at Mt. Vernon Place.

18. In fact, the Democratic National Convention of 1928 was held at Houston, and the Republican National Convention at Kansas City.

19. HLM refers to the fact that the office of the *Smart Set*, which he coedited from 1914 to 1923, was located at 25 West Forty-fifth Street (between Fifth and Sixth Avenues).

3. American Politics, Morality, and Religion

1. HLM refers to *Theodore Roosevelt: An Autobiography* (1913). See HLM's reviews of several biographies of Roosevelt (SS, March 1920; rpt. in P2 as "Roosevelt: An Autopsy").

2. Peruna was a patent medicine devised by Dr. Samuel B. Hartman in 1879; by 1900 it was one of the most popular medicines in the country. HLM frequently used the word peruna to refer to a bogus remedy or panacea.

3. HLM refers to Parley Parker Christensen (1869–1954), candidate of the Farmer Labor party for president in 1920.

4. William Allen White, "These United States," *Nation* 114, 19 April 1922, 460–62.

5. The *Witenagemot* was the national council in Britain in Anglo-Saxon times.

6. "Drink no longer water, but use a little wine for thy stomach's sake and thine often infirmities" (1 Timothy 5:23).

7. Campbellites were followers of the British religious leader Thomas Campbell (1763–1854) and his son Alexander (1788–1866), who came to the United States in the early nineteenth century and evolved a version of Christianity that emphasized baptism by immersion and the sufficiency of the Bible as a guide to life and doctrine. The followers called themselves the Disciples of Christ; the term Campbellites was bestowed upon them by outsiders.

8. Nathan Leopold and Richard Loeb were sentenced to life imprisonment for the kidnapping and murder of Bobby Franks in 1924. An impassioned defense by Clarence Darrow saved them from the death penalty.

9. The reference is to a Ku Klux Klan parade in Washington, D.C., on 8 August 1925, in which an estimated forty thousand Klansmen marched. It was the largest rally in the Klan's history up to that time.

10. That is, the presidential election of 1928, in which the Republican Herbert Hoover defeated the Democrat (and Catholic) Al Smith.

4. American Art, Literature, and Culture

1. *American Literature*, tr. by Julia Franklin; New York, Doubleday, Page & Co., 1915. [HLM]

2. HLM refers to various works by Theodore Roosevelt (*The Strenuous Life*, 1900; *The New Nationalism*, 1910; *The Great Adventure*, 1918) and William Howard Taft (*Four Aspects of Civic Duty*, 1906; *Present Day Problems*, 1908; *Ethics in Service*, 1915).

3. Actually, Twain's late essay *Is Shakespeare Dead?* (1909) is a satire on the Shakespeare-Bacon controversy, jokingly affirming that the known facts of Shakespeare's life are too meager to support the view that he could have written the plays attributed to him.

4. The Scotch Covenanters were groups of Presbyterians in Scotland who flourished in the sixteenth and seventeenth centuries and who maintained that God offers grace and salvation to human beings by means of covenants. Covenanters exercised a significant influence in America during the seventeenth century, especially among Baptists and Congregationalists.

5. HLM refers to Edgar Allan Poe, who was found dead in a gutter in Baltimore. For an expansion of HLM's notions of the cultural barrenness of the South, see his celebrated essay "The Sahara of the Bozart" (P2).

6. "Yes-sayer," a conception from Nietzsche, who urged a vigorous saying "Yes" to life and its potentialities of thought and action.

7. New York, Dodd, Mead & Co., 1916. [HLM]

8. HLM refers to "The Blue and the Gray" (1867), a popular poem on the Civil War by Frances Miles Finch (1827–1907), and "The Battle Hymn of the Republic" (1862), a poem by Julia Ward Howe (1819–1910).

9. *Die Gartenlaube* was a German illustrated weekly (1853–1918) intended for family consumption.

10. [Ralph Waldo Emerson], "The Editors to the Reader," *Dial* 1, no. 1 (July 1840): 1–2. Emerson cofounded the *Dial* (with Theodore Parker, A. Bronson Alcott, Margaret Fuller, and others) and edited it during the last two years of its short run (1840–44). Fuller edited it during the first two years.

11. HLM refers to the magazine founded in 1880, which became a forum for the promotion of avant-garde literature in the 1910s.

12. The first edition for public sale did not appear until June, 1917, and in it the preface was suppressed. [HLM]

13. HLM refers to "3,000 Years among the Microbes," written in 1905, a satirical autobiography of a microbe living on the person of a tramp. A brief excerpt of it was published in an appendix of Paine's biography; the full text was first published in Twain's *Which Was the Dream? and Other Symbolic Writings of the Later Years* (1967). The other work referred to is "1601," a bawdy *jeu d'esprit* written in 1876 and portraying Queen Elizabeth engaging in coarse sexual discussions with Sir Francis Bacon, Sir Walter Ralegh, and others. It was privately printed in 1882 but not widely distributed until 1939.

14. See n. 47 below.

15. The next two sections of the essay comprise a reworked version of "The American: His New Puritanism," and are here omitted.

16. New York, (1914). [HLM]

17. I quote from page 157 of *Anthony Comstock, Fighter*, the official biography. On page 239 the number of his prosecutions is given as 3,646, with 2,682 convictions, which works out to but 73 per cent. He is credited with having destroyed 50 tons of books, 28,425 pounds of stereotype plates, 16,900 photographic negatives, and 3,984,063 photographs — enough to fill "sixteen freight cars, fifteen loaded with ten tons each, and the other nearly full." [HLM]

18. By Charles Gallaudet Trumbull; New York, Fleming H. Revell Co. (1913). [HLM]

19. An example: "All the evil men in New York cannot harm a hair of my head, were it not the will of God. If it be His will, what right have I or any one to say aught? I am only a speck, a mite, before God, yet not a hair of my head can be harmed unless it be His will. Oh, to live, to feel, to be — Thy will be done!" (pp. 84–85). Again: "I prayed that, if my bill might not pass, I might go back to New York submissive to God's will, feeling that it was for the best. I asked for forgiveness and asked that my bill might pass, if possible; but over and above all, that the will of God be done" (p. 6). Nevertheless, Comstock neglected no chance to apply his backstairs pressure to the members of both Houses. [HLM]

20. Now, with amendments, sections 211, 212 and 245 of the United States Criminal Code. [HLM]

21. *Vide Anthony Comstock, Fighter*, pp. 81, 85, 94. [HLM]

22. *The Memoirs of a Woman of Pleasure* (1748–49; commonly known as *Fanny Hill*) is a well-known erotic novel by British novelist John Cleland (1709–1789). *Only a Boy* (1899?) is a mildly pornographic tale attributed to Eugene Field (1850–1895).

23. Now sections 1141, 1142 and 1143 of the Penal Laws of New York. [HLM]

24. Maria Monk (d. 1850?), *Awful Disclosures of Maria Monk* (1836), an account of Monk's life in a convent in Montreal. Alfred Trumble, *Mabille Unmasked; or, The Wickedest Place in the World: A Lurid Panorama of the Night Life of Paris* (1882).

25. U.S. *vs.* Casper, reported in the *Twentieth Century*, Feb. 11, 1892. [HLM]

26. The trial court dodged the issue by directing the jury to find the prisoner not guilty on the ground of insanity. The necessary implication, of course, was that the publication complained of was actually obscene. In 1895, one Wise, of Clay Center, Kansas, sent a quotation from the Bible through the mails and was found guilty of mailing obscene matter. *The Free Press Anthology*, compiled by Theodore Schroeder; New York, Truth Seeker Pub. Co., 1909, p. 258. [HLM]

27. U.S. *vs.* Bennett, 16 Blatchford, 368–9 (1877). [HLM]

28. *Idem*, 362; People *vs.* Muller, 96 N.Y., 411; U.S. *vs.* Clark, 38 Fed. Rep. 734. [HLM]

29. U.S. *vs.* Moore, 129 Fed., 160–1 (1904). [HLM]

30. U.S. *vs.* Heywood, judge's charge, Boston, 1877. Quoted in U.S. *vs.* Bennett, 16 Blatchford. [HLM]

31. U.S. *vs.* Slenker, 32 Fed. Rep., 693; People *vs.* Muller, 96 N.Y. 408–414; Anti-Vice Motional Picture Co. *vs.* Bell, reported in the *New York Law Journal*, Sept. 22, 1916; Sociological Research Film Corporation *vs.* the City of New York, 83 Misc. 815; Steele *vs.* Bannon, 7 L. R. C. L. Series, 267; U.S. *vs.* Means, 42 Fed. Rep. 605, etc. [HLM]

32. U.S. *vs.* Cheseman, 19 Fed. Rep., 597 (1884). [HLM]

33. People *vs.* Muller, 96 N.Y., 413. [HLM]

34. U.S. *vs.* Bennett, 16 Blatchford, 368–9. [HLM]

35. U.S. *vs.* Smith, 45 Fed. Rep. 478. [HLM]

36. U.S. *vs.* Bennett, 16 Blatchford, 360–1; People *vs.* Berry, 1 N.Y., Crim. R., 32. [HLM]

37. People *vs.* Muller, 32 Hun., 212–215. [HLM]

38. U.S. *vs.* Bennett, 16 Blatchford, 361. [HLM]

39. U.S. *vs.* Moore, 16 Fed Rep., 39; U.S. *vs.* Wright, 38 Fed. Rep., 106; U.S. *vs.* Dorsey, 40 Fed. Rep., 752; U.S. *vs.* Baker, 155 Mass., 287; U.S. *vs.* Grimm, 15 Supreme Court Rep., 472. [HLM]

40. Various cases in point are cited in the Brief on Behalf of Plaintiff in Dreiser *vs.* John Lane Co., App. Div. 1st Dept. N.Y., 1917. I cite a few: People *vs.* Eastman, 188 N.Y., 478; U.S. *vs.* Swearingen, 161, U.S., 446; People *vs.* Tylkoff, 212 N.Y., 197; In the matter of Worthington Co., 62 St. Rep. 116–7; St. Hubert Guild *vs.* Quinn, 64 Misc., 336–341. But nearly all such decisions are in New York cases. In the Federal courts the Comstocks usually have their way. [HLM]

41. St. Hubert Guild *vs.* Quinn, 64 Misc., 339. [HLM]

42. For example, Judge Chas. L. Benedict, sitting in U.S. *vs.* Bennett, *op. cit.* This is a leading case, and the Comstocks make much of it. Nevertheless, a contemporary newspaper denounces Judge Benedict for his "intense bigotry" and alleges that "the only evidence which he permitted to be given was on the side of the prosecution." (Port Jervis, N.Y., *Evening Gazette*, March 22, 1879.) Moreover, a juror in the case, Alfred A. Valentine, thought it necessary to inform the newspapers that he voted guilty only in obedience to the judicial instructions. [HLM]

43. *Vide* "Newspaper Morals," by H. L. Mencken, the *Atlantic Monthly*, March, 1914. [HLM]

44. *Trilby* (1895) is a popular play by Paul M. Potter, based on the novel of the same name by British novelist George Du Maurier (1834–1896), about an artist's model who falls under the spell of a German-Polish musician, Svengali. *Sapho* (1886) is a play by Alphonse Daudet (1840–1897), based on his novel of the same name (1884), dealing with sexual obsession.

45. As a fair specimen of the sort of reasoning that prevails among the consecrated brethren I offer the following extract from an argument against birth control delivered by the present active head of the New York Society for the Suppression of Vice before the Women's City Club of New York, Nov. 17, 1916:

"Natural and inevitable conditions, over which we can have no control, will assert themselves wherever population becomes too dense. This has been exemplified time after time in the history of the world where over-population has been corrected by manifestations of nature or by war, flood or pestilence. . . . Belgium may have been regarded as an over-populated country. Is it a coincidence that, during the past two years, the territory of Belgium has been devastated and its population scattered throughout the other countries of the world?" [HLM]

46. For example, the printed contract of the John Lane Co., publisher of Dreiser's *The "Genius,"* contains this provision: "The author hereby guarantees . . . that the work . . . contains nothing of a scandalous, an immoral or a libelous nature." The contract for the publication of *The "Genius"* was signed on July 30, 1914. The manuscript had been carefully read by representatives of the publisher, and presumably passed as not scandalous or immoral, inasmuch as the publication of a scandalous or immoral book would have exposed the publisher to prosecution. About 8,000 copies were sold under this contract. Two years later, in July, 1916, the Society for the Suppression of Vice threatened to begin a prosecution unless the book was withdrawn. It was withdrawn forthwith, and Dreiser was compelled to enter suit for a performance of the contract. The withdrawal, it will be noticed, was not in obedience to a court order, but followed a mere Comstockian threat. Yet Dreiser was at once deprived of his royalties, and forced into expensive litigation. Had it not been that eminent counsel volunteered for his defense, his personal means would have been insufficient to have got him even a day in court. [HLM]

47. HLM refers to the attempted suppression of Dreiser's *The "Genius"* (1915) by the New York Society for the Suppression of Vice. HLM spearheaded a public protest, signed by dozens of prominent American and British authors.

48. Apparently a reference to *The Yoke* (1907) by British novelist Hubert Wales (1870–1943).

49. *Hagar Revelly* (1913), by Daniel Carson Goodman (b. 1883), is a novel about a working-class woman's struggles against poverty. HLM reviewed it in SS, October 1913, and discussed Anthony Comstock's attack upon it in "The Free Lance" (BES, 14 October 1913). *Love's Pilgrimage* (1911) is a novel in which Upton Sinclair sought to speak frankly about love, sex, marriage, pregnancy, and related issues. *One Man* (1915), by Robert Steele (b. 1880), is a novel about a man's struggle against his Puritan

upbringing. HLM reviewed it lavishly in SS, June 1915 (rpt. as "Portrait of an Immortal Soul," P1).

50. Stanisław Przybyszewski's (1868–1927) Homo Sapiens (1905; Eng. tr. 1915) is a novel of psychological realism dealing with the hidden sexual motives of human action. Mikhail Artzibashef's (1878–1927) Sanin (1907; Eng. tr. as Sanine, 1915) is a novel featuring a protagonist given over to selfishness and cynical hedonism. It was published in the United States by the firm B. W. Huebsch, which also issued Artzibashef's novel Breaking-Point (Eng. tr. 1912; Huebsch, 1915), a nihilistic work about the futility of life.

51. HLM alludes to Phillips's Susan Lenox (1917), which was decreed to have violated the obscenity laws when an action was brought against it by the New York Society for the Suppression of Vice in 1917. British novelist Elinor Glyn (1864–1943) wrote a popular novel, Three Weeks (1907), in which an Englishman conducts a torrid love affair with the queen of a Russian dependency.

52. The chief sufferers from this conflict are the authors of moving pictures. What they face at the hands of imbecile State boards of censorship is described at length by Channing Pollock in an article entitled "Swinging the Censor" in the Bulletin of the Author's League of America for March, 1917. [HLM]

53. Paul et Virginie (1788), by Jacques Henri Bernadin de Saint-Pierre (1737–1814), is a sentimental adventure novel about two chaste young lovers; it enjoyed tremendous popularity in the late eighteenth and early nineteenth centuries.

54. For example, the magazine which printed David Graham Phillips' Susan Lenox: Her Rise and Fall as a serial prefaced it with a moral encomium by the Rev. Charles H. Parkhurst. Later, when the novel appeared in book form, the Comstocks began an action to have it suppressed, and forced the publisher to bowdlerize it. [HLM]

55. An account of a typical prosecution, arbitrary, unintelligent and disingenuous, is to be found in "Sumner and Indecency," by Frank Harris, in Pearson's Magazine for June, 1917, p. 556. [HLM]

56. For further discussions of this point consult "Art in America," by Aleister Crowley, The English Review, Nov., 1913; "Life, Art and America," by Theodore Dreiser, The Seven Arts, Feb., 1917; and "The American: His Ideas of Beauty," by H. L. Mencken, The Smart Set, Sept., 1913. [HLM]

57. Vide The Cambridge History of English Literature, vol. XI, p. 225. [HLM]

58. The point is discussed by H. V. Routh in The Cambridge History of English Literature, vol. XI, p. 290. [HLM]

59. In Boon; New York, George H. Doran Co., 1915. [HLM]

60. "The well-worn way is the safest."

61. HLM alludes to John S. Sumner (1876–1971), who succeeded Comstock as secretary of the New York Society for the Suppression of Vice (1915–50).

62. In a letter to Felix Shay, Nov. 24, 1916. [HLM]

63. Doughty published his comments in an issue of Alcalde, a monthly magazine of the ex-students of the University of Texas. He responded to HLM's attack on him with an indignant letter, published as "Doughty vs. Mencken," Literary Review (New York Evening Post), 19 January 1924, p. 466.

64. A reference to Julia Moore (1847–1920), who published a popular volume of

poetry, *The Sweet Singer of Michigan Salutes the Public* (1876), for the centennial of American independence. It was ridiculed by critics and reviewers of the day.

65. *What Price Glory* (Fox, 1926), directed by Raoul Walsh, starred Victor McLaglen, Edmund Lowe, and Dolores del Rio. Adapted from the play by Maxwell Anderson and Laurence Stallings (1924), it concerns American soldiers in World War I.

66. HLM refers to three best-sellers of a former day. *David Harum* (1899) by Edward Noyes Westcott (1846–1898) is a novel about a successful but illiterate banker. For *Ben Hur* see Section II, n. 7; for *Three Weeks* see n. 51 above.

67. Nick Carter is a detective hero featured in a long succession of dime novels and pulp adventure stories initially written by John R. Coryell (1848–1924) beginning in 1886 and continued by other hands for many years thereafter.

68. The reference is to Theodore Dreiser's *An American Tragedy* (1925). In 1927 Dreiser sold the film rights to the book for $90,000 to Famous Players–Lasky, but the rights were for a silent film only; the film was never produced. A few years later Dreiser sold the rights again to Paramount for $55,000. *An American Tragedy* (Paramount, 1931), was directed by Joseph von Sternberg, with a screenplay by Sternberg and Samuel Hoffenstein (an earlier screenplay by Sergei Eisenstein was rejected because of his communist leanings). A later film version is *A Place in the Sun* (Paramount, 1951), directed by George Stevens.

69. HLM refers to *La Révolte des anges* (1914; Eng. tr. as *Revolt of the Angels*, 1914) by Anatole France (pseud. of Jacques-Anatole-François Thibault, 1844–1924) and *Lord Jim* (1900) by Joseph Conrad (1857–1924).

70. There were at this time two long-running annual series of best American short stories: *Best American Short Stories* (1915–), edited by Edward J. O'Brien (1890–1941), and *O. Henry Memorial Award Prize Stories* (1920–), edited by Blanche Colton Williams (1879–1944).

Epilogue: Testament

1. Nicola Sacco and Bartolomeo Vanzetti were working-class Italian Americans and self-proclaimed anarchists who in 1920 were arrested and tried for murder; they were convicted, even though there was strong evidence of innocence on the part of Sacco. They were executed in 1927. HLM wrote about the case on several occasions, including the article "Sacco and Vanzetti" (*BES*, 18 April 1927). He also contributed to a symposium on the case, "Those Two Men!" *Lantern* (Boston) 2, no. 3 (August 1929): 5–6.

2. The Woman's Christian Temperance Union was founded in 1874.

3. HLM alludes to *Men versus the Man: A Correspondence between Robert Rives La Monte, Socialist, and H. L. Mencken, Individualist* (1910) and *Notes on Democracy* (1926).

Glossary of Names

All names, save where indicated, are of Americans.

ABBOTT, LYMAN (1835–1922), Congregationalist minister and longtime editor of the influential magazine the *Christian Union* (later the *Outlook*). Abbott became acquainted with Theodore Roosevelt in the first decade of the twentieth century, and Roosevelt joined the staff of the *Outlook* in 1909, after leaving the presidency.

ADE, GEORGE (1866–1944), fabulist and journalist who achieved tremendous celebrity with *Fables in Slang* (1900) and its numerous sequels. HLM consistently regarded him as one of the leading wits and satirists of his time. See "George Ade" (P1).

AGASSIZ, LOUIS (1807–1873), Swiss-born naturalist who came to the United States in 1846 and remained there for the rest of his life, becoming a professor at Harvard and curator of the Agassiz Museum in Cambridge, Massachusetts. His chief work was *Contributions to the Natural History of the United States of America* (1857–62; 4 vols.).

ALEXANDER, JOHN WHITE (1856–1915), painter and illustrator. He began his career as an illustrator for *Harper's Magazine*; later he executed a well-known portrait of Walt Whitman (1886–89) as well as a celebrated series of murals in the Library of Congress (1895).

ALLEN, JAMES LANE (1849–1925), Kentucky novelist who enjoyed great popularity from the 1890s to the 1920s. HLM tended to dismiss him as a second-rater. See his reviews of *The Doctor's Christmas Eve* (1910; rev. in *SS*, March 1911) and *The Heroine in Bronze* (1912; rev. in *SS*, February 1913). HLM refers to Allen's *A Cathedral Singer* (1916), a novel that takes place in and around the Cathedral of St. John the Divine in New York City, and to *A Summer in Arcady* (1896), a frank novelette about a young woman's sexual awakening.

ANDERSON, WILLIAM H. (1874–1959), prohibitionist long associated with the Anti-Saloon League in Illinois, New York, and Maryland, and a member of the executive and legislative committee of the Anti-Saloon League of America (1912–24).

ASBURY, FRANCIS (1745–1816), British-born theologian who converted to Methodism in 1767 and came to the United States in 1771, leading revivals in many cities and becoming the founder of American Methodism. He was made a bishop in 1785.

ATHERTON, GERTRUDE (1857–1948), California novelist who enjoyed a great vogue in her day, outselling Edith Wharton and Willa Cather. HLM reviewed her novels *Tower of Ivory* (1910; rev. in SS, June 1910), *Julia France and Her Times* (1912; rev. in SS, September 1912), *Mrs. Balfame* (1916; rev. in SS, July 1916), her best-selling *Black Oxen* (1923; rev. in SS, May 1923), and *The Crystal Cup* (1925; rev. in AM, October 1925). In general he found her fluent and entertaining but insubstantial.

BALTIMORE, CECILIUS CALVERT, second Lord (1606?–1675), first proprietor of the province of Maryland (1632–75). In 1657 he came to terms with the powerful Maryland Puritans who had settled on the Severn River (on the site later occupied by Annapolis) to end a religious conflict and to decree toleration for Protestants and Catholics.

BANGS, JOHN KENDRICK (1862–1922), journalist and humorist best known for a series of sketches, *A Houseboat on the Styx* (1895), presenting caricatures of historical figures.

BARNUM, P. T. (1810–1891), showman who, after achieving spectacular success as the proprietor of the American Museum in New York City, organized a circus in 1870 that later became the Ringling Brothers and Barnum & Bailey Circus. See his autobiography, *The Life of P. T. Barnum* (1854; revised as *Struggles and Triumphs*, 1869).

BARRETT, E. BOYD (b. 1883), Jesuit writer on psychology and author of *The Jesuit Enigma* (1927), which HLM reviewed favorably in AM, January 1928.

BARRYMORE, LIONEL (1878–1954), stage actor who began appearing in films in 1911 and remained an immensely popular leading man for the next quarter-century.

BARTLETT, JOHN RUSSELL (1805–1886), antiquarian and bibliographer, and compiler of a *Dictionary of Americanisms* (1848), one of several forerunners of HLM's own *American Language* (1919). Bartlett also did much bibliographical and historical work on his native state, Rhode Island.

BECK, JAMES M. (1861–1936), U.S. assistant attorney general (1900–1903) and solicitor general (1921–25). At the outbreak of World War I he vigorously supported the Allied cause and was critical of Woodrow Wilson's stance of neutrality.

BEERS, HENRY A. (1847–1926), professor of English at Yale and author of several influential works of literary history, including *A Century of American Literature* (1878) and *History of English Romanticism in the Nineteenth Century* (1899).

BEHRING, EMIL VON (1854–1917), German bacteriologist who is regarded as the founder of immunology. He received the first Nobel Prize for physiology or medicine in 1901.

BELASCO, DAVID (1859–1931), actor, producer, and playwright who wrote numerous plays that enjoyed great popularity on Broadway in the late nineteenth and early twentieth centuries.

BELLAMY, EDWARD (1850–1898), novelist and short story writer whose utopian novel, *Looking Backward: 2000–1887* (1888), was immensely popular and led to the formation of "Bellamy clubs" to promote the radical political and economic ideas embodied in it.

BERKELEY, SIR WILLIAM (1606–1677), colonial governor of Virginia (1642–77). Berkeley, as a Cavalier, was violently opposed to the Puritans who battled the Royalist forces in the English Civil War, and was forced to retreat to his plantation for the period 1652–60; but upon the Restoration, Charles II reappointed him as royal governor.

BERNHARDT, SARAH (1844–1923), French stage actress considered the finest of her time. Her first performance in the United States occurred in 1880.

BIERCE, AMBROSE (1842–1914?), short story writer and satirist. Although HLM did not think highly of Bierce's tales—even the Civil War tales gathered in *Tales of Soldiers and Civilians* (1891; later titled *In the Midst of Life*)—he greatly relished *The Devil's Dictionary* (1906). Bierce's *Collected Works* (edited by himself) appeared in twelve volumes in 1909–12. HLM corresponded briefly with Bierce in 1913. His most exhaustive analysis occurred in an article in CST (1 March 1925; rpt. as "Ambrose Bierce," P6).

BJØRNSON, BJØRNSTJENE (1832–1910), Norwegian playwright and novelist who won the Nobel Prize for literature in 1903.

BLANKENBURG, RUDOLPH (1843–1918), German-born businessman (founder of the manufacturing company, Rudolph Blankenburg & Co., 1875) and mayor of Philadelphia (1912–16).

BLEASE, COLEMAN L. (1868–1942), governor (1910–16) and U.S. senator (1924–30) from South Carolina who defended lynching and denounced African Americans.

BOARDMAN, ELEANOR (1898–1991), actress known as the Kodak Girl after appearing in advertising posters for Eastman Kodak. At the time HLM visited Hollywood, she was married to the director King Vidor.

BOAS, FRANZ (1858–1942), German-born anthropologist and the founder of American cultural anthropology. More than any other individual, Boas amassed the scientific support to overturn notions of the biological superiority and inferiority of races. HLM alludes to Boas's article, "The History of the American Race," *Annals of the New York Academy of Sciences* 21 (1912): 177–83.

BORDEAUX, HENRY (1870–1963), French novelist and essayist whose novels emphasize traditional moral and religious values.

BORGLUM, GUTZON (1867–1941), sculptor and painter now best known for executing the busts of Washington, Jefferson, Lincoln, and Roosevelt on Mount Rushmore. He began the work in 1927 and had nearly finished it when he died; it was completed shortly thereafter by his son, Lincoln.

BOYD, ERNEST A. (1887–1946), critic who became one of HLM's best friends. HLM thought highly of *Ireland's Literary Renaissance* (1916; rev. in SS, March 1917), *Appreciations and Depreciations* (1918; rev. in SS, February 1918), *Studies in Ten Literatures* (1925; rev. in AM, June 1925), and *Literary Blasphemies* (1927; rev. in AM, February 1928). Boyd also wrote a monograph, *H. L. Mencken* (1925).

BOY-ED, KARL (1872–1930), a captain who was Germany's naval attaché to the United States at the outbreak of World War I. He was compelled to leave the US in 1915 after numerous allegations that he was giving covert aid to Germany and compromising U.S. neutrality during the war.

BOYNTON, PERCY H. (1875–1946), literary critic and professor long associated with the University of Chicago. HLM tended to find his criticism unadventurous and academic.

BRAGG, GEORGE FREEMAN (1863–1940), African American clergyman and rector of St. James Church (Episcopal) in Baltimore. He was the author of *Men of Maryland* (1914), *The History of the Afro-American Group of the Episcopal Church* (1922), and other works.

BRANDES, GEORG (1842–1907), Danish critic whose works of literary criticism were highly influential in Europe and the United States.

BRIEUX, EUGÈNE (1858–1932), French playwright and a pioneer in realistic drama. HLM thought highly of his plays, reviewing several English translations of them, including *Three Plays* (1911; rev. in SS, October 1911). He also wrote a substantial preface to an edition of *Blanchette and The Escape: Two Plays by Brieux* (1913). *Les Avariés* (1901; Eng. tr. as *Damaged Goods*) caused a scandal in its frank discussion of veneral disease. It appeared in *Three Plays*.

BRILLAT-SAVARIN, ANTHELME (1755–1826), French lawyer and politician who wrote one of the most celebrated treatises on gastronomy, *Physiologue du goût* (1825; Eng. tr. as *The Physiology of Taste*).

BRISBANE, ARTHUR (1864–1936), prolific journalist and editor who worked initially for the *New York Sun* (1883–90), then became managing editor of the *New York World* (1890–97), then worked for the Hearst newspapers.

BROOKS, VAN WYCK (1886–1963), critic and biographer whose *Letters and Leadership* (1918; rev. in SS, February 1919) and *The Ordeal of Mark Twain* (1920; rev. in SS, October 1920) were favorably reviewed by HLM. He is best known for *The Flowering of New England* (1936) and *New England: Indian Summer* (1940).

BROWN, ALICE (1857–1948), novelist, poet, and playwright who wrote chiefly of New England life.

BROWN, JOHN (1800–1859), white abolitionist who led an abortive slave uprising at Harpers Ferry, Virginia, in 1859 and was hanged for treason later that year.

BROWNELL, W. C. (1851–1928), editor and critic who emphasized moral qualities in literature. HLM did not think much of his criticism; he frequently cited *Stan-*

dards (1917)—a plea for the retention of conventional aesthetic and moral standards in literature—as emblematic of his work.

BRYAN, WILLIAM JENNINGS (1860–1925), leading Democratic politician of the later nineteenth and early twentieth centuries. He was Democratic candidate for president in 1896, 1900, and 1908, and secretary of state under Woodrow Wilson (1912–15). His role in the prosecution of the Scopes trial of 1925 is infamous, made the more so by HLM's pungent and cynical coverage of it.

BRYANT, WILLIAM CULLEN (1794–1878), poet who attained celebrity with the early poem "Thanatopsis" (1817) and continued to write poetry prolifically for the remainder of his long career.

BÜLOW, HANS VON (1830–1894), German pianist and conductor who toured extensively in the United States in 1875–76 and 1889–90.

BURLESON, ALBERT SIDNEY (1863–1937), U.S. postmaster general (1913–21) who gained infamy for his prejudice against African American postal workers and for his crackdown on purportedly "seditious" materials sent through the mail.

BURNETT, FRANCES HODGSON (1849–1924), British-born author of *Little Lord Fauntleroy* (1886) and other sentimental works for children and adults.

BURNS, ROBERT (1759–1796), Scottish poet. In 1785 he fell in love with Jean (not Jane) Armour; but because he had developed a reputation for religious heterodoxy, her father did not permit them to marry. They finally married in 1788.

BURR, AARON (1756–1836), vice president under Thomas Jefferson (1801–5). He was tried for treason in 1807 but acquitted. HLM alludes to the fact that Burr, who had early developed a reputation as a libertine, was thought by the residents of Princeton, New Jersey (where Burr was a student at Princeton College), to have abandoned a young woman named Catherine Bullock, who then died of a broken heart and was buried in the Princeton cemetery.

BUSONI, FERRUCCIO (1866–1924), Italian pianist and composer (author of the opera *Turandot*, 1917). He toured the United States as a pianist in 1890.

BUTLER, NICHOLAS MURRAY (1862–1947), longtime president of Columbia University and author of many books on education, politics, and other subjects. Although a Republican, he did not support Prohibition.

CABELL, JAMES BRANCH (1879–1958), Virginia novelist whom HLM regarded as one of the leading authors of his day. HLM reviewed almost every one of his works from 1909 to the late 1920s; he also helped to defend Cabell when his novel *Jurgen* (1919) came under attack from the New York Society for the Suppression of Vice. See HLM's brief monograph, *James Branch Cabell* (1927).

CAHAN, ABRAHAM (1860–1951), Jewish journalist and novelist born in Russia who settled in the United States in 1882. Cahan worked on a number of Yiddish journals in New York, notably the socialist daily *Vorwaerts* (later the *Jewish Daily Forward*), which he established as a major Jewish-American paper. He wrote several novels and story collections aside from his best-known work, *The Rise of David Levinsky* (1917; rev. in *SS*, May 1918), a well-received novel about the Jewish community in New York.

CAINE, HALL (1853–1931), popular British novelist whose work HLM regularly ridiculed. See his reviews of *The White Prophet* (1909; rev. in *SS*, December 1909), *The Woman Thou Gavest Me* (1913; rev. in *SS*, November 1913), and Caine's autobiography, *My Story* (1908; rev. in *SS*, September 1909).

CALLAHAN, PATRICK H. (1865–1940), businessman and Catholic layman. He established the successful Louisville Varnish Company in 1915. He advocated the repudiation of religious bigotry, but supported Prohibition and William Jennings Bryan's fundamentalism at the Scopes trial.

CANNON, JAMES (1864–1944), perhaps the leading Methodist clergyman of his time, was elected bishop in 1918. He was a vigorous proponent of temperance, being the leading lobbyist for the Anti-Saloon League both before and after the passage of the Eighteenth Amendment.

CARNEGIE, ANDREW (1835–1919), financier who gradually gained nearly total control of the U.S. steel industry until he sold the Carnegie Steel Company to J. P. Morgan in 1907. He later became a noted philanthropist.

CARROLL, CHARLES (1737–1832), Maryland politician who was elected a delegate to the Continental Congress in 1776 (where he signed the Declaration of Independence) and to the Constitutional Convention in 1787.

CARTER, MRS. LESLIE (Caroline Louise Dudley, 1862–1937), stage actress who starred in many plays from the 1890s to the 1920s.

CARUSO, ENRICO (1873–1921), Italian tenor hailed as the finest of his era. He toured the United States on many occasions, including a visit to San Francisco during the earthquake and fire of 1906.

CATHER, WILLA (1876–1947), novelist and poet whom HLM considered the best American woman writer of her age. She won the Pulitzer Prize for *One of Ours* (1922). Aside from numerous reviews of her novels, HLM also wrote a brief essay, "Willa Cather" (in *The Borzoi 1920* [1920]).

CATT, CARRIE CHAPMAN (1859–1947), advocate of woman suffrage who succeeded Susan B. Anthony as head of the National American Woman Suffrage Association (1900–1904, 1915–20).

CHAMBERS, ROBERT W. (1865–1933), best-selling novelist whose shopgirl romances enjoyed a tremendous vogue in the 1910s and 1920s. HLM heaped abuse upon him in his reviews of *Ailsa Page* (1910; rev. in *SS*, January 1911), *The Adventures of a Modest Man* (1911; rev. in *SS*, May 1911), *The Gay Rebellion* (1913; rev. in *SS*, July 1913), and *The Business of Life* (1913; rev. in *SS*, December 1913). HLM did not, however, review Chambers's best-selling novel *The Common Law* (1911).

CHANNING, WILLIAM ELLERY (1780–1842), Unitarian minister and vigorous opponent of slavery. HLM appears to allude to some of Channing's polemical abolitionist works, such as *The Duty of the Free States* (1842).

CHAPLIN, CHARLES (1889–1977), British actor who became the first "movie star" after emigrating to the United States in 1912 and starring in many silent films. HLM wrote an article on him, "The Chaplin Case" (*BES*, 24 January 1927), concerning his bitter and much-publicized divorce from his second wife, Lita Grey, which led to a million-dollar settlement.

CHESTERTON, G. K. (1874–1936), British novelist and critic best known today for his Father Brown detective stories. Although HLM initially found Chesterton's wit stimulating, he later came to weary of Chesterton's religiosity and overuse of paradox. See his reviews of *Orthodoxy* (1908; rev. in *SS*, February 1909), *The Ball and the Cross* (1909; rev. in *SS*, March 1910), and *The Flying Inn* (1914; rev. in *SS*, April 1914).

CHURCHILL, WINSTON (1871–1947), prolific and popular novelist of his day. He achieved best-seller status with *Richard Carvel* (1899) and other historical novels and melodramas. HLM regarded him as, at best, a second-rater; see his reviews of *A Modern Chronicle* (1910; rev. in *SS*, July 1910), *The Inside of the Cup* (1913; rev. in *SS*, September 1913), and *A Far Country* (1915; rev. in *SS*, August 1915).

COBB, IRVIN S. (1876–1944), popular writer of humorous short stories, included in such volumes as *The Escape of Mr. Trimm* (1913), *Old Judge Priest* (1915), and many others. See his autobiography, *Exit Laughing* (1941). HLM had a low opinion of his work; see his essay, "The Heir of Mark Twain" (*P1*).

COHALAN, DANIEL FLORENCE (1865–1946), justice of the New York State Supreme Court (1911–24) intimately involved with the Tammany organization.

COMSTOCK, ANTHONY (1844–1915), founder of the New York Society for the Suppression of Vice in 1873. Attaining tremendous power and influence, Comstock and his allies carried on numerous campaigns to prevent the distribution of "obscene" books and other matter. He was one of HLM's *bêtes noires*. See his review of Charles Gallaudet Trumbull's *Anthony Comstock, Fighter* (1913; rev. in *SS*, April 1914), and the essay "Comstockery" (*P5*).

COOLIDGE, CALVIN (1872–1933), thirtieth president of the United States (1923–29). HLM relentlessly criticized his support of Prohibition, his subsidies to farmers, and other perceived derelictions. He tartly reviewed his tract, *The Price of Freedom* (1924; rev. in *BES*, 19 April 1924 and in *AM*, June 1924).

CORELLI, MARIE (pseud. of Mary Mackay, 1855–1924), British novelist whose mix of spiritualism and melodrama made many of her novels best-sellers, beginning with *The Sorrows of Satan* (1895). HLM reviewed *Holy Orders* (1908; rev. in *SS*, November 1908) and *Innocent, Her Fancy and His Fact* (1914; rev. in *SS*, February

1915), remarking of the latter: "Sadness . . . stalks through it like some great murrain through the countryside; it is a sure cure for joy in every form. I myself, a mocker at all sweet and lovely things, a professional snickerer, a saucy fellow by trade, have moaned and blubbered over it like a fat woman at *La Dame aux Camélias*."

COULEVAIN, PIERRE DE (pseud. of Hélène Favre de Coulevain, 1871–1913), French novelist whose tales of married life enjoyed a brief vogue in the 1910s. HLM reviewed her novel *On the Branch* (Eng. tr. 1910; rev. in *SS*, April 1910).

COX, JAMES M. (1870–1957), U.S. representative (1909–13) and governor (1913–15, 1917–21) from Ohio and Democratic candidate for president in 1920.

CRANE, FRANK (1861–1928), clergyman and journalist and one of the most widely syndicated columnists of his day. HLM regarded his work as trite and naively optimistic.

CRANE, STEPHEN (1871–1900), novelist, short story writer, and poet whose short novel *The Red Badge of Courage* (1895) is considered the finest literary treatment of the Civil War. HLM wrote an introduction to Crane's *Major Conflicts: George's Mother; The Blue Hotel; Maggie* (1926).

CREEL, GEORGE (1876–1953), journalist whom President Woodrow Wilson appointed chairman of the Committee on Public Information in 1917 to write pro-Allied propaganda as a means of eliciting American support for the war. HLM habitually referred to it as the Creel Press Bureau.

CROCE, BENEDETTO (1866–1952), Italian philosopher, literary theorist, and author of numerous influential treatises on aesthetics and poetry.

CROSS, VICTORIA (pseud. of Vivian Cory), a prolific popular novelist of the first three decades of the twentieth century. Her novels chiefly feature female protagonists in romantic scenarios.

CURTIS, CYRUS H. K. (1850–1933), publisher who purchased the *Saturday Evening Post* in 1897 and transformed it into one of the most successful magazines in American history and the Curtis Publishing Company into one of the richest publishers in the world. He later acquired the *Philadelphia Public Ledger* and the *New York Evening Post*, but was not successful with them.

DANIELS, JOSEPHUS (1862–1948), secretary of the navy under Woodrow Wilson (1913–21). He earned HLM's wrath by prohibiting the use of alcohol on navy vessels in 1914 and by an extensive build-up of the navy in accordance with the Naval Appropriation Act of 1916, which HLM believed was part of the U.S. government's covert support of the Allies against Germany in World War I.

D'ANNUNZIO, GABRIELE (1863–1938), Italian poet, novelist, and playwright who enjoyed a vogue in the English-speaking world at the turn of the century.

DAVIS, RICHARD HARDING (1864–1916), journalist and novelist whose novels and tales of adventure and romance enjoyed great popularity in his time. HLM took note of only one of them: the story collection *The Man Who Could Not Lose* (1911; rev. in SS, December 1911), most of whose contents HLM found "silly beyond description."

DAWES, CHESTER GATES (1865–1951), vice president under Calvin Coolidge (1925–29). He was cowinner of the Nobel Peace Prize in 1925 for his work on the Allied Reparations Commission, which helped stabilize the German economy following World War I.

DEBS, EUGENE V. (1855–1926), labor leader and socialist candidate for president. He helped found the Industrial Workers of the World (1905), a radical labor organization, and served two years in prison (1919–21) for protesting the government's repression of civil liberties during World War I.

DELL, ETHEL M. (d. 1939), prolific author of popular sentimental novels from the 1910s to the 1930s.

DEMPSEY, JACK (1896–1983), heavyweight champion of the world from 1919 to 1926, when he lost to Gene Tunney. HLM covered the fight between Dempsey and the French boxer Georges Carpentier in 1921; see "How Legends Are Made" (*BES*, 5 July 1921).

DEPEW, CHAUNCEY M. (1834–1928), president of the New York Central Railroad and US senator from New York (1899–1911). During his second term Depew was revealed to have accepted a retainer from the Equitable Life Assurance Company; but, contrary to HLM's assertion, he eventually regained his popular standing, although he did not again run for office.

DESLYS, GABY (1884–1920), French dancer who attained great popularity in the United States after her debut there in 1911.

DREISER, THEODORE (1871–1945), pioneering novelist; HLM became his chief advocate. Dreiser's first novel was the controversial *Sister Carrie* (1900), a grim naturalistic work about a working-class woman. HLM wrote substantial reviews of many of Dreiser's subsequent books, including *Jennie Gerhardt* (1911; rev. in SS, November 1911), *The Financier* (1912; rev. in the *New York Times Review of Books*, 10 November 1912), *The Titan* (1914; rev. in *Town Topics*, 18 June 1914, and in SS, August 1914), *The "Genius"* (1915; rev. in SS, December 1915), *A Hoosier Holiday* (1916; rev. in SS, October 1916), and *An American Tragedy* (1925; rev. in AM, March 1926). He devoted a substantial chapter to Dreiser in *A Book of Prefaces* (1917). For their tortured personal relationship see *Dreiser-Mencken Letters* (1977; 2 vols.) as well as HLM's *My Life as Author and Editor* (1993).

DU BOIS, W. E. B. (1868–1963), African American leader and prolific author. His most celebrated volume is *The Souls of Black Folk* (1903). In 1910 he helped found the NAACP and edited its journal, *The Crisis*.

DUSE, ELEONORA (1858–1924), Italian stage actress who first toured the United States in 1893.

EASTMAN, MONK (1873–1920), Jewish gang leader who became a powerful force in the control of gambling and prostitution in New York City. Serving a ten-year prison term (1904–14), he was pardoned by Governor Alfred E. Smith after serving bravely in World War I. He was killed by a Prohibition enforcement agent.

EDDY, MARY BAKER (1821–1910), founder of Christian Science and author of the Christian Science Bible, *Science and Health* (1875). HLM wrote copiously about Christian Science over his career; see, e.g., "On Christian Science" (*BES*, 23 October 1916), "The Career of a Divinity" (*AM*, November 1929), and "Christian Science Technique" (*BES*, 3 March 1930).

EDWARDS, JONATHAN (1703–1758), Calvinist theologian who fostered the Great Awakening in the 1740s. His best-known sermon, "Sinners in the Hands of an Angry God" (1741), is not considered representative of his religious thought.

ELIOT, GEORGE (pseud. of Mary Ann Evans, 1819–1880), British novelist who created a scandal by living with the philosopher George Henry Lewes (who was married) from the mid-1850s until his death in 1878.

ELLIS, HAVELOCK (1859–1939), British essayist and psychologist whose landmark treatise, *Studies in the Psychology of Sex* (1897–1928; 7 vols.), HLM greatly admired as a sane, balanced account of the subject. Ellis wrote a substantial essay on Nietzsche in *Affirmations* (1898). HLM wrote of him on several occasions; see the section "Havelock Ellis" (originally a review in the *New York Evening Post*, 24 September 1921) in the essay "Five Men at Random" (*P3*) and "Havelock Ellis" (*BES*, 11 July 1926).

EMERSON, RALPH WALDO (1803–1882), a leading poet and essayist of the nineteenth century. For HLM's early evaluation of him, see "An Unheeded Law-Giver" (*P1*). Later he reviewed Régis Michaud's biography, *Emerson: The Enraptured Yankee* (1930; rev. in *AM*, October 1930).

ERSKINE, JOHN (1879–1951), novelist and essayist who attained celebrity with *The Private Life of Helen of Troy* (1925) and other works treating historical figures irreverently. He was a longtime professor of English at Columbia University (1906–37).

FAIRBANKS, DOUGLAS, SR. (pseud. of Douglas Elton Ulman, 1883–1939), stage and film actor who achieved tremendous popularity for his wholesome good looks and his devil-may-care persona. He appeared in films from 1915 to 1934.

FAIRFAX, THOMAS, 6TH BARON (1692–1782), British nobleman and friend of Addison, Steele, and Bolingbroke who retired to America in 1746, settling in the Northern Neck of Virginia and becoming friendly with George Washington and his family.

FARRAR, GERALDINE (1882–1967), soprano who made her debut at the Royal Opera in Berlin in 1901. She sang at the Metropolitan Opera from 1906 to 1922.

FISKE, JOHN (1842–1901), philosopher and historian whose works of popular science and history—including *Myths and Myth-Makers* (1872) and *The Beginnings of New England* (1889)—were highly popular and influential in their day.

FOLLEN, CHARLES (KARL) (1796–1840), German-born scholar who was dismissed as the first professor of German literature at Harvard when he delivered an "Address to the People of the United States" (1834) opposing slavery. HLM appears to be referring either to this address or to a later article, "The Cause of Freedom in Our Country" (*Quarterly Anti-Slavery Magazine*, October 1836).

FOREL, AUGUSTE (1848–1931), German physician and author of pioneering works on human and animal sexuality, including *Die sexuelle Frage* (1905; Eng. tr. as *The Sexual Question*, 1908).

FOSTER, WILLIAM Z. (1881–1961), communist and labor leader who helped to unionize workers in the meat packing and steel industries. He joined the American Communist party in 1921 and became its driving force for the next forty years.

FRANK, WALDO (1889–1967), journalist and novelist whose avant-garde work attracted much attention in the 1920s and 1930s.

FREDERIC, HAROLD (1856–1898), novelist and journalist and author of several novels that anticipate the naturalism of Stephen Crane and Theodore Dreiser, including *The Damnation of Theron Ware* (1896), a controversial work about a clergyman's loss of faith.

FREEMAN, MARY E. WILKINS (1852–1930), short story writer and novelist known for her homely tales of New England life, including *A Humble Romance and Other Stories* (1887) and *A New England Nun and Other Stories* (1891).

FREUD, SIGMUND (1856–1939), Viennese founder of psychoanalysis. HLM wrote a review-article on several works by Freud and his colleagues: "Rattling the Subconscious" (SS, September 1918).

FULLER, HENRY BLAKE (1857–1929), pioneering writer of naturalist fiction. He wrote novels prolifically from 1890 to 1908, then devoted himself chiefly to literary criticism for Chicago newspapers.

GARDEN, MARY (1874–1967), Scottish-born soprano who specialized in debuts of the music of Debussy, Prokofiev, and other contemporary composers.

GARLAND, HAMLIN (1860–1940), novelist and essayist. HLM poked fun at his study of spiritualism, *The Shadow World* (1908; rev. in SS, February 1909), but was more charitable toward Garland's autobiography, *A Son of the Middle Border* (1917; rev. in the *New York Evening Mail*, 29 September 1917). HLM also thought well of *Rose of Dutcher's Coolly* (1895), widely considered the best of Garland's novels, about the attempt of a young woman to escape the drudgery of farm life in Wisconsin.

GARRISON, WILLIAM LLOYD (1805–1879), journalist whose fiery abolitionist paper, the *Liberator* (1831–65), spearheaded the movement for ending African American slavery.

GARY, ELBERT HENRY (1846–1927), president of the Federal Steel Company and later a major organizer of J. P. Morgan's United States Steel Corporation; he was chairman of the board of directors from 1903 to 1927. Earlier he had been a county judge (1882–90) and president of the Chicago Bar Association (1893–94).

GASKELL, ELIZABETH (1810–1865), British novelist and author of *Cranford* (1853), *Wives and Daughters* (1866), and other novels probing social relations among the industrial working class.

GAYNOR, WILLIAM J. (1849–1913), jurist who, as member of the appellate division of the New York State Supreme Court (1905–09), vigorously supported individual rights against misuse of power by the government, especially the police. He pursued further campaigns of reform as mayor of New York City (1909–13).

GIBBONS, JAMES, CARDINAL (1834–1921), archbishop of Baltimore (1877–1921) and one of the most prominent Catholic theologians of his day. Early in his career HLM wrote an effusive article on him: "Cardinal Gibbons," *AM* 69, No. 2 (December 1909): 168, 170–72.

GILBERT, JOHN (JACK) (1895–1936), actor who broke into films in 1916 and appeared as a dashing leading man in numerous films of the 1920s, notably three films with Greta Garbo, *Flesh and the Devil* (1927), *Love* (1927), and *A Woman of Affairs* (1928). His popularity declined with the advent of the talkies.

GILMAN, DANIEL COIT (1831–1908), educator who, after founding the Sheffield Scientific School at Yale and serving as the president of the University of California (1872–75), became the first president of Johns Hopkins University (1876–1902).

GLASGOW, ELLEN (1873–1945), Virginia novelist. HLM did not care for her earlier work—see, e.g., his review of *The Romance of a Plain Man* (1909; rev. in *SS*, August 1909)—but felt that her novels of the 1920s, such as *They Stooped to Folly* (1929; rev. in *AM*, October 1929), revealed an incisive dissection of Southern society. He expansively reviewed a collected edition of her work (1933; rev. in *AM*, August 1933).

GODFREY, STUART C. (1886–1945), U.S. army officer who attained the rank of brigadier general in 1942. He developed a specialty in military engineering.

GORKY, MAXIM (1868–1936), Russian novelist and short story writer. He and his companion, Maria Andreyeva, arrived in the United States in April 1906 and remained until September, staying mostly in New York. They created a scandal because they were not married.

GOURMONT, REMY DE (1858–1915), iconoclastic French author and intellectual whose challenging symbolist novels and essays (especially *Une Nuit au Luxembourg*, 1906; Eng. tr. as *A Night in the Luxembourg*, 1912) enjoyed a vogue in the United States and United Kingdom in the early twentieth century.

GRANT, MADISON (1865–1937), lawyer and president of the Immigration Restriction League who wrote a best-selling treatise, *The Passing of the Great Race* (1916), in which he argued that the white race in Europe and the United States was being overwhelmed by an influx of immigrants from other races.

GRANT, PERCY STICKNEY (1860–1927), Protestant Episcopal clergyman and rector of the Church of the Ascension in New York City (1893–1924). His planned marriage to Rita de Acosta Lydig in 1921 was forbidden by Bishop William T. Manning because Lydig had been previously married and divorced.

GREUZE, JEAN-BAPTISTE (1725–1805), the leading French painter of the mid-eighteenth century. He specialized in portraits, historical tableaux, and genre paintings, and laid the foundations for the neoclassicism of the later eighteenth century. HLM refers to Greuze's later painting, "The Broken Jug" (late 1770s), in which the jug is a metaphor for the initial sexual experience of the young woman carrying it.

GREY, ZANE (1875–1939), prolific author of westerns, notably *Riders of the Purple Sage* (1912). Many of his novels were adapted into films.

GRISWOLD, RUFUS WILMOT (1815–1857), journalist and editor of an important anthology, *The Poets and Poetry of America* (1842). He gained eternal infamy by a vicious obituary of Edgar Allan Poe (who had named him his literary executor), full of falsehoods that tarnished Poe's reputation for generations.

GUEST, EDGAR A. (1881–1959), English-born journalist and poet whose endless array of sentimental and homiletic poems, syndicated widely in newspapers, earned him great popularity among the masses but scorn from critics as a prototypical hack. His *Collected Verse* appeared in 1934.

HACKETT, JAMES K. (1869–1926), stage actor who starred in many plays in the later nineteenth and early twentieth centuries, most notably *The Prisoner of Zenda* (1895).

HAECKEL, ERNST (1834–1919), German zoologist and enthusiastic proponent of Darwin's theory of evolution, today best known for a widely influential popular treatise on biology and physics, *Die Weltrathsel* (1899; Eng. tr. as *The Riddle of the Universe*, 1900).

HALDEMAN-JULIUS, EMANUEL (1889–1951), author and publisher who established the Haldeman-Julius Company in Girard, Kansas, for the purpose of issuing inexpensive books for the masses, many of them on secularism, atheism, and freethought.

HANNA, MARK (1837–1904), a leading Republican politician of the later nineteenth century. He was U.S. senator from Ohio (1897–1904) and vigorously supported William McKinley for president. Although an ally of big business, he advocated the right of labor to organize as a means of efficiently dealing with disputes between labor and capital.

HARDING, WARREN GAMALIEL (1865–1923), twenty-ninth president of the United States (1921–23). He died suddenly of coronory thrombosis while in office. For

HLM's snide account of Harding's florid oratory, see "A Short View of Gamalielese," *Nation* 112, 27 April 1921, 621–22.

HARDY, THOMAS (1840–1928), British novelist and poet. HLM refers to *Jude the Obscure* (1895), his last novel, which provoked a firestorm of controversy in its depiction of the dismal life and death of a young married man who falls in love with his cousin.

HARRIMAN, EDWARD HENRY (1848–1909), financier who obtained control of the Union Pacific, Southern Pacific, and other major railroads.

HARRIS, FRANK (1855–1931), Irish-born literary critic and essayist who settled in London and wrote prolifically for British magazines. His biography *Oscar Wilde: His Life and Confession* was published by the author in 1916; see HLM's review (*SS*, September 1916), in which he elaborates upon the rumor that a publisher had accepted the book but was warned that publication of it in any form would lead to prosecution. HLM also thought highly of other works by Harris, including *The Man Shakespeare* (1909; rev. in SS, January 1910) and *Bernard Shaw* (1931; rev. in AM, February 1932).

HARRIS, JOEL CHANDLER (1848–1908), journalist and short story writer who achieved celebrity and critical renown for his tales of Uncle Remus, with their faithful recreations of African American dialect and folk myth.

HARRISON, CARTER HENRY, JR. (1860–1953), mayor of Chicago (1897–1905, 1911–15) who resisted the recommendations of the Chicago Vice Commission and other reform groups to wipe out prostitution in the city. Instead, he chose to segregate prostitution within certain districts, a policy HLM supported.

HARTE, BRET (1936–1902), poet, short story writer, and novelist who became the first California author to achieve national and international fame. His first collection of tales, *The Luck of Roaring Camp* (1868), remained his most popular.

HASSAM, CHILDE (1859–1936), painter who illustrated many volumes of children's stories in the 1870s and 1880s. He later gained celebrity for his watercolors, exhibiting frequently in Boston. A trip to France (1886–89) led to his falling under the influence of the French impressionists. By the 1890s he was regarded as a leading American painter. Late in life he turned to printmaking, executing many etchings and lithographs.

HAUPTMANN, GERHART (1862–1946), German dramatist whom HLM regarded as a leading playwright of the period. HLM refers to *Hanneles Himmelfahrt* (1893; Eng. tr. as *Hannele*, 1894), a play mingling Naturalism and fantasy and dealing with the dream-fantasies of an impoverished young woman in a poorhouse. See HLM's successive reviews of the multivolume *Dramatic Works of Gerhart Hauptmann*, translated by Ludwig Lewisohn (1912–24; rev. in SS, March 1913, December 1913, September 1914, and April 1915); also his reviews of *The Weavers* (1899, 1911; rev. in SS, August 1911), *The Fool in Christ* (1911; rev. in SS, February

1912), *The Sunken Bell* (1899, 1914; rev. in SS, September 1914), and the novel *Atlantis* (1912; rev. in SS, March 1913).

HAY, JOHN (1838–1905), secretary of state under William McKinley and Theodore Roosevelt (1898–1905) and initiator of the Open Door policy in China. He was also the author of several novels of social realism, notably *The Breadwinners* (1884), in which he defended the principle of property ownership.

HEARST, WILLIAM RANDOLPH (1863–1951), one of the most influential newspaper and magazine publishers of his day, whose career began at the age of twenty-three when his father gave him the *San Francisco Examiner* in 1887. HLM reviewed a biography of Hearst, John Kennedy Winkler's *W. R. Hearst: An American Phenomenon* (1928; rev. in AM, July 1928).

HEMPHILL, JOHN, friend of HLM and Democratic candidate for governor of Pennsylvania.

HENRY, O. (pseud. of William Sydney Porter, 1862–1910), short story writer who attained tremendous popularity in the first decade of the twentieth century. HLM generally considered his work facile and hackneyed. See his reviews of *Cabbages and Kings* (1904; rev. in the *Baltimore Sunday Herald*, 18 December 1904), *Roads of Destiny* (1909; rev. in SS, July 1909), and *Strictly Business* (1910; rev. in SS, May 1910). See also "O. Henry" (CST, 25 October 1925).

HERGESHEIMER, JOSEPH (1880–1954), novelist whose work enjoyed both critical and popular esteem in his day. HLM regularly reviewed his novels as they appeared and considered him a leading writer of his day; see his reviews of *The Lay Anthony* (1914; rev. in *Town Topics*, 22 October 1914, and SS, December 1914), *The Three Black Pennys* (1917; rev. in SS, December 1917), *Java Head* (1919; rev. in SS, March 1919), and *Cytherea* (1922; rev. in SS, April 1922). Hergesheimer became a close friend of HLM in the 1920s.

HERRICK, ROBERT (1868–1938), novelist and short story writer whose novels of middle-class society enjoyed considerable popularity in the first two decades of the twentieth century. HLM did not regard his work highly. See his reviews of *One Woman's Life* (1913; rev. in SS, June 1913) and *His Great Adventure* (1913; rev. in SS, January 1914). HLM refers to his novel *Together* (1908), a strong story of the lives of four married couples.

HOMER, WINSLOW (1836–1910), painter, illustrator, and etcher, perhaps the most celebrated American painter of his day.

HOPE, LAURENCE (pseudonym of Adela Florence [Cory] Nicolson, 1865–1904), author of *India's Love Lyrics* (1902)—also published as *The Garden of Kama*—a hugely popular poetic adaptation of the *Kama Sutra*.

HOWELLS, WILLIAM DEAN (1837–1920), novelist, editor, and critic who was perhaps the most highly regarded American writer of the later nineteenth century, chiefly on the strength of *The Rise of Silas Lapham* (1885) and other novels of social realism. HLM, however, considered him only a second-rater. By the time HLM began reviewing, Howells's best days were over, and HLM's reviews of *New Leaf Mills* (1913; rev. in SS, June 1913) and *The Leatherwood God* (1916; rev. in SS, January 1917) are condescending at best. HLM did not think much of the memoir *My Mark Twain* (1910; rev. in SS, January 1911).

HUNEKER, JAMES GIBBONS (1860–1921), critic, novelist, and memoirist who befriended HLM in the 1910s and exercised a considerable influence on his critical style and manner. HLM considered Huneker a pioneering American critic, especially in the realm of music criticism, and admired the vigor and iconoclasm of his writing. He regularly reviewed Huneker's works as they appeared and devoted a lengthy chapter to him in *A Book of Prefaces* (1917). See also "James Huneker" (*Century Magazine*, June 1921; rpt. with revisions as "Huneker," *P3*). HLM also edited a selection of Huneker's *Essays* (1929).

HUXLEY, THOMAS HENRY (1825–1895), pioneering naturalist and enthusiastic supporter of Darwin whose "plain English" and fearless challenging of religious orthodoxy were much appreciated by HLM. See HLM's "Huxley" (*CST*, 2 August 1925).

HYLAN, JOHN F. (1868–1936), mayor of New York City (1917–25), a Tammany politician often involved in controversy for his municipal appointments.

IBSEN, HENRIK (1828–1906), Norwegian dramatist. See HLM's extensive introductions to new translations of *A Doll's House* (1909), *Little Eyolf* (1909), and *The Master Builder, Pillars of Society, and Hedda Gabler* (1918).

INGERSOLL, ROBERT G. (1833–1899), voluminous author and one of the most popular lecturers of the later nineteenth century. His pungent attacks on religion and his espousal of agnosticism were embodied in numerous volumes, including *The Mistakes of Moses* (1879) and *The Christian Religion* (1882).

JAMES, HENRY (1843–1916), novelist and short story writer who left the United States in 1875 to reside in Europe, chiefly in England. By the time HLM began reviewing, most of James's major works had already been written, and HLM managed to review only such minor volumes as *Julia Bride* (1909; rev. in SS, January 1910), *The Finer Grain* (1910; rev. in SS, March 1911), and *The Outcry* (1911; rev. in SS, January 1912). It becomes evident that HLM had little patience with James's mincing style or the detailed psychological analyses of his characters, although he frequently praised *What Maisie Knew* (1897).

JANNINGS, EMIL (1884–1950), Swiss-born actor who, after several years as a sailor, began acting in films in Germany in 1914. He was the star of Murnau's *The Last Laugh* (1924).

JESUP, MORRIS K. (1830–1908), a wealthy banker who became a leading philanthropist, giving large amounts of money to a variety of organizations, notably the American Museum of Natural History.

JEWETT, SARAH ORNE (1849–1909), short story writer whose tales and sketches of her native Maine, gathered in such collections as *Deephaven* (1877) and *The Country of the Pointed Firs* (1896), are highly regarded.

JOHNSON, JACK (1878–1946), the first African American heavyweight champion of the world; he held the title from 1908 to 1915. Johnson provoked anger among whites by his lavish and flamboyant lifestyle, which frequently involved his driving around the country with a variety of white girlfriends. In 1913 he was convicted of violating the Mann Act, which prohibited the transportation of women across state lines for the purpose of "prostitution and debauchery." Johnson fled the United States, returning only in 1920, serving a year in prison. Johnson's second wife was Lucille Cameron, a white woman with "a big bust, wide hips, and heavy thighs" (Randy Roberts, *Papa Jack: Jack Johnson and the Era of White Hopes* [New York: Free Press, 1983], p. 143).

KAHN, OTTO H. (1867–1934), German-born banker and philanthropist who contributed generously to the Allies during World War I. In 1921 France bestowed upon him the Legion of Honor.

KAUFFMANN, ANGELICA (1741–1807), Swiss painter who worked both in Italy and England and became a member of the Royal Academy. Her portraits of society figures were highly regarded.

KELLNER, LEON (1859–1928), Polish literary historian whose *American Literature* (1915; rev. in SS, October 1915) HLM regarded with approbation. It is a translation of *Geschichte der nordamerikanischen literatur* (1913). Among other works by Kellner translated into English are *Historical Outlines of English Syntax* (1892) and *Restoring Shakespeare* (1925).

KEY, FRANCIS SCOTT (1779–1843), lawyer and poet who wrote "The Star-Spangled Banner" on the night of 13–14 September 1814, while British warships were attacking Fort McHenry in Baltimore. It was officially adopted as the U.S. national anthem in 1931.

KIPLING, RUDYARD (1865–1936), British novelist, short story writer, and poet. Much of HLM's early verse—collected in his first book, *Ventures into Verse* (1903)—and the short stories he wrote in the first decade of the twentieth century were heavily influenced by Kipling.

KOCK, [CHARLES] PAUL DE (1793–1871), prolific French author of slyly pornographic novels of Parisian life; they were hugely popular throughout Europe in the first half of the nineteenth century.

KREYMBORG, ALFRED (1883–1966), poet, critic, editor, and promoter of Modernist literature, especially by way of little magazines, including *Others* and *Broom*. HLM refers to Kreymborg's novelette *Edna Vitek: A Study in Morals* (1914), an unvarnished account of a waitress in a New York restaurant.

LA FOLLETTE, ROBERT (1855–1925), governor (1901–5) and U.S. senator (1906–25) from Wisconsin, and vigorous proponent of Progressive causes such as the direct primary and fairness in taxation. He ran for president in 1924, obtaining more votes than any third-party candidate up to that time.

LAMBERT, GERARD B. (1886–1967), businessman who operated a number of pharmaceutical companies, notably the Lambert Company (1926–55; later Warner-Lambert), which developed the mouthwash Listerine.

LAWRENCE, D. H. (1885–1930), British novelist whose work HLM reviewed with consistent hostility; see his reviews of *The Lost Girl* (1920; rev. in *BES*, 26 February 1921, and in *SS*, May 1921), *Psychoanalysis and the Unconscious* (1921; rev. in *SS*, July 1922), and *Women in Love* (1921; rev. in *SS*, February 1923). HLM alludes to Lawrence's novel *The Rainbow* (1915), an expurgated version of which was scheduled for publication in the United States by B. W. Huebsch but was never distributed. Several later novels by Lawrence—especially *Lady Chatterley's Lover* (1928)—were also plagued by attempts at censorship and suppression.

LEARY, JOHN JOSEPH, JR. (b. 1874), journalist who befriended Theodore Roosevelt in the latter's later years, and wrote *Talks with T. R., from the Diaries of John J. Leary, Jr.* (1920).

LEE, GERALD STANLEY (1862–1944), prolific social and literary commentator, author of such works as *The Shadow Christ* (1896), *The Lost Art of Reading* (1902), and *Crowds: A Moving-Picture of Democracy* (1913). HLM thought his work vitiated by platitudinousness and conventionality.

LEWIS, SINCLAIR (1885–1951), novelist who, after several poorly received early works, achieved celebrity and critical renown with a succession of novels that HLM considered landmarks in social, political, and religious satire: *Main Street* (1920; rev. in *SS*, January 1921), *Babbitt* (1922; rev. in *SS*, October 1922), *Arrowsmith* (1925; rev. in *CST*, 8 March 1925, and *AM*, April 1925), *Mantrap* (1926; rev. in *AM*, August 1926), *Elmer Gantry* (1927; rev. in *AM*, April 1927), *The Man Who Knew Coolidge* (1928; rev. in *AM*, June 1928), *Dodsworth* (1929; rev. in *AM*, April 1929), *Ann Vickers* (1933; rev. in *AM*, March 1933), and *It Can't Happen Here* (1936). Lewis received the Nobel Prize for literature in 1930.

LIND, JENNY (1820–1887), Swedish soprano nicknamed "the Swedish nightingale." She gave a series of concerts in the United States in 1850–51 under the management of P. T. Barnum.

LOUNSBURY, THOMAS R. (1838–1915), philologist and author of the widely read *History of the English Language* (1879). Lounsbury also wrote on Chaucer and Shakespeare and was a proponent of simplified spelling; see also his treatise, *The Standard of Usage in English* (1908).

LOW, A. MAURICE (1860–1929), British author of *The American People* (1909–11; 2 vols.), *Woodrow Wilson: An Interpretation* (1918), and other works on politics and warfare.

LOWELL, AMY (1874–1925), poet and critic who fostered the imagist movement in poetry during the 1910s. HLM, with his generally conservative views on poetry, did not look with favor upon her work.

LUSK, CLAYTON R. (1872–1959), state senator from New York (1919–24) who sponsored a number of anti-sedition and censorship bills in 1921–22, but came under scrutiny for having allegedly accepted gifts from various companies to support or oppose legislation in the Senate. He was the guiding force behind the Lusk Committee in its investigation of "seditious" activities (1919–22).

MABIE, HAMILTON WRIGHT (1845–1916), editor and critic whose work HLM always regarded as prototypical of conventional, moralizing, unimaginative criticism.

MACLANE, MARY (1881–1929), memoirist who wrote a scandalous autobiography, *The Story of Mary MacLane* (1902), which candidly discussed her frequent sexual escapades. HLM took note of its revision, *I, Mary MacLane* (1917; rev. in SS, July 1917). In 1918 she starred in a silent film adaptation of this work, playing herself.

MAETERLINCK, MAURICE (1862–1949), Belgian playwright and essayist whose work—notably the plays *Pelléas et Mélisande* (1889) and *The Blue Bird* (1908)—enjoyed great popularity at the turn of the century. HLM expressed irritation at his vague mysticism and melancholy.

MANSFIELD, RICHARD (1854–1907), stage actor and producer who attained tremendous popularity and critical esteem in the last two decades of the nineteenth century. He played Baron Chevrial in A. M. Palmer's production of *A Parisian Romance* (1883).

MARTINEAU, HARRIET (1802–1876), British essayist and novelist who visited the United States in 1834 and recorded her observations in *Society in America* (1837).

MASTERS, EDGAR LEE (1868–1950), poet whose *Spoon River Anthology* (1915) was a pioneering volume in its use of free verse and in its grim psychological realism. HLM appreciated it even before it appeared in book form, but had less regard for its sequel, *The New Spoon River* (1924; reviewed in AM, October 1925). He was also cool toward such other poetry collections as *The Great Valley* (1916; rev. in SS, November 1917) and *Toward the Gulf* (1918; rev. in SS, June 1918) and the novels *Mitch Miller* (1920) and *Mirage* (1924; rev. in AM, June 1924), but he spoke glowingly of Masters's controversial biography, *Lincoln, the Man* (1931; rev. in *New York Herald Tribune Books*, 8 February 1931).

MATTHEWS, BRANDER (1852–1929), well-known literary critic whose work HLM considered pedantic and hackneyed; but he praised *A Study of the Drama* (1910; rev. in SS, August 1910) as a "book showing keen observation, wide knowledge, profitable reflection and good sense."

MAYER, LOUIS B. (1885–1957), film executive who became vice president and general manager of MGM in 1924 and remained one of the most powerful figures in the film industry until his dismissal from MGM in 1951.

McPherson, Aimée Semple (1890–1944), popular Pentecostal evangelist based in Los Angeles. In 1926 she disappeared for five weeks; upon her return she claimed to have been kidnapped. The Los Angeles district attorney accused her of spending time with a married man, Kenneth G. Ormiston, and indicted her on charges of obstruction of justice and subornation of perjury. Although the charges were eventually dropped, McPherson's reputation suffered seious damage. During his trip to southern California in late 1926 HLM wrote a pungent article about her, "Sister Aimée" (*BES*, 13 December 1926).

Milholland, Inez (1886–1916), feminist who vigorously advocated the cause of woman suffrage as a member of the Woman's Party in the few years preceding her early death.

Miller, Kelly (1863–1939), African American historian and educator, longtime professor of sociology at Howard University (1890–1934), and author of numerous books and articles on African Americans, including *Out of the House of Bondage* (1917) and *The Everlasting Stain* (1924).

Mistral, Frédéric (1830–1914), French poet who led the revival of the study of the Provençal language and shared the Nobel Prize for literature in 1904.

Mitchell, Donald G. (1822–1908), journalist, essayist, and editor who became the first editor of the department The Easy Chair for *Harper's Magazine*. Of his many books, *The Reveries of a Bachelor* (1850) is the best known.

Mitchell, S. Weir (1829–1914), physician whose historical and other novels enjoyed popularity in their day. HLM reviewed *The Red City* (1907; rev. in SS, January 1909) and *Westways* (1913; rev. in SS, December 1913), finding it "second rate but workmanlike."

Mix, Tom (1880–1940), actor in many western silent and early talkie films from 1909 to 1935.

Moore, George (1862–1933), Anglo-Irish novelist and memoirist whom HLM regarded as one of the leading writers of his age. He sympathetically reviewed the three volumes of Moore's autobiography, *Hail and Farewell: Ave* (1911; rev. in SS, March 1912), *Salve* (1912; rev. in SS, February 1913), and *Vale* (1914; rev. in SS, October 1914). He also reviewed *A Story-Teller's Holiday* (1918; rev. in SS, December 1918) and *An Anthology of Pure Poetry* (1924; rev. in AM, October 1925). HLM refers to Moore's *Memoirs of My Dead Life* (1906), an autobiographical work that was published in expurgated form in the U.S. by D. Appleton & Co. (1906). In the lengthy chapter 9 of that work, Moore writes of his affair with a woman named Doris, whom he met in the south of France. Although she was engaged to be married, she gave up her virginity to Moore.

More, Paul Elmer (1864–1937), prominent literary critic who achieved critical esteem with his eleven-volume series, *Shelburne Essays* (1904–21). HLM considered him a proponent of an attenuated and timorous classicism. HLM reviewed the last two volumes of the *Shelburne Essays: With the Wits* (1919; rev. in *SS*, February 1920) and *A New England Group* (1921; rev. in *SS*, June 1921), as well as *The Catholic Faith* (1931; rev. in *AM*, April 1932).

MORGAN, J. P. (1837–1913), banker and financier who invested heavily in railroads and helped to form the United States Steel Corporation. He was also a noted philanthropist, contributing substantially to the Metropolitan Museum of Art and the American Museum of Natural History.

MÜHLBACH, LUISE (pseud. of Klara Müller, 1814–1873), prolific German author of conventional historical novels.

MUNSEY, FRANK A. (1854–1925), owner of a chain of popular magazines (beginning with the *Golden Argosy* in 1882) that became immensely successful. He also bought several newspapers, including the *New York Sun* (1916) and the *New York Herald* (1920).

MÜNSTERBERG, HUGO (1863–1916), German-born psychologist and director of the then newly established psychological laboratory at Harvard. He wrote several studies of American culture: *American Traits* (1901), *The Americans* (1904), *American Problems* (1910), and *American Patriotism* (1913).

MUNYON, JAMES M. (1848–1918), a hugely popular and successful manufacturer of homeopathic patent medicines. Although not an actual physician, he always referred to himself as "Dr. Munyon." His pet phrase, circulated widely through advertisements, was: "There is hope."

MURNAU, F. W. (1888–1931), German film director whose *Nosferatu* (1922) is a classic adaptation of Bram Stoker's *Dracula*. He also directed *The Last Laugh* (1924), a landmark in silent film in its depiction of the spiritual collapse of an old man after he is demoted from hotel porter to lavatory attendant.

NEARING, SCOTT (1883–1983), socialist and prolific author on politics and society. In 1915 he was dismissed as professor of economics at the University of Pennsylvania for speaking out against child labor. Although he subsequently served for two years (1915–17) as professor of social sciences at the University of Toledo, he then found it impossible to secure a teaching position. In 1932 he and his wife Helen retired to a farm in Vermont. HLM later reviewed his *Where Is Civilization Going?* (1927; rev. in *AM*, January 1929).

NIETZSCHE, FRIEDRICH (1844–1900), revolutionary German philosopher whose anticlericalism and theories of the superman significantly influenced HLM. See HLM's *The Philosophy of Friedrich Nietzsche* (1908), his slim selection, *The Gist of Nietzsche* (1910), and his translation of *The Antichrist* (1920). HLM wrote frequently of Nietzsche in *SS* (see the issues of November 1909, March 1910, March 1912, August 1913, and August 1915). See also "Nietzsche" (*CST*, 23 August 1925).

NORRIS, FRANK (1870–1902), novelist whose early novels, *McTeague* (1899), *The Oc-topus* (1901), and *The Pit* (1903) were pioneering works of naturalism. HLM appreciatively reviewed the posthumous novel *Vandover and the Brute* (1914; rev. in *Town Topics*, 18 June 1914, and in *SS*, August 1914).

NYE, BILL (pseud. of Edgar Wilson, 1850–1896), voluminous humorist who attracted a wide following in the last quarter of the nineteenth century with widely syndicated newspaper sketches.

O'CONNELL, WILLIAM HENRY (1859–1944), Roman Catholic clergyman who was made archbishop of Boston (1907) and subsequently a cardinal (1911). He aggressively exercised both religious and political influence during much of his tenure.

O'HARE, KATE RICHARDS (1877–1948), prominent socialist who was convicted under the Espionage Act for protesting U.S. involvement in World War I; her sentence was later commuted and she was eventually pardoned by President Calvin Coolidge.

OPPENHEIM, E. PHILLIPS (1866–1946), voluminous British author of novels of adventure and suspense. HLM reviewed several of them—*The Illustrious Prince* (1910; rev. in *SS*, September 1910), *The Moving Finger* (1910; rev. in *SS*, July 1911), *The Mischief-Maker* (1912; rev. in *SS*, May 1913), *A People's Man* (1914; rev. in *SS*, March 1914), and others—remarking of the first: "There is something going on every second."

ORNSTEIN, LEO (1893–2002), Ukrainian-born pianist and composer who created controversy with his avant-garde compositions of the 1910s and 1920s. In 1920 he became head of the piano department of the Philadelphia Musical Academy.

PADEREWSKI, IGNACE JAN (1860–1941), Polish pianist and composer hailed as one of the most technically accomplished (and flamboyant) pianists of his day. He toured the United States many times from 1890 onward.

PAINE, ALBERT BIGELOW (1861–1937), Mark Twain's secretary, whose official biography, *Mark Twain: A Biography* (1912; 3 vols.) was reviewed enthusiastically by HLM (*SS*, February 1913). Paine edited many of Twain's posthumous publications.

PAINE, THOMAS (1737–1809), British-born pamphleteer who wrote in support of American independence in the tract *Common Sense* (1776) but whose religious skepticism, exhibited in *The Age of Reason* (1795–96), earned him notoriety as an "infidel."

PALMER, A. MITCHELL (1872–1936), U.S. attorney general (1919–21) who gained notoriety for his vigorous prosecution of supposed Communists and anarchists, mostly foreign nationals, following the end of World War I; three thousand persons were arrested and many of them were deported.

PARKHURST, CHARLES H. (1842–1933), Presbyterian clergyman who attacked the political corruption of the Tammany organization in New York City. He wrote several books on religion, politics, and other issues, including *Our Fight with Tammany* (1895) and *My Forty Years in New York* (1923).

PATTEE, FRED LEWIS (1863–1950), professor of English at Pennsylvania State University and author of *A History of American Literature Since 1870* (1915) and other works on American literary history.

PATTERSON, JOSEPH MEDILL (1879–1946), socialist and author of social protest novels including *A Little Brother of the Rich* (1908) and *Rebellion* (1911).

PEAY, AUSTIN (1876–1927), Democratic governor of Tennessee (1923–27) who reluctantly signed the anti-evolution bill that triggered the Scopes trial in 1925.

PHELPS, WILLIAM LYON (1865–1943), longtime professor at Yale University (1891–1933) and a prominent literary critic of his day. Although praising Phelps's early championing of Mark Twain, HLM condemned him for the superficiality of his critical judgments and his neglect of important modern poets, novelists, and dramatists. See his reviews of *Essays on Modern Novelists* (1910; rev. in SS, June 1910), *Essays on Russian Novelists* (1911; rev. in SS, June 1911), *The Advance of the English Novel* (1916; rev. in SS, June 1917), *The Advance of English Poetry* (1918; rev. in SS, January 1919), *Essays on Modern Dramatists* (1921; rev. in BES, 23 April 1921), and other works.

PHILLIPS, DAVID GRAHAM (1867–1911), novelist and journalist who wrote more than twenty novels in just over a decade (1901–11). Although HLM felt that some of his work was marred by appeals to popular taste, he maintained that the novels *The Hungry Heart* (1909; rev. in SS, December 1909) and *The Husband's Story* (1911; rev. in SS, January 1911) were among the best novels of their time; at this time he even pronounced Phillips the leading American novelist. HLM also reviewed *The Grain of Dust* (1911; rev. in SS, July 1911). Phillips was murdered in Gramercy Park in New York. HLM makes frequent reference to Phillips's posthumously published novel, *Susan Lenox: Her Fall and Rise* (1917), a controversial work about a woman who becomes a prostitute at an early age but eventually manages to leave the profession and become an actress.

PHILLIPS, WENDELL (1811–1884), prominent American abolitionist and social reformer.

POE, EDGAR ALLAN (1809–1849), poet, short story writer, and critic about whom HLM had mixed feelings. Scorning his poetry as singsong and his tales as shilling shockers, HLM nonetheless felt that Poe—chiefly on the strength of his trenchant and often vituperative essays and reviews—was one of the leading American writers of the nineteenth century, with Twain and Whitman.

POOLE, ERNEST (1880–1950), journalist and novelist whose proletarian novels—notably his first, *The Harbor* (1915; rev. in SS, June 1915)—were well received in their day. HLM found this novel disappointing, and found *His Second Wife* (1918; rev. in SS, August 1918) "a piece of mush."

PORTER, GENE STRATTON (1863–1924), popular novelist whose sentimental novels of Indiana life were leavened by a love of nature. HLM reviewed one of her best-known novels, *Laddie* (1913; rev. in *SS*, November 1913), remarking that she wrote deftly but that her story was "commonplace and tedious."

POUND, EZRA (1885–1972), poet and critic whose revolutionary work was early appreciated by HLM; see his reviews of *Provença* (1910; rev. in *SS*, April 1911) and *Lustra* (1917; rev. in *SS*, June 1918) and of the essay collection *The Instigations of Ezra Pound* (1920; rev. in *SS*, August 1920). HLM also found his treatise, *Antheil and the Treatise on Harmony* (1924, 1927; rev. in *AM*, August 1928), entertaining. Pound left the United States in 1908 to reside in Europe, chiefly Italy.

PRINGLE, AILEEN (1895–1989), a leading actress in silent films in the 1920s. She was married (1912–33) to Sir Charles MacKenzie Pringle, governor of the Bahamas, but during the later 1920s she had an affair with HLM.

QUIRK, JAMES ROBERT (1884–1932), journalist and editor of *Photoplay*, at the time the leading magazine devoted to film.

RAINSFORD, WILLIAM STEPHEN (1850–1933), Protestant Episcopal clergyman born in Dublin. He came to the United States in 1870 and was minister at St. George's in New York City (1882–1904). During this time he created a scandal by recommending the reform, not the abolition, of saloons and dance halls.

RANDALL, JAMES RYDER (1839–1908), journalist and poet born in Baltimore. He wrote "Maryland, My Maryland" in 1861 while in Louisiana at the outbreak of the Civil War.

REESE, LIZETTE WOODWORTH (1856–1935), Baltimore poet whose lyric poems HLM regarded highly. See his review of *A Wayside Lute* (1913; rev. in *SS*, May 1910), in which he singled out the sonnet "Tears" as one of the finest poems written by an American.

RIDER, FREMONT (1885–1962), genealogist and travel writer, and author of *Rider's New York City: A Guide for Travelers* (1916; 2nd ed. 1923). See his autobiography, *And Master of None* (1955).

ROBINS, ELIZABETH (1865?-1952), actress and novelist who was the first woman to play the title role in *Hedda Gabler* in London. She published novels under the pseudonym C. E. Raimond. Under her own name she wrote a sentimental novel about white slavery, *My Little Sister* (1913; rev. in *SS*, May 1913), which HLM ridiculed.

ROBINSON, EDWIN ARLINGTON (1869–1935), prolific and highly regarded poet. His *Collected Poems* (1921) won the Pulitzer Prize. A revised edition appeared in 1937.

ROCKEFELLER, JOHN D. (1839–1937), founder of the Standard Oil Company, which was declared a trust and dissolved by the Supreme Court in 1911.

ROGERS, MAX (d. 1932), popular vaudeville comedian who performed chiefly in New York City from the 1880s to the 1910s.

ROOSEVELT, THEODORE (1858–1919), vice president under William McKinley; he became the twenty-sixth U.S. president (1901–9) when McKinley was assassinated. HLM heaped scorn upon his bluff persona and was particularly hostile to Roosevelt's vehement calls for the United States to enter World War I on the side of the Allies. See HLM's "Roosevelt: An Autopsy" (P2).

ROOSEVELT, THEODORE, JR. (1887–1944), eldest son of Theodore Roosevelt. After serving in World War I, he helped organize the American Legion and in 1921 was appointed assistant secretary of the navy, a position his father had held.

ROSENTHAL, MORIZ (1862–1946), highly regarded Polish pianist who toured the United States in 1888–89.

ROSEY, GEORGE (1864–1936), composer of marches, piano pieces, and other works in the late nineteenth and early twentieth centuries.

RUSSELL, WILLIAM T. (1863–1927), rector of St. Patrick's Church in Washington, D.C. (1908–17), and later bishop of Charleston. Born in Baltimore and secretary to James, Cardinal Gibbons there (1894–1908), Russell was the author of *Maryland, the Land of Sanctuary* (1907).

RYAN, THOMAS FORTUNE (1851–1928), American financier involved in the organization of the Metropolitan Street Railway Company (1892) and other mergers in transportation, tobacco, and other industries.

SAGE, RUSSELL (1816–1906), financier who helped to organize the nation's railroads and telegraph systems, making millions in the process. After his death his widow established the Russell Sage Foundation, a leading charitable organization.

SAND, GEORGE (pseud. of Aurore Dupin, Baronne Dudevant, 1804–1876), French novelist who, after separating from her husband in 1831, engaged in liaisons with Frédéric Chopin, Alfred de Musset, and others.

SANDBURG, CARL (1878–1967), poet and biographer. HLM found much merit in his *Chicago Poems* (1916; rev. in SS, February 1917) as well as in his collection of updated fairy tales, *Rootabaga Stories* (1922; rev. in SS, March 1923), and his collection of folksongs, *The American Songbag* (1927; rev. in AM, March 1928). Of the first installment of Sandburg's biography of Lincoln, *Abraham Lincoln: The Prairie Years* (1926; rev. in AM, July 1926), HLM remarked: "No man has ever written of the young Lincoln with a finer insight, or with greater eloquence."

SANDERSON, JULIA (1887–1975), tremendously popular star in musical comedies of the 1910s and 1920s, including *No, No, Nanette* (1925).

SANGER, MARGARET (1879–1966), birth control pioneer (she coined the term birth control in 1914) who frequently endured prison terms in her quest to legalize the sale and distribution of contraceptive devices and to permit the dissemination of information on family planning.

SARGENT, JOHN SINGER (1856–1925), painter who settled in England in 1884, although he traveled widely and visited the United States on many occasions, sometimes for lengthy stays.

SCHEFFEL, JOSEPH VICTOR VON (1826–1886), German poet and novelist best known for the humorous epic poem *Der Trompeter von Säckingen* (1854) and the novel *Ekkehard* (1855).

SCHUYLER, GEORGE S. (1895–1977), African American journalist who wrote widely on African American matters in the *Messenger*, the *Crisis*, HLM's *American Mercury*, and the *Pittsburgh Courier*. In his gradual political evolution from socialism to conservatism, he angered many African Americans by his controversial and deliberately provocative views. He also published two novels.

SCHWAB, CHARLES M. (1862–1939), president of the Carnegie Steel Company and the first president of the United States Steel Corporation (founded 1901). In 1904 he formed the rival Bethlehem Steel Corporation. Although at one time having assets of $200 million, he died insolvent.

SEMBRICH, MARCELLA (1858–1935), Polish soprano who first toured the United States in 1883. She later became a U.S. citizen.

SHAW, GEORGE BERNARD (1856–1950), Anglo-Irish playwright. HLM's first treatise was *George Bernard Shaw: His Plays* (1905). He consistently reviewed Shaw's new plays as they appeared in book form: *Man and Superman* (1903; rev. in the *Baltimore Sunday Herald*, 30 October 1904); *The Doctor's Dilemma* (1907), *Getting Married* (1910), and other works (rev. in SS, August 1911); *Misalliance* (1911) and other works (rev. in *Town Topics*, 16 July 1914); *Androcles and the Lion* (1912; rev. in SS, August 1916); etc. HLM refers to *Mrs. Warren's Profession* (1898), about a middle-class woman who runs a whorehouse. HLM generally concluded that Shaw, with his immense technical skill in dramaturgy, had a penchant for uttering the obvious in terms of the scandalous, thereby provoking controversy.

SHERMAN, STUART P. (1881–1926), critic and editor who earned HLM's scorn for the superficiality and parochialism of his judgments, especially in his championing of a narrowly "American" ideal of literature. HLM savaged his *Americans* (1922; rev. in SS, March 1923) and also heaped abuse on a small pamphlet issued at the end of World War I, *American and Allied Ideals* (1918), which he felt embodied the worst of Sherman's thought. Later he reviewed Sherman's *Life and Letters*, edited by Jacob Zeitlin and Homer Woodbridge (1929; rev. in AM, December 1929).

SIGOURNEY, LYDIA HOWARD HUNTLEY (1791–1865), prolific Connecticut poet and novelist who in her day was called the "Sweet Singer of Hartford." Her *Poetical Works* appeared in 1850.

SINCLAIR, UPTON (1878–1968), novelist, journalist, and political activist whose numerous and multifarious attempts at social and economic reform (chiefly of a socialist variety) earned HLM's continual scorn and amusement. He attained celebrity with the novel *The Jungle* (1906), exposing the appalling conditions of the Chicago stockyards. HLM took note of many of his subsequent works, including the novel *The Moneychangers* (1908; rev. in SS, November 1908); *The Brass Check: A Study of American Journalism* (1919; rev. in SS, April 1920); *The Book of Life, Mind and Body* (1921; rev. in SS, July 1922); *The Goose-Step: A Study of American Education* (1923; rev. in SS, May 1923); *Money Writes!* (1927; rev. in AM, February 1928); and *The Wet Parade* (1931; rev. in the *Nation*, 23 September 1931). HLM did not review the early novel *The Metropolis* (1908), a satire on the selfishness of New York high society.

SMALL, LEN (1862–1936), governor of Illinois (1921–29) who was a defendant in several civil and criminal suits during his term of office; he was forced to repay $650,000 to the state treasury.

SMITH, F. HOPKINSON (1838–1915), short story writer and novelist whose novels and tales were popular from the 1890s to the 1910s. HLM took note of some of his later works, *Peter* (1908; rev. in SS, November 1908), *Forty Minutes Late* (1909; rev. in SS, January 1910), and *Kennedy Square* (1911; rev. in SS, November 1911), finding them saccharine and lacking in ingenuity and wit.

SORMA, AGNES (1865–1927), German actress who first toured the United States in 1897.

SOUSA, JOHN PHILIP (1854–1932), composer and bandmaster celebrated for his marches. See HLM's article, "Sousa, et Cetera" (*BES*, 31 May 1910).

SPENCER, HERBERT (1820–1903), British philosopher and social scientist, and author of numerous works using Darwin's theory of evolution as the basis for speculations on the nature of human psychology and society.

STEARNS, HAROLD (1891–1943), journalist and essayist. HLM reviewed his *Liberalism in America* (1919; rev. in SS, May 1920), finding it "a capital piece of work — temperate, well-informed, well-reasoned, extremely well-written." HLM also read (but did not review) *America and the Young Intellectual* (1921) and contributed a chapter on "Politics" to Stearns's compilation *Civilization in the United States* (1922), included in the present volume under the title "The American Politician." Stearns was among the American expatriates living in Paris in the 1920s. See his autobiography, *The Street I Know* (1935).

STILLMAN, JAMES (1850–1918), capitalist and president of the National City Bank, which for a time during the late nineteenth century was the leading bank in the United States in its support of industrial and financial combines.

STOWE, HARRIET BEECHER (1811–1886), author of *Uncle Tom's Cabin* (1852), a novel that was instrumental in convincing Northerners of the iniquity of slavery.

STRINDBERG, AUGUST (1849–1912), renowned Swedish playwright. HLM frequently reviewed English translations of his plays, notably in the articles "The Terrible Swede" (SS, June 1912) and "A Counterblast to Buncombe" (SS, August 1913).

SUCKOW, RUTH (1892–1960), novelist and short story writer whose work HLM encouraged and promoted. Among her volumes are *Country People* (1924), *The Odyssey of a Nice Girl* (1925), and *The Folks* (1934).

SUDERMANN, HERMANN (1857–1928), German novelist and playwright and pioneer of naturalism. HLM refers to *Das hohe Lied* (1908; Eng. tr. as *The Song of Songs*), a stark novel about a young woman's entry into society.

SULLIVAN, JOHN L. (1858–1918), bare-knuckle boxer who held the American heavyweight crown from 1882 until 1892, when he fought (wearing gloves) and lost to James J. Corbett.

SUNDAY, BILLY (1862?–1935), itinerant evangelist who became immensely popular in the first two decades of the twentieth century for his histrionic outdoor sermons. HLM discussed his witnessing of one of Sunday's lecture tours in *BES* (17 February, 14 and 27 March, 2 May 1916); see also "Savonarolas A-Sweat" (*SS*, July 1916).

TANEY, ROGER B. (1777–1864), chief justice of the Supreme Court (1836–64) who wrote the majority opinion in the notorious Dred Scott case of 1857, in which the Supreme Court ruled that no African American descended from slaves could ever be a U.S. citizen and that Congress lacked the authority to exclude slavery in the territories.

TAYLOR, BAYARD (1825–1878), journalist and poet. His translation of Goethe's *Faust* (1870–71) long remained popular and led to his appointment as U.S. minister to Germany (1878).

THALBERG, IRVING G. (1899–1936), production executive who first worked for Carl Laemmle and then became vice president of MGM (1924–36).

THAW, HARRY (1871–1947), wealthy New York socialite who killed the architect Stanford White in 1906 because of his jealousy of his wife Evelyn Nesbit's former attachment to White. Thaw was found innocent by reason of insanity, but escaped from the Matteawan State Hospital for the Criminally Insane in 1913. He was recaptured and released in 1915. His attempted suicide in 1917 led to a seven-year confinement at various insane asylums in Pennsylvania.

THOMA, LUDWIG (1867–1921), German journalist (editor of the satirical magazine *Simplicissimus*, 1900–1903), novelist, dramatist, poet, and short story writer best known for his satirical and humorous tales.

THOMPSON, WILLIAM HALE (1867–1944), mayor of Chicago (1915–23, 1927–31) whose second term was tarnished by the conviction of several members of his administration for defrauding the city of more than $1 million in "experts'" fees.

THURMAN, ALLEN G. (1813–1895), U.S. senator from Ohio (1869–81) and Grover Cleveland's vice-presidential running mate in their unsuccessful campaign of 1888.

TOCQUEVILLE, ALEXIS DE (1805–1859), French sociologist and author of the landmark treatise *De la Démocratie en Amérique* (1835–40; Eng. tr. as *Democracy in America*, 1835–40).

TOLSTOY, LEO (1828–1910), Russian novelist best known for the novels *War and Peace* (1863–69) and *Anna Karenina* (1873–77). HLM cites *The Kreutzer Sonata* (1889), a novella about a man who murders his wife out of jealousy. It created controversy for its frank discussion of sexual topics.

TRAIN, GEORGE FRANCIS (1829–1904), businessman who did important work in the development of railroads in the United States, Europe, Asia, and Australia; he was also an author and journalist. See his autobiography, *My Life in Many States and in Foreign Lands* (1902).

TULLY, JIM (1891–1947), a hobo whom HLM discovered and whose work he encouraged. Tully went on to become a prolific novelist. He went to Hollywood in the mid-1920s and became a colorful personality there, although he did very little work as a screenwriter and actor.

TUNNEY, JAMES JOSEPH ("Gene") (1898–1978), boxer who defeated Jack Dempsey twice (in 1926 and 1927) for the heavyweight championship of the world. He retired undefeated in 1928.

TURQUAN, JOSEPH (1854–1928), French historian and biographer, and author of *Napoléon amoureux* (1897; Eng. tr. as *The Love Affairs of Napoleon*, 1909) and other works about Napoleon's family.

TWAIN, MARK (pseud. of Samuel Langhorne Clemens, 1835–1910), novelist, short story writer, and essayist. HLM vaunted *Adventures of Huckleberry Finn* (1885) as one of the great works of American literature, and had much praise for *Life on the Mississippi* (1883), *A Connecticut Yankee in King Arthur's Court* (1889), *Extract from Captain Stormfield's Visit to Heaven* (1909), *The Mysterious Stranger* (posthumously published in 1916), and the philosophical dialogue *What Is Man?* (privately published in 1905). Other works discussed by HLM are the short story "The Celebrated Jumping Frog of Calaveras County" (1865); the travel books *The Innocents Abroad* (1869), *A Tramp Abroad* (1880), and *Following the Equator* (1897); the sensational novel *The Gilded Age* (1873; with Charles Dudley Warner); and the fictional biography *Personal Recollections of Joan of Arc* (1896).

TYLER, WAT (d. 1381), leader of the first popular rebellion in England in 1381, in protest against harsh taxation of the poor.

VALENTINO, RUDOLPH (1895–1926), Italian-born actor who went to Hollywood in 1917 and was a screen idol for a decade preceding his sudden death. HLM wrote a touching obituary, "Valentino" (*BES*, 30 August 1926).

VAN DYKE, HENRY (1852–1933), clergyman and essayist who achieved tremendous popularity with a succession of volumes on religion, nature, and personal conduct. HLM felt that his work was a byword for unoriginal and superficial thought.

HLM excoriated him in his reviews of the story collection *The Unknown Quantity* (1912; rev. in SS, February 1913) and of *Six Days of the Week: A Book of Thoughts about Life and Religion* (1924; rev. in SS, March 1925). The latter review consists of nothing but quotations of banal utterances from the volume.

VARDAMAN, JAMES KIMBALL (1861–1930), governor (1904–08) and U.S. senator from Mississippi (1913–19) who opposed the education of African Americans as a threat to white supremacy.

VIDOR, KING (1894–1982), director of numerous films from 1919 to 1959, including *The Big Parade* (1925), *The Crowd* (1928), and *Duel in the Sun* (1947). He was briefly married to the actress Eleanor Boardman, who starred in several of his films.

VOLSTEAD, ANDREW JOHN (1860–1947), U.S. representative from Minnesota (1903–23) and author of the Volstead Act (1919) that allowed the enforcement of the Eighteenth Amendment prohibiting the sale and consumption of alcoholic beverages.

WANAMAKER, JOHN (1838–1922), businessman who opened his first department store in Philadelphia in 1871. Wanamaker's was immediately successful as a result of innovative marketing methods. Wanamaker devoted considerable time and money to charitable and religious work.

WANGER, WALTER (1894–1968), film producer whose credits include such films as *Queen Christina* (1934), *Stagecoach* (1939), and *Cleopatra* (1962). At the time of HLM's visit to Hollywood, Wanger was an executive at Famous Players–Lasky.

WARD, ARTEMUS (pseud. of Charles Farrar Browne, 1834–1867), prolific journalist and humorist who enjoyed tremendous popularity in the 1860s for his sketches mixing colloquialism, puns, and social commentary.

WELLS, H. G. (1866–1946), prolific British novelist and historian. HLM dismissed his early science fiction novels, but regarded his later novels of social realism—*Tono-Bungay* (1909; rev. in SS, April 1909), *Ann Veronica* (1909; rev. in SS, February 1910), *The History of Mr. Polly* (1910; rev. in SS, July 1910), *The New Machiavelli* (1911; rev. in SS, April 1911), *Marriage* (1912; rev. in SS, January 1913)—as some of the best novels of the period. HLM felt that Wells's subsequent novels revealed a disastrous falling off, an opinion recorded in the essay "The Late Mr. Wells" (SS, August 1918; in P1). But HLM felt that Wells made a striking comeback with the treatises *The Outline of History* (1920; rev. in BES, 10 January 1921, and in SS, March 1921), *The Science of Life* (1931; rev. in AM, March 1931), and *The Work, Wealth and Happiness of Mankind* (1931; rev. in AM, April 1932). He also reviewed Wells's *Experiment in Autobiography* (1934; rev. in the *Nation*, 14 November 1934).

WEMBRIDGE, ELEANOR ROWLAND (b. 1882), psychologist and social commentator, and author of such works as *The Right to Believe* (1909), *Other People's Daugh-*

ters (1926), and *Life among the Lowbrows* (1931). She wrote several articles for HLM's *American Mercury*. HLM refers to her article "Negroes in Custody" (*AM*, September 1930).

WESLEY, JOHN (1703–1791), British religious leader who, with his brother Charles (1707–1788), founded Methodism while at Oxford in the late 1720s. He undertook an unsuccessful evangelical mission to Georgia in 1735–37.

WHEELER, WAYNE B. (1869–1927), superintendent of the Anti-Saloon League of Ohio (1904–15), general counsel for the Anti-Saloon League of America (1915–27), and vigorous supporter of Prohibition.

WHISTLER, JAMES MCNEILL (1834–1903), painter who moved to Paris in 1855 and then to London in 1860, remaining there for the rest of his life.

WHITE, WILLIAM ALLEN (1868–1944), Kansas journalist who purchased the *Emporia Gazette* and published in it a celebrated editorial, "What's the Matter with Kansas?" (15 August 1896), a defense of William McKinley against the attacks of William Jennings Bryan in the presidential campaign. He won the Pulitzer Prize in 1922. He also wrote novels, short stories, poetry, and biographies of Woodrow Wilson and Calvin Coolidge.

WHITEFIELD, GEORGE (1714–1770), British Methodist evangelist who came to the United States frequently from the 1740s onward, becoming one of the leaders of the religious revival known as the Great Awakening.

WHITLOCK, BRAND (1869–1934), mayor of Toledo, Ohio (1905–13), and U.S. minister to Belgium. HLM frequently recommended Whitlock's essay *On the Enforcement of Law in Cities* (1910), which outraged doctrinaire reformers in its urging of moderation in the pursuit of moral infractions.

WHITMAN, WALT (1819–1892), poet and journalist and one of the leading writers of the nineteenth century, chiefly on the strength of *Leaves of Grass* (1855). Whitman was dismissed as a clerk in the Department of the Interior in 1865 by the new secretary, James Harlan, apparently because some of the poems in *Leaves of Grass* were considered obscene; but Whitman's friends quickly obtained a position for him in the attorney general's office. HLM had high regard for Whitman; his most exhaustive comments on Whitman's place in American literature occur sporadically through the long essay "The National Letters" (*P2*). HLM also took note of the posthumous compilation *Uncollected Poetry and Prose*, edited by Emory Holloway (1921; rev. in *SS*, January 1922).

WILDE, OSCAR (1854–1900), British novelist, poet, and playwright whose name fell under a cloud for a generation following his conviction for homosexuality in 1895. HLM refers to *The Picture of Dorian Gray* (first published in the Philadelphia magazine *Lippincott's* in 1890), a supernatural novel that created a scandal in its depiction of the protagonist's dissolute lifestyle.

WILLIS, N. P. (1806–1867), poet, short story writer, and journalist who was once highly regarded (he was the subject of an effusive article by Edgar Allan Poe) but has now lapsed into obscurity.

WILSON, HARRY LEON (1867–1939), novelist, short story writer, and playwright whose humorous tales HLM found stimulating: *Bunker Bean* (1912; rev. in SS, May 1913), *Ruggles of Red Gap* (1915; rev. in SS, June 1915), and *Somewhere in Red Gap* (1916; rev. in SS, December 1916).

WILSON, WOODROW (1856–1924), twenty-eighth president of the United States (1913–21). HLM regarded him with great hostility because of what he believed to be Wilson's doctrinaire moralism and his covert support of the Allies in World War I under the guise of a false neutrality. He reviewed the first four volumes of Ray Stannard Baker's *Woodrow Wilson: Life and Letters* (1927–31; rev. in AM, February 1928 and February 1932) with characteristic pungency.

WOOD, LEONARD (1860–1927), brigadier general, military governor of Cuba (1899–1902), and chief of staff of the U.S. army (1910–14). He unsuccessfully sought the Republican nomination for the presidency in 1916 and 1920.

WOODBERRY, GEORGE E. (1855–1930), critic, poet, and editor best known for his biographies of Hawthorne (1902), Emerson (1907), and Poe (1909). HLM regarded his poetry as academic and lifeless.

WYSPIAŃSKI, STANISŁAW (1869–1907), Polish playwright and painter best known for the play *Wesele* (1901; Eng. tr. as *The Wedding*).

ZIEGFELD, FLORENZ (1869–1932), Broadway producer and founder in 1907 of the Ziegfeld Follies, one of the most popular revues of its time.

Sources

"On Living in the United States." *Nation*, 7 December 1921, 655–56.

"The American." SS 40, no. 2 (June 1913): 87–94.

"The American: His Morals." SS 40, no. 3 (July 1913): 89–91.

"The American: His Language." SS 40, no. 4 (August 1913): 89–96.

"The American: His Ideas of Beauty." SS 41, no. 1 (September 1913): 91–98.

"The American: His Freedom." SS 41, no. 2 (October 1913): 81–88.

"The American: His New Puritanism." SS 42, no. 2 (February 1914): 87–94.

"Good Old Baltimore." SS 40, no. 1 (May 1913): 107–14.

"Maryland: Apex of Normalcy." *Nation*, 3 May 1922, 517–19.

"The City of Seven Sundays." SS 44, no. 3 (November 1914): 71–78 (as by "Owen Hatteras").

"Along the Potomac." SS 60, no. 1 (September 1919): 73–75 (as by "C. Farley Anderson").

"San Francisco: A Memory." BES, 21 July 1920, 6.

"San Francisco." CST, 20 November 1927, Section 5, p. 1.

"New York." SS 72, no. 1 (September 1923): 138–44.

"Meditation in E Minor." *New Republic*, 8 September 1920, 38–40.

"What Ails the Republic." BES, 17 April 1922, 6.

["The American Politician."] "Politics." In *Civilization in the United States*, ed. Harold Edmund Stearns, pp. 21–34. New York: Harcourt, 1922.

["Religion in America."] ["1. Evangelical Pastors."] "Editorial." AM 6, no. 3 (November 1925): 286–88. ["2. Church and State."] "Editorial." AM 15, no. 2 (October 1928): 156–58. ["3. The American Religion."] "Editorials: The American Religion." AM 23, no. 1 (May 1931): 31–34.

"The Burden of Credulity." *Opportunity* 9, no. 2 (February 1931): 40–41.

"Notes on Negro Strategy." *Crisis* 41, no. 10 (October 1934): 289, 304.

"Puritanism as a Literary Force." In *A Book of Prefaces*. 1917; rev. ed., pp. 197–225, 253–83. New York: Alfred A. Knopf, 1922.

"The American Tradition." *Literary Review (New York Evening Post)*, 24 November 1923, 277–78.

"The Low-Down on Hollywood." *Photoplay* 32, no. 5 (April 1927): 36–37, 118–20.

["Palmy Days for Authors."] "Editorial." AM 12, no. 1 (September 1927): 34–36.

"Testament." *American Review of Reviews* 76, no. 4 (October 1927): 413–16.

Index

Roman Catholicism, 22, 73, 77, 81, 133–36, 138–39, 141, 142, 186
Rookwood pottery, 47
Roosevelt, Theodore, 9, 21, 55, 114, 123, 194n25, 197n2, 203, 217, 220, 227
Roosevelt, Theodore, Jr., 5, 82, 227
Rose of Dutcher's Coolly (Garland), 158
Rosenthal, Moriz, 41, 227
Rosey, George, 46, 227
Rotary Club, 1, 3, 82, 114, 185, 187
Russell, H. H., 191n1
Russell, William T., 70, 227
Ryan, Thomas Fortune, 12, 227

Sacco, Nicola, 186, 187, 189
Sage, Russell, 12, 227
"Sahara of the Bozart, The," viii
St. Louis, Mo., 147
Salvation Army, 61, 119
Samson and Delilah (Saint-Saëns), 94
Sand, George, 27, 227
Sandburg, Carl, 170, 227
Sanderson, Julia, 88, 227
San Francisco, Cal., xiv, 100–105, 107, 208
Sanger, Margaret, 82, 227
Sanine (Artzibashef), 165
Sankey, Ira David, 61
Sapho (Daudet), 164
Sappho, 74
Sargent, John Singer, 43, 227–28
Saturday Evening Post, xvi, 3, 157, 181, 210
Savannah, Ga., 68
Scheffel, Joseph Victor von, 41, 228
Schuyler, George S., 143, 228
Schwab, Charles M., 3, 184, 228
Scopes trial, xii, xvii
Seabury, Samuel, 163
Sembrich, Marcella, 41, 228
Sexual Question, The (Forel), 165
Shakespeare, William, 37, 51, 148, 150, 177, 178
Shaw, George Bernard, 40, 89, 164, 228
Sherman, Stuart P., 171, 173, 228
Sigourney, Lydia Howard Huntley, 171, 228
Simmons, William J., 191n1
Sinclair, Upton, 82, 108, 156, 158, 166, 228–29
Sister Carrie (Dreiser), 149, 183
Small, Len, 82, 229
Smart Set, viii, xiv, xvi, 196n19
Smith, Alfred E., xii, 135, 138
Smith, F. Hopkinson, 156, 229

Smith, Fred B., 195n39
Smoot, Reed, 66
Song of Songs (Sudermann), 90
Sorma, Agnes, 41, 229
Sousa, John Philip, 46, 229
Southey, Robert, 169
S.P.C.A., 52
Spencer, Herbert, 15, 29, 229
Spoon River Anthology (Masters), 170
"Spring Song" (Mendelssohn), 46
Standards (Brownell), 169, 172
"Star-Spangled Banner, The" (Key), 10, 43
Stearns, Harold, xi, 2, 229
Steinheil, Marguerite, 90
Stillman, James, 82, 229
Stowe, Harriet Beecher, 42, 229
Strindberg, August, 41, 90, 196n10, 229
Student Volunteer Movement for Foreign Missions, 64
Suckow, Ruth, 183, 230
Sudermann, Hermann, 90, 230
Sullivan, John L., 161, 230
Summer in Arcady, A (Allen), 165
Sumner, John S., 201n61
Sunday, Billy, 4, 96, 130, 171, 230
Susan Lenox (Phillips), 148
Swift, Jonathan, 43, 169
Swinburne, Algernon Charles, 42, 169
Synge, J. M., 169

Taft, William Howard, 194n25, 197n2
Taney, Roger B., 14, 230
Tannhäuser (Wagner), 46
Tassin, Algernon, 154
Taylor, Bayard, 171, 230
Tchaikovsky, Peter Ilich, 58
Tennyson, Alfred, Lord, 41
Terre Haute, Ind., 87
Thalberg, Irving G., 178, 230
Thaw, Harry, 82, 127, 165, 230
Thoma, Ludwig, 169, 230
Thompson, William Hale, 82, 230
Three Weeks (Glyn), 181
Thurman, Allen G., 185, 230
Times (London), 29, 124
Titan, The (Dreiser), 149, 166
Titian (Tiziano Vecellio), 150
Tocqueville, Alexis de, 18, 230–31
Together (Herrick), 166
Tolstoy, Leo, 42, 65, 155, 231
To M. L. G., 90
Train, George Francis, 161–62, 231